Against
Pure
Reason

FORTRESS TEXTS IN
MODERN THEOLOGY

IN THE SERIES

FORTRESS TEXTS IN MODERN THEOLOGY

Against Pure Reason

Writings on Religion, Language, and History

Johann Gottfried Herder

Translated, edited, and with an introduction by Marcia Bunge

Fortress Press　　　　　　　　**Minneapolis**

AGAINST PURE REASON
Writings on Religion, Language, and History

Scripture quotations unless otherwise noted are from the New Revised Standard Version of the Bible, copyright © 1989 by the Division of Christian Education of the National Council of Churches. They have been adapted to more closely reflect Herder's text.

Library of Congress Cataloging-in-Publication Data

Herder, Johann Gottfried, 1744-1803.
  [Selections. English. 1993]
  Against pure reason: writings on religion, language, and
history / by J. G. Herder; translated, edited, and
introduced by Marcia Bunge.
    p. cm (Fortress texts in modern theology)
  Includes bibliographical references
  ISBN 0-8006-3212-5 (alk. paper)
  1. Religion-Philosophy-Early works to 1800.
  2. Theology-18th century. 3.History (Theology) Early works to 1800. I. Bunge. Marcia J.
(Marcia JoAnn), . II. Title. III. Series.
BLH51, H4695 1992
200-dc20
                                                    92-360
                                                     CIP

The paper used in this publication meets the minimum requirements of American National Standard for Information Sciences—Permanence of Paper for Printed Library Materials, ANSI Z329.48-1984.   (∞)™

Manufactured in the U.S.A.   AF 1-3212

97   96   95   94   93   1   2   3   5   6   7   8   9   10

Contents

Preface

Twelve years ago, when I was first introduced to the writings of Johann Gottfried Herder in a seminar at the University of Tübingen, I was fascinated by this eighteenth century thinker's insights, his compassion, the breadth of his interests, and his influence on diverse areas of nineteenth century thought. He also intrigued me because he raised many questions central to twentieth century thought. He wrote about history, literature, language, culture, religion, and the Bible in terms more familiar to our century than his own. Unlike many of his contemporaries, who viewed the ideals of European Enlightenment as the sole standard by which to judge all other cultures, Herder possessed a broader, more pluralistic outlook on history. He insisted that other cultures and periods of history be studied in relation to their own contexts, and he treasured and respected their individuality. He felt that the arrogance of the Enlightenment world-view not only blinded his contemporaries to the richness of history but also fed the oppression of the peoples whom Europe was so busily colonizing. He coupled this emphasis on cultural integrity with a concern for human rights and universal peace. He struggled, just as the European community and the new Commonwealth of Independent States do today, to create a vision that values ethnic and religious diversity as well as our common humanity.

I was also struck by the contemporary flavor of Herder's ideas about language and his interpretations of literature and the Bible. Like many philosophers of language today, Herder believed that human beings cannot think without language and that reason is shaped by one's historical context. Furthermore, at a time when many critics sought universal categories by which to evaluate literature, Herder studied it in its historical context. His work helped to foster a new appreciation of the Bible and non-European literature in his own time and anticipated the kind of historical approach found within biblical and literary criticism today.

When I returned to the United States in 1981, I entered a doctoral program at the University of Chicago and, since my interest in Herder continued to grow, decided to write my dissertation on him. While pursuing my research, I was surprised to discover that few of Herder's works were translated into English. Moreover, much of the secondary literature written in English on the eighteenth century either mentioned Herder only in passing or mistakenly characterized him as an irrationalist. This caricature stems from Herder's emphasis on the importance of passion and imagination and his critique of Enlightenment thinkers who viewed reason as sovereign. Although these ideas did play a role in early German Romanticism, Herder's critique of reason did not mean that he rejected it altogether. Rather, he argued against those who overemphasized the role of reason and who believed that it is an autonomous faculty unaffected by language, tradition, or other aspects of human experience. Herder was "against pure reason" in these senses but never "against reason itself." In many ways he was a child of the Enlightenment. Yet in contrast to many of his contemporaries, he advocated a more comprehensive understanding of human nature and history, believing that human beings are not merely rational but also historical, social, linguistic, emotional, and religious creatures. Herder's attempts to outline a fuller vision of humanity explain the breadth of his interests and influence in a diverse range of disciplines.

Although recent secondary literature is helping to provide a more accurate picture of Herder, several primary texts are still unavailable in English. This is the case in regard to one of the most important aspects of Herder's writings—his religious thought. Only two major works in this area have been translated into English: *The Spirit of Hebrew Poetry* and *God, Some Conversations*. Although the former (translated in 1833 in a style somewhat inaccessible to readers today) provides an understanding of his interpretation of the Bible and the latter his view of God, these works present only a narrow slice of the broad spectrum of his religious ideas. The selections in this anthology are chosen from several major works in order to provide in one volume a fuller picture of the scope of Herder's religious thought. This volume serves not only as an introduction to Herder but also to the Enlightenment, nineteenth century religious thought, and key questions that have occupied theologians for the last two hundred years.

One of my most difficult tasks in editing this anthology was selecting noteworthy and representative texts from Herder's vast collected writings and letters. In selecting texts that would best capture the central themes, major works, and the extensive range of Herder's religious thought, I chose, wherever possible, writings from different periods of his life and lengthy sections of several major works, rather than paragraphs and sentences from numerous several major works, rather than paragraphs and sentences from numerous writings. I excluded texts with too many obscure literary or historical allusions and texts too difficult to grasp in translation, such as Herder's theological poems. In the introduction I have referred to several important texts that could not be included in the anthology for those who wish to read them in German.

Translating Herder's works was also challenging. Although Herder is one of Germany's great prose writers, his style is unusual and sometimes confusing, even for native German speakers. It is filled with incomplete sentences, inventive metaphors, and exclamations. I have retained some elements of Herder's unique style, but not at the expense of translating the passages as clearly and accurately as possible. Although I had access to handwritten manuscripts and consulted them, I have based my translation on the standard edition of his collected works edited by Bernhard Suphan.

Since Herder expresses some strikingly mature views about women for his time and an acute awareness of the limitations of language about God, I have been especially attentive to issues of inclusive language in my translation. In those passages in which Herder refers to both males and females, I have translated singular nouns into the plural to avoid using masculine pronouns (for example, I usually translate *der Mensch* as "human beings"). In passages in which Herder refers exclusively to men, however, such as in his discussions of ordained ministers, I have used terms that reflect Herder's own historical context. Herder often speaks of God in masculine terms, such as "father," and in those passages I have used masculine pronouns to refer to God. In those instances where he uses other expressions for God, I have followed his own warning about the dangers of anthropomorphisms and thus tried to avoid feminine and masculine pronouns.

This project called for the talents of many people whom I would like to thank. Annette Richter, Norbert Kraft, Susanne Siegl, Daniel Dahlstrom, Mary Preus, Roy Harrisville, James Limburg, and Ekkehard Rudolph all provided me with insights that greatly strengthened the translation. I deeply appreciate their help and their ability to maintain a marvelous sense of humor, even while struggling over difficult passages. Any weaknesses that may remain in the translation are, of course, my own responsibility. I am also grateful to Joanne Engquist and Janet Wheelock for their work as research assistants and to Diane Bartles and Robert Gerdes for their help in preparing the manuscript. I benefited greatly from the advice and comments of several Herder scholars: Günter Arnold, Herbert von Hintzenstern, Hans-Dietrich Irmscher, Wulf Koepke, Ernest Menze, and John Rogerson. I also want to thank Brian Gerrish and the series editors for their support and the Association of Theological Schools for a generous grant that enabled me to begin the project and to spend several months in Bonn and Weimar. All of the people whom I have mentioned brought a great degree of energy, warmth, and comradery to this project, for which I am deeply grateful.   *Marcia Bunge*

Abbreviations

( )	Herder's parenthetical remarks.
[ ]	Translator's insertions.
Briefe	Collected letters of Herder (See *Select Bibliography*)
HWP	*Historisches Wörterbuch der Philosophie*. Edited by Joachim Ritter. Basel: Schwabe, 1974.
NRSV	*New Revised Standard Version of the Bible*. Edited by Bruce Metzger and Roland Murphy. New York: Oxford University Press, 1991.
RS	*Riverside Shakespeare*. Edited by G. Blakemore Evans. Introduction by Harry Lovin. Notes to plays by Herschel Baker. Boston: Houghton Mufflin, 1974.
SW	*Sämmtliche Werke*. The Suphan edition of Herder's collected writings (see *Select Bibliography*).

Select Bibliography

For a comprehensive bibliography see: Günther, Gottfried, Albina Volgina, Siegfried Seifert, eds. *Herder Bibliographie*. Berlin/Weimar: Aufbau, 1978.
For secondary works after 1977 see: Markworth, Tino, ed. *Johann Gottfried Herder: A Bibliographical Survey 1977-87*. Hürth-Effern: Gabel, 1990.

PRIMARY TEXTS

Briefe: Gesamtausgabe 1763-1803. Wilhelm Dobbek and Günter Arnold, eds. Published under the direction of Karl-Heinz Hann (Goethe-und-Schiller-Archiv). Weimar: Böhlau, 1977-86. [The complete edition of Herder's letters.]
Der Handschriftliche Nachlass Johann Gottfried Herders. Hans Dietrich Irmscher and Emil Adler, eds. Wiesbaden: Otto Harrassowitz, 1979. [A catalog of Herder's handwritten manuscripts in the *Staatsbibliothek Preussischer Kulturbesitz*. Many of them have never been published.]
Sämmtliche Werke. Bernhard Suphan, ed. (Carl Redlich and Reinhold Steig). Berlin: Wiedmannsche Buchhandlung, 1877-1913. 33 vols. Reprint. Hildesheim: Georg Olms, 1967-68. [The standard and most complete edition of Herder's writings.]
Werke. Frankfurt: Deutscher Klassiker Verlag, 1985- . 10 vols. [This edition, not yet complete, contains extensive commentaries and will become a standard reference.]
Werke. Wolfgang Pross and Pierre Penisson, eds. München: Carl Hanser, 1984-85. 3 vols. [This is another recent edition of selected texts with helpful commentaries.]
[See the *Herder Bibliographie* for other editions of Herder's writings.]

TRANSLATIONS OF HERDER'S WRITINGS INTO ENGLISH

"The Book of Job Considered as a Work of Art." *Journal of Speculative Philosophy*. 4 (1870): 284-88.
A Brief Commentary on the Revelation of St. John. London: John Hatchard and Son, 1821.

"The Divinity and Right Use of the Bible." *History and Repository of Pulpit Eloquence*. Henry Clay Fish, ed. New York: M. W. Dodd, 1857.

"Essay on the Origin of Language." *Milestones of Thought*. John Moran and Alex Gode, trans., New York: Unger, 1966. [Part one only is translated.]

God, Some Conversations. Frederick Burkhardt, trans. New York: Veritas, 1940. Reprint. Indianapolis: Bobbs-Merrill, 1962.

J. G. Herder on Social and Political Culture. Frederick Barnard, trans. London: Cambridge University Press, 1969. [A selection of Herder's writings.]

Journal of My Travels in the Year 1769. John Harrison, trans. Ann Arbor: University Microfilms, 1952. Ph.D. diss., Columbia University.

Letters Relating to the Study of Divinity [Letters 1 and 2]. *Christian Disciple* 8, 9 (1820-21).

Outlines of a Philosophy of the History of Man. T. O. Churchill, trans. London: J. Johnson, 1880. [A translation of the *Ideen zur Philosophie der Geschichte der Menschheit*.]

Reflections on the Philosophy of the History of Mankind. Frank E. Manuel, ed. Chicago: University of Chicago, 1968. [An abridgement of Churchill's translation.]

Selected Works, 1764-1767: Early Addresses, Essays, and Drafts; Fragments on German Literature. Ernest Menze and Karl Menges, eds. Ernest Menze and Michael Palma, trans. University Park: Pennsylvania State University Press, 1991.

The Spirit of Hebrew Poetry. James Marsh, trans. Burlington: Smith, 1933.

Treatise upon the Origin of Language. London: Longman, 1827. [Entire essay is translated.]

Yet Another Philosophy of History of the Education of Humanity. Eva Herzfield, trans. Ph.D. diss. Columbia University, 1968.

[Several of his poems have been translated into English. See *Herder Bibliographie*.]

SECONDARY TEXTS IN ENGLISH

Aarsleff, Hans. "The Tradition of Condillac: The Problem of the Origin of Language in the Eighteenth Century and the Debate in the Berlin Academy before Herder." *Studies in the History of Linguistics: Traditions of Paradigms*, Dell Hymes, ed., Bloomington: Indiana University Press, 1974.

Barnard, F. M. "The Hebrews and Herder's Political Creed." *Modern Language Review* 54 (1959): 533-46.

————. *Herder's Social and Political Thought: From Enlightenment to Nationalism*. Oxford: Clarendon Press, 1965.

————. "Natural Culture and Political Legitimacy: Herder and Rousseau." *Journal of the History of Ideas* 44 (1983):231-53.

————. "Natural Growth and Purposive Development: Vico and Herder." *History and Theory: Studies in the Philosophy of History* 18 (1979): 16-36.

————. "Particularity, Universality, and the Hebraic Spirit: Heine and Herder." *Jewish Social Studies* 43 (1981): 121-36.

————. *Self-Direction and Political Legitimacy: Rousseau and Herder*. Oxford: Oxford University Press, 1988.

Barth, Karl. *Protestant Thought: From Rosseau to Ritschl*. Brian Cozens, trans. New York: Harper & Row, 1959.

Berlin, Isaiah. *The Crooked Timber of Humanity: Chapters in the History of Ideas*, Henry Hardy, ed. New York: Knopf, 1991.

————. *Vico and Herder: Two Studies in the History of Ideas.* New York: The Viking Press, 1976.

————. "Herder and the Enlightenment." *Aspects of the 18th Century.* Earl R. Wasserman, ed. Baltimore: Johns Hopkins, 1965.

Clark, Robert T. *Herder: His Life and Thought.* Berkeley: University of California Press, 1955.

————. "Herder, Percy, and the Song of Songs." *Publications of the Modern Language Association of America* 61 (1946): 1087-1100.

————. "Herder's Conception of *Kraft.*" *Publications of the Modern Language Association of America* 57 (1942): 737-52.

Bunge, Marcia. "Herder and the Origins of a Historical View of Religion: An Informative Perspective for Historical Theology Today." *Revisioning the Past: Prospects in Historical Theology.* Mary Potter Engel and Walter E. Wyman, eds. Minneapolis: Fortress 1992.

————. *The Restless Reader: Johann Gottfried Herder's Interpretation of the New Testament.* Ph.D. diss. University of Chicago, 1986.

Ergang, Robert Reinhold. *Herder and the Foundations of German Nationalism.* New York: Columbia University Press, 1931 Reprint. New York: Octagon Books, 1976.

Frei, Hans. *The Eclipse of Biblical Narrative: A Study in Eighteenth and Nineteenth Century Hermeneutics.* New Haven: Yale University Press, 1974.

Gerrish, Brian. "The Secret Religion of Germany: Christian Piety and the Pantheism Controversy." *The Journal of Religion* 67 (1987): 437-55.

Gillies, A. *Herder.* Oxford: Blackwell, 1945.

————. "Herder's Essay on Shakespeare: 'Das Herz der Untersuchung.' " *Modern Language Review* 32 (1937): 262-80.

Iggers, Georg G. *The German Conception of History: The National Tradition of Historical Thought from Herder to the Present.* Middletown: Wesleyan University Press, 1968.

Keopke, Wulf. *Johann Gottfried Herder.* Boston: Twayne, 1987.

————, ed. *Johann Gottfried Herder: Innovator through the Ages.* Bonn: Bouvier, 1982.

————, ed. *Herder: Language, History, and the Enlightenment.* Columbia: Camden House, 1990.

Kümmel, Werner Georg. *The New Testament: The History of the Investigation of Its Problems,* S. McLean Gilmour and Howard C. Kee, trans. Nashville: Abingdon, 1972.

Lovejoy, Arthur O. *Essays in the History of Ideas.* Baltimore: J. Hopkins Press, 1948.

————. *The Great Chain of Being: A Study of the History of an Idea.* New York: Harper & Row, 1960.

Manuel, Frank E. *The Eighteenth Century Confronts the Gods.* Cambridge: Harvard University Press, 1959.

Mayo, Robert. *Herder and the Beginnings of Comparative Literature.* Chapel Hill: University of N. Carolina, 1969.

McEachran, Frank. *The Life and Philosophy of Johann Gottfried Herder.* Oxford: Clarendon, 1939.

McGiffert, Arthur Cushman. "The God of Spinoza as Interpreted by Herder." *Hibbert Journal* 3 (1904-5): 706-26.

Meinecke, Friedrich. *Historicism: The Rise of a New Historical Outlook.* J. E. Anderson, trans. New York: Herder & Herder, 1972.

Morton, Michael. *Herder and the Poetics of Thought: Unity and Diversity in "On Diligence in Several Learned Languages."* University Park: Pennsylvania State University Press, 1989.

Müller-Vollmer, Kurt, ed. *Herder Today: Contributions from the International Herder Conference.* Berlin: Walter de Gruyter, 1990.

Nisbet, H. B. *Herder and the Philosophy and History of Science.* Cambridge: Modern Humanities Research Association, 1970.

Norton, Robert Edward. *Herder's Aesthetics and the European Enlightenment.* Ithaca: Cornell University Press, 1991.

Pfleiderer, Otto. *The Philosophy of Religion on the Basis of Its History,* Alexander Stewart and Allan Menzies, trans. London: Williams & Norgate, 1886. Vol. I.

Purdie, Edna. "Introduction." *Von Deutscher Art und Kunst.* Oxford: Clarendon, 1924.

———. *Studies in German Literature of the Eighteenth Century: Some Aspects of Literary Affiliation.* London: Athlone Press, 1965.

Rogerson, John. *Old Testament Criticism in the Nineteenth Century: England and Germany.* London: S.P.C.K., 1984.

Sapir, Edward, "Herder's 'Ursprung der Sprache.' " *Modern Philology* 5 (1907): 109-42.

Schütze, Martin. "The Fundamental Ideas in Herder's Thought." *Modern Philology* 18 (1920): 65-78, 289-302; 19 (1921-22): 113-30, 361-82; 21 (1923): 29-48, 113-32.

The Spinoza Conversations between Lessing and Jacobi: Text with Excerpts from the Ensuing Controversy. G. Vallée, J. B. Lawson, and C. G. Chapple, trans. New York: University Press of America, 1988.

Vallée, Gérhard. "Introduction." In *The Spinoza Conversations between Lessing and Jacobi.* New York: University Press of America, 1988.

Wells, G. A. "Condillac, Rousseau and Herder on the Origin of Language." *Studies on Voltaire and the Eighteenth Century* 230 (1985): 233-46.

———. *Herder and After: A Study in the Development of Sociology.* Hague: Mouton, 1959.

———. "Herder's Resistance to the Idea That Language Is an Invention." *Journal of English and Germanic Philology,* 85 (1986): 167-90.

SECONDARY TEXTS IN GERMAN

Adler, Emil. *Herder und die Deutsche Aufklärung.* Frankfurt: Europa Verlag, 1968.

Adler, Hans. *Die Prägung des Dunklen.* Hamburg: Meiner, 1990.

Arnold, Gunter. *Johann Gottfried Herder.* Leipzig: Bibliographisches Institut Leipzig, 1988.

Baur, Ernst. *Johann Gottfried Herder: Leben und Werk.* Stuttgart: Kohlhammer, 1960.

Bluhm, Heinz. "Herders Stellung zu Luther." *Publications of the Modern Language Association of America* 64 (1948): 158-82.

Brändle, Johann. *Das Problem der Innerlichkeit: Hamann, Herder, und Goethe.* Bern: A. Franke, 1950.

Bunge, Marcia. "Johann Gottfried Herders Auslegung des Neuen Testaments," *Historische Kritik und biblischer Kanon in der deutschen Aufklärung.* Henning Graf Reventlow, Walter Sparn, John Woodbridge, eds. Wolfenbütteler Forschungen 41. Wiesbaden: Harrossowitz, 1988.

Cillien, Ursula. *Johann Gottfried Herder-Christlicher Humanismus.* Ratingen: A. Henn Verlag, 1972.

Dietterle, Joh. A. "Die Grundgedanken in Herder's Schrift 'Gott' und ihr Verhältnis zu Spinozas Philosophie." *Theologische Studien und Kritiken* (1914): 505-55.

Dietze, Walter. *Johann Gottfried Herder: Abriss seines Lebens und Schaffens.* Berlin: Aufbau Verlag, 1980.

————, ed. *Herder Kolloquium 1978.* Weimar: Hermann Böhlaus, 1980.

Dobbek, Wilhelm. *J. G. Herders Weltbild.* Köln: Böhlau Verlag, 1969.

Doerne, Martin. *Die Religion in Herders Geschichtsphilosophie.* Leipzig: Felix Meiner, 1927.

Dreike, Beate Monika. *Herders Naturauffassung in ihrer Beeinflussung durch Leibniz' Philosophie.* Wiesbaden: Steiner, 1973.

Drews, Peter. *Herder und die Slawen.* München: Sagner, 1990.

Embach, Michael. *Das Lutherbild Johann Gottfried Herders.* Frankfurt am Main: Peter Lang, 1987.

Faust, Ulrich. *Mythologien und Religionen des Ostens bei Johann Gottfried Herder.* Münster: Aschendorff, 1977.

Federlin, Wilhelm-Ludwig. "Predigt und Volksbildung. Marginalien zu J. G. Herders Predigtverständnis." *Deutsches Pfarrerblatt,* 11 (1981): 506-14.

————. "Das Reformationsbild in der Geschichtsphilosophie Herders." *Bückeburger Gespräche über Johann Gottfried Herder 1983.* Rinteln, 1984.

————. *Vom Nutzen des Geistlichen Amtes.* Göttingen: Vandenhoeck & Ruprecht, 1982.

Frenz, Peter. *Studien zu traditionellen Elementen des Geschichtsdenkens und der Bildlichkeit im Werk Johann Gottfried Herders.* Frankfurt/M: Lang, 1983.

Gadamer, Hans-Georg. "Herder und die geschichtliche Welt." *Kleine Schriften* 3. Tübingen: J.C.B. Mohr, 1972.

————. "Herder als Wegbereiter des Historischen Bewusstseins." *Geist der Zeit* 19 (1941): 661-70.

————. "Nachwort." *Auch eine Philosophie der Geschichte zur Bildung der Menschheit.* J. G. Herder. Frankfurt A.M.: Suhrkamp Verlag, 1967.

Gaier, Ulrich. *Herders Sprachphilosophie und Erkenntniskritik.* Stuttgart: Frommann-Holzboog, 1988.

Germer, Hanfried. *Das Problem der Absolutheit des Christentums bei Herder und Schleiermacher.* Marburg: Buchdruckerei J. Hamel, 1937.

Goebel, Louis. *Herder und Schleiermachers Reden über die Religion.* Gotha: F. A. Perthes, 1904.

Grawe, Christian. *Herders Kulturanthropologie.* Bonn: Bouvier, 1967.

Gronau, Eduard. "Herders religiöse Jugendentwicklung: Dargestellt unter besonderer Berücksichtigung seiner Anschauungen von der Sünde." *Zeitschrift für systematische Theologie* 8 (1930): 308-46.

Güttgemann, Erhardt. *Offene Fragen zur Formgeschichte des Evangeliums.* München: Kaiser Verlag, 1970.

Gulyga, Arseni. *Johann Gottfried Herder. Eine Einführung in seine Philosophie.* Frankfurt a.M.: Röderberg, 1978.

Haym, Rudolf. *Herder nach seinem Leben und seinen Werken Dargestellt.* 2 vols. Berlin: R. Gaertner, 1877-85. Reprint. Berlin: Aufbau, 1954.

Heintel, Erich. "Einleitung." *Johann Gottfried Herder: Sprachphilosophische Schriften.* Johann Gottfried Herder. Erich Heintel, ed. Hamburg: Felix Meiner, 1960.

Hintzenstern, Herbert von. "Herders Lutherbild." In *Bückeburger Gespräche über Johann Gottfried Herder 1983.* Rinteln: C. Bösendahl, 1984.

————. "Theologische Arbeiten des Schriftstellers und Dichters Johann Gottfried Herder." *Amtsblatt der Evangelisch-Lutherischen Kirche in Thüringen* 35, no. 15 (10 August 1982): 128-38.

Hirsch, Emanuel. *Geschichte der neueren evangelischen Theologie im Zusammenhang mit den allgemeinen Bewegungen des europäischen Denkens.* Volume 4. Gütersloh: Gerd Mohn, 1968.

Hoffart, Elizabeth. *Herders "Gott."* Halle: Niemeyer, 1918.

Hornig, Gottfried. *Die Anfänge der historisch-kritischen Theologie: Johann Semlers Schriftverständnis und seine Stellung zu Luther.* Göttingen: Vandenhoeck & Ruprecht, 1961.

Irmscher, Hans-Dietrich. "Beobachtungen zur Funktion der Analogie im Denken Herders." *Deutsche Vierteljahresschrift für Literaturwissenschaft und Geistesgeschichte* (March, 1981): 64-97.

————. "Grundzüge der Hermeneutik Herders." *Bückeburger Gespräche über Johann Gottfried Herder 1971.* Schaumburger Studien, Heft 33. Bückeburg: Grimme, 1973.

————. "Der handschriftliche Nachlass Herders und seine Neuordnung." *Herder-Studien.* Walter Wiora and H.D. Irmscher, eds. Marburger Ostforschungen, 10. Würzburg: Holzner, 1960.

————. "Herder über das Verhältnis des Autors zum Publikum." *Bückeburger Gespräche über Johann Gottfried Herder 1975.* Schaumburger Studien, Heft 37. Rinteln: Bösendahl, 1976.

————. "Johann Gottfried Herder." *Deutsche Dichter des 18. Jahrhunderts.* Benno von Wiese, ed. Berlin: Erich Schmidt, 1977.

————. "Nachwort." *Abhandlung über den Ursprung der Sprache.* Johann Gottfried Herder. Hans-Dietrich Irmscher. ed. Stuttgart: Reclam, 1966.

————. "Probleme der Herder-Forschung." *Deutsche Vierteljahrsschrift für Literaturwissenschaft und Geistesgeschichte* 37 (1963): 266-317.

Jacoby, Günter. *Herders und Kants Aesthetik.* Leipzig: Dürr'sche Buchhandlung, 1907.

Johann Gottfried Herder: Zum 175. Todestag am 18. Dezember 1978. Sitzungberichte der Akademie der Wissenschaften der DDR. Berlin: Akademie Verlag, 1978.

Jöns, Dietrich Walter. *Begriff und Problem der historischen Zeit bei Johann Gottfried Herder.* Göteborgs Universitets Arsskrift, vol. 62. Stockholm: Almquist & Wiksell, 1956.

Kantzenbach, Friedrich Wilhelm. "Herders Briefe das Studium der Theologie betreffend." *Bückeburger Gespräche über Johann Gottfried Herder 1975.* Schaumburger Studien, Heft 37. Rinteln: Bösendahl, 1976.

————. *Johann Gottfried Herder in Selbstzeugnissen und Bilddokumenten.* Reinbek bei Hamburg: Rowohlt Taschenbuch Verlag, 1970.

————. "Konturen eines neuen Herder-Bildes: Theologie und Zeitgeist an der Schwelle zum 19. Jahrhundert." *Religion und Zeitgeist im 19. Jahrhundert.* Julius Schoeps. ed. Stuttgart-Bonn: Burg, 1982.

Kathan, Anton. *Herders Literaturkritik: Untersuchungen zu Methodik und Struktur am Beispiel der frühen Werke.* Göppingen: A. Kümmerle, 1969.

Kelletat, Andreas. *Herder und die Weltliteratur.* Frankfurt/M: Peter Lang, 1984.

Kohlschmidt, Werner. "Untersuchungen zu Herders kritischem Stil und zu seinen literaturkritischen Grundeinsichten." *Herder Studien.* Berlin: Junker & Dünnhaupt, 1929.

Knodt, Eva M. *"Negative Philosophie" und dialogische Kritik: zur Struktur poetischer Theorie bei Lessing und Herder.* Tübingen: Niemeyer, 1988.

Kraus, Hans-Joachim. *Geschichte der historisch-kritischen Erforschung des Alten Testaments*. Neukirchen: Neukirchner Verlag, 1956.

Kühnemann, Eugen. *Herders Leben*. München: Beck, 1895.

Lehmann, Rudolf von. "Herders Humanitätsbegriff." *Kant-Studien* 24 (1920): 242-60.

Lilje, Hanns. "Herder, Theologie im Weimarer Kreis." *Goethe und seine grossen Zeitgenossen*. Albert Schaefer, ed. München: C. H. Beck, 1968.

Litt, Theodor. *Die Befreiung des geschichtlichen Bewusstseins durch J. G. Herder*. Kleine Bücherei zur Geistesgeschichte, no. 11. Leipzig: Seemann, 1942.

———. *Kant und Herder als Deuter der geistigen Welt*. Heidelberg: Quelle & Meyer, 1949. (2d edition).

Maltusch, Johann Gottfried, ed. *Bückeburger Gespräche über Johann Gottfried Herder 1971*. Bückeburg: Grimme, 1973.

———. *Bückeburger Gespräche über Johann Gottfried Herder 1975*. Rinteln: Bösendahl, 1976.

Merkel, R. F. "Lessing und Herder als Religions-Historiker." *Niew theologisch Tijdschrift* 25 (1936): 129-43.

Möller, Michael. *Theologische Aspekte des anthropologischen Ansatzes bei Johann Gottfried Herder, dargestellt an seinen Schriften aus der Bückeburger Zeit*. Diss. Karl-Marx-Universität Leipzig, 1986.

Müller, Johann Georg. *Aus dem Herder'schen Hause*. Jakob Baechtold, ed. Berlin: Weidmann, 1881.

Niederstrasser, H. "Herder-der 'Redner Gottes'." *Zeitschrift für Kirchengeschichte* 71 (1954/55): 97-125.

Pannenberg, Wolfhart. *Anthropologie in theologischer Perspektive*. Göttingen: Vandenhoeck & Ruprecht, 1983.

Pfleiderer, Otto. "Herder und Kant." *Jahrbuch für protestantische Theologie* 1 (1875): 636 ff.

Pross, Wolfgang. "Spinoza, Herder, Büchner: Über 'Gesetz' und 'Erscheinung'." *Georg Büchner Jahrbuch* 2 (1982): 62-91

———, ed. "Kommentar" and "Materialien." *Johann Gottfried Herder: Abhandlung über den Ursprung der Sprache*. München: Carl Hanser, 1978.

Puschmann, Joachim. *Alttestamentliche Auslegung und geschichtliches Denken bei Semler, Herder, Eichhorn, Schleiermacher und unter besonderer Berucksichtigung de Wette's*. Lunebyrg, 1959.

Ruprecht, Erich. "Vernunft und Sprache. Zum Grundproblem der Sprachphilosophie Johann Gottfried Herders." *Bückeburger Gespräche über Johann Gottfried Herder 1975*. Schaumburger Studien, Heft 37. Rinteln: Bösendahl, 1976.

Sapir, Edward. "Herder's 'Ursprung der Sprache.'" *Modern Philology* 5: (1907) 109-42.

Sauder, Gerhard, ed. *Johann Gottfried Herder 1744-1803*. Hamburg: Felix Meiner, 1987. [Papers delivered at the conference on Herder held on November 21-23, 1984 in Saarbrücken and sponsored by the "Deutsche Gesellschaft für die Erforschung des achtzehnten Jahrhunderts."]

Schaede, Ernst. "Herders Schrift 'Gott' und ihre Aufnahme bei Goethe." *Germanische Studien* 149. Berlin: Ebering, 1934.

Schmidt, Eva, ed. *Herder im Geistlichen Amt: Untersuchungen, Quellen, Dokumente*. Leipzig: Köhler & Amelang, 1956.

Schmidt, Wolff. "Berührungspunkte der Geschichtsphilosophien Herders und Friedrich Schlegels." *Zeitschrift für Religions- und Geistesgeschichte* 33 (1981): 127-54.

————. "Mythologie und Uroffenbarung bei Herder und Friedrich Schlegel." *Zeitschrift für Religions- und Geistesgeschichte* 25 (1973): 32-45.

Schmitt, Albert R. *Herder und Amerika.* Hague: Mouton, 1967.

Schöffler, Herbert. "Johann Gottfried Herder aus Mohrungen." *Deutscher Geist im 18. Jahrhundert.* Gotz von Selle, ed. Göttingen: Vandenhoeck & Ruprecht, 1956. 2d edition, 1967.

Scholder, Klaus. "Herder und die Anfänge der historischen Theologie." *Evangelische Theologie* 22 (1962): 425-40.

Scholz, Heinrich, ed. *Die Hauptschriften zum Pantheismusstreit zwischen Jacobi und Mendelssohn.* Berlin: Reuther und Reichard, 1916.

Schott, Uwe. *Die Jugendentwicklung Ludwig Feuerbachs bis zum Fakultätswechsel 1825.* Göttingen: Vandenhoeck & Ruprecht, 1973.

Sell, Karl. *Die Religion unserer Klassiker: Lessing, Herder, Schiller, Goethe.* Tübingen: J.C.B. Mohr, 1904.

Siegel, Carl. *Herder als Philosoph.* Stuttgart: Cotta, 1907.

Stadelmann, Rudolf. *Der historische Sinn bei Herder.* Halle/Saale: Max Niemeyer, 1928.

Stellmacher, Wolfgang. *Herders Shakespeare-Bild.* Berlin: Rütten und Loening, 1978.

Stephan, Horst. *Herder in Bückeburg und seine Bedeutung für die Kirchengeschichte.* Tübingen: J. C. B. Mohr, 1905.

————. "Schleiermachers Reden über die Religion und Herders Religion, Lehermeinungen, und Gebräuche." In *Zeitschrift für Theologie und Kirche,* 16 (1906): 484-505.

————, ed. *Herders Philosophie.* Leipzig: Dürr'sche Buchhandlung, 1906.

Strothmann, F. W. "Das scholastische Erbe im Herderschen 'Pantheismus.' " *Dichtung und Volkstum* 37 (1936): 174-87.

Timm, Hermann. *Gott und die Freiheit.* Frankfurt am Main: Vittorio Klostermann, 1974.

Troeltsch, Ernst. *Der Historismus und seine Probleme.* Volume 3 of *Gesammelte Schriften.* Tübingen: J.C.B. Mohr, 1922.

Ungar, Rudolf. *Herder, Novalis und Kleist.* Frankfurt: Diesterweg, 1922.

Vollrath, Wilhelm. *Die Auseinandersetzung Herders mit Spinoza.* Darmstadt: C.F. Winter, 1911.

Werner, August Wilhelm Ernst. *Herder als Theologe.* Berlin: F. Henschel, 1871.

————. "J. G. Herder's Verhalten zum Alten Testament." *Zeitschrift für wissenschaftliche Theologie* 14 (1871): 351-83.

Willi, Thomas: *Herders Beitrag zum Verstehen des Alten Testaments.* Beiträge zur Geschichte der biblischen Hermeneutik, no. 8. Tübingen: J.C.B. Mohr, 1971.

Wolff, Hans M. "Der junge Herder und die Entwicklungsidee Rousseaus." *Publications of the Modern Language Association of America* 57 (1942): 753-819.

Ziegengeist, Gerhard ed. *Johann Gottfried Herder: Zur Herder-Rezeption in Ost und Südosteuropa.* Berlin: Akademie Verlag, 1978.

Introduction

Johann Gottfried Herder (1744-1803) was depicted by Friedrich Nietzsche as an unquiet guest of the eighteenth century.[1] Although Nietzsche used this image to describe some negative aspects of Herder's personality, from our perspective today, the image actually captures some of the most positive and intriguing characteristics of this complex German figure. Herder is an unquiet guest of the eighteenth century for several reasons. He was a restless, active thinker whose range of interests were so broad that it is difficult to categorize him easily. Furthermore, many of his ideas placed him in uneasy opposition to intellectual trends of his day. He sharply criticized Enlightenment philosophers who held reason to be sovereign and unaffected by history or language. Although he was "against pure reason" in these senses, he was not an irrationalist, as some of his critics have claimed. He also disagreed with enthusiasts and romantics who overemphasized the role of emotion. In addition, Herder was unquiet because he was greatly disturbed by the inhumanity and arrogance of his "enlightened" contemporaries who were oppressing and colonizing peoples of other countries. Herder's unquietness in all of these respects are trademarks of a thinker who would challenge and expand the eighteenth-century world. His provocative ideas also led to significant changes in several areas of nineteenth-century thought and have played a role in our own century.

Herder is best known for his contributions to the philosophy of history, German literature, and the philosophy of language. His writings on history emphasized the historical character of all human existence. This radical historical perspective led him to appreciate the uniqueness and integrity of diverse

1. Friedrich Nietzsche, *Menschliches Allzumenschliches,* vol. 1 of *Werke in drei Bänden,* ed. Karl Schlechta (München: Hanser, 1966), 924-25.

cultures and historical periods. In contrast to many thinkers of the Enlightenment, he warned against judging other cultures according to European standards. His ideas about history played a significant role in the emergence of historical consciousness and historicism in the nineteenth century.[2]

Herder expressed his lifelong interest in art and literature in his work as a poet, translator, and literary critic. In an age of prose, he reminded readers of the value of poetry. He also highlighted the individuality of the literature of various cultures by viewing it from a historical perspective. He thereby prompted a new appreciation not only for German folk songs and poetry but also for the indigenous literature of other cultures and periods. He wrote poetry and translated literature from various countries.[3] His work made him one of Germany's most significant literary critics and an initiator of the field of comparative literature.[4]

Herder's writings on language challenged the widely held view of reason as an autonomous faculty, clearly rejecting Immanuel Kant's notion of "pure reason." Herder claimed that reason is linguistic and historical: It is shaped by a particular language and by a particular historical situation. This emphasis on the linguistic character of human understanding played a formative role in the emergence of linguistics and the philosophy of language,[5] and several of his ideas are still echoed in modern language philosophy.[6]

In addition, Herder was a theologian, exegete, and Lutheran pastor whose views on history, literature, and language were tightly interwoven with his ideas about religion. These ideas were provocative in his own time and contributed to the development of several disciplines in the nineteenth century.

2. Friedrich Meinecke devotes a chapter of his book about historicism to Herder, and he cites Herder, Goethe, and Möser as "the three greatest and most effective among the first pioneers of a new sense of history in the eighteenth century." *Historicism: The Rise of a New Historical Outlook*, trans. J. E. Anderson (New York: Herder & Herder, 1972), 295.

3. For a discussion of Herder's work as a translator, see Andreas Kelletat, *Herder und die Weltliteratur* (Frankfurt/M.: Peter Lang, 1984).

4. Rene Wellek says that Herder is "the first modern historian of literature who has clearly conceived of the ideal of universal literary history"; *The History of Modern Criticism: 1750-1950* (New Haven: Yale University Press, 1955), 1:195. Robert Mayo argues that although Herder did not bring any fundamentally new ideas or methods to the study of comparative literature, he "expressed ideas which were already current more forcefully than any previous critic and put them forward at the right historical moment"; his "tremendous enthusiasm and eagerness to understand the literature of many different nations exercised a profound influence on succeeding generations"; *Herder and the Beginnings of Comparative Literature* (Chapel Hill: University of North Carolina, 1969), 146.

5. Ernst Cassirer called Herder's "Treatise on the Origin of Language" the first "psychological and philosophical beginnings" of a theory of language; *Freiheit und Form* (Berlin: Cassirer, 1916), 199. See also Rudolf Jung, "Sprachkritik bei Lichtenberg und Herder," *Jahrbuch des Wiener Goethe-Vereins*, Neue Folge der Chronik 70 (1966): 51; and R. H. Robins, *A Short History of Linguistics* (Bloomington: Indiana University Press, 1967), 151-53.

6. See James Marchand, "Herder: Precursor of Humboldt, Whorf, and Modern Language Philosophy" in *Johann Gottfried Herder: Innovator through the Ages*, ed. Wulf Koepke (Bonn: Bouvier, 1982), 20-34.

For example, he viewed religion historically, respected the individuality of diverse religions, and was convinced that all peoples possess religion. These insights helped to inspire the modern discipline of the history of religions,[7] to generate interest in myths and symbolic thinking,[8] and to disclose relationships between religion and culture. His ideas thereby contributed to the development of the fields of anthropology and the sociology of religion.

In the realm of biblical criticism, Herder prompted a historical examination of the texts and attention to their individuality. His insights into the Bible have placed him among the founders of literary-historical criticism.[9] Hans-Joachim Kraus claims that Herder's work anticipated almost every area of modern biblical criticism.[10] In Hebrew Bible studies, Herder's historical approach inspired a new appreciation of Hebrew language and poetry.[11] His writings on the New Testament discussed the theological and historical diversity of the Gospels, postulated an oral tradition behind them, and assumed that Mark was the first written expression of this tradition. Herder thereby "prepared the ground for the recognition of the priority of Mark and the emergence of the two-document hypothesis of gospel origins."[12]

Major German historians of Protestant thought, such as Karl Barth and Emanuel Hirsch,[13] recognize the importance of Herder's insights for theology. Karl Barth, for example, claims that Herder's penetrating understanding of the concrete reality of history opened the way to central theological developments of the nineteenth century. Barth calls Herder "the inaugurator

7. Ulrich Faust, *Mythologien und Religionen des Ostens bei Johann Gottfried Herder* (Münster: Aschendorff, 1977), 228-29; Claude Welch, *Protestant Thought in the Nineteenth Century* (New Haven: Yale University Press, 1985), 2:104-105; Gunther Stephenson, "Geschichte und Religionswissenschaft im Ausgehenden 18. Jahrhundert" in *Numen: International Review for the History of Religions* 13 (1966): 43-79; Gustav Mensching, *Geschichte der Religionswissenschaft* (Bonn: Universitätsverlag, 1948), 53-55, 66; and Joachim Wach, *Types of Religious Experience: Christian and Non-Christian* (Chicago: University of Chicago Press, 1951), 50.

8. He has been called "the first modern student of myth"; "Religion, The Study and Classification of" in *Encyclopedia Britannica*, 15th ed., 26:551.

9. Erhardt Güttgemann, *Offene Fragen zur Formgeschichte des Evangeliums* (München: Kaiser, 1970), 120.

10. Hans-Joachim Kraus, "Herders Alttestamentliche Forschungen" in *Bückeburger Gespräche über Johann Gottfried Herder 1971*, ed. by Johann Gottfried Maltusch (Bückeburg: Grimme, 1973), 59, 75. P. P. Miller believes "there is a clear anticipation of Kugel's interpretation of parallelism in the work of Herder"; "Meter, Parallelism, and Tropes: The Search for Poetic Style," *Journal for the Study of the Old Testament* 28 (1984): 101.

11. See, for example, C. Kuhl, "Bibel-Wisssenschaft des AT," *Die Religion in Geschichte und Gegenwart*, 3d ed., 1:1231.

12. Werner Georg Kümmel, *The New Testament: The History of the Investigation of Its Problems*, trans. S. McLean Gilmour and Howard C. Kee (New York: Abingdon, 1972), 82.

13. Karl Barth, *Protestant Thought: From Rousseau to Ritschl*, trans. Brian Cozens (New York: Harper and Row, 1959), 197-224; Emanuel Hirsch, *Geschichte der neueren evangelischen Theologie im Zusammenhang mit den allgemeinen Bewegungen des europäischen Denkens* (Gütersloh: Gerd Mohn, 1952), 4:224 ff.

of typical nineteenth century theology before its inauguration by Schleiermacher"[14] and states his significance in these bold terms:

> Herder's significance for those theologians who came after him can scarcely be
> rated highly enough. Without him the work of Schleiermacher and de Wette
> would have been impossible, and also the peculiar pathos of the course of
> theology in the nineteenth century. Without Herder there would have been no
> Erlangen group and no school of religious history. But for Herder, there would
> have been no Troeltsch.[15]

Although Herder's religious thought played a significant role in the history
of Western thought, this aspect of his work has gone almost unnoticed in the
English-speaking world. Few of his religious writings have been translated
into English,[16] and secondary literature is scarce. If English-speaking historians of Western religious thought write about Herder, then they either mention
him only in passing or falsely characterize him as an irrationalist.[17]

The purpose of this anthology is to introduce English-speaking readers to
the central themes, major works, and extensive breadth of Herder's religious
thought. Writings were selected that would help readers gain a fuller appreciation not only for the complexity of Herder's religious thought but also for
his place in the late eighteenth century and his influence in several areas of
nineteenth-century thought. Although the texts are of historical interest, they
also highlight Herder's continued importance as a thinker.

The anthology is divided into five chapters representing five areas that
were central to Herder's religious thought and influential in the nineteenth
century. Selections within each chapter are arranged, in general, chronolog-
ically. His writings typically interweave several themes and strongly resist
such a division. Nonetheless, this arrangement was the clearest way, in the
available space, to highlight central ideas in his works, to emphasize the range
of his ideas, and to encourage readers to explore more fully those areas of
his writing they find most compelling. One understands an author best by
reading an entire work. It is hoped that this selection of texts will prompt
readers to "go back to the sources" and study some of his texts in their entirety.

14. Barth, 223.
15. Ibid., 200.
16. Although a number of Herder's writings have been translated into English, there are
English translations of only two major works of his religious thought: *The Spirit of Hebrew
Poetry* and *God, Some Conversations*. (See the list of English translations in the Select Bibliography.)
17. Compare, for example, the extended treatment of Herder in Karl Barth's *Protestant
Thought: From Rousseau to Ritschl*; Otto Pfleiderer's *The Development of Theology in Germany
since Kant*, trans. J. Frederick Smith (New York: Macmillan, 1890); and Emanuel Hirsch's
Geschichte der neueren evangelischen Theologie to studies of this period in English. Hans Frei,
an exception, devotes an entire chapter to Herder's interpretation of the Bible in *The Eclipse of
Biblical Narrative* (New Haven: Yale, 1974). See also chapter 6 of Frank E. Manuel, *The
Eighteenth Century Confronts the Gods* (Cambridge: Harvard University Press, 1959).

This introduction is divided into two parts. The first provides a brief summary of Herder's life; the second introduces five major themes in Herder's religious thought, which correspond to the five chapters of this anthology. Part two considers Herder's treatment of these themes in more detail and introduces the selections of each chapter. Although these themes do not exhaust the content of Herder's religious thought, they were chosen because they are important themes in his writings, in nineteenth-century thought, and in religious thought today.

HERDER'S LIFE

Herder was born August 25, 1744, in the small town of Mohrungen, East Prussia (now Morag, Poland).[18] The region was at that time heavily influenced by Pietism.[19] The local pastor, Christian Reinhold Willamovius, had strong Pietistic tendencies, and Herder was brought up in a pious household in which the Bible was central. His father was a schoolmaster and the cantor at the Lutheran church. His mother was the daughter of a schoolmaster.

Herder showed much promise in school at an early age. Nonetheless, his father's salary was low, and his parents were unable to support their son's education financially. Fortunately, he did have access to the extensive library of a local pastor, Sebastian Friedrich Trescho, a Pietist with some appreciation for Enlightenment ideas. Early in 1761 Trescho offered Herder free lodging in exchange for his services as a copyist. In this setting, Herder had the opportunity to read the ancient classics, German authors, and theological writings. Herder's chance for a university education came in 1762, when he met a Baltic surgeon who was returning from the Seven Years' War. The doctor was so impressed with Herder's intelligence that he offered to take Herder to Königsberg and to pay for his medical education. The doctor also agreed to operate on Herder's eye, which had an ailment that would trouble him the rest of his life. Herder's only obligation was to translate an article by the doctor into Latin.

Herder went to Königsberg in the summer of 1762 and enrolled in medicine. He was queasy over the sight of blood, however, and soon switched to theology. There is little information about Herder's formal theological training. The most powerful intellectual influences on Herder occurred outside the theology

18. The standard biography is Rudolf Haym's *Herder nach seinem Leben und seinen Werken Dargestellt* (Berlin: R. Gaertner, 1877-85), 2 vols. The most comprehensive biography in English is Robert Clark's *Herder: His Life and Thought* (Berkeley: University of California Press, 1955). Shorter introductions to Herder's life and thought in English are A. Gillies, *Herder* (Oxford: Blackwell, 1945) and Wulf Koepke, *Johann Gottfried Herder* (Boston: Twayne, 1987).

19. Herbert Schöffler, "Johann Gottfried Herder aus Mohrungen" in *Deutscher Geist im 18. Jahrhundert*, 2d ed. (Göttingen: Vandenhoeck and Ruprecht, 1956), 62; Emil Adler, *Herder und die deutsche Aufklärung* (Frankfurt: Europa Verlag, 1968), 265.

faculty: in the lecture hall of Immanuel Kant (1724-1804) and in the home of Johann Georg Hamann (1730-87).

Herder went to hear Kant lecture for the first time in the fall of 1762 and soon became one of his most faithful students. Kant also respected Herder, permitted him to read manuscripts, and exempted him from tuition for classes. Kant had not yet written his three major critiques, and he lectured on a wide range of topics from mathematics and geography to ethics and metaphysics. His gift to Herder was less his own philosophy than a lively introduction to philosophers such as David Hume, Jean-Jacques Rousseau, Gottfried Wilhelm Leibniz, and John Locke. Above all, in the great tradition of the Enlightenment, Kant inspired Herder to think for himself. Later in his life Herder would criticize Kant's view of reason and the arts, and Kant would grow impatient with the poetic spirit in which Herder wrote about philosophy and history. Yet despite their later, often bitter differences, Herder always admired Kant.

During this period Herder also began a lifelong friendship with Hamann, whose insights were far different from those of Kant. Hamann, one of the great opponents of the Enlightenment, was well-versed in literature and a deeply religious man. His creative and at times enigmatic ideas played a complex role in several areas of Herder's thought. Hamann inspired in Herder a love of poetry, taught him English, and introduced him to English literature, particularly Shakespeare. Hamann also emphasized the role of faith, intuition, and feeling in religion. In addition, he provided a holistic view of the human personality, which influenced not only Herder's thought but also German Romanticism. Contrary to popular conceptions of his time, Hamann believed the human personality can be divided neither into mind and body nor into isolated faculties such as will, reason, and feeling. Goethe summarized Hamann's principle in this way: "Everything that we undertake to perform, whether by deed, by word, or otherwise, must arise from all our powers united together; everything in isolation is worthless."[20]

In 1764, after his education in Königsberg, Herder moved to Riga, now the capital of Latvia but then part of the Russian Empire. Initially, he was a teacher at the Cathedral School *(Domschule)*. After his ordination in the Lutheran church in 1767, he was also pastor of Riga's two principal churches and a popular preacher.

During this period of his life, from 1764 to 1769, Herder became well known through two of his works on literature and aesthetics: *Fragmente über die neuere deutsche Literatur* (1767) [Fragments concerning recent German

20. Johann Wolfgang von Goethe, *Aus meinem Leben: Dichtung und Wahrheit*, ed. Rich. Wülker (Leipzig: Seemann, 1903), 363 (Book 12).

literature] and *Kritische Wälder* (1769) [Critical forests].[21] The *Fragmente* aimed to produce a general history of literature and, at the same time, called for a renewal of German literature. In his historical survey of literature, Herder sought examples that could stimulate authors of his own day. Yet he rejected absolute standards of taste and criticized contemporary authors who imitated authors of the past or of other cultures. He was especially critical of the tendency of German authors of his time to neglect the German language and to import styles of writing from other countries instead. The *Fragmente* also dealt with language and the nature and value of poetry. Whereas many of his contemporaries viewed language as static and considered poetry merely a form of amusement, Herder believed that language constantly changes and that poetry reflects a people's deepest traits and very spirit.

Kritische Wälder was a response to various aesthetic theories of his time, including those of Gotthold Ephraim Lessing (1729-81), Johann Joachim Winckelmann (1717-68, who had written extensively on Greek art), Friedrich Justus Riedel (1742-86), and Christian Adolf Klotz (1738-71). The first section of the *Wälder* critiques Lessing's *Laokoon, oder, über die Grenzen der Malerei und Poesie* (1766). Although Herder admired Lessing and was greatly influenced by him, he criticized Lessing's failure to judge artistic expression in relation to its historical context. He also disagreed with Lessing's distinctions between literature and the visual arts. Finally, Herder emphasized the expressive qualities of the arts and their uniqueness in different times and cultures.[22]

During this period in Riga, Herder also became intimately acquainted with the literature and the suffering of the Latvian, Lithuanian, and Estonian peoples. Their lands were part of the Russian Empire at that time but were ruled by the German-speaking aristocracy. Herder saw how the aristocracy exploited the people and drove them from their land. Within this context Herder developed these themes, which are found throughout his writings: criticism of the exploitation of native peoples and respect for their unique cultures.[23]

Herder left Riga in the summer of 1769, planning to take a journey to France that would bring him new perspectives on the world. His thoughts on the voyage to France were recorded in Nantes in his "travel journal."[24] He traveled from France to Holland and Germany. During these travels, his ideas about literature and history continued to develop, and he met several leading

21. For a valuable discussion of Herder's aesthetic philosophy as expressed in his writings from 1763 to 1778, see Robert Norton's *Herder's Aesthetics and the European Enlightenment* (Ithaca: Cornell University Press, 1991).
22. The fourth section of the *Wälder* was not published during Herder's lifetime but is central to his aesthetics.
23. See also, for example: SW 4:413; 5:533-34, 546, 550; 18:222-24, 236-37, 255-57, 288-89.
24. *Journal meiner Reise im Jahr 1769* (SW 4:345-461).

figures of his time, such as Jean Le Rond d'Alembert (1717-1783) and Denis
Diderot (1713-1784) in Paris and the German poet Matthias Claudius (1740-
1815) and Lessing in Hamburg. After serving for a brief time as a tutor,
Herder went to Strassburg in the fall of 1770 and met Johann Wolfgang von
Goethe, who would become Germany's most renowned poet. Goethe and
Herder exchanged many ideas on literature and, despite a few periods of
estrangement, remained lifelong friends. During his stay in Strassburg, Herder
also wrote his most famous work on language, *Abhandlung über den Ursprung
der Sprache* (1772) [*Treatise upon the Origin of Language*, 1827].

In 1771 Herder accepted a position as court preacher in the town of Bückeburg, now part of northwest Germany, and stayed there until 1776. His years
in Bückeburg were difficult. The court of Count Wilhelm of Schaumburg-
Lippe, whose background was almost entirely military, was void of lively
literary and intellectual conversation. Herder also felt isolated among the
highly orthodox clergy of the region. He wrote to Johann W. L. Gleim on
August 9, 1772, that he was experiencing in Bückeburg "a living death."[25]
Herder's marriage to Karoline Flachsland (1750-1809) on May 2, 1773, in
Darmstadt, however, brought Herder much happiness at this time and throughout his life. These years also brought important developments in his views
of religion, history, and literature.

Herder's view of religion deepened, and he began to emphasize the emotional, inner life of faith and to criticize the rationalist theology of his day.
According to Horst Stephan, these new, mystical elements of Herder's thought
may have been prompted, in part, by his loneliness and dissatisfaction with
Bückeburg.[26] His turn to a less intellectual view of religion was, above all,
the outcome of his contact with two women: Karoline and Countess Maria.[27]
Although his wife's faith was not deeply mystical, she had an experiential
view of faith that had been fostered by her earlier contact with a group of
"sentimentalists" in Darmstadt. Herder also developed a friendship with the
Countess Maria, who had been brought up in the Pietistic school of Herrnhut.
Her deep humility and sincere Christian piety greatly influenced Herder. Their
relationship deepened when her twin brother died, and she and Herder exchanged several thought-provoking letters about religion.

Herder's emphasis on the inner life of faith was also strengthened by his
correspondence with Johann Kaspar Lavater (1741-1801), a Swiss enthusiast,
and with Matthias Claudius, who expressed mystical themes in his writings.
In addition, Herder was influenced by his reading of Pascal's *Pensées*:

> He found in Pascal an ally in his self-imposed task of defeating the rationalist
> and academic pedants, of cleansing religion from the corrosive influences of

25. *Briefe* 2:198.
26. Horst Stephan, *Herder in Bückeburg* (Tübingen: J.C.B. Mohr, 1905), 71. This book
provides the most extensive treatment of Herder's years in Bückeburg.
27. *Ibid.*; Clark, *Herder*, 183.

the professional commentators, and of restoring that harmony between the world and the will of God, the loss of which he saw increasingly clearly to the spiritual degeneration of the day.[28]

In these years, Herder wrote two significant theological texts that reflect his new attitude toward religion: *Älteste Urkunde des Menschengeschlechts* (1774, 1776) [The oldest document of the human race] and *An Prediger, Fünfzehn Provinzialblätter* (1774) [To preachers: Fifteen provincial letters]. The former, a translation and interpretation of Genesis 1-2, is a difficult text to read, in part because Herder tries to express himself in a way that reflects ancient Hebrew. Nonetheless, it is significant because of its historical approach to the Bible and its attack on rationalistic theology. Herder attempts to show that Genesis is neither the work of manipulative priests nor a faulty treatise on physics, as some Deists claimed, but rather a poetic work that depicts the early human experience of God's revelation in nature. In his interpretation he points out its similarities to Ancient Near Eastern accounts of creation. The work also contains some intriguing ideas about the origins of human language and consciousness.

In the *Provinzialblätter*, Herder's criticizes those who fail to grasp the power of religion. He denounces excessive preoccupation with reason and the rationalistic tendency to equate religion with morality. He especially attacks Johann Joachin Spalding (1714-1804), a respected Lutheran theologian of the time, for viewing the church as a tool of the state and tying sermons too closely to moral discourses.[29] Herder assumes here and later that religion is sui generis, affecting all our powers. This emphasis on the unique character of religion, which Herder outlines more precisely in later works, helped restore religion to a central place in the late eighteenth century.[30]

At this time Herder also wrote several other interpretations of the Bible: *Erläuterungen zum Neuen Testament* (1775) [Elucidations of the New Testament], *Briefe zweener Brüder Jesu* (1775) [Letters of two brothers of Jesus], and *Johannes Offenbarung* (1774) [The Revelation of John].

In addition to writing these theological texts, Herder wrote his first major historical work, *Auch eine Philosophie der Geschichte zur Bildung der Menschheit* (1774) [*Yet Another Philosophy of History of the Education of Humanity,* 1968]. This revolutionary work laid the foundation for historicism and "directly contributed to the reawakening of historical interest."[31] In this work Herder most clearly expresses his belief in the importance of the integrity

28. A. Gillies, *Herder* (Oxford: Basil Blackwell, 1945), 58.
29. Herder's early essay, "Der Redner Gottes," also emphasizes that sermons cannot be equated with moral discourses. See SW 32:3-11.
30. Barth, 201-2.
31. Georg Iggers, *The German Conception of History* (Middletown: Wesleyan University Press, 1983), 37.

and individuality of all peoples and ages of history. They are not to be judged
or ranked in relation to one another but rather studied on their own terms.
He resists textbook generalizations, common in his time (and our own), about
the course of history. He insists that historians must simultaneously carefully
study all significant historical data and imaginatively enter the unique spirit
of an age or culture.

While in Bückeburg, Herder also continued his work in the area of literature
and became a leading figure in the *Sturm und Drang* [Storm and Stress]. He
wrote several poems and collected folksongs from various cultures, showing
a particular interest in the sagas and early poetry of Northern Europe, such
as the Nordic *Edda*, Thomas Percy's collection of English ballads,[32] and
"Ossian." Herder also wrote essays on literature, including one of his most
famous, entitled "Shakespeare." The essay was part of the volume, *Von
deutscher Art und Kunst*, (1773) [On German style and art], which contains
two essays by Herder, one by Goethe, and another by Justus Möser (1720-
94). This revolutionary volume became a manifesto of the *Sturm und Drang*.[33]

In August of 1775 Herder was delighted to receive an offer to be professor
of theology and chaplain at the University of Göttingen. Christian Gottlob
Heyne, professor of philology at Göttingen, had helped initiate the offer, and
negotiations had been going on for about two years. Herder wrote the *Erläuterungen zum Neuen Testament* in order to satisfy the faculty and the court
that he was orthodox enough for the position. Later that fall, however, he
was called to a "colloquium" to explain his religious beliefs. Herder found
the request insulting and, despite encouragement from Heyne, refused to go.
He pointed out that he was, after all, the highest ranking pastor in Schaumburg-
Lippe and had taken up his office with the promise to uphold the faith according
to the Augsburg Confessions.[34] In the meantime, Goethe had helped him
secure a position as *Generalsuperintendent* in Weimar. Herder accepted the
position from Duke Karl August of Sachsen-Weimar and moved to Weimar
in October of 1776.

Herder stayed in Weimar from 1776 until his death in 1803. As *Generalsuperintendent* he served as the chief pastor of the region, court preacher,
and superintendent of schools. He performed his tasks well but was never
quite satisfied with the position. This dissatisfaction was due, in part, to lack
of financial support and to the government's reluctance to adopt all of his
proposed ecclesiastical and educational reforms. During this period he wrote
his most mature works on history, theology, and the Bible.

32. Thomas Percy, *Reliques of Ancient English Poetry* (1765).
33. For a discussion of the work and its historical context, see Edna Purdie's "Introduction"
to *Von deutscher Art und Kunst* (Oxford: Clarendon, 1924), 5-41.
34. Letter to Georg Friedrich Brandes (January 5, 1776); *Briefe* 3:243-46.

Herder's major historical work in Weimar was *Ideen zur Philosophie der Geschichte der Menschheit* [Ideas toward a philosophy of the history of humanity], published in four parts between 1784 and 1791. Lengthy yet unfinished, it is an ambitious work, in which Herder begins with reflections on the planet earth and the evolution of its many forms of life. He then turns to prehistoric cultures and a summary of recorded history to the sixteenth century. He devotes special attention to the ancient Hebrew people and to Greek civilization. He emphasizes the influence of climatic and geographic conditions as well as historical circumstances on the development of cultures. Several sections also criticize elements of his own age. In this work Herder stresses, as he did in *Yet Another Philosophy of History*, the immanent value of each historical culture and age. Yet he also seeks to discover patterns and laws in history.

His major works in theology during his years in Weimar were *Briefe, das Studium der Theologie betreffend* (1780-81) [Letters concerning the study of theology], *Gott, einige Gespräche* (1787) [*God, Some Conversations* (1940)], and *Christliche Schriften* (1794-98) [Christian writings]. The *Briefe, das Studium der Theologie betreffend*, were written as a practical guide for theology students. *God, Some Conversations* is Herder's most philosophical treatment of the concept of God.[35] The *Christliche Schriften* were published in five volumes. The first volume addresses the biblical themes of the gift of tongues and the resurrection while the second and third interpret the gospels. The fourth describes the spirit of Christianity, and the fifth the nature of religion.

Herder wrote several additional interpretations of the Bible during this period. *Lieder der Liebe* (1778) [Songs of love] is Herder's translation of and commentary on the Song of Solomon. *Maran Atha* (1779) is a historical interpretation of the book of Revelation. His most extensive and significant interpretation of the Hebrew Bible is *Vom Geist der hebräischen Poesie* [The spirit of Hebrew poetry, 1833], published in 1782-83. It was directed to a broad audience and quickly established Herder's reputation as an exegete in both Europe and North America.

During the last years of his life Herder continued to write on many subjects. He published some of his most important texts on human understanding. In *Vom Erkennen und Empfinden der menschlichen Seele* (1778) [On knowing and feeling in the human soul], which went through several drafts beginning in 1774, he argued that knowledge is not possible without sensation and experience. Later, in *Verstand und Erfahrung; Vernunft und Sprache. Eine Metakritik zur Kritik der reinen Vernunft* (1799) [Understanding and experience; reason and language: A metacritique of *The Critique of Pure Reason*],

35. For Herder's view of God, see also the "Thirtieth Letter" of his *Briefe, das Studium der Theologie betreffend* (in chap. 5 of this anthology).

he directly challenged Kant's view of human understanding and his separation of thought and language.

He also published his most important collection of *Volkslieder* (1778-79) [Folksongs], which contains translations of literature from a wide range of cultures, including German, English, Spanish, Scottish, Italian, Scandinavian, ancient Greek and Latin, Slavic, and Baltic. It was the "first comprehensive anthology of world literature"[36] and did much to prompt the research of *Volkslieder*. He continued to write about aesthetics and literature in several other works. His *Zerstreute Blätter* (1785-97) [Scattered leaves] are six collections that include some of his poems, translations of literature from several countries, and short essays on history, religion, and literary theory. *Kalligone* (1799) is a criticism of Kant's aesthetics as expressed in his *Critique of Judgment*.

In the light of the French Revolution, Herder offered a commentary on the contemporary situation and hopes for the human race in his *Briefe zu Beförderung der Humanität* (1793-97) [Letters for the advancement of humanity]. The letters, compiled into ten collections, are filled with his ideas about literature, history, and the possibilities for peace and social justice.[37] They express his lifelong rejection of tyranny and his affirmation of human rights and all that fosters human integrity. The journal *Adrastea* (1801-04), is a continuation of the *Briefe* and aims to provide a critical assessment of the eighteenth century. A journal of political and social history, it includes one of Herder's most popular translations: a Spanish epic poem entitled *El Cid*.

In addition to preaching and writing on such a vast array of subjects, Herder initiated several positive reforms in the Weimar schools. Despite his achievements, he was somewhat isolated during the last years of his life. His friendship with Goethe waned as Goethe's relationship to Schiller grew. He was also disturbed by political events of the late eighteenth century. Nevertheless, Herder continued to find much happiness in his family life and developed a close friendship with the young author Jean Paul Richter, who lived in Weimar from 1798 to 1800. Herder died on December 18, 1803.

CENTRAL THEMES IN HERDER'S RELIGIOUS THOUGHT

Human Nature, Language, and History

History is a central theme throughout Herder's writings, deeply connected to his religious ideas. Although his writings on history are diverse, three

36. Wellek, 192.
37. For his idea about ways to foster peace, see SW 18:267-274.

elements remain consistent: individuality, unity, and application. Herder pays attention, above all, to the individuality of every period or culture. He believes that each possesses the center of its own happiness and should be understood within its own context. No historical period, whether the Enlightenment or ancient Greece, may serve as the basis for judging others.

This individuality may be discovered by setting preconceptions aside and entering the spirit of a past age or people—by empathizing with it and understanding it on its own terms. Herder is not so naive as to believe that we can successfully set aside all prejudices; he is simply stressing the necessity of an openness to difference. This openness demands not only empathy and imagination but also the rigorous and disciplined collection of facts and data. Further, it requires a familiarity with the literature of a people and the traditions of its surrounding cultures.

Although Herder uncovers individuality in history, he also discovers its unity. To describe this unity he uses natural metaphors, such as the growth of a tree or the course of a river, as well as terms such as "continuity," "development," and "continuation" *(Fortgang)*.[38] In discussions of this unity Herder emphasizes, on the one hand, one culture's dependence on another and on its own past. Cultures rarely develop in isolation but rather emerge out of their history and in contact with other cultures. Since phases of human history grow out of one another, they have an organic unity. He emphasizes the unity of history, on the other hand, by pointing to God's providence. Herder believes that God has a plan and purpose for human history.[39] Even if human beings cannot perceive this plan, they can find glimpses of it within the individual scenes of history.[40]

A third element in Herder's approach to history is his application of the past to the present and the future. Although he seeks to understand a period on its own terms, he does not simply attempt to reconstruct the past. He recognizes that history is always understood from the present and must be interpreted for the present. With a historical perspective one can see not only the impact of history on the present but also possibilities for the future.[41]

38. SW 5:512, 530, 559.
39. SW 5:512-13, 559-61.
40. According to Irmscher, this understanding of history is similar to Martin Luther's notion of "masks" of the hidden God, which seems to have influenced Herder directly; "Johann Gottfried Herder," *Deutsche Dichter des 18. Jahrhunderts*, ed. Benno von Wiese (Berlin: Erich Schmidt, 1977), 537.
41. Both Hans-Georg Gadamer and Hans-Dietrich Irmscher have emphasized Herder's application of the past to the present. Irmscher clearly argues that Herder sees history in three ways: "1. als Fremdheit, 2. als Herkunft und 3. als fortwirkende Kraft"; "Grundzüge der Hermeneutik Herders," *Bückeburger Gespräche über Johann Gottfried Herder 1971* (Bückeburg: Grimme, 1973), 42. See Gadamer's "Nachwort" to Herder's *Auch eine Philosophie der Geschichte* (Frankfurt: Suhrkamp Verlag, 1967).

These elements of Herder's view of history are seen in the selection from his early, major work on history, *Yet Another Philosophy of History*. Herder's work directly attacks two popular views of history of his time. One view, represented by Isaak Iselin (1738-82), depicts history as a steady progression from superstition and barbarism to Enlightenment and a Golden Age of Reason. Iselin believes that history is progressing toward ever greater "virtue and happiness" and likens this progression to the ages of a human being, glorifying the Enlightenment as history's adulthood in its prime. The standard by which to judge history is, therefore, the present. For Herder, this view treats all other periods and cultures as simply a means to an end. He finds Iselin's scheme of the "ages" of history absurd and claims, "Each period has in itself the center of its own happiness. The youth is not happier than the innocent, contented child; nor is the peaceful old man unhappier than the energetic man in his prime."[42]

In addition, Herder claims that the idea that all periods of history progress toward the Enlightenment is not only false but also oppressive. He specifically mentions the European oppression of Jews, North and South American Indians, and European colonies. He complains that Europeans preach tolerance but live in greed at the expense of other cultures. He is disgusted by the arrogant claims of "philosophers in the northern valley of the earth" in the face of Europe's oppressive colonizations, threatening military build-ups, and slave-trade. Warning that there will come a time when these oppressed peoples will turn European ideals against the Europeans, Herder says, "We forge the chains with which they will bind us."[43]

In *Yet Another Philosophy of History* Herder also criticizes a skeptical view of history, represented by Voltaire, which sees no meaning or unity in history. Noting the variety of cultures and truth-claims represented within history, skeptics point out its inconsistencies and conclude that it has no unifying purpose. Although Herder also pays attention to the diversity found within history, he believes that history is guided by a divine purpose. His response to the skeptics is that although human beings cannot draw a complete picture of history's course, it nevertheless offers glimpses of a divine purpose "through the openings and ruins of individual scenes."[44]

Herder's view of history is linked to his understanding of human nature. He stresses the uniqueness and individuality of cultures because he recognizes that human beings are historical creatures. In other words, they are temporal beings who are shaped by the specific culture, traditions, and circumstances in which they are born. They can neither avoid nor change these "givens." As historical creatures, they are also, however, always in the process of

42. SW 5:512.
43. SW 5:579.
44. SW 5:513.

becoming. They use their own unique powers to appropriate and redefine that which has been handed down to them.

Although Herder emphasizes the diversity and uniqueness of human beings, he also believes that all human beings are one because they are made in God's image. This aspect of Herder's view of human nature is the foundation of his emphasis on tolerance. Because all people are made in God's image, they must not oppress one another. Herder is, at times, interpreted as a man who fostered extreme nationalism. Yet his emphasis on the individuality of a people was consistently coupled with the themes of tolerance, humanity, and the unity of the human race.[45]

This understanding of human nature is reflected in Herder's notion of *Bildung*, as expressed in the selection from the *Ideen zur Philosophie der Geschichte der Menschheit*. *Bildung* is, of course, a complex concept that has been interpreted in many ways. In German, it can mean "formation," "cultivation," or "education," and has been used in many ways to speak about how we develop as human beings. There are three basic elements in Herder's use of the term *Bildung*, however, that can help us understand some of its general characteristics in his writings.

The first element of *Bildung* is "tradition." Tradition underscores the limited historical nature of human beings. It is a way of saying that the thoughts and actions of human beings are shaped both by immediate historical circumstances and by all that has come before them. No one, according to Herder, becomes a human being alone. We are connected to parents, teachers, and friends, to the circumstances of our life, and to our culture. Herder recognizes that this culture has been, in turn, influenced by its history and by other surrounding cultures and their past.

Beyond tradition, the process of *Bildung* has a second principle: "organic powers." These are the unique powers possessed by all individual human beings that enable them to receive that which has been transmitted to them by tradition and to appropriate it in their own unique ways. Through these powers they can apply tradition to the needs of the present situation. Without such a power, history would be an endless imitation of what has already been.

Herder also believes that this process is guided by a universal purpose— humanity *(Humanität)*.[46] This is a broadly defined and significant term in

45. Since World War II Herder has sometimes been viewed as an extreme nationalist because the Nazis distorted and appropriated some of his ideas about the distinctiveness of peoples. However, it is clear in Herder's writings that he believed "that a nation based on a genuine culture would be peaceful, because it would respect other nations, and that concern for humanity as a whole was more important than concern for one's own nation." Wulf Koepke, *Johann Gottfried Herder*, iv. As Robert Ergang argues, "Herder's nationalism was in its essence humanitarian; it was built around the principle of the essential unity of mankind as a whole." *Herder and the Foundations of German Nationalism*, 1931 (Reprint, New York: Octagon, 1976), 263.
46. SW 14:235-52. See also: 13:154-65; 17:150-82, 343-44, 354.

Herder's writings. It expresses the notion that all human beings share a common purpose and direction and is based on the conviction that all human beings are made in the image of God. Herder often equates humanity with religion, claiming that both give direction to human development in all its diversity.[47] "Humanity" describes both the full development of one's unique capabilities and the normative goal toward which all human beings strive.[48] Herder believes that all people develop humanity in their own distinct ways and yet are united by it. Thus, the term encompasses both the unity and diversity of human beings.[49]

Herder believes that the process of *Bildung* is universal, whereby human beings simultaneously are formed by tradition and transform tradition anew. This does not imply that all human beings are the same. For Herder, they are shaped by differing traditions and possess differing gifts. No one person or culture is the same as another. Nevertheless, Herder believes that all human beings experience this process of *Bildung*.

Expanding on and historicizing the notion of a "chain of being,"[50] he speaks about a *Kette der Bildung*—a "chain of *Bildung*"—that can be seen throughout history. This "chain" is the process of history by which human beings are influenced by what has come before them and yet reshape history in new ways, according to their unique gifts. This process is not to be equated with "progress" in the sense that each generation becomes "better" or more "civilized" than the former. Rather, it finds ever new expression and God's continual guidance in diverse cultures and historical periods.

This view of *Bildung* corresponds to one aspect of Herder's understanding of immortality,[51] expressed in his *Über die menschliche Unsterblichkeit* (1791)

47. SW 13:154, 161; Herder says that the purer a religion, the more it advances humanity (SW 17:121).

48. Frederick Barnard suggests that Herder's definition of humanity contains two elements that constantly intermingle: 1) the capacity of human beings to achieve what human beings are able to achieve using their knowledge and skill to the best advantage in the course of one's historical development; 2) normative goals of human striving which involve general values. "Particularity, Universality, and the Hebraic Spirit," *Jewish Social Studies* 43 (1981): 132-33.

49. Michael Morton helps to describe this apparent contradiction in this way:
For Herder . . . as for his successors, the "home" to which we return is itself irreducibly twofold in nature: on the one hand, the condition of unity from which we all began; on the other, by virtue of incorporating multiplicity and diversity-indeed, contrariety—differing qualitatively from that original state.
Michael Morton, *Herder and the Poetics of Thought: Unity and Diversity in "On Diligence in Several Learned Languages"* (University Park: Pennsylvania University Press, 1989), 125-26.

50. The "chain of being" is a conception of the universe as a continuous gradation of types of being in order of perfection, stretching from God through a hierarchy of finite beings to nothingness. For a full discussion of the meaning of this idea in the history of Western thought, see Arthur Lovejoy, *The Great Chain of Being* (Cambridge: Harvard University Press, 1961).

51. For a fuller picture of his view of immortality see also: "Gespräche über die Seelen Wanderung," "Palingenesie," "Tithon und Aurora," "Von Wissen und Nichtwissen der Zukunft." For a discussion of the development of Herder's view of immortality see Rudolf Ungar, *Herder, Novalis und Kleist* (Frankfurt: Diesterweg, 1922), 1-23.

[On human immortality]. Although in other contexts Herder speaks of immortality as eternal life, in this lecture he defines the essence of immortality as one's positive influence on later generations. Since human beings are historical, they are bound to influence the future. Those who contribute to it in ways that foster human dignity and integrity are immortal. They pass on those most noble elements in life that are taken up by later generations. Although their names may be forgotten, their positive contributions, passed on through texts, deeds, institutions, or personal examples, live on in history, in the *Kette der Bildung*.

The *Abhandlung über den Ursprung der Sprache* [*Treatise upon the Origin of Language*] emphasizes the historical nature of human beings and clearly expresses another central dimension of Herder's view of human nature, making it an important work for the beginnings of modern philosophical anthropology.[52] In this work and several others,[53] he defines human beings as essentially linguistic creatures.[54] Because they think through a certain language, their worldview is shaped by their native tongue. Language is thereby integrally related to human consciousness and to cultural identity. For Herder, human beings are essentially creatures of language. This view stood in contrast to the contemporary views that did not recognize the linguistic nature of understanding and tended to perceive language as merely an instrument of thought.

The essay was written in the context of widespread interest in the origin of language.[55] In 1769 the Berlin Academy of Science offered a prize for the best essay on the subject.[56] Herder's essay, which won the prize in 1771, has two parts. The first part rejects contemporary theories about the origin of language and posits a new view. One theory, represented by Johann Peter Süssmilch (1707-67), a theologian and member of the Academy, claims that

52. Wolfhart Pannenberg, *Anthropologie in theologischen Perspektive* (Göttingen: Vandenhoeck and Ruprecht), 40-76. Pannenberg points out the considerable influence of Herder on Arnold Gehlen.

53. Herder's texts on language have been collected by Erich Heintel in *Johann Gottfried Herder: Sprachphilosophische Schriften* (Hamburg: Felix Meiner, 1960).

54. SW 30:144.

55. For a discussion of the context and argument of Herder's essay see: Edward Sapir, "Herder's 'Ursprung der Sprache,' " *Modern Philology* 5 (1907): 109-42. It is important to remember that Herder's own ideas about language arose within a rich and complex discussion, and he combines elements of already existing linguistic theories. As Robert Norton notes, "Little justice would be done to either Herder's essay or the Enlightenment philosophies of language if one would interpret the *Abhandlung* as a profoundly original repudiation of shallow contemporary ideas," *Herder's Aesthetics*, 103.

56. The precise questions proposed by the Academy were: "En supposant les hommes abandonnés à leurs facultés naturelles, sont-ils en état d'inventer le langage? Et par quels moyens parviendront-ils d'eux-mêmes à cette invention? On demanderoit une hypothèse qui expliquat la chose clairement et qui satisfît à toutes les difficultés." Adolf von Harnack, *Geschichte der Königlich Preussischen Akademie der Wissenschaft zu Berlin* (Berlin: Reichsdruckerei, 1900), 2:306.

language has a divine origin.[57] Herder interprets this to mean that it was taught to human beings by God.[58] Herder dismisses this hypothesis as muddled and claims that Süssmilch's theory actually refutes itself.

Other theories, represented by E. Bonnot de Condillac and Jean-Jacques Rousseau, try to explain how human beings transformed instinctive animal sounds or cries into human speech. Condillac, a French thinker, asserts that various instinctive cries and gestures came to be used by human beings as signs and were then gradually replaced by more articulate sounds.[59] Other sounds were added by analogy and associated with the objects to which they referred. According to Herder, Rousseau follows Condillac in suggesting that human language originated from inarticulate cries and gestures.[60] Yet Rosseau adds that an almost deliberate agreement was made between human beings when gestures were substituted by speech.

Herder admits that the instinctive sounds of human beings could be called language. These sounds are a kind of "natural language" that human beings share with sentient creatures. They are expressed today in interjections and cries of emotion. Yet Herder denies that this "language of feeling" or "animal language" is the root of human language. He argues that involuntary utterances of emotional states or sensations are very different from human language and that no transition between the two is possible.

In contrast to such theories, Herder assumes that human beings possessed language from the beginning. Language is part of human nature itself, for the ability to reflect, a characteristic unique to human beings, is possible only through language. For Herder, thinking and language are coterminous. Reflective consciousness arises only in the development of language. As reflective creatures, human beings are also creatures of language. Their self-consciousness and consciousness as a community—in essence, "their world"—is constituted only through language. Thus, the question of the origin of language is no longer central to Herder because human beings are seen as essentially linguistic creatures.

The second part of the essay provides four "laws" or observations concerning actual languages and their historical development. The first law emphasizes the ability of individuals to increase the power of their use of language.

57. His essay was entitled *Versuch eines Beweises, dass die erste Sprache ihren Ursprung nicht von Menschen, sondern allein vom Schöpfer erhalten habe* (Berlin, 1766).

58. For a reevaluation of Süssmilch's theory of language and Herder's possible misinterpretation of it see: Bruce Kieffer, "Herder's Treatment of Süssmilch's Theory of the Origin of Language in the *Abhandlung über den Ursprung der Sprache*: A Re-evaluation," *The Germanic Review* 53 (1978): 96-105. Kieffer believes that both Herder and Süssmilch assert that human beings possessed language from the beginning of their existence.

59. Herder refers to Bonnot de Condillac's, *De l'origine et du progres du langage* (vol. 2 of *Essai sur l'origine des connaissances humaines*, (Amsterdam: Pierre Mortier, 1746).

60. See Rousseau's *Discours sur l'origine et les fondements de l'inégalité parmi les hommes*, (Amsterdam: M. M. Rey, 1755).

The second law outlines the ways that language develops within the family. The third addresses the development of distinct languages within cultures, claiming that a countless variety of languages is bound to exist because of the diverse conditions and needs of individual peoples. Despite his emphasis on diversity, Herder states in his fourth law that all languages have common roots. He bases his claim on the similarity of grammatical structures and the almost universal use of similar alphabets. This argument for the unity and diversity of human language conforms to his understanding of both the unity and diversity of the human race.

Myth and Religion

Herder's historical perspective is clearly evident in his understanding of myth and religion, for he views them, like all aspects of culture, as historical phenomena. He studies religions in relation to their immediate historical contexts and to the surrounding traditions that have influenced them. When he discusses the New Testament and early Christianity, for example, he takes into account both the historical circumstances of first century Christians and the influences of Hellenistic, Jewish, and even gnostic traditions on them. Through this historical approach, he recognizes the political and social roles of religion in a particular culture.

This historical view enables Herder to appreciate the individuality of the religious expression of any culture. He says that peoples differ from one another in every respect; hence their religions also differ.[61] He also discovers individuality and, therefore, diversity within the various forms that one religion may take over time, in a variety of cultural contexts, and even among individuals of the same culture. This appreciation for the individuality of religious expression leads him to insist that religious beliefs and texts be studied without prejudice and without judging them according to foreign standards. For example, he criticizes those who ridicule the religion of the ancient Hebrews as mere superstition.[62] Further, in contrast to many thinkers of the Enlightenment, he respects and appreciates primitive religions.[63] Although he tends to praise Christianity as a religion of humanity, he, unlike Friedrich Schleiermacher (1768-1834) and G. W. F. Hegel (1770-1831), neither "ranks" religions nor classifies them in relation to one another.

Herder's historical perspective on religion can be found throughout all periods of his career. For example, the early fragment, "Über die verschiedenen Religionen," ca. 1764 [Concerning the various religions] expresses

---

61. SW 24:49.
62. SW 5:483-87.
63. Herder says we have much to learn from them. See, for example, SW 32:148-52.

Herder's desire to write a history of religions.[64] In this essay he emphasizes
that religions are diverse and should be studied historically. He also underlines
the social and political dimensions of religion. He insists that one must study
the religion of a people in relation to its political structure because religions
are woven into a culture's fabric and have always played a political role.

Herder's historical approach is also evident in his *Fragment einer Abhandlung über die Mythologie* [Fragment of an essay on mythology], published
posthumously and written sometime between 1782 and 1792.[65] In the essay
he criticizes those who label myths as "blind superstition" and claims that
myths are "activities of human reason." They express ways that human beings
have attempted to understand their world and to express their feelings about
it. Instead of viewing these myths with prejudice, we can use them to learn
much about a people's thought and culture.

In a much later work entitled *Über National-Religionen: Erstes Gespräch*
(1802) [First dialogue concerning national religions], Herder emphasizes that
religions develop within particular contexts and thereby reflect and inform
the culture, language, and spirit of a people. He explains that the religion of
a people emerges in relation to the deepest traits of that people's character.
Although one member of Herder's dialogue treasures Christianity as the highest
expression of Jesus' "religion of humanity," the essay clearly urges readers
not to compare or judge religions in relation to one another. Herder closes
his dialogue with a vision in which the unique and diverse religions of the
world are respected and religious tyranny no longer exists.

In addition to viewing religion as an historical phenomenon, Herder provides in his writings at least three further characteristics of religion. First, he
claims that religion is as central to human nature as reason and language and
that all people possess religion. He believes that religions are expressions of
our humanity and reflect a divine plan and purpose for history. He recognizes
many negative elements in the history of religions, and yet he affirms that
religions can express and help foster what is most noble in human beings.

Second, he believes that religion affects one's entire being. It provides the
center of one's approach to the world. In his sermons, *An Prediger, Fünfzehn
Provinzialblätter* [To preachers: Fifteen provincial letters], *Briefe, das Studium
der Theologie betreffend* [Letters concerning the study of theology], and other
texts, he emphasizes the emotional, experiential nature of faith, arguing against
tendencies to equate religion with either "correct doctrine" or morality. Nevertheless, he does not focus on emotion alone. He believes religion engages

64. Rudolf Haym believes the text was written in 1765 (*Herder*, 1:309) but Otto Hoffmann
dates it 1764 (SW 33:41).

65. Ulrich Faust, *Mythologien und Religionen des Ostens bei Johann Gottfried Herder*
(Münster: Aschendorff, 1977), 42. The first publication of Herder's fragment is found in Faust's
volume, 43-46, 154-64.

one's entire being and all of one's powers. He therefore criticizes Pietists or Enthusiasts who have reduced religion to a matter of inward, private feelings or to the mystical experience of unity with God.

The selection on religion from the *Ideen zur Philosophie der Geschichte der Menschheit* [Ideas toward a philosophy of history] emphasizes this point. He claims that, on the one hand, religion engages the mind. It is introduced through the endeavor to find causes of events and discover their relationships. Human beings search for causes, and where they see no visible ones in nature they seek invisible ones. On the other hand, religion is also an exercise of the heart. It engages human feelings, emotions, and convictions.[66] Religion is tightly interwoven into a person's way of ordering and experiencing the world and thereby informs a culture's values, language, morals, and entire character.

The volume *Von Religion, Lehrmeinungen und Gebräuchen* [Concerning religion, doctrines, and practices] also underscores the depth of religious experience by distinguishing religion from doctrine and from natural science. This text is the last volume of the *Christliche Schriften*. It is addressed to Christians as well as non-Christians and is Herder's most extensive text on the nature of religion. He fears that in his own time religion was reduced to right thinking by the orthodox; to feeling by the radical Pietists; and to ethics by the rationalists. Herder insists that religion is "a matter of our entire being, or our innermost consciousness."[67] "It is the innermost consciousness of what we are as human beings and of what we ought to be and do as human beings."[68] If one understands religion in this way, then one will neither confuse religion with a set of doctrines and rules nor be fearful of scientific discoveries.

Third, this text and several others indicate that according to Herder, religion arises out of a sense of God's power in nature and of one's own place in it. In one section of *The Spirit of Hebrew Poetry*,[69] for example, he speaks about the feeling of God's power in nature as the origin of religion. He claims that fear and ignorance did not invent religion, as some thinkers of his time and as even some of Herder's early writings suggested. He believes religion arises from the feeling of adoration or wonder in the presence of a mighty "spirit" whose power is witnessed in nature. Even among the most primitive peoples, a sublime poetry and sensibility exist that are created by the "all-pervading feeling of this great, invisible spirit."[70] Some religions may mix this feeling with terror and fear, and yet the belief in the existence of a powerful, good,

66. SW 13:161-65.
67. SW 20:141. Another text that defines religion is SW 21:604-7. Herder does admire those Pietists, such as Spener, Zinzendorf, and Arndt, who separated religion from dogma; SW 20:250, 251; 23:490, 492; 24:32, 35.
68. SW 20:159.
69. SW 11:248-60.
70. SW 11:248. cf. SW:32:148-52 (his earlier view of religion).

spirit is never completely annihilated. All peoples, to greater and lesser degrees, still have a sense of this "great spirit" and the goodness of existence.

God and Nature

One cannot appreciate Herder's views about religion apart from his understanding of God and nature. Herder rejects several popular conceptions of God: the distant God of the Deists, the moral God of Kant and of the rationalists, the naively personal God of the Pietists, and the pantheist equation of God and the world. Herder speaks of God in terms of being *(Dasein)* and in terms of a power or energy *(Kraft)* that moves through all things. God is the source of all existence and the dynamic power that orders and unites it.[71]

Nature reflects this ordering activity of God. The laws of nature are expressive symbols of the divine.[72] All parts of nature are also interrelated because they are guided by and are expressions of the wise and good ordering power of God. Further, nature is a dynamic, unified complex of forces. Matter is not "dead" but rather a system of active forces that change and form a whole. This view of nature as a dynamic, living organism stands in contrast to the mechanistic, static view of the world that was common during the Enlightenment.[73]

This understanding of God and nature affects Herder's view of revelation. Although Herder emphasizes the Bible as God's revelation, his view of revelation is much more encompassing. In his *Briefe, das Studium der Theologie betreffend,* he calls revelation the "education of the human race."[74] He believes that God has acted in and through history in diverse ways to help guide human understanding. Thus, revelation cannot be limited to the Bible. Nature, too, is a form of God's revelation.[75] Although it can be confusing,[76] it declares the glory of God. Herder believes that history and other texts, such as those by ancient Greek philosophers, have also disclosed God's activity and purpose.[77] Given his broad understanding of revelation, Herder does not want to

---

71. SW 16:539-41, 543-45, 566-71.

72. SW 16:529.

73. For a fuller discussion of his view of nature, see Walter D. Wetzels, "Herders Organismusbegriff und Newtons Allgemeine Mechanik" and Martin Bollacher, "'Natur' und 'Vernunft' in Herders Entwurf einer Philosophie der Geschichte der Menschheit" in *Johann Gottfried Herder 1744-1803* (Hamburg: Felix Meiner, 1987), 177-85, 114-24; Friedrich von Bärenbach, *Herder als Vorgänger Darwin's und der modernen Naturphilosophie* (Berlin: Grieben, 1877); and H. B. Nisbet, *Herder and the Philosophy and History of Science* (Cambridge: Modern Humanities Research Association, 1970). For Herder's view of the unity and diversity of nature, see also SW 6:318-19.

74. SW 10:285-86.

75. See also SW 6:234, 258; 10:292-97; 16:535. Note that Herder does not equate God and nature; SW 10:330-31.

76. SW 10:297.

77. SW 10:298.

set reason and nature in opposition to Scripture. All, he claims, are gifts from
God and, as such, all are meant to be used.

The selection from the *Älteste Urkunde des Menschengeschlechts* [Oldest
document of the human race] depicts the powerful revelation of God that
Herder finds in nature. The text is an interpretation of Genesis that describes
the dawn as God's revelation. The delight and wonder of the morning light
grasps all of God's creatures. This revelation is given to all peoples, and thus
all have a sense of the divine—a sense of the ordering power that moves
through all things.

In his essay, *Liebe und Selbstheit* (1785) [Love and selfhood] Herder speaks
further about the sense of God that all creatures possess. He believes that
God has created in all of them a longing for and feeling of God. This feeling
is inevitable because God has given life to all that exists; God's love and
wisdom have created all things. God is the "great universal mother," the
"tender supreme father," the "all in all." Thus, all things are bound to point
to God's presence and possess an intimation of it.

The essay also addresses the way in which human beings relate to God.
Herder criticizes Enthusiasts, who are fascinated with seeking unity with God.
The essay builds on the views of Frans Hemsterhuis (1721-90), a Dutch
philosopher who visited Herder in 1785 and whose treatises influenced the
philosophy of Germany's *Sturm und Drang*. Hemsterhuis believes that happiness comes through union with the object of one's desire (whether a work
of art, a person, or God). This union is possible through love, understood in
the platonic sense of eros. Yet he criticizes Enthusiasts who claim that the
highest expression of love of God is the immediate experience of unity with
the divine.

Herder specifies the limitations of the Enthusiasts' view of love. For him,
anything that annihilates one's individuality or consciousness cannot be love,
for without them, a relationship is impossible. Herder sees that our relationships to others and to God, if they are to remain relationships, are limited by
our individual existence. He believes true love of God and neighbor begin
with one's individual existence and not with the attempt to be united with
God and all things. He warns the cosmopolitans of his time, "Those who
embrace the whole universe with love usually love nothing but their own
narrow selves."[78] He also claims that God wants to be loved by our whole
being (both head and heart) and not simply by our emotions.

God, Some Conversations offers Herder's most philosophical and explicit
treatment of God and nature. The text must be understood in the context of

78. SW 15:323.

the "Pantheism Controversy."[79] The controversy began in 1783 when Moses Mendelssohn (1729-86), who was planning to write a work on Lessing's character, learned that Friedrich Heinrich Jacobi (1743-1819) believed that Lessing had been a Spinozist. At that time Benedict Spinoza (1632-77) was despised and generally considered to be an atheist, and his work was either rejected or ignored. Thus, Mendelssohn questioned the charge and asked Jacobi for more information. Jacobi then wrote him an account of his meeting with Lessing on July 6, 1780 in Wolfenbüttel.[80] Jacobi claimed that during a discussion of Goethe's poem, *Prometheus* (1774), Lessing confessed his disappointment with the orthodox conceptions of God and said that he knew nothing other than *hen kai pan*.[81] When Jacobi said that this sounded like Spinoza, Lessing expressed his sympathy with the philosopher. This confession shocked Jacobi because he believed that Spinoza's system led to atheism and determinism.

After receiving Jacobi's letter, Mendelssohn decided to write a work that would clarify Lessing's relation to Spinoza. Jacobi feared that Mendelssohn would misrepresent both Lessing and Spinoza and therefore decided to write his own book on the two thinkers. He wrote to Herder for advice. The two letters in this anthology are Herder's response to Jacobi. In them, Herder confesses his own agreement with *hen kai pan* and criticizes Jacobi's narrow view of God. The letters also indicate Herder's extensive occupation with Spinoza's philosophy and Goethe's appreciation of it.[82] Despite Herder's critique, Jacobi published his book in 1785, the same year that Mendelssohn's work was published.[83] With the publication of these two works, the controversy became public.

79. See Emil Adler, "Pantheismus-Humanität-Promethie" in *Bückeburger Gespräche 1971*, 77-90; Frederick H. Burkhardt's introduction to his translation of *God, Some Conversations*; A. C. McGiffert, "The God of Spinoza as Interpreted by Herder," *Hibbert Journal* 3 (1904-05): 706-26; Max Grunwald, *Spinoza in Deutschland* (Berlin: S. Calvary, 1897); Brian Gerrish, "The Secret Religion of Germany," *Journal of Religion* 67 (1987): 437-55; and A. Altmann *Moses Mendelssohn: A Biographical Study* (Tuscaloosa: University of Alabama Press, 1973), 553-759. The chief material of the controversy has been collected by Heinrich Scholz in *Die Hauptschriften zum Pantheismusstreit* (Berlin: Kantgesellschaft, 1916). Selections from this documentation have been translated into English by G. Vallée, J. B. Lawson, and C. G. Chapple in *The Spinoza Conversations Between Lessing and Jacobi* (New York: University Press of America, 1988).

80. See Jacobi's letter of November 4, 1783 in *Über die Lehre des Spinoza, in Briefen an den Herrn Moses Mendelssohn* (Breslau, 1785).

81. Greek for "one and all." It suggests that God and all that exists are one.

82. Herder had been familiar with Spinoza's writings for several years. He mentions Spinoza in his writings as early as 1765, although negatively (SW 32:32). He probably read Spinoza for himself sometime before 1769 and speaks highly of him already in the 1770s (SW 8:202; 32:228; *Briefe* 3:151). See also: David Bell, *Spinoza in Germany from 1679 to the Age of Goethe* (London: Bithell series of Dissertations, 1984), 38 ff.; Martin Bollacher, "Der junge Goethe und Spinoza," *Studien zur Geschichte des Spinozismus in der Epoche des Sturms und Drangs* (Tübingen, 1969).

83. Jacobi's book was *Über die Lehre* (cited above). Mendelssohn's work was entitled: *Morgenstunden, oder Vorlesungen über das Daseyn Gottes* (Berlin: C. F. Voss und Sohn: 1785).

Herder's work, *God, Some Conversations* (1787), is his own contribution to the controversy. It is written in the form of five dialogues that build on the ideas of Leibniz, Spinoza, and the Earl of Shaftesbury. The work provides, in the first place, a more positive and accurate understanding of Spinoza than other works of the period.[84] It was "the first extensive work in Germany to justify Spinoza's system and to acclaim him as a great thinker."[85] McGiffert claims that the work also "did more than any other to bring Spinoza into favour with the thinkers of the day, and to prepare the way for the tremendous influence which he exerted in Germany in the first half of the nineteenth century."[86] The work thereby provided "one of the most important roots of the nineteenth century emphasis on divine immanence."[87]

The primary source of information about Spinoza at that time was through Pierre Bayle's article on Spinoza in his *Dictionnaire Historique et Critique* (1697), in which Bayle mentions Spinoza's exemplary character but denounces him as an atheist. Herder encourages people to read Spinoza's writings themselves. If they do, then they will find that Spinoza is neither an atheist nor a pantheist. For Herder, Spinoza was a moral Enthusiast for whom God was central. In his writings, God is the immanent cause of things, but God and nature are not identical.

In the second place, the *Conversations* provide Herder's own view of God. Herder integrates many of Spinoza's ideas, such as the immanence of God in all things. Yet Herder questions Spinoza's notion that thought and extension are the attributes of God that the human intellect grasps. He believes that God is revealed in an infinite number of forces in an infinite number of ways. Herder also incorporates into his view of God Leibniz's category of active force *(vis viva)* and Shaftesbury's emphasis on the order and harmony of the world. Herder speaks of God as the ground and source of all things, as the active power that gives life to all things; he believes God's goodness and wisdom move in and through all aspects of existence. The organic interrelationship of all things in nature is a sign of this powerful, active, primal force.

This view of God and God's manifestation in nature implies a new understanding of God's relation to human beings. If one explores nature and discovers its laws, then God's wise rule and sacred necessity will be disclosed. One cannot demonstrate the existence of God. Yet through feeling and intuition and through the keen observation of nature, one can be certain of God's existence and ordering power through all things. Happiness comes to those

84. Roger Scruton claims that Herder's view of Spinoza was more discriminating than that of Jacobi and Mendelssohn; *Spinoza* (Oxford: Oxford University Press, 1986), 111.
85. Burkhardt, "Introduction" to *God*, 34.
86. McGiffert, "The God of Spinoza as Interpreted by Herder," 710.
87. Ibid., 711.

who willingly follow divine necessity and sense their own place in the whole. This emphasis on the place of humanity in the cosmos has implications, as Gerrish argues, for a new understanding of the religious quest. "Without saying so, Herder moves the religious goal closer to the ancient Chinese ideal of harmony with the forces of nature, or with their underlying principle or way."[88]

In addition to providing a concept of God, the text also criticizes particular ways of speaking about God in Herder's own time. For example, he criticizes Jacobi (both in his letters and in the *Conversations*) for referring to God as "extramundane" and as a "person."[89] Since "person" and "personality" are terms that indicate particularity, they can mislead people into believing that God is more *a* being than the ground of all existence. Furthermore, "extramundane" implies God exists "outside of the world," whereas for Herder God acts in, under, and through all existence.[90] Herder also criticizes some anthropomorphic images of God from Leibniz,[91] the image of God as the "world-soul,"[92] and the language of expansion and contraction for God's creative activity.[93] The way these words are used can imply that God is a being encompassed by space and time instead of the ground of being and the active, organizing power working through it.

In both his writings about God and religion Herder discusses the complex nature of religious language.[94] He believes that language about God is diverse. He claims that it differs according to a people's language, tradition, historical circumstances, concepts, needs, and even geographic location. There is no absolute religious language that can be used universally. All peoples have a unique way of speaking about God. In *Über National-Religionen: Erstes Gespräch* [National religions] he says every people has its own religious language because it springs from that people's distinctive character, tradition, language, and way of thinking and feeling.

For Herder, this inevitable diversity demands our respect. The religious language of various peoples is bound to differ, and this diversity calls for understanding rather than judgment. He criticizes those who claim that ancient religions and their literature are nonsense simply because they differ from

88. Gerrish, 454. This attitude is expressed very early, in 1768, in a prayer from a sermon (SW 31:86).
89. SW 16:497-99; letters to Jacobi of February 6 and December 20, 1784 in *Briefe* 5:27-29, 89-91.
90. *Briefe* 5:90.
91. SW 16:481-84.
92. SW 16:526-28.
93. SW 16:506-07; *Briefe* 5:28.
94. For a fuller discussion of this theme see Marcia Bunge, "Human Language of the Divine: Herder on Ways of Speaking about God," *Herder Today*, ed. Kurt Mueller-Vollmer (Berlin: Gruyter, 1990), 304-18.

one's own.[95] For example, he questions those who attack ancient Hebrew personifications of God, such as shepherd and father,[96] and those who expect the sayings of Jesus to be written in the style of a modern-day dogmatic theology.

Although Herder is enthusiastic about diverse ways of speaking about God, he does not say that all ways are meaningful. His writings imply three specific criteria for meaningful discourse about God. First, words about God are meaningful if they point beyond themselves to God as the ground of being and as the active power that unites and orders all existence. Second, meaningful discourse about God engages both thought and feeling. In other words, it is both cognitive and emotive, reflective and affective. Finally, meaningful language about God should have a relation to the tradition it addresses, otherwise it will be unintelligible to the people. For example, Herder criticizes the Jesuit missionaries in South America and especially those in China for not understanding the traditions of these peoples and thereby failing to proclaim the Christian message to them in a meaningful way.[97]

Literature and the Bible

Herder's historical perspective also shapes his approach toward both literature and the Bible. He examines all texts in relation to their historical contexts, investigating not only their immediate historical setting but also the broader influence of other ancient religions and traditions on them. For example, he encourages his readers of the Bible to study not only the immediate historical contexts of specific works but also the geography, literature, history, and languages of Ancient Near Eastern cultures.

Herder also appreciates the individuality of each work, refusing to judge texts according to foreign standards or to compare them to one another. In speaking of the Hebrew Bible prophets, for example, he says that each has a particular spirit, history, and language.[98] Even the various parts of one prophet's writing should be treated individually because they arise out of different circumstances.[99] In the same way, he claims that the Gospels are highly individual, for each reflects the unique interests and gifts of the authors and their particular audiences. Herder uncovers this individuality both through empathy with the author and through rigorous historical and philological investigation.

Herder's historical approach to literature is clearly expressed in the text, *"Resultat der Vergleichung der Poesie verschiedener Völker alter und neuer*

95. SW 11:12-13; 10:287.
96. SW 12:10-12.
97. SW 24:7-8, 23-25.
98. SW 10:98-99.
99. SW 10:99-100.

Zeit" [Conclusions drawn from the comparison of the poetry of diverse peoples of ancient and modern times.][100] Although the text was published late in Herder's career (1796) and stresses the moral dimension of poetry more than Herder's earlier writings, it reveals the historical view of literature that is also found throughout his works. The essay points out the diversity and uniqueness of the literature of various peoples. Herder takes issue with those who were caught up in the *Querelle des Anciens et des Modernes*, disputing whether ancient literature, especially Homer, or modern should beheld in highest esteem.[101] Herder argues that no piece of world literature is "ideal" for all cultures. Literature of diverse cultures should not be compared to one another; attention should be given to their natural distinctions.

Herder also criticizes two common approaches to literature. One approach classifies literature according to genres and literary forms. He asks: How can the tragedy of Greece be fairly compared to the tragedy of Shakespeare? He is convinced that the precise nature of these literary forms differs according to various cultures, and thus genres cannot provide a fruitful approach.

Another approach, represented by Friedrich Schiller, attempts to classify literature according to the basic sentiments of the poets. Schiller's essay, "Über naive und sentimentalische Dichtung" (1795) [Naive and sentimental poetry], classifies poets according to different "modes of perception." Although Herder is intrigued by Schiller's insights, he believes that such classifications of poets or their poetry are superficial. The true method of understanding poetry, for Herder, is the "natural method": "to leave each flower in its own context and from here to study it from its roots to its top just as it is, in reference to its own time and nature."[102]

This "natural" approach is seen in Herder's most famous essay on literature, "Shakespeare." At this time in Germany, Shakespeare's work was criticized by those, such as Johann Christoph Gottsched (1700-66), who took the conventions of French theatre as the norm by which all drama was to be judged. Others, such as Lessing, defended Shakespeare by explaining that his works conformed to the standards for tragedy set by Aristotle.

Herder's essay takes a radically new turn by attempting to appreciate Shakespeare's plays on their own terms and in relation to their historical context. He claims that every form of drama—whether of ancient Greece, Elizabethan England, or eighteenth-century France—develops in a particular context with distinctive characteristics and should not be judged, therefore,

100. The essay is the 107th letter of the "Eighth Collection" of the *Briefe zu Beförderung der Humanität* (1796) [Letters for the advancement of humanity] SW 18:134-40.

101. For a discussion of the *Querelle des Anciens et des Modernes* see Robert Jauss, "Aesthetische Normen und geschichtliche Reflexion in der 'Querelle des Anciens et des Modernes,' " in *Parallèle des Anciens et des Modernes* by M. Perrault (Munich: Eidos, 1964).

102. SW 18:138.

according to foreign standards or conventions. Through his "genetic" approach, Herder discusses the qualities of Shakespeare's genius without dismissing his particular historical context and his dependence on popular English ballads, legends, romances, and folksongs. Thus, as A. Gillies points out, the plays were, in Herder's eyes, "often dramatizations of traditional romance material." This in no way diminishes Shakespeare's genius because, for Herder, it was the nature of creative genius "to be part and parcel of the very source of things."[103]

Herder's historical approach is also evident in his most important interpretation of the Hebrew Bible, *The Spirit of Hebrew Poetry*. This work is divided into two parts: the first is in the form of a dialogue and the second is an expository analysis of specific texts. Both parts refute common, negative views of the ancient Hebrew texts. Enlightenment critics tended to compare them to ancient Greek and Roman poetry, complaining that the Hebrew language was crude and its poetry lacked proper aesthetic form. Herder rejects such comparisons on the basis of his historical approach.

He also applies his historical approach to the New Testament. The two texts on the Gospels from the *Christliche Schriften*, *Vom Erlöser der Menschen* (1796) [Concerning the Savior of the human race] and *Vom Gottes Sohn der Welt Heiland* (1797) [Concerning God's Son, the Redeemer of the world], are Herder's most mature interpretations of the New Testament. As in his earlier writings, he approaches the Bible from an historical perspective and with attention to their individuality. Yet more than in his earlier works, he studies the diversity stemming from the concerns and style of each author and the kind of audience each author addressed. In addition, he discusses the oral tradition that informed the written Gospels. He believes the gospel began as oral proclamation and was only later committed to writing. This insight helps Herder to explain the diversity of the four Gospels and leads him to suspect that Mark was the first written expression of this oral tradition.

Although Herder says that the Bible must be read "humanly,"[104] that is, historically and in the same way as all literature, he emphasizes the Bible's uniqueness and its meaning for modern readers. He considers the Bible to be God's revelation because it teaches human beings about God's plan and purpose in history. He calls the Bible a "fatherly explanation," "a voice of God,"[105] that helps them realize who they are in God's creation and what they are to become.[106] It reveals that all human beings are created in God's image. This

103. A. Gillies, "Herder's Essay on Shakespeare: 'Das Herz der Untersuchung,' " *Modern Language Review* 32 (1937): 273, 279.
104. SW 10:7.
105. SW 10:297.
106. SW 10:347.

image is, for Herder, most clearly depicted in Jesus, who proclaimed the genuine "religion of humanity."[107]

Herder is aware of the limitations and possibilities of the interpretation of the Bible. Since human beings are shaped by a particular culture and think through a particular language, they come to the text with certain presuppositions. They cannot go "outside" language or rise to some point "beyond" their particular historical context. Thus, their interpretations of the Bible, and any text, will always be limited.

Yet Herder believes that interpretation of the Bible also offers new possibilities for the present. This conviction is grounded in Herder's view of the Bible and the "organic powers" of human beings. He believes the Bible is a guide for all generations, yet people are to appropriate the Bible in new ways according to their own capacities and historical circumstances. For example, in his interpretation of the Gospels, he does not end with an historical analysis of the texts alone but rather points readers to "the gospel itself," which contains a message of humanity that can still be appropriated today.

Christianity and Theology

Although Herder expresses a broad interest in religion, he also was a Lutheran pastor and church official who was concerned about his congregation, the church, and the education of clergy. During the late eighteenth century both the clergy and the church were under attack. In many areas of Germany, the pastor often appeared to be simply a functionary of the state.[108] The close relationship between the church and the state caused many pastors to perform duties that are now fulfilled by state officials, such as conducting the census, reporting illnesses, directing the school system, promoting morality, and providing channels of communication between the government and the people. Many of the educated laity, influenced by rationalism, regarded the church and the clergy with indifference or as anachronisms.

In both his own ministry and in his writings addressed to theologians, Herder attempts to bring new life into every area of the church and its ministry. For example, he hopes for a more authentic understanding of the church by calling for its separation from the state. He denounces preaching that is not biblically based and does not speak meaningfully to the congregation. He suggests immediate and gradual changes in the liturgy.[109] He recognizes the power of hymns to open the heart,[110] encourages the singing of hymns at

107. SW 10:295.
108. W. H. Bruford, *Germany in the 18th Century: The Social Background of the Literary Revival* (Cambridge: Cambridge University Press, 1965), 251-56.
109. SW 31:761-74.
110. SW 31:721.

home,[111] writes prefaces to existing hymnals,[112] and edits a new hymnal which incorporates both unaltered hymns of the Reformation and more recent ones.[113] He also writes about the importance of meaningful materials for confirmation and insists that it be a "dynamic exercise" *(lebendige Übung),* in which students appropriate truths of Christianity and not simply repeat them.[114] To this end he publishes Martin Luther's catechism with commentary.[115] Further, he is concerned about the number of immature and ill-prepared pastors and expresses the deep desire to establish a type of internship for theology students after their exams and provide them with further training in practical theology.[116]

His concern for the church can be understood in the light of his understanding of Christianity.[117] For Herder, Christianity is centered in the work and teachings of Jesus Christ.[118] Herder believes that Christ's life and death expressed humanity and fostered it in others.[119] He was a teacher of "purest humanity,"[120] the image of God. He helped the poor and oppressed and healed the sick; love of others was central to his teaching and his actions. He preached the kingdom of God and the practical renewal of society. Knowledge of God was, for him, "blessedness and eternal life."[121]

As the pure expression of the image of God, Jesus Christ is a model for others,[122] for all people are made in the image of God. Jesus is presented by the apostles as filled with the gifts of the spirit; the power of God enlivened every part of his being. In this sense he was an "ideal," a representation of the "supreme character of humanity."[123] Christ is not a model in the sense that later generations should "copy" him. Rather, he is a model who inspires all people to develop according to their own capacities and to express humanity and love to others in their own unique settings.[124]

Furthermore, Jesus Christ is a savior. Herder speaks of him as the "messenger of God" and as a "sacrifice for the world."[125] Herder does not discuss

111. SW 31:722.
112. SW 31:707-17.
113. SW 31:717-22. See also 31:778-82.
114. SW 31:786-87.
115. SW 30:302-6.
116. SW 31:782-86.
117. A central text on the nature of Christianity that could not be included in this volume is *Geist des Christenthums* [The Spirit of Christianity]; SW 20:3-131.
118. Central texts on Herder's view of Christ are the following: SW 7:197-210; 10:235-48; 11:190-91; 20:23-29; and 31:433-49.
119. SW 14:290-91. For one account by Herder of the beginnings of Christianity, see SW 14:290-305.
120. SW 14:502.
121. SW 11:190.
122. SW 7:200, 207-8, 222.
123. SW 20:26.
124. Herder clearly describes this sense of a model in a sermon from 1772 entitled "Von den Schranken und Misslichkeiten bei Nachahmung auch guter Beispiele und Vorbilder" (SW 31:172-94).
125. SW 7:199.

the nature of this sacrifice in detail. He prefers to use Luther's simple explanation of the Second Article of the Apostle's Creed.[126] Yet Herder does emphasize that a pastor should believe in the truth of Jesus' resurrection from the dead.[127] This is part of the history passed on by the early church, and certainty about the resurrection brings comfort. He assumes that later generations can neither prove nor rationally understand all that the apostles have written. As he says in a later text concerning miracles in general, the way of thinking in the contemporary world differs greatly from the way of thinking of the first century.[128] Therefore, the present generation cannot judge what early Christians called "miracles."

The religion that Christ inspired is "Christianity." According to Herder, Christianity is a "religion of humanity."[129] It is humanity itself.[130] Herder acknowledges and criticizes instances of inhumanity in the history of Christianity, but he also believes that it is an instrument for the advancement of what is most noble in human beings.

Although he indicates that Christianity is a religion for all nations that calls for "purest humanity in the purest way,"[131] he does not believe it should be forced on anyone. In the spirit of Lessing, whom Herder admired,[132] he insists that the heart of Christianity embodies tolerance. He also criticizes missionary work that destroys a people's culture. He is disappointed with aspects of the missionary work in South America, for example, because it destroyed the spirit and culture of the native peoples. He deplores instances of oppression in the church and recognizes its destructive results, especially when the church has been used as a tool of the state.[133] Herder advises one to let God enlighten the pagans in God's own way; a person's own task is to live according to the truth—to become a light.[134] Although aspects of his view of modern Jews are confusing, Herder also clearly criticizes attempts to convert them, denounces their persecution and suggests that they have the privileges and respect of other citizens.[135] He praises Lessing's play, *Nathan the Wise,* for its more accurate picture of Jews.[136]

Herder believes that the Bible is central to the Christian religion. Although he treats the Bible historically, he also believes it is God's revelation. The

126. SW 10:394.
127. SW 10:169-71.
128. SW 20:63-64.
129. SW 20:191; see also 5:519; 13:290-341; and Letter 124 of *Briefe zu Beförderung der Humanität* (SW 18:301-2).
130. SW 17:121.
131. SW 18:301.
132. For Herder's view of Lessing's work and significance, see SW 15:486-512.
133. SW 24:22-32; 18:222.
134. SW 20:75.
135. SW 24:61-75; 15:129-130.
136. SW 24:71. See also his letter to Lessing from June 1, 1779, in which Herder praises the play and expresses his great respect for Lessing (*Briefe* 4:93-94).

centrality of the Bible in Herder's theology can be seen in his sermon *"Über die Göttlichkeit und Gebrauch der Bibel"* [Concerning the divinity and use of the Bible], delivered in 1768, in which he insists that Christians, to be Christians, confess that the Bible is divine revelation.[137] God is revealed to human beings in a way that they could understand: through human language in a particular time and place. The Bible therefore carries the traces of the ancient Hebrew way of thinking and must be studied in its historical context. When studied in this light, God's revelation still speaks to modern readers in an edifying and powerful way.

The centrality of the Bible for Christianity is also seen in Herder's most important text addressed to theologians, the *Briefe, das Studium der Theologie betreffend*. The work is written, as the title indicates, in the form of letters to a young theology student. Thus, it is written in a conversational style and does not aim to present a systematic position. Within the four parts of the letters, Herder addresses three topics. The first two parts are an introduction to the Bible; part three explores the task of theology and the nature of dogmatics; part four discusses practical theology, especially preaching. The Bible is central to all four parts because dogmatics and preaching, for Herder, are built on the Bible.[138]

The central task in preaching is to relate the Bible to the situation of those in the congregation.[139] In the section on preaching, he claims that preaching must be based on the Bible and yet speak directly to the situation of people today. He criticizes preachers in his own time who either focus on style, creating flamboyant sermons without content, or lecture on doctrine alone, referring neither to the Bible nor the concerns of the congregation. The best sermons relate the biblical text to the questions and experiences of the listeners. Sermons shape and edify the soul in ways that lead to concrete actions of love and service. Apparently Herder himself paid attention to the experiences of those in the pew, for he was known as one of the best preachers of his time. Even as early as 1769, he said that a preacher must know "all sides of the human soul" and offer it the word of God—a word which can "make the human soul happy."[140]

The *Briefe, das Studium der Theologie betreffend* also indicate that dogmatics, like preaching, is based on the Bible. Like many theologians before him, Herder believes that dogmatics is a science that is based on the Bible and that shows the relationship between doctrines of the church. It is a "sacred philosophy," "a system of the noblest truths for the human race concerning

137. SW 31:96-121.
138. SW 10:314; 11:17-18.
139. Other central texts on Herder's view of preaching are: "Der Redner Gottes" (SW 32:3-11) and his farewell sermon in Riga (SW 31:122-43).
140. SW 31:126-29.

the happiness of the human spirit and its eternal salvation."[141] He is impatient
with theologians who begin with their own doctrines and use the Bible only
to illustrate them.[142] He felt this false approach to dogmatics was taken especially by followers of Christian Wolff (1679-1754), a rationalist philosopher
who attempted to explain everything by means of logical analysis and whose
system was popular in the last half of the eighteenth century. As early as
1766, Herder claims that the best path for dogmatics is by way of hermeneutics.[143]

In addition to being centered on the Bible, dogmatics must be historical.
Herder says that dogmatics should include an understanding of the history of
dogmatics. He wants theologians to study the development of particular doctrines in their historical contexts so that they can understand the original
meaning of doctrinal terms. The theologian must then determine whether these
terms should still be used in the present situation or be changed so that they
are more intelligible today. If they are changed, then the theologian must have
a keen sense of both the content of the doctrine and the use of contemporary
terms.

In both the *Briefe, das Studium der Theologie betreffend* and the *Briefe
an Theophron*, Herder tries to create a space for theologians somewhere
between the intellectualism of the rationalists, who squeeze the life and truth
out of Christianity, and the emotionalism of the extreme Pietists, who use
neither the tools of biblical criticism nor the resources of other sciences. He
wants to hold onto the truth of Christianity while, at the same time, prompting
the free spirit of inquiry into all aspects of theology. His writings seek, in the
sense of Paul Ricoeur, a "second naiveté" that moves beyond the first naiveté
of faith and incorporates ordered reflection upon it.

It is precisely this kind of informed naiveté that Herder apparently inspired
in Johann Georg Müller, to whom the *Briefe an Theophron* were addressed.
Müller was a pious Swiss Calvinist who had been influenced by Lavater and
was very comfortable in the Pietistic circles of Zurich, where he spent his
first year as a theology student. When he went to Göttingen a year later and
was confronted with biblical criticism and enlightenment theology, he experienced a religious crisis. Hermann Samuel Reimarus's *Fragmente des Wol-
fenbüttelschen Ungenannten* (1774-78) [Wolfenbüttel fragments] had recently
been published by Lessing. They pointed out contradictions in the biblical

141. SW 10:279.
142. See also the first of Herder's aphorisms in which he criticizes a type of dogmatics that
does not study the books of the Bible individually and "pulls words from the sky" (SW 32:197-
98).
143. SW 1:32-33.

texts, accused the biblical writers of conscious fraud, and raised many questions about the Bible.[144] Torn between faith and doubt, Müller decided to visit Herder during his fall break in 1780 and stayed with him a week. Herder had just finished the first two parts of *Briefe, das Studium der Theologie betreffend.* Müller's reading of the first section, his conversations with Herder, and his deep admiration of Herder's sincere piety and personal integrity helped to address his fears and to inspire in him a new sense of intellectual freedom. He completed his studies and became a pastor and leader of the church.

Throughout his theological writings Herder builds on his Lutheran heritage in the sense that he emphasizes *sola scriptura* and the centrality of the Bible for dogmatics, calling for a return to biblically based theology. He also identifies the learning of the biblical languages and the careful interpretation of the text as central to the training of a Lutheran theologian.[145] He even favors Luther's catechism above all others[146] and praises the soul and passion of his hymns.[147]

Herder does not focus, however, on the doctrine of justification, which is the central doctrine of Lutheran theology. In a late text, he even appears to reject this doctrine when he regrets that Luther was influenced by Augustine's doctrine of the will and his distinctions between nature and grace, and grace and works.[148] Herder is much more attracted to and speaks more frequently about other aspects of Luther's thought.[149] He admires his passionate character, the power of his translations of the Bible and their importance for the German language, and the significance of the Reformation for European history and culture. He believes that Luther recognized more clearly than theologians of his own time that a preacher must speak to the people in terms that they can understand.[150] Herder is especially impressed with Luther's emphasis on the freedom of conscience and of thought. In one passage, for example, Herder says that the spirit of Luther's thinking is that no one should hinder another in the knowledge of the truth.[151]

144. The *Briefe an Theophron* were supposed to be published as the fifth part of *Briefe, das Studium der Theologie betreffend.* They were not published, however, until 1808 in J. G. Müller's edition of Herder's theological writings. For the context of the *Briefe an Theophron* and Herder's relation to Müller see: Haym, 2:160-71; and Clark, *Herder*, 279-81. For Herder's response to Lessing's publication of the *Fragmente*, see SW 15:506-7.

145. SW 11:119.

146. Haym, 2:617.

147. SW 31:709-10, 712.

148. SW 20:69.

149. For a discussion of Herder's relation to Luther see: Heinz Bluhm, "Herders Stellung zu Luther," PLMA 64 (1948): 158-82; Herbert von Hintzenstern, "Herders Lutherbild," *Bückeburger Gespräche über Johann Gottfried Herder 1983* (Rinteln: Bösendahl, 1984), 159-73; and Michael Embach, *Das Lutherbild Johann Gottfried Herders* (Frankfurt am Main: Peter Lang, 1987).

150. SW 20:99.

151. SW 24:100. See also: 11:203, 19:52.

CONCLUSION

Through his insights in the five areas mentioned above and through his
protest "against pure reason," Herder created a new and profound perspective
on humanity and religion. Instead of characterizing human beings mainly in
terms of reason, he underscored the central role of language, history, and
religion in human experience. From this perspective, he appreciated the diversity of contemporary religious beliefs as well as the complexity of the
history of religions and the history of Christian thought. Unlike G. W. F. Hegel
after him, who drew the progression of history and religious thought in clean
lines, Herder hesitated to replace this complexity with abstractions.

Herder's new understanding of religion and history valued diversity and
individuality. At every point in his writings, however, he held together this
love of diversity with a belief in the unity and interrelation of all human
beings. He believed that they share a common humanity, for they are all
created in the image of God. Thus, although Herder recognized radical differences between ethnic groups and their religious beliefs, he envisioned that
they could all have compassion for one another and strive to live together in
peace.

One weakness of Herder's religious thought is that he does not develop
the concept of truth that shapes this vision. Although he appears to believe
that truth is expressed in all religions, he does not clarify his position by
discussing the precise relationship between Christianity and other religions.[152]
Furthermore, even though his radically historical view is tempered by a conviction that God is active throughout history and unites its vast course, Herder
does not thoroughly address suspicions that his position could lead to rela-
tivism. He even fails to outline the relation of his ideas to his own Lutheran
heritage, for his theology lacks central elements such as clear christology and
a detailed discussion of the doctrine of justification.

Herder never claimed, however, to be a systematician, and his service to
Western religious thought is not so much the development of a coherent
theological position, but rather an ability to dispel old categories of thought
and inspire a fresh examination of the significance and intricate nature of
religion. In this respect, as the discussion above has shown, he made several
contributions. During a time when religion was reduced to morality, criticized,
or simply treated with indifference, Herder emphasized the historical dimension as well as the power and centrality of religion. His view of God and
revelation generated new debates on the nature of the divine and the ways

152. Herder's lack of clarity in this area has especially generated debate about his attitude
to the Jews. See, for example, Emil Adler, "Johann Gottfried Herder und das Judentum," *Herder
Today*, 382-401; F. M. Barnard, "The Hebrews and Herder's Political Creed," *Modern Language
Review* 54 (1959): 533-46; Paul L. Rose, *Revolutionary Antisemitism in Germany: From Kant
to Wagner* (Princeton: Princeton University Press, 1990).

one speaks about God. He strengthened the historical interpretation of the Bible and, at the same time, emphasized its meaning for today. He grounded dogmatics historically and biblically but also insisted that it be directed toward the concerns and questions of the present generation.

Although Herder's ideas were not completely original and depended on many thinkers who came before him, his religious thought is particularly striking because he took up such a wide range of ideas generated in the seventeenth and eighteenth centuries and transformed them into a much deeper understanding of the nature of religion. In this way, he provided his own generation with new perspectives on religion and passed on ideas that dominated theological discussions during the nineteenth century. Many of these ideas, especially about language, history, individuality, and pluralism continue to inform and challenge religious thought today.

1

Human Nature, Language, and History

YET ANOTHER PHILOSOPHY
OF HISTORY

1. No one in the world feels *the weakness of generalizing* more than I.[1] If you depict *an entire* people, age, or region, what have you depicted? If you group together peoples and periods that succeed one another in *perpetual flux* like waves of the sea, what have you described? To whom does the descriptive term apply? If you then summarize all this in nothing but a *generality*, whereby everyone probably thinks and feels whatever they please, what an *imperfect means of description!* How easily can you be *misunderstood!*

Who has noticed how *inexpressible* the *individuality* of one human being is—how impossible it is *to express distinctly* an individual's *distinctive characteristics*? To express how that individual feels and lives? To express how different and particular all things are to an individual because they are seen by the eyes, measured by the soul, and felt by the heart of *that individual?* Who has noticed what *depth* lies in the character of any *single nation?* No matter how often this nation is studied and admired, it still evades the one word that could capture it. Even if a word is found, it rarely enables the character of that nation to be recognized in such a way that everyone can comprehend it and empathize with it. Since this is the case, how can one possibly survey the ocean of entire peoples, times, and countries, and capture them in *one glance, one feeling,* or *one word*?! What a lifeless, incomplete *phantom* of a word it would be! The whole *tableau vivant* of manners, customs, necessities, particularities of the land and the sky must either be *added* to that word or *precede* it. You must first enter the spirit of a nation in order to

1. [SW 5:501-13; 557-61.]

38

empathize completely with even one of its thoughts or deeds. You must discover a characterizing word through which you can understand everything in depth. Otherwise, you simply read a word.

We all believe that we still possess the paternal, domestic, and humane instincts of the Hebrew, and that we are still able to possess the loyalty and artistic diligence of the Egyptian, the vivacity of the Phoenician, the Greek love of liberty, the Roman strength of character. Who does not believe we sense a predisposition toward all of these *characteristics* and lack only the *time* and the *opportunity* to develop them? And you see, my reader, this is exactly the problem. Without a doubt the most cowardly villain still has a remote tendency toward and chance of becoming the most courageous hero. But between these potentialities and such a character's entire sense of being and of existence—what an immense gulf! Even if you lack nothing but the *time* and the *opportunity* to translate your predispositions into the actual accomplishments and noble instincts of a Hebrew, a Greek, or a Roman— what an immense gulf! For the instincts and actual accomplishments alone are the subjects at hand. In order to empathize with the soul's *entire nature*, which *reigns* in everything, which forms all other tendencies and human powers after itself, and which colors even the most trivial actions, do not base your response on that one word; rather, enter the century, the region, the entire history—empathize with every part of it. Only then will you be on your way to understanding that word. Only then will you also give up imagining that "you are the sum of each and every thing." Do you think you are the sum of all things? *The quintessence of all times and all peoples?* This is surely the sign of a fool!

The character of nations! This must be determined alone by *data* about their *disposition* and *history.* Did not, or could not, a patriarch have other tendencies besides those which you attribute to him? To this double question, I reply simply: *yes, indeed!* He did indeed have other *secondary traits,* which are self-evident from what I say or do not say, and which I, and perhaps others with me who have his history in mind, already imply in the generality. Moreover, he could have vastly different traits in a different place, at a later period of cultural development, and under different circumstances. Could not Leonidas, Caesar, and Abraham be celebrities of our century? But they were not! Ask history about it! This is the subject at hand.

Thus, I am prepared to come across minor contradictions in the *wealth of detail* of peoples and times. No people stayed or could have stayed the same for any extended period of time; every people, like the arts and sciences and everything else in the world, had its period of growth, blossoming, and decay; each of these changes lasted only the *minimum amount of time* that could be given to it on the wheel of human destiny; finally, *no two moments in the world are ever identical;* and, therefore, the Egyptians, the Romans, and the

Greeks did not stay the same *in every period*. I shudder to think about the kind of clever arguments that clever people, especially historians, can make of such observations! They say: Although Greece was composed of many peoples, Athenians and Boeotians, Spartans and Corinthians were nothing less than identical. They ask: Was not agriculture already practiced in Asia? Did not the Egyptians once trade as skillfully as the Phoenicians? Were not the Macedonians as much conquerors as the Romans? Did not Aristotle have as speculative a mind as Leibniz? Did not our Nordic peoples surpass the Romans in bravery? Were all Egyptians, Greeks, Romans—are all rats and mice—identical? No! For after all, they are rats and mice!

It becomes tiresome to address the public if you always have to be prepared for remarks of this kind and worse, which are delivered by the vociferous section of the public—and in what a tone! (The more noble-thinking section keeps quiet!) At the same time, you must be aware that the great herd of sheep that cannot tell left from right will bleat in concert! Can a *general picture* exist without *arrangement and order?* Can you have a *broad perspective* without *height?* If you hold your face right up against a painting, if you chip off this piece of it, glue your eyes to that little lump of paint, then you will never see the whole picture—indeed you will not see a picture at all. If your head is full of one particular group with which you are infatuated, then how can you possibly view the flux of ever-changing historical events as a whole? How can you order them, gently follow their course, distinguish only the *main action* in each scene, quietly trace the influences, and finally give a name to all of this? If you cannot do all of this, however, then history just flickers and wavers before your eyes—a confusion of scenes, peoples, and times. First you must read and learn to see. I know as well as you do, by the way, that every *general picture*, every *generalization*, is only an *abstraction*. The Creator alone is the One who conceives the entire *unity* of one and all nations, conceiving them in all their *diversity* without losing sight of the *unity*.

2. Away then with these narrow-minded remarks that lack purpose and perspective! Viewed from the perspective of the purpose of the vast course of history as a whole, how shallow are some *popular judgments of our century about the advantages, virtues, and happiness of such distant and such diverse nations—judgments based on mere textbook generalizations!*

Human nature, even at its best, is not some *independent deity:* It must learn everything, be shaped through continuous processes, advance further through gradual struggle. Naturally it will develop mainly, or exclusively, those aspects which are given occasions for virtue, struggle, or process. Each form of human perfection is, in a certain sense, national, time-bound, and, most specifically, individual. We develop only that which is occasioned by time, climate, necessity, *world,* or accidents of fate. We disregard the rest.

Tendencies or talents slumbering in the heart can never become actual accomplishments. It is possible, therefore, for a nation to possess both the most sublime virtues and weaknesses; it can contain irregularities and reveal astonishing contradictions and incongruities. These will only be astonishing, however, to those carrying an idealistic picture of virtue according to the manual of their own century and to those who are so obsessed with philosophy that they seek to discover the whole earth in a single corner of it. For those who want to understand the human heart out of the elements of life's circumstances, such irregularities and contradictions are perfectly human. They are the proportion of human powers and tendencies related to a certain purpose that could never be attained without them. Thus, they are not exceptions, but the rule.

Suppose, my friend, that the childlike religion of the Ancient Near East,[2] the very faithfulness to the most delicate feeling of human life, contained weaknesses that you condemn according to the standard of other periods. A patriarch cannot be a Roman hero, or a Greek runner, or a coastal merchant; just as he cannot be that which your academic ideal or your mood dictates in order to falsely praise or bitterly condemn him. Suppose that according to models of later times he appeared to you to be faint-hearted, fearful of death, flabby, ignorant, idle, superstitious, and, when you are seeing red, even wicked. He has become what God, climate, time, and the stage of world history could fashion: a patriarch! Consequently, he possesses qualities that later ages lost: innocence, fear of God, and humanity. These qualities will always make him a god in the eyes of later generations! What a figure the Egyptian becomes when compared, on the one hand, to the cheerful Greek who creates everything so beautifully and, on the other, to the humanists of our time who have such fine taste and who carry all wisdom in their heads and the whole world in their hearts! Through such comparison, the Egyptian appears to be grovelling, slavish, bestial, superstitious, depressed, cruel to strangers, and a thoughtless creature of habit. But what about the perseverance, loyalty, and composure of the Egyptians? Can you compare these qualities to the pederasty among the Greeks and to the brutal competition for beauty and pleasure among their youth? If you were to take an ideal, it does not matter whose, could you fail to recognize Greek frivolity, impiety, and their lack of love, rearing, and decency? Could those perfect qualities have been developed to the extent they were, however, without the imperfect ones? Providence itself, you see, required no ideal. It wanted to achieve its aim only in change, in the process of tradition which takes place through the waking of new powers

2. [*orientalische Religion. Orient* and *Morgenland* have been translated as "Ancient Near East" (a standard term in biblical scholarship) when Herder clearly refers to the ancient Hebrews and the Hebrew Bible. The terms are translated as "Near East" when Herder refers to this region and not the Far East].

and dying of others. Oh, you philosopher in the northern valley of the earth, holding the toy scale of your century, are you wiser than providence?

We create arbitrary verdicts of praise and blame on the basis of a favorite people of antiquity with whom we have become infatuated, and we use them to judge the whole world. What justifies such verdicts? Those Romans could be like no other nation. They did what *no one could imitate:* they were Romans. They stood at the pinnacle of a world, and everything surrounding them was valley. From their youth they were formed in the spirit of Rome, and they acted according to it from that lofty plain. What is so astonishing about that? Is it so astonishing that a small shepherding and farming people in one valley of the earth was not an iron beast who could act like the Romans? Is it so astonishing that this people would, in turn, possess virtues which the noblest Roman could not possess? That the noblest Roman from his height, under pressure of necessity, could in cold blood resolve to perform cruelties that the shepherd in the small valley could not imagine? From the peak of that great political system the sacrifice of human life was, alas, often considered to be of little consequence, a necessity, and (poor humanity, what situations are you capable of creating!) even good. The very system that made widespread vice possible also lifted up virtues and made a broad impact on human history. Is humankind in any context ever capable of pure perfection? The summit borders on the valley. Around the noble Spartans dwell the inhumanely treated Helots. The triumphal Roman, painted in the red of the gods, is also tinctured invisibly with blood: Robbery, sacrilege, and debauchery surround his chariot. Oppression goes before him; misery and poverty follow after him. Defect and virtue, then, always dwell together under one human roof.

Conjuring up a favorite people of the earth in superhuman splendor can create fine poetry. Such poetry can also be useful, for human beings are also ennobled by beautiful prejudices. What if the poet is, however, a historian or a philosopher, as most pretend to be, modeling every century according to the *one pattern of their time* (a pattern frequently inadequate and weak)? Hume! Voltaire! Robertson! Classical ghosts of the twilight! What are you in the light of truth?

A learned society of our time,[3] doubtless with the best intentions, posed the following question: "Which was the happiest people in history?" If I understand the question correctly, and if it does not lie beyond the horizon of human response, then I can only say that such a moment of happiness existed for every people at a certain time and under certain circumstances. Otherwise, it was never a people at all. Indeed, human nature is not the vessel for an absolute, independent, and immutable happiness, as philosophers define

3. The gentlemen must have cherished a terribly high ideal because, to my knowledge, none of the philosophical problems they posed ever proved soluble. [Herder is referring here to the Berlin Academy.]

it. Rather, it always attracts that measure of happiness of which it is capable: It is a pliant clay which assumes a different shape under different circumstances, needs, and burdens. Even the image of happiness changes with each context and climate. (For what is this image but the sum of "the satisfaction of desires, the achievement of goals, and the quiet surmounting of needs" that take shape according to country, time, and place?) Basically, then, all comparison is disastrous. As soon as the internal sense of happiness or the disposition changes, as soon as the external circumstances and needs fashion and fortify this new sense, who can then compare the *different* forms of happiness perceived by *different* senses in *different* worlds? Who can compare the Hebrew shepherd and patriarch with the [Egyptian] farmer and artist, the [Phoenician] sailor, the [Greek] runner, the [Roman] conqueror?[4] Happiness does not depend on a laurel wreath, on a view of the blessed herd, on a cargo ship, or on a captured battle flag, but on the soul that needed this, aspired to this, attained this, and wanted to attain nothing more. Each nation has its own *center* of happiness *within itself,* just as every sphere has its own center of gravity.

The good Mother has taken good care of this, too. She placed tendencies toward *diversity* in our hearts. Not one of these tendencies, however, was made all-compelling. In this way, if only some of them are satisfied, then the soul soon creates a concert out of these awakened notes and does not feel the unawakened ones except in so far as they mutely and obscurely support the sounding melody. She placed tendencies toward diversity in our hearts; she then placed a part of the diversity in a circle around us, ready at hand; and then she restricted the human view so that after a short time by force of habit this circle became a horizon, beyond which we can neither see nor scarcely speculate! I envy and strive for all that is akin to my nature, all that can be assimilated by it, and I make it my own; beyond that, kind nature has armed me with insensitivity, coldness, and blindness, which can even turn into contempt and disgust. Nature's only aim, however, is to force me back on *myself,* to offer me satisfaction in my own center. The Greeks adopt as much from the Egyptians as they need for themselves, and the Romans adopt what they need from the Greeks; when they are satisfied, the rest falls to the ground, and they do not strive for it. In this development of particular national tendencies toward particular forms of national happiness, the distance between one people and another can grow too great. Look how the Egyptian detests the nomadic shepherd and equally despises the frivolous Greek! Whenever the dispositions and spheres of happiness of two nations collide, there arises what we call prejudice, mob judgment, and narrow nationalism! But in its

4. [In version "a" the text reads: Do not ask, therefore, whether the Hebrew shepherd, or the Egyptian farmer and artist, or the Phoenician sailor, or the Greek runner, or the Roman hero was happier!]

proper time and place prejudice is good, for happiness can spring from it. It thrusts peoples together toward their center, attaches them more firmly to their roots, causes them to flourish more fully in their own way, and makes them more ardent and therefore happier with their own tendencies and purposes. In this respect the most ignorant, most prejudiced nation is often the happiest. The age that wanders toward the desires and hopes of foreign lands is already an age of disease, flatulence, unhealthy opulence, approaching death!

3. The universal, philosophical, philanthropic tone of our century readily applies "our own ideal" of virtue and happiness to each distant nation, to each remote period in history. But can one such single ideal be the sole standard for judging, condemning, or praising the customs of other nations or periods? Is not the good scattered throughout the earth? Since one form of humanity and one region cannot encompass the good, it has been distributed in a thousand forms, continually changing shape like an eternal Proteus[5] throughout all continents and centuries. Further, as this Proteus changes and continues to change, humankind always remains only humankind, even if it does not strive for greater virtue or individual happiness.[6] Nevertheless, a *plan in this continual striving* is evident. My great theme!

Those who so far have attempted to unfold the progress of the centuries have usually treasured the following idea: Progress is toward greater virtue and happiness of individual human beings. In support of this idea they have embellished or invented facts, minimized or suppressed other contrary facts, covered entire aspects of the situation, and substituted words like "enlightenment" for "happiness" and "more and better ideas" for "virtue." In this way they invented the fiction of the "universal, progressive improvement of the world" which no one believed, at least not the true student of history and the human heart.

Others, who recognized the trouble with this illusion without knowing a better one, saw vices and virtues varying like climates, perfections sprouting like spring leaves and then perishing, human customs and tendencies flying and turning like the leaves of fate. No plan! No progress! Nothing but endless change! Nothing but weaving and unraveling, like Penelope's work![7] These people fell into a whirlpool, into doubt about all virtue, happiness, and human purpose, and they laced all history, religion, and ethics with skepticism. The latest fad of recent philosophy (especially in France) is doubt! This doubt appears in a hundred forms, but always sporting the dazzling title: "based on

5. [In Greek mythology Proteus was a sea god who could assume different shapes.]

6. [Herder is referring here and below to Isaak Iselin's theory of historical progress. See Iselin, *Über die Geschichte der Menschheit*, (Frankfurt : J. H. Harscher, 1764).]

7. [Penelope, the wife of Odysseus, had agreed to choose a suitor during her husband's absence as soon as she finished weaving a cloak for Laertes, Odysseus's father. But to avoid that decision, each night she unraveled what she had woven during the day.]

world history!" Contradictions in history are like waves in the sea: Either they sink your ship completely or the scrap of morality and philosophy that you save from the wreck is hardly worth mentioning.

Could there not exist manifest *progress and development,* but in some higher sense than we usually think? Do you see this flowing river? Look how it springs from a tiny source, swells, divides here, rejoins there, winds in and out, and cuts wider and deeper. Yet, regardless of its course, it still remains *water! River! Drops of water!* Mere drops of water, until it plunges into the sea! Might it not be the same with the human race? Do you see that growing tree? Those striving human beings? Human beings must pass through different periods of life! All periods are obviously in *progress*! All strive together in *continuity*! Between each period are apparent *resting places, revolutions, changes!* Nevertheless, each period has in itself the *center* of its own happiness. The youth is not happier than the innocent, contented child; nor is the peaceful old man unhappier than the energetic man in his prime. The pendulum swings with the same force, whether swinging more quickly as it moves toward its widest arc or more slowly as it approaches a state of rest. Yet all the while the striving never ceases! We never exist in our own period alone; we build on what has *gone before,* and this simply becomes the foundation of the *future* and does not attempt to be more. This is the way *analogy* speaks in nature— the expressive *pattern of God in all creation.* Evidently, this is the way analogy speaks in the *human race!* The Egyptian could not have existed without the Hebrew; the Greek built on the work of the Egyptian; the Romans lifted themselves on the shoulders of the whole world. This is the genuine sense of "progress" and "continuous development," even if no individual were to prosper from it! The human race enters into the magnificent whole! The human race becomes something about which a shallow account of history boasts so much and reveals so little: It becomes the *theater of a guiding purpose on earth!* It becomes so, even if we are not immediately able to espy its final purpose; it becomes the theater of God, even if presented only through the *openings* and *ruins of individual scenes.*

At least this view is broader than the philosophy that mixes everything together arbitrarily, dwelling here and there on isolated historical perplexities in order to make all of history into an ant's game, an aimless striving of isolated tendencies and powers, a chaos, in which one gives up hope in the existence of virtue, purpose, and God. If only I were able to bind these disparate scenes together without tangling them up! If only I were able to show how they relate to one another, develop out of one another, and blend into one another—to show that individually they are but moments in history and that only through historical progress do they become *means to higher ends.* If this could be done, then what a view this would be! What a *noble use of human history! What a way to encourage us to hope, act, and believe even when we do not see everything or see nothing at all! . . .*

In general, the philosopher is never more of a brute than when he most faithfully wishes to play God and when he confidently calculates the perfection of the world. He is wholly convinced that everything moves very nicely in a straight line and that every succeeding individual and every succeeding generation reaches perfection in a lovely progression according to *his* ideal! He alone is able to reveal the exponents of virtue and happiness in this progression. It so happens that everything always comes back to him: He is the final, the highest link in the chain of being in which everything culminates. "Look! To what enlightenment, virtue, and happiness the world has ascended! And look at me! I am high atop the pendulum! The gilded tongue of the world's scales!"

Such a philosopher has not taken into account what even the faintest echo from heaven to earth should have taught him: In reality human beings always remain human beings, and by analogy to all things they are nothing but human. To perceive the form of angels or devils in human beings is an illusion! Human beings are but halfway between the two: defiant and despondent; aspiring in need, but growing weary in idleness and opulence. Human beings are nothing without talents and the exercise of them; with these talents, however, they gradually improve and near perfection. Human beings are a hieroglyph of good and evil, filling the annals of history! Human beings! Always mere instruments of fate!

The philosopher has not considered that this elusive double creature can be modified in a thousand ways and almost has to be, given the structure of our earth; that in a creation with various climates and temporal circumstances, there are bound to be virtues unique to a nation and a period that blossom and thrive almost untended in one place and die out or wither miserably in another; that all this is possible and necessary, but that underneath the ever-changing husk, the same kernel of human substance and happiness could still be, and in all probability will be, preserved (that is, a physics of history, psychology, and politics, about which our century certainly has already indulged in much fantasy and reflection).

The philosopher has not considered that infinitely greater care on the part of the *Father of us all* would be shown if an *invisible kernel of susceptibility to happiness and virtue were found in all humanity throughout the whole earth and throughout all ages.* Even if it developed differently and naturally appeared in different forms, the kernel would inwardly be but one single measure and mixture of forces.

Finally, this philosopher—this omniscient creature—has not considered that a greater divine plan for the whole human race could exist which no individual creature could survey precisely because nothing moves toward something merely individual as its final purpose, least of all toward a philosopher or monarch of the eighteenth century. All scenes together, in which each actor has only one role in which to strive and to be happy, form a whole. This whole is certainly unknown and invisible to the individual, self-centered actor, but it is evident to the spectator who has the proper perspective and who calmly and patiently observes the process of the whole performance.

Look at the entire universe from heaven to earth! What are the means, the ends? Is not everything a means to a million ends? Is not everything an end for a million means? The chain of almighty and omniscient goodness is braided and twisted in a thousand ways. Nevertheless, every link in the chain is a link in its own place; it is attached to the chain, but is unaware of the end to which the chain is finally attached. Every link is under the illusion that it is the center, falsely perceiving everything around it only in so far as these things direct their rays or waves toward this center. A fine illusion! But where is the outer circumference of all these waves, rays, and apparent centers? Who is it? What is its purpose?

In the history of the human race, even with all the waves and all the times to come, is there likely to be anything other than the "blueprint of almighty wisdom"? If the earth, our dwelling, manifests itself down to the minutest detail as the "painting of God," would not the history of its inhabitants do the same? The dwelling is only decor! A painting of one scene, one view! The history of its inhabitants, in contrast, is an *unending drama with many scenes! God's epic* throughout all *centuries, continents,* and *generations—a fable with a thousand variations replete with one great meaning!*

This meaning—this universal perspective—is bound to lie beyond the grasp of the human race. You, insect on a clump of clay, look once again at heaven and earth! As you observe all that lives and dies in the active universe, do you see yourself as the absolute center affected by all things? Do you not instead participate in higher, unknown purposes? (No one asked you where, how, or when.) Are they not purposes in which the morning star and the small cloud beside it, you and the worm you just smashed with your foot, all participate? It is undeniable and yet beyond our comprehension that all things participate with purpose in the great, vast, harmonious world of an individual moment and in the great, vast course of history. They participate in all immediate events and all developments of the human race, in the Creator's wise and confusing drama. Can you suspect anything less or anything different? Even if all of history were for you a labyrinth with hundreds of closed and hundreds of opened passages, the labyrinth would still be the "palace of God, created for God's purposes and perhaps for the pleasure of God's eye, but not for yours!"

The whole world is an abyss that God can view in a single moment. I stand in this abyss and am lost no matter where I turn! I see a great work without a name, and yet it is full of names, voices, and powers! I do not feel as if I am standing at that place where the harmony of all these voices converge. I am able to hear, however, in my own context that the diminished, confusing sounds have a certain harmony. This much I know and hear indeed. This harmony also resonates in hymns of praise in the ears of the one for whom time and place have no meaning. The human ear lingers only a few moments and hears only a few tones, often only as a vexing chord of dissonant notes. For perhaps this ear appeared just as the chord was being tuned and found itself unfortunately hurled into a whirlwind of dissonance. The modern, "enlightened" human being wants to be not only one who can hear all these tones at once but also the loftiest tone of all! One who reflects the entire past and represents the purpose of the entire composition in all its variety! What a slanderous child! It just might be that this precocious child is only an echo of the former, mortal tone or only a part of the chord!

I am under the great tree of the almighty Father[8] whose top extends beyond all heavens and whose roots reach beneath all worlds and hell. Am I an eagle that soars above this tree? Or a raven that sits on the shoulder of God, daily bringing him evening greetings from the worlds below? Oh, that I might be a tiny fiber of one leaf on this tree! Or a small comma or dash in the great book of the universe!

Whatever I am, a voice from heaven says that I, like all things, have meaning in my place. All things are given powers that contribute to the whole; all have a feeling of happiness according to the measure of these powers! Who among my fellow-creatures has priority above the others before coming into existence? Even if the purpose and harmony of all things demands that my neighbor is a golden vessel and I am an earthen one (for I am an earthen vessel in terms of my purpose, tone, durability, feeling, and abilities), can I quarrel with the master craftsman? I am neither ignored nor given priority over others. Sensibility, action, and ability are divided among the whole human race. Here the current breaks off, there it begins. Those to whom much is given must produce much. Those who enjoy many senses must strive with these many senses. I believe that nothing can broaden our sensibilities more than reflecting on what the current of history says and does not say, what it reveals and conceals. This reflection is offered to us in the light of universal history!

IDEAS TOWARD A PHILOSOPHY
OF HISTORY

As ready as human beings are to imagine that they are self-made, they are nevertheless dependent on others for the development of their capacities.[9]

8. This is a magnificent image found in the Nordic *Edda*. [The *Eddas* are two Icelandic accounts of Scandinavian and Teutonic mythology, both from the Middle Ages.]
9. [SW 13:343-53; 14:207-13, 225, 235, 244.]

It is not only the philosophers who have exalted human reason to a pure power that is autonomous and independent of the senses and organs. The sensualists also imagine as they dream their way through life that they have become everything they are entirely by their own efforts. This illusion can be explained, especially in relation to the sensualists. The feeling of autonomy, given to them by the Creator, rouses them to act and rewards them with the most pleasing payment of experiencing an action that they have completed on their own. They forget the days of their childhood; the seeds that they received then and still receive daily lie dormant in their souls; they see and enjoy only the budding plant and take pleasure in its flourishing growth, in its fruit-laden branches. Philosophers, however, who know from experience the origin and dimensions of human life and who could also trace the entire chain of human development in history, should, I think, leave behind their ideal world in which they feel isolated and all-sufficient and quickly return to our world of reality, because everything in history reminds them of our dependence on others.

Just as human beings do not spring from their own wombs at birth, they themselves do not give birth to the use of their own mental powers. Not only is the seed of our internal disposition, like the structure of our body, genetic; but each development of this seed also depends on fate, which planted us in this or that place and supplied us according to time and circumstances with the means of our formation [*Bildung*]. Even the eye must learn to see, the ear to hear; and it should be no secret what skill is needed to acquire the principle instrument of our thought—language. Nature has obviously arranged our whole organism [*Mechanismus*], including the character and length of our stages in life, for this external aid. An infant's brain is soft and still adheres to the skull; the strata of the brain are formed slowly; it grows firmer over the years, until at length it hardens and receives no more new impressions. It is the same with the bodily limbs and the instincts of a child. The limbs are fragile and develop through imitation. The instincts perceive what they see and hear with the aid of a wonderful, active attention and an inner life force. Thus, the human being is an organism that must be skillfully crafted. It is, to be sure, endowed with a genetic disposition and an abundance of life, but the organism does not work automatically, and even the most gifted person must learn how to work it. Reason is an aggregate of observations and exercises of the soul; it is the sum of the education of our race. The pupil, like a foreign artist, completes this education within the self according to given, external models.

Herein lies the principle of the history of humanity without which no such history could exist. If human beings were self-made and developed everything independently of external circumstances, then it might be possible to have a history *of one* individual, but not of human beings, not of their entire species.

Our specific character, however, lies in this: We are born almost without instinct, we become what we should and can be only through lifelong training toward humanity, and this is the reason our species is both perfectible and corruptible. It follows that the history of humanity is necessarily a whole, that is, from the first link to the last it is a chain consisting of social life and of the dynamic tradition that shapes us.

We can speak, therefore, of an education of the human race [*Erziehung des Menschengeschlechts*], for every individual becomes a human being only by means of education, and the whole human race lives solely within this chain of individuals. Of course, if someone said that the human race—not the individual—is educated, then this would be nonsense because "race" and "genus" are only abstract concepts except insofar as they exist in individual entities. Were I to define "human race" with reference to all the most perfect qualities of humanity, culture, and the greatest enlightenment that an idealistic concept would allow, I would have said as much about the actual history of our species as if I had spoken about "animal-kind," "stone-kind," and "metal-kind" in general and had decorated these terms with all the most noble attributes, but with attributes that would contradict those of actual, individual entities. Our philosophy of history should not wander along this path of Averroan philosophy,[10] according to which the whole human race possesses but one intellect (of a very low order) that is distributed to individuals in a merely piecemeal fashion. Were I, however, to confine everything to the individual and to deny the existence of the chain that connects individuals both to one another and to the whole, then I would equally contradict human nature and actual human history. This is because not one of us becomes a human being autonomously. An intellectual genesis, that is, education, connects the whole formation of an individual's humanity to that individual's parents, teachers, and friends, to all the circumstances in the course of that individual's life, consequently to that individual's people and their ancestors, and in the end to the whole chain of the human race, for some links of the chain are bound to influence one of the powers of that individual. In this way, peoples can be traced back to families and families to their founders; the stream of history becomes narrower as we approach its source, and our whole earthly dwelling ultimately becomes one schoolhouse of our human family. It contains, of course, many divisions, classes, and rooms, but it still offers one kind of instruction that has been transmitted with various alterations and additions from our ancestors to all peoples. If we trust that a human teacher,

10. [Averroes was a Muslim philosopher of the twelfth century whose commentaries on Aristotle were very influential in Western thought. One distinctive trait of his philosophy was this belief in the oneness of the possible intellect for the whole human race. Averroism was a philosophical movement of the thirteenth century whose main source was the philosophy of Aristotle as interpreted by Averroes.]

whose understanding is limited, does not separate students into classes for no reason, and if we think that the human race everywhere finds a kind of education beyond birth according to the necessities of time and place, then what intelligent person observing the structure of the earth and the relation of human beings to it would not suspect that the Father of our race, who has determined how long and to what extent nations should exist, did not also, as the teacher of our race, create us with this characteristic? Will one who observes a ship deny the purpose of its builder? Whoever examines the formation of our nature through external means in relation to each inhabited climate cannot avoid thinking that the diverse climates of diverse peoples also had a purpose in the design of the intellectual education of human beings. We are not, however, the product of local climate alone, for living creatures like ourselves contribute to our education, habits, and development. It seems to me, therefore, that there is an education of the human race and a philosophy of history as surely and truly as there is one humanity, that is, a continuous interaction of individuals that alone makes us human beings.

On this foundation, the principles of this philosophy of history become immediately as evident, simple, and unmistakable to us as the natural history of humanity itself is. These principles are called *tradition* and *organic powers*. All education exists only by means of imitation and training, that is, by means of the transmission of a model into an imitation. What better word for this transmission than "tradition"? Imitators must have powers, however, to receive what has and can be transmitted and to convert it, like the food whereby they live, into their own natures. Accordingly, their own receptive powers determine what and how much they receive, from whom they acquire it, and how they make it their own, use it, and apply it. Consequently, the education of our race can be said to be both "genetic" and "organic." It is genetic by virtue of its process of transmission. It is organic by virtue of its process of assimilating and applying that which is transmitted. The name of this second genesis, which permeates a person's entire life, is open. We are free to call it either "culture," for it is like the cultivation of the soil; or "enlightenment," for it brings to mind the image of light. If we do use these terms, then we can say that the chain of culture and enlightenment [*Kette der Cultur und Aufklärung*] stretches to the ends of the earth. Even the natives of California and Tierra del Fuego learned to make and use the bow and arrow; they learned their language and concepts, practices and arts, just as we learn ours. In this sense they were, therefore, in fact cultured and enlightened, although at the simplest level. The difference, then, between so-called "enlightened" and "unenlightened," or between "cultivated" and "uncultivated" peoples is not a difference of kind, but only of degree. The painting of the nations has infinite shades, changing with time and place; and, as in all pictures, everything depends on the point of view from which we examine it. If we take the idea of European culture as our standard, then we will indeed discover culture only in Europe. If we go even further, establishing arbitrary distinctions between culture and enlightenment, neither of which, if they be genuine, can exist independently of the other, then we lose ourselves still further in the clouds. If we keep our feet on the ground, however, and take the broadest view of what nature itself, which is bound to know the purpose and character of its creatures best, displays to us as human development [*menschliche Bildung*], then this is none other than *the tradition of an education toward some form or other of human happiness and way of life*. This process is as universal as the human species. It is often even active to the highest degree among primitive people, although only in a narrower sphere. Human beings living among human beings cannot avoid being improved or harmed by culture: Tradition takes hold of them, forms their minds, and fashions their limbs. They become what they are, they are fashioned, according to tradition and according to the ways the mind and body can be shaped. Even children living by chance among animals have acquired some form of human culture after living for a time among human beings, as most known cases show. In contrast, a child living among wolves from the moment of birth would be the only uncultivated human being on the earth.

What conclusions can be drawn from this well-grounded perspective, which is confirmed by the entire history of the human race? First, we discover the following principle that encourages and comforts our lives as well as our present reflection: Whereas the human race is not self-made, and whereas there are dispositions in its nature that cannot be praised highly enough, the Creator must have appointed means for the development of these dispositions, and these means in turn reveal his most wise, paternal goodness. Is the corporeal eye so beautifully formed in vain? Does not the eye discover the golden beams of the sun? These rays were created for the eye, as the eye for them, and they fulfill the wisdom of the eye's design. It is the same with all the senses and with all parts of the body. They find the means for their education, the medium for which they were created. And can it be otherwise with the spiritual senses and organs on whose use the character of the human race and the nature and measure of its happiness depend? Could the Creator have failed to attain his purpose for all of nature because this purpose depends on the use of human powers? Impossible! Any foolish hypothesis of this kind is of our own making. Either we are attributing erroneous ends to the Creator, or we are trying as much as possible to frustrate these ends. But because our attempts are bound to be limited, and because no design of the omniscient Creator can be thwarted by a creature of God's thoughts, let us be confident and certain that even during the most perplexing parts of history, God's purpose for the human race on earth continues to be evident. All God's works have this particular quality in common: Although they all belong to a whole which no eye can scan, each is a whole in itself and bears the divine character of its determination. This is the case with plants and animals. Would it be otherwise with human beings and their determination? Is it possible that thousands were created merely for the sake of one? That all past generations were created merely for the last? That all individuals were created merely for the species, that is, for the image of an abstract name? The omniscient Creator does not play games in this way! God does not create abstract, shadowy illusions. God loves and cares for each of his children with paternal affection, as if each creature were the only one in the world. All of his means are ends. All of his ends are means to higher ends whereby the infinite most richly reveals himself. The purpose of the human race must then be what an individual is and can be. And what is this? It is humanity and happiness in a specific place, to a specific degree, as a specific link, and no other, in the chain of the development [*Kette der Bildung*] of the whole human race. Wherever and as whoever you were born, you are the one you are meant to be. Neither leave this chain nor raise yourself above it! Rather, embrace it! Life and peace dwell for you only in the interconnection of this chain, in what you both actively receive and actively impart.

Second, as much as it flatters human beings that the deity has accepted them as assistants and left their formation [*Bildung*] here below to themselves, it is precisely this divinely chosen means of our formation that reveals the imperfection of our earthly existence, inasmuch as we *are* not yet human beings, but are daily *becoming* so. The human being is a pitiable creature indeed! We possess nothing on our own. We receive everything through imitation, instruction, and practice, whereby we are molded like wax! If you are proud of your reason, take a look at the latitude of your fellow beings throughout the wide earth, or listen to their polyphonic, dissonant history! Is there any kind of inhumanity, to which a person, a nation, and frequently a number of nations could not become accustomed? Many, and perhaps most, nations have even eaten the flesh of their compatriots! Can you think of any foolish illusion that has not actually been made sacred by some inherited tradition in one place or another? No rational creature, therefore, can stand lower than human beings, for throughout their whole lives they are not only children in regard to reason but also pupils of the reason of others. Into whatever hands they fall, these hands form them. I doubt that there could possibly be a human custom that some nation or some individual of that nation has not adopted. Every kind of vice and cruelty is exhausted in history, until here and there a nobler form of human sentiments and virtues finally appears. This could not possibly be otherwise because of the divinely chosen means of the formation of our race that takes place only through our own race. Both the follies and the rare treasures of wisdom must be inherited. The path of humanity was shaped like a labyrinth with misleading passages on all sides and where few footsteps lead to the innermost goal. Happy the mortal who reaches the goal or leads others to it, whose thoughts, inclinations, and wishes, or even whose silent example, have promoted the humanity of others. God acts upon earth only by means of chosen, exemplary human beings: Religion and language, the arts and sciences, even governments themselves cannot be adorned with a nobler crown than with the laurels gathered from the moral, continual development [*Fortbildung*] of human souls. Our body rots in the grave, and our name is soon a mere shadow on the earth. We can continue, even through anonymous influence, to live actively in the souls of later generations only when we are incorporated into the voice of God, that is, into the dynamic tradition [*bildende Tradition*] that shapes us.

Third, the philosophy of history that pays attention to the chain of tradition [*Kette der Tradition*] is, strictly speaking, the true history of humankind. Without this chain all the external events of this world are but clouds or terrifying deformities. It is a dreadful prospect to behold nothing in the earth's revolutions except ruins upon ruins, eternal beginnings without end, radical changes of fate without an enduring purpose. The chain of human development [*Kette der Bildung*] alone forms the ruins into a whole structure in which human figures do indeed vanish, but where the human spirit lives on immortally. There are glorious names that shine in the history of culture as geniuses of the human race, as brilliant stars in the mortal night! Although the course of time destroyed many of their edifices, and although much gold sank in the mire of forgetfulness, the labors of their lives were not in vain, for their works that providence thought fit to save have been preserved in other forms. Besides, no human monument on earth can endure intact and eternal, for it was formed in the stream of generations only by the hands of a certain time for that time. It is allowed to crumble as soon as it delays the aims of future generations or makes those aims unnecessary. Thus, the variable form and the imperfection of all human activity was also part of the Creator's plan. Folly appeared so that wisdom might overcome it. Even the noblest works decay and crumble so that human beings might be able to exert new labors in improving or building upon their ruins, for we all exist here but on a training ground. Every individual must depart from this place. Since one can be, therefore, indifferent about what posterity may do with one's works, good people would be appalled if succeeding generations venerated their works with listless stupidity and undertook no projects of their own. The good wish them to undertake these new labors, for what the good carry out of the world is their increased power, the inner, ripe fruit of their human activity.

Oh, golden chain of human development that surrounds the earth and extends from all individuals to the throne of providence! Ever since I first perceived you and traced you in your finest links—in the feelings of father, mother, friends, and teachers—history no longer appears to me as it once did, that is, as a horrifying scene of devastation on the sacred earth. History includes a thousand crimes veiled in detestable praise, and a thousand more disclosed in all their ugliness stand beside them. These crimes nevertheless accentuate the rare and genuine service of active humanity. This service proceeded on its way quietly and obscurely, seldom aware of the effects that providence created from it, just as providence created spirit from matter. The noble plant could flourish only amid storms. Analogously, the sweet labor of human beings could be victorious only by struggling against false presumptions. This labor often seemed to be defeated by its own pure intentions, but this was not the case. The seed emerges and grows more beautifully from the ashes of the good, and when watered by blood, it becomes an unfading flower. Therefore, I am no longer confused by the workings of historical changes: They are as necessary for our race as a current for a stream that prevents it from becoming a stagnant pool. The genius of humanity blooms in ever new forms, and it is regenerated in peoples, generations, and lineages as it proceeds. . . .

The purpose [Zweck] *of human nature is humanity [Humanität]; and with this purpose God has put the fate of our race in our own hands.*

The end of something that is not merely a lifeless means must lie within itself. Had we been created to strive with ever-vain attempts to an unattainable point of perfection that were external to our nature, as the magnet turns to the north, we would not only pity ourselves as blind machines but also pity the being who condemned us to such a tantalic fate by creating our race merely for its diabolical eyes, which delight in others' misfortunes. Should we try to excuse this being by saying that these empty endeavors, which never attain their goal, promote some good and keep our nature in perpetual activity, it would nevertheless be an imperfect, ferocious being who deserved such an excuse. For no good lies in an activity that never attains its goal, and this being would have deceived us, weakly or maliciously, by intentionally placing before us such an illusion. Fortunately, the nature of things teaches us no such foolishness. If we observe humankind, as we know it, and according to the laws intrinsic to it, then we perceive nothing higher in human beings than humanity. Even if we think about angels or gods, we think of them as ideal, superior human beings.

Human nature is organized to this apparent end, as we have seen. To this end we have been given our finer senses and instincts, our reason and freedom, our delicate and durable health, our language, arts, and religion. In all situations and societies human beings have had nothing in mind and could aim at nothing other than humanity, as they themselves have conceived of it. For the benefit of humanity nature made differences between the sexes and different periods of life so that our childhood might last longer, and we might learn a kind of humanity by means of education. All of the different modes of life

throughout the whole wide world have been established and all forms of
society have been introduced for the benefit of humanity. Whether hunter or
fisher, shepherd or farmer and citizen, human beings have learned in all
situations to discriminate food and to build homes for themselves and their
families. They have learned to raise clothing to the level of adornment for
both sexes and to arrange their households. They have invented various laws
and forms of government, which all aimed to allow individuals, undisturbed
by others, to exercise their powers and acquire a more pleasing and freer
enjoyment of life. To this end property was acquired and work, arts, trade,
and contact between various parties were made easier. Punishments were
created for criminals and rewards for the deserving, and thousands of moral
practices were established for people of different ranks in public and private
life, and even in religion. For this, wars were carried out, treaties were made;
by degrees a kind of international law of war and human rights, along with
various agreements about hospitality and economy, were achieved so that
human beings would be protected and respected outside the borders of their
own countries. Thus, whatever good appears to have been accomplished in
history, it has been done for the sake of humanity; whatever foolish, vicious,
or abominable has been perpetuated, this was done against humanity. Human
beings can conceive of no other end of all their earthly institutions than what
lies in themselves, that is, in the weak and strong, the base and noble nature
that God has given them. If we recognize each thing in the whole creation
only by what it is and what it affects, then the purpose of the human race on
earth is given to us, as if by the clearest demonstration, by its nature and
history.

Let us look back at the regions of the earth which we have surveyed thus
far [in this work]. In all of the institutions of peoples from China to Rome,
in all of the varieties of their political constitutions, in each one of their
inventions of war and peace, even in all of the faults and mistakes of nations,
we can recognize the main law of nature: Let human beings be human beings!
Let them shape their situation according to what they hold to be best. For
this, peoples took possession of their lands and established themselves in
them as they were able. In the different parts of the earth, marriage, the state,
slaves, clothing, houses, recreation, food, science, and art have been made
into what people thought was best for their own or for the general good. Thus,
everywhere we find human beings possessing and exercising the right to form
themselves into a kind of humanity that they themselves recognize. If they
have erred or stopped halfway on the road of tradition that was handed down
to them, then they have suffered the consequences of their error and have
done penance for their own failings. God in no way bound their hands any
further than they were bound by time, place, and their own intrinsic powers.
When they failed, God never came to their aid through miracles but rather

allowed these failings to produce their effects so that human beings might learn to correct them on their own.

As simple as this law of nature is, as worthy as it is of God, so consistent and fertile are its consequences for the human race. If the human race is to be what it is and become what it is capable of becoming, then it must preserve a nature that is effective on its own and a sphere of free activity that is disturbed by no supernatural miracle. All inanimate substances, every species directed by instincts, have remained what they were from the beginning of creation. God made human beings gods on earth, implanting in them the principle of self-activity and setting this principle in motion from the beginning by means of human nature's internal and external needs. Human beings could not live and support themselves, if they had not learned to use reason. As soon as they used it, the door was opened to thousands of errors and failed attempts. Yet through these same errors and failed attempts, the way was also opened to a better use of reason. The faster they recognized their mistakes and the greater energy they used to correct them; the further they advanced, and the more they formed their humanity. They must form it. Otherwise, they groan for centuries under the load of their own mistakes.

We see, too, that in order to establish this law nature has chosen as broad a field as the dwelling of our race would allow. Nature has organized human beings as diversely as one human race could be organized on this earth. . . .

The fundamental principle of this divine law of nature reconciles us beautifully not only with the form of our race worldwide but also with its variations throughout different periods of time. Everywhere human beings are what they have made of themselves, what they had the desire and power to become. If they were content with their situation or if the means to their improvement were not yet mature in the grand sowing of time, then they remained what they had been for centuries and did not change. However, if they used the tools that their God had given them to use—their understanding, their power, and all of the opportunities to which a favorable wind directed them—then they raised themselves skillfully higher and improved themselves courageously. If they did not do this, then their indolence became so apparent that they did not even feel this misfortune. For every lively feeling of injustice that is accompanied by understanding and power must become a liberating power. Long submission to despotism, for example, was not established by the might of the despots. The easy, trusting weakness of their subjects and, later, their patient indolence were its strong and only supports. For it is, of course, easier to bear with patience than to act with vigor. This is why so many peoples have not used the right that God gave to them through the divine gift of their reason.

Nonetheless, there is no doubt, generally speaking, that what has not yet happened on earth will happen in the future. For the rights of human beings

are imprescriptible, and the powers that God placed within them are inerad-
icable. We are astonished to see how far the Greeks and the Romans advanced
in their contexts in a few centuries, for even though the goal of their activity
was not always the most pure, they proved that they could achieve it. Their
image shines in history and encourages anyone like them, under similar and
more favorable assistance of fate, to similar and greater activities. The whole
of history of people becomes in this respect a school for instructing us in the
course by which we are to achieve the beautiful goal of humanity and human
dignity. So many celebrated, ancient nations attained an inferior goal. Why
should we not achieve a purer, more noble goal? They were human beings
like us. Their vocation—to achieve the best form of humanity—is our own,
according to our temporal circumstances, according to our conscience, according to our duties. What they achieved without miracles, we can and may
achieve. God helps us through our own industry, our own understanding, our
own powers. When God created the earth and all nonrational creatures, God
formed human beings and said to them: "Be my image, a god on earth! Rule
and govern! Whatever you can create from your nature that is noble and
excellent, do so. I may not help you through miracles, for I have placed your
fate in your own, human hands, but all of my holy, eternal laws of nature
will assist you."

Let us consider a few of these natural laws that, even according to the
testimony of history, have promoted the course of humanity in the human
race; and, as truly as they are the natural laws of God, they will continue to
promote it.

*All of the destructive powers in nature must, over the course of time, not
only yield to the maintaining forces but also finally serve the education of
the whole. . . .*

*The human race is destined to go through all kinds of states of culture in
all kinds of variations; yet the permanency of its welfare is founded solely
and essentially on reason and justice. . . .*

*According to the laws of their internal nature, reason and justice must
gain more ground among human beings over the course of time and promote
a more durable humanity. . . .*

*A wise goodness rules human fate; for this reason there is no more greater
dignity, no more durable and purer happiness than to act according to it.*

ON HUMAN IMMORTALITY

. . . Our noblest possessions do not come from ourselves; our understanding
along with its powers, the way in which we think, act, and exist, is, as it
were, inherited.[11] We think in a *language* that our ancestors invented. We

11. [SW 16:34-43.]

think in a way that was shaped and formed by many thinkers, enriched by the finest geniuses of the human race, including those of other languages, who thereby graciously bequeathed to us the noblest part of their existence— their innermost being, their acquired treasures of thought. Each day we enjoy and use thousands of *inventions* that have come to us from the past and in part from the most distant regions of the earth, and without which we would have been forced to lead a bleak and paltry life. We have inherited *maxims and morals* which not only illuminate the natural law that lies obscurely within us, but also inspire and empower us to soar above depression and the daily grind, to shake off prejudices, and, by feeling other souls who are filled with the same light of truth, goodness, and beauty, to unite ourselves with them in friendship and action far more intimately than irrational, inanimate objects could ever unite. This chain of effects [*Kette der Wirkungen*] has reached us; it has surrounded and embraced us; against our will we are bound to hold onto it and to continue to influence the present and the future, be it for better or worse, in an effective or an obstructive way. This is the invisible, hidden medium that links together minds through thoughts; hearts through inclinations and drives; senses through impressions and forms; societies through laws and institutions; families through examples, life-styles, and education; lovers through love; and friends through harmonious friendship. Within this binding medium we are, then, bound to and will influence our own and others' descendants. This is the essence of genuine human immortality. Every other image of immortality is merely a name, a label.

In order to become fully aware of this, let us simply think about the most lively moments of our life, especially of our childhood and youth. Because we enjoyed these moments, did we not let go of ourselves and open ourselves to others? Did we not receive from others and feel that they were a part of us and we were a part of them? In those moments we forgot our limited, mortal form; we were in the realm of eternal truths, of pure goodness, of undying pleasure and existence. In this way, we appropriated in our youth the thoughts of those who most influenced us; their tones flowed into our own; we saw their forms, worshiped their shadows; and the effect that their innermost voice made upon us developed into the shape of our own soul. We continue to think with the thoughts of those great and wise people whose bodies have long since decayed; not just what they thought, but how they thought, was imparted to us; we appropriate this and in turn pass it on to others. Even if it seems that some of these thoughts lie dead and buried in the deep floor of the sea of our thoughts, at the proper time they will emerge and be formulated in relation to other thoughts, for nothing is dead in the human soul. Everything either lives or waits to be raised to life. One soul animates and wakes another because the realm of human souls is linked together in the most intimate way. The passions, life-styles, and morals of human beings—especially of those people with whom we deal daily, people we either hate or love, abhor or respect—continue to affect us at a deeper level. We revolt against those whom we hate while impressions left by those whom we love blend gently into our own nature. We become accustomed to the voice, mien, glance, and expression of the other in such a way that we unconsciously appropriate them and transmit them to others. This is the invisible, magic cord that ties together even human gestures; it is an endless transmission of characteristics—a palingenesis and metempsychosis of thoughts, inclinations of our hearts, and drives that we assimilate and then reject, and vice versa. We believe we exist in isolation from others, but this is never the case; we do not even exist in isolation when by ourselves, for we are affected by the spirits of the dead, of ancient deified heroes,[12] or by the spirits of our teachers, friends, foes, those who form us, those who deform us, and a thousand people who influence us. We cannot avoid seeing their faces and hearing their voices; even the spasms of their deformed creations are passed on to us. Happy are those to whom fate allots an Elysium and not a Tartarus as the heaven of their thoughts,[13] as the realm of their feelings, principles, and behavior; their souls are grounded in a happy immortality.

In order for you to understand my view of immortality, I offer the following:

1. The purer and nobler an element of our nature, the more it opens itself to others, renounces its narrow bounds, and becomes expressive, infinite, and eternal. If we impose a form that oppresses us upon other people, then it will oppress them even more so because this form is not their own. In contrast, whatever gives them room to breathe and creates joy in them, whatever allows them to breathe freely and offers them an Elysium in which flowers freely bloom, this is the pure ether of immortality. I am referring, for example, to clear, genuine thoughts, to every scientific development in which we forget ourselves and focus our attention only on the laws of the object of study. I am referring to rational, moral, and legal principles in which every individual recognizes, even unwillingly, what is universally valid and dignified and sees in them, as it were, "formulas of eternity." Wherever chords of this kind sound, all pure, human souls resonate with them; we take pleasure in these chords until that point at which, without our knowing, they become the strings of our own inner being. This is the way all virtuous people of the human race have affected later generations; this is the way we are affected by parents, teachers, lawmakers, friends, and anyone else who promotes the process of our thinking, the structure of our life, toward the purest, most

12. [*Dämonen.* In Greek mythology a demon is an inferior divinity such as a deified hero.]

13. [In Greek mythology Elysium was the dwelling place after death of virtuous mortals or those given immortality by divine favor. Later accounts placed Elysium in the underworld. Tartarus was the lowest region of the underworld to which the wicked were condemned to torment.]

noble humanity. Oh, how happy beyond all others are the heroes and geniuses of humankind when goodness of heart is allotted them in addition to their power and wisdom, their wisdom and power. They possess thousands of means for becoming immortal in the most beautiful and most certain way. Whether or not their names are known by the oppressed, helpless, or orphaned, as long as these people enjoy protection, help, encouragement, support, and joy through the organizations of these heroes and geniuses, then the latter live immortally in their institutions. Their work that they promote and institute includes improved education for the neglected, the kind reception of the abandoned, a purpose for which these people are trained, a sense of gratitude and joy, and all the good influences that God passes on anew. The fruits that have grown from the seeds that these heroes and geniuses planted for the pure benefit of humanity have an immortal nature, are sustained by an ever-renewing power, and grow on ever-thriving branches. In contrast, anything that becomes distorted in and through our mortal form descends to the realm of Orcus.[14]

2. The passage of such contributions into the whole eternal treasure of humanity requires a *rejection of our own ego*, that is, a renunciation of self and of the prejudices that cling to the self. Would we, if we could, want to bestow our weaknesses to the present and to posterity? No, indeed! The nectar of immortality, the sap of life through which the true and the good grow, is a pure liquid; everything that is mixed with personality must descend to the abyss; it must be refined in the vessels and workings of the great machinery of the world until the dregs settle. Truth rests upon itself; even if a die is rolled on all six sides, it still remains a die. A pyramid, in contrast, when placed on its point, must either collapse or with great effort be rolled this way and that until it finds its steady ground. This self-denial comes easily once one has enjoyed the air of that higher region and is transported into the realm of permanence and truth. We would gladly discard the mortal shell of our personality if we knew that the present world and posterity would only remember our imperfection. The premise of a universal law is the necessary absence of a passion for the personal; in the same way, every pure form of the good and the beautiful requires an ideal instead of a personal portrait. Those who are able to be their own greatest critics are the only ones who are children of the gods, who are immortal in their nature and their deeds. Perhaps I will someday have the opportunity to say something about the deified heroes, mortal heroes, and geniuses of antiquity whose divine forms seem to me to be abstract concepts and categories under which all that is immortal in human thoughts, deeds, and traits is arranged in a tangible way.

3. Because a thing can be the best of its kind in one way alone, however, and because the forms of things must return according to eternal laws, and

14. [In Greek mythology Orcus is the god of the underworld.]

because nothing internal can exist without something external (that is, no thought or movement of the will can exist without an outward sign), we see that the *art* of the eternally true, good, and beautiful necessarily finds a place in the garden of immortality. Amidst all of the misleading paths, there is only one that is straight and true. If a masterpiece appears only after endless practice in youth, we cannot doubt that it possesses a permanent and lasting character. The eyes of the initiated recognize this character. Even if jealousy throws a cloud over it, or barbarism a thick fog, the cloud will pass, the fog will lift, and the light of the eternal work will shine forth again for centuries. If you examine history closely, it is amazing how few unique forms appear in the realm of human thoughts and actions. There are far fewer leaders in the world of sciences, arts, inventions, laws, and maxims than political leaders; some of them continued to be influential for hundreds of years through the power of some sweet error. Finally, however, the buried treasure was rediscovered; after a long winter, the eternal power of nature started a new and beautiful spring. The beautiful and best of every sort in the history of all times and peoples is marked with the seal of immortality—with the mark and character of that which continually returns; the beautiful and best strike the happy medium of their kind, they provide a formula that could only have been understood in this way.

If I am not mistaken, and if we are thinking soundly, then this perspective has to instill in us a new taste for life, a new appreciation of the position we hold in life, and the desire not only to enjoy eternity from this position but also to work in the best way possible for that which endures in humanity. We cannot help but take part; we stand in the current of time where one wave pushes the next; we are bound to affect the future either in a useful or a harmful way, just as the past affects us. The reward of life is that even in darkness and fog we achieve the goal where the crown hangs; we strike the chords where sweet-sounding harmonies resonate as they rise and fall into infinity. Even if our mortal ears could not immediately hear them, they would nevertheless be there, continuing to resound and to strike new harmonies. We do not affect the future through texts alone; we can affect it more profoundly through institutions, words, deeds, and through our example and the way we live. In this way we vividly impress our image upon others; they receive it and pass it on. This is the way the tree of humanity rose up above the peoples; innumerable hands contributed to its maintenance and care. We enjoy its fruits and must assist its further cultivation. Our eyes cannot take in how far it extends; but our hands are active; our short life is lengthened and becomes eternal through this process of participation and sharing. It seems to me that we will easily forget our own name when caught up in this noble and proper feeling; we do not want to bequeath to our contemporaries and to posterity our personal portrait, but rather our mind, our heart, the best efforts of our life, and the noblest form that we appropriated and passed onto others.

TREATISE ON THE ORIGIN OF LANGUAGE

Part One: Could Human Beings, Left to Their Own Natural Capabilities, Have Invented Language?

Even as animals, human beings have language.[15] All strong sensations of the body, including the most violent and painful ones, and all fervent passions of the soul are immediately expressed in cries, tones, and wild, inarticulate sounds. The suffering animal as well as the hero, Philoctetes,[16] will whimper and groan when overcome by pain, even if abandoned on a desert island without sight, trace, or hope of help from a fellow creature. It is as if a creature breathes more freely when it vents its burning anguish. It is as if it sighs away part of the pain and at least inhales new strength to endure as it fills the empty air with groans. Nature certainly did not create us as isolated blocks of stone or as egoistic monads! Even the most delicate chords of animal feeling (I must use this image because I know no better one for expressing the mechanics of sentient bodies), even the chords whose sound and intensity do not originate in the will and in mature reflection, whose nature cannot be penetrated by all the probings of reason, are chords expressed toward other creatures. This is the case even when there is no consciousness of sympathy from other creatures. The chord is struck and performs its natural duty: It sounds, it calls for a sympathetic echo even when none exists, even when it can neither hope for nor expect a response.

If physiology ever advanced to a point where it could explain human psychology (which I very much doubt), it would throw some light on this phenomenon through an analysis of the nervous system. It might, however, also divide this phenomenon into individual parts that are too minute and insensitive. For now let us regard this phenomenon in its entirety as a clear law of nature: *A sentient being cannot confine any of its vivid feelings to itself and must immediately express each one involuntarily and unintentionally by a sound.* Nature gave this law to all things on earth: "Do not feel for yourself alone, but let your feeling resound." This was, as it were, the final motherly touch from the formative hand of nature. Because this last creative touch was peculiar to all in the same species, this law became a blessing: "Let your feelings resound in a way that is peculiar to your species, and let it be heard

15. [SW 5:5-9, 17-18, 21-26, 28-32, 34-41, 46-48.]
16. [Philoctetes is the hero of Greek mythology who slew Paris, an act that led to the conquest of Troy.]

sympathetically by one and all." Suppose that no one comes in contact with this weak, sensitive creature! No matter how alone, isolated, and exposed to the cruel storms of the universe it appears to be, it is not alone. It is related to all of nature. . . . *These sighs, these tones, are language. There exists, therefore, a language of feeling that is a direct law of nature.*

Today, of course, certain remnants of this language, more than great outbursts, prove that *human beings have had this language in common with animals.* These remnants are, nevertheless, irrefutable. Although the language that we create may have suppressed the language of nature, and although our civilized life-style and social conventions may have dammed up, dried up, and diverted the torrent and tide of passions, the strongest moment of feeling, no matter where or how seldom it occurs, nevertheless claims its rights and resounds directly in accentuated tones in its maternal language. The flare-up of passion, the sudden onslaught of joy or happiness, pain and sorrow that dig deep furrows in the soul, the overpowering feeling of revenge, despair, rage, terror, horror, and so on—all these feelings announce themselves, and each one does so in its own way. Every kind of emotion sleeping in our nature has a corresponding kind of sound. I have observed that the remoter the affinity between human beings and a certain kind of animal and the greater the dissimilarity in the structure of their nervous systems; the less we can understand each other's natural language. As land mammals, we are able to understand land animals better than sea animals; we understand land animals that live in herds better than land animals that live in the forest; and we best understand the herds that live closest to us. . . . In fact this natural language is a community language for the members of each species among themselves, and hence human beings also possess their own kind of natural language.

The sounds of this language are certainly very simple. When they are articulated and written down on paper as interjections, the most contrary feelings are expressed almost in the same way. The faint "ah" is the sound of melting love as well as sinking despair; the fiery "oh" is the expression of sudden joy as well as flaming rage, of mounting admiration as well as overwhelming sorrow. Were these sounds intended, however, just to be written on paper as interjections? The tear that fills the sad, dim eye and seeks comfort is very moving when seen within the entire portrait of sorrow. Taken alone, however, it is a cold drop of water; place it under a microscope, and I would rather not know what it might be! The weary breath, the half sigh that dies on the lips distorted by pain, moves us very deeply. But if you separate this sigh from its living context, then it is an empty puff of wind. Can it be otherwise with the sounds of feeling? In their living context, in the total picture of active nature, accompanied by so many other phenomena, they are moving and sufficient unto themselves. Separated and torn from this context, robbed of their life, they are obviously nothing but ciphers! . . .

Remnants of these natural sounds resound in all primitive languages. They do not, of course, compose the main threads of human language. They are not the roots as such, but rather the sap that enlivens the roots of language. . . .

If we decide to call these immediate sounds of feeling "language," then I do indeed find its origin very natural. *Not only is this origin not superhuman but it is also obviously animal: the natural law of a sentient organism.*[17]

But I cannot conceal my astonishment that philosophers, that is, people with conceptual clarity, could have ever thought that *the origin of human language could be explained from this cry of emotions.* For is not human language something totally different? All animals, down to the mute fish, give sound to their feelings. No animal, however, not even the most perfect one, possesses the slightest, true beginnings of a human language. Shape, refine, and arrange this cry of natural language in any way you please. If understanding is not present to use this sound intentionally, then according to the natural law cited above, I do not see how human, volitional language could ever arise. Children, like animals, speak with the sounds of emotion. But is not the language they learn from other human beings a totally different language? . . .

Human beings are for us the only creatures of language that we know. They differ from all animals precisely through language. Thus, there is no more secure way to begin the investigation of the origin of human language than with experiences about the distinction between animals and human beings. Condillac and Rousseau were bound to err in their discussion of the origin of language because they were mistaken in such customary and different ways about this distinction. The former[18] turned animals into human beings, the latter[19] turned human beings into animals. I must, therefore, discuss this distinction more thoroughly.

We are certain that the strength and reliability of human instincts are vastly inferior to those of animal instincts and that human beings do not at all possess what in many species of animals are called "innate technical skills and instincts" [angeborne Kunstfähigkeiten und Kunsttriebe]. However, most philosophers, including one of the most profound German philosophers,[20] have

17. [*Maschine.* This is an eighteenth century expression for organism.]

18. [Étienne Bonnot de Condillac,] *Traité des animaux* [Amsterdam de Bire, 1755].

19. [Jean Jacques Rousseau,] *Discours sur l'origine [et les fondements] de l'inegalité [parmi les hommes* (Amsterdam: M. M. Rey, 1755)].

20. [Hermann Samuel] Reimarus, *Allgemeine Betrachtungen über die Triebe der Thiere, hauptsächlich über ihre Kunst-Triebe* [Hamburg: J. C. Bohn 1760]. For some opinions on it see [Lessing's] *Briefe, die neueste Litteratur betreffend.* [The latter is a journal published between 1759 and 1766 and edited by C.F. Nicolai. It contained contributions from several authors, including G.E. Lessing and M. Mendelssohn. The articles to which Herder refers are the following: 8 (October 30, 1760): 233-40; 8 (November 6, 1760): 240-56; 8 (November 13, 1760): 257-72; 8 (November 20, 1760): 273-79; 15 (July 1 and 8, 1762): 3-30.]

not yet explained these technical instincts or the reason for their absence in human nature. It appears that a major perspective has been overlooked from which we can, if not completely explain the nature of animals, at least make some observations about it that may, as I hope to show in another context, throw great light on human psychology. This perspective is the *sphere of the animals*.

Each animal has a sphere in which it belongs from birth, instantly enters, spends its entire life, and dies. It is a strange fact that *the keener the senses of an animal, the stronger and more certain its instincts, and the more marvelous the products of its technical skill; the narrower its sphere is, the more uniform its product*. I have investigated this relationship and have discovered that a wonderful inverse proportion can be observed everywhere between, on the one hand, the limited scope of an animal's movements, habitat, food, self-preservation, mating, training, and social behavior and, on the other, its instincts and technical skills. The bee in its hive builds a honeycomb with a wisdom that Egeria could not teach her Numa.[21] But apart from these cells and from its proper task within them, the bee is nothing. The spider weaves its web with the art of Minerva. But all its skill is woven into this narrow space in which it spins: This is its universe! How marvelous is the insect, yet how narrow the sphere of its activity!

Contrariwise, *the more manifold the activities and purposes of an animal, the more diverted its attention toward several objects, the more variable its way of life, in short, the greater and the more diversified its sphere; the more its senses are divided and weakened*. It is beyond the scope of this essay to demonstrate with examples this great relationship which pervades the chain of all living creatures. I must either leave the demonstration to others or postpone it until later. For now, I will proceed with my argument.

In all probability and by analogy it is, therefore, possible to explain all technical instincts and skills by referring to the imaginative powers of the animals without assuming blind determinism (of the kind assumed even by Reimarus that is ruining philosophy entirely). Extremely keen senses are bound to become very penetrating when they are confined within a narrow circle and directed to one kind of object, and when all the rest of the world does not exist for them! The powers of the imagination are bound to operate very strongly when they are confined to a narrow circle and endowed with similar powers of the senses! When senses and conception are directed to *one* point, what can result but instinct? The senses and conceptions, then, account for the sensitivity, the skills, and the instincts of animals according to their species and stages.

21. [In Roman mythology, Pompilius Numa was reputed to have been the wise second king of Rome. He received counsel from the nymph Egeria about forms of worship.]

Hence I may state the following thesis: *The sensitivity, skills, and technical instincts of animals increase in strength and intensity in inverse relation to the size and diversity of their sphere of activity.*

Human beings, however, do not have such a uniform and narrow sphere in which only *one* task awaits them; instead, a world of activities and tasks surrounds them.

The senses and organization of human beings are not focused on one single object; instead, human beings have senses for all things, and hence for each individual thing their senses are weaker and duller.

The powers of the human soul embrace the whole world; human conceptions are not directed toward one single object. Consequently, human beings have no technical instincts, no innate technical skills, and—a point more pertinent to our subject—no *animal language.*

Apart from the sounds of sentient organisms mentioned above, what is that which in some species is called "animal language" but the result of the observations I have just made? What is it but *an obscure, sentient agreement between animals of the same species about their proper task within the sphere of their activity?*

The smaller the sphere of the animals, the less is their need for language. The keener their senses, the more focused on *one object* their conceptions, and the more compelling their instincts; the more constricted is the agreement of their possible sounds, signs, or utterances. A living mechanism, a governing instinct, is speaking and perceiving here. How little speech is necessary for it to be understood!

Animals belonging to the narrowest sphere are therefore even without hearing; for their own world they are all touch, smell, or sight; they have a uniform image, a uniform trait, a uniform activity. They therefore have very little, if any, language.

The larger the sphere of animals, the more varied their senses—but why repeat myself? With human beings the situation changes completely. Of what use would the language of animals be, even of those that are most eloquent and command the greatest variety of sounds, in the human sphere of activity, even under the poorest conditions? Of what use could the dark language of all animals as a whole be to the sporadic desires of human beings, to their divided attention, to their more dully perceptive senses? To human beings this language would be neither rich nor clear, neither sufficient for specifying many objects nor adapted to human organs. It is altogether not *their* language. For, if we do not wish to play with words, what is the proper language of any creature but the one appropriate to the sphere of its needs and its activities, to the organization of its senses, to the direction of its conceptions, and to the strength of its desires? *And with respect to human beings, which animal language meets these requirements?*

The following question is also unnecessary: What language, apart from the automatic language mentioned above, do human beings possess as instinctively as every species of animal does within and according to its sphere? The answer is brief: None! Precisely this short answer is the decisive one.

With every animal, as we have seen, its language is an expression of sensory perceptions, which are so strong that they develop into instincts. Hence, this language (like senses, perceptions, and instincts) is *inborn* and *immediately natural* to the animal. The bee buzzes as it sucks; the bird sings as it nests; but how do human beings speak by nature? Not at all! Just as they do nothing or very little entirely by instinct as the animals do. With the exception of the cries of its sentient organism, a newborn child is mute. It expresses neither conceptions nor instincts by sounds as every animal does in its own way. Therefore, placed among animals alone, it would be the most abandoned child of nature—naked and exposed, weak and needy, timid and unarmed, and, what sums up its misery, deprived of all guides to life. It is born with such diffused and weakened senses, with such indefinite and slumbering skills, with such divided and enfeebled instincts that it is obviously geared toward a thousand needs and destined for a large sphere of activity. And yet it is so orphaned and abandoned that it is not even endowed with a language to express its needs. No! Such a contradiction is not the way that nature operates! Other hidden powers, instead of instincts, must lie dormant in the child. It is born mute, but—!

. . . If human senses, when applied to a limited patch of the earth, to the activity and the enjoyment within a sphere in the universe, are less keen than the senses of the animal that lives within this sphere, then it is precisely this that gives human senses the *advantage of freedom*. Human senses, precisely because they are not intended to serve any one point, are the more universal senses of the world.

If human powers of imagination are not confined to the construction of a honeycomb or a spider web and are as such inferior to the technical skills of the animals in this sphere, then it is precisely for this reason that these powers gain a *wider perspective*. There is no single product of human skill that cannot be improved. Human beings have, however, the free space to exercise their powers in many ways and hence to improve themselves. Every thought is not the immediate product of nature; yet for that reason it can be a human being's own creation.

If instinct, understood as a result of the organization of the senses and of the sphere of imagination alone and not as a product of blind determinism, is bound to be absent in human beings, then they thereby gain *greater clarity*. Because they do not fall blindly upon one particular point and remain fixed there, they are independent, they can seek for themselves a sphere of self-reflection, they can mirror themselves in themselves. No longer an infallible organism in the hands of nature, they themselves become the purpose and end of their efforts.

Call the entire disposition of human powers what you will: *understanding, reason, reflection*,[22] and so on; it does not matter to me, as long as you do not use these terms to denote disconnected powers or merely advancing degrees of animal powers. *It is the entire arrangement of all human powers, the entire economy of human sensory and cognitive, of human cognitive and volitional nature.* More precisely, *it is the sole positive power of thinking*, combined with a certain organization of the body, that is called *reason* in human beings and *innate technical skill* in animals; in human beings it is called *freedom*, and in animals it is called *instinct*. The difference, however, is *not one of degree or of additional powers*, but rather *one of an entirely dissimilar direction and development of all powers*. Whether you are a follower of Leibniz or Locke, Search or Know-all,[23] whether an idealist or materialist, you must admit (as a result of the above and once we agree on our use of terms) that the distinctive character of humanity consists in this and nothing else.

All those who have raised objections against this position have been deceived by erroneous conceptions or by unclear ideas. There are those who have understood human reason as an additional, entirely disconnected faculty of the soul, bestowed on human beings like an additional power exceeding that of the animals, and which, like the forth rung of a ladder with three below, must be singled out for separate consideration. Clearly this position is—no matter how great the philosophers who affirm it—philosophical nonsense. All individual faculties of our soul or of that of animals are nothing but metaphysical abstractions, impressions! We separate them because our feeble minds cannot study them as a whole; they are arranged in chapters not because they operate in nature chapter by chapter, but rather because a student finds it easiest to explain them in this way. The fact that we classify certain activities of the soul under certain major terms such as "wit," "sagacity," "imagination," or "reason," does not mean that a single act of the mind is ever possible in which wit or reason alone operates. We classify them in this way only because we primarily discern in the act, such as in the comparison or clarification of ideas, that abstraction which we call "wit" or "reason." Nevertheless, the entire undivided soul is always at work. If a person could ever perform a single act while thinking completely like an animal, then that person would most decidedly no longer be a human being, no longer even be capable of any human acts. If a person were ever devoid of reason for a

---

22. [*Verstand, Vernunft, Besinnung*. In the second version of the text *Besinnung* is changed to *Reflexion*.]

23. A distinction favored in a recent metaphysical work, *Search's Light of Nature Pursued* (London: T. Jones, 1768). [Written by Abraham Tucker (1705-74) under the pseudonym, Edward Search. Tucker used Know-all as a fictive character in his philosophical dispute.]

single moment, then I cannot see how that person could think reasonably ever again, unless the entire soul, the entire economy of that individual's nature, would have been changed.

According to sounder conceptions of the matter, human rationality, the character of the human species, is something quite different: *It is the overall determination of our power of thought in relation to our senses and instincts.* If we take all previous analogies into account, then it necessarily follows that:

- If human beings had the instincts of animals, then they could not possess what we now call reason. These instincts would sweep human powers so obscurely to one single point that they would have no free sphere of reflection. It must follow that
- If human beings had the senses of animals, then they would not possess reason. The keen sensitivity of animal senses and the powerful flood of perceptions they bring would stifle all calm reflection. But conversely, according to these very laws of correlation belonging to the economy of nature, it must follow that
- If animalistic senses and instincts that confine the powers to one point are absent, then another creature would come into being whose positive powers would operate in a much wider sphere, owing to its more complex organization: a distinctive and free creature not only *capable* of cognition, volition and action, but also *conscious* of knowing, willing, and acting. This creature is the human being. In order to avoid the confusion resulting from the notion of individual faculties of reason and the like, we shall call this entire disposition of human nature "reflective discernment" [*Besonnenheit*].[24] According to these same laws of correlation, because all terms such as "senses," "instinct," "imagination," and "reason" are often only connotations of one single vital force in which opposites cancel each other out, it follows that
- If human beings were not intended to be instinctual animals, then by virtue of the more freely operating positive power of their souls, human beings had to be creatures of reflective discernment.

By carrying this series of syllogisms a few steps further, I can perhaps anticipate some objections.

If reason is not a separate power that operates in isolation but rather an orientation of all powers that is peculiar to the human species, then *human beings must possess reason from the first moment of their existence as human*

24. [*Besonnenheit* has also been translated as consciousness, reflection, or mind. It has been translated here as "reflective discernment" so that its relation to, yet distinction from, *Reflexion* (another term used in this essay) can be shown. *Besonnenheit* stems from the Greek word *sophrosyne*, which means "soundness of mind." See HWP.]

beings. This reflective discernment is apparent in the very first thought of a child, just as an insect is an insect from the start. More than one writer has been unable to comprehend this, and this is why the subject at hand is crammed with the crudest, most disgusting objections. They misunderstood the subject and thus could not comprehend it. Does thinking with reason necessarily mean thinking with fully developed reason? Does the claim that infants think with reflective discernment mean that they reason like sophists from their academic chairs or politicians in their cabinets? Blessed is the child who as yet knows nothing of this tiring maze of subtleties! Is it not evident, however, that this objection refers only to one particular cultivated use of human powers and does not disclaim the positive reality of a human power? What fool would claim that human beings think at the moment of birth in the same way as after many years of practice—unless at the same time one denies the development of all human powers and thereby confesses by implication to be an intellectual minor? This development means nothing but the use of these human powers with greater ease, strength, and versatility. Does this not then presuppose that something already exists to which this development applies? Must not the seed of what is to grow exist from the start? Is not the whole tree contained in the seed? Just as a child does not possess the claws of a griffin nor the mane of a lion, neither can it think as griffins and lions think. However, if it is thinking in a human way, then reflective discernment, that is, the determination of all its powers in this major direction, is as much a part of its lot at its first moment in life as it is at its last. Reason reveals itself amidst the sensations of a child in such a definite way that the omniscient one who created this soul already perceived in the child's earliest state the whole web of life's activities. This is analogous to the geometrician who finds the whole structure of a given class from *one* part of the series. . . .

I regret having lost so much time defining and arranging mere concepts. It was necessary to do so, however, because people have recently wreaked utter havoc on this area of psychology. French philosophers have thrown everything in confusion through their discussion of a few peculiarities that supposedly distinguish human from animal nature, and German philosophers have arranged most concepts of this kind more for the benefit of their own philosophical systems and in accordance with their own points of view than for the sake of avoiding confusion within the perspective of the common way of thinking. Besides, my clarification of these concepts did not actually lead us astray, for we now come directly to the matter at hand!

Human beings, endowed with reflective discernment—a characteristic peculiar to them alone—and allowing this reflective discernment (reflection) [*Besonnenheit (Reflexion)*]* to operate freely for the first time, invented language. But what is reflection? What is language?*

Reflective discernment is characteristically peculiar to human beings and essential to their species. The same can be said about language and their own invention of language.

The invention of language is as natural to human beings as it is for them to be human beings. Let us elaborate these two concepts: reflection and language [*Reflexion und Sprache*].

Human beings exhibit reflection when the power of the soul acts so freely that, in the vast ocean of sensations rushing in on it by way of the senses, it can, so to speak, isolate and retain *one* single wave, direct its attention to it, and be wholly conscious of doing so. They exhibit reflection when, from the fleeting dreams of images that pass before the senses, they can rouse themselves to a moment of alertness, concentrate deliberately on one image, observe it clearly and calmly, and isolate some of its distinguishing marks so that it is identified as a specific object and no other. Human beings exhibit reflection, then, not simply by vividly or clearly perceiving all the characteristics of objects, but by apperceiving[25] one or several characteristics as distinctive. This first act of apperception renders a clear concept: It is the first judgment of the soul.[26]

And how did this apperception take place? By means of a distinguishing mark, which human beings had to isolate and which, as a distinguishing mark for consciousness, was clearly impressed upon them. Come, let us applaud them with a shout of "Eureka!" This first distinguishing mark for consciousness was a word from the soul. With it, human language was invented!

Suppose that lamb, as an image, passes before their eyes. It appears to them as it appears to no other animal. Not as to the hungry, prowling wolf! Not as to the bloodthirsty lion! These animals already smell and taste the lamb in their minds! Their senses overpower them! Their instincts overwhelm them! Sheep appear differently to human eyes than to the bullish ram that senses the ewe only as an object of instinctive desire! Again, the senses overpower, and the instincts overwhelm. It appears not as to any animal to which the lamb is indifferent; it allows the animal to pass because the animal's instincts are directed toward something else. Not so with human beings! As soon as the need arises to know the lamb, no instinct interrupts them, no sense draws them toward or away from it. The lamb stands there just as it manifests itself to the senses. White, soft, woolly—the reflective soul searches for a distinguishing mark. The sheep bleats! The soul has found a distinguishing mark. Its inward sense is at work. The soul retains this bleating; it made the

25. [*Erkennen* for "perceiving" and *anerkennen* for "apperceiving." Herder is referring to Leibniz's distinction between perception and apperception.]

26. One of the most beautiful treatises to illuminate the nature of apperception on the basis of physical experiments (which only rarely serve to elucidate the metaphysics of the soul) is to be found in the publication of the Berlin Academy of 1764.

greatest impression on the mind, broke away from all other qualities of sight and touch, and sprang into relief. The sheep returns. White, soft, woolly— again the soul sees, touches, reflects, seeks a distinguishing mark. The sheep bleats, and the soul recognizes it again. The soul inwardly feels, "Aha, you are the bleating one!" The soul has recognized the sheep in a human way when it recognizes and names the sheep clearly, that is, with a distinguishing mark. If known any less clearly, the lamb would not have been perceived at all because no senses and no instinct for the sheep could replace the lack of distinctiveness with a more vivid clarity. Could it be known distinctly and directly, without a distinguishing mark? No creature with senses can feel apart from itself in this way because it must always repress, annihilate as it were, other sensations, and it must always recognize the difference between two objects through a third. Through a distinguishing mark, then? What was this other than an *inner distinguishing word?* The *sound* of the bleating, perceived by one human soul as the distinguishing mark of the sheep, became the name of the sheep, even if that soul never tried to stammer it.

The sheep was known by its bleating. This was a fixed sign, by which the soul clearly reflected upon an idea. What is this other than a word? And what is the whole of human language other than a collection of such words? Even if no opportunity had arisen for communicating this idea to another creature or for wanting or being able to "bleat" this distinguishing mark of reflection with the lips, the soul would have "bleated" it internally when it chose this sound as a sign for the memory and later when it recognized the sheep through it. *Language, therefore, was invented by human beings as naturally and as necessarily as it is for human beings to be human.*

Most of those who have written about the origin of language did not search for it in the one place in which it could be found. Many people had numerous doubts, therefore, whether it could be found anywhere within the human soul. It has been sought in the better articulation of the organs of speech, as if an orangutan with precisely the same organs as human beings could have ever invented a language! It has been sought in the cries of passion, as if all animals did not possess these cries, and as if any animal ever had invented a language from them! Others have adopted a principle that claims that human beings imitated nature and hence her sounds, as though thinking could be combined with such a blind inclination! As if the monkey gifted with the same inclination, or the blackbird so skilled in imitating voices, could have invented a language! Most people have posited a mere convention, a contract. It was against this position that Rousseau argued most vigorously. After all, what an obscure, tangled expression it is: "a natural contract to form language"! These numerous, intolerable, fallacious theories concerning the human origin of language have contributed in making the opposite theory [of its divine origin] almost universally held. I hope, however, it will not remain so. It is not the structure of the mouth that creates language, for even a man born mute, if capable of conscious reflection, would form a language in his soul. It is not a matter of the cries of emotion, for language was not invented by a breathing organism but by a creature of conscious reflection. Nor was it a principle of imitation, for the incidental imitation of nature is merely a means to one end and one end only, as will be explained later. Least of all can it be an agreement, an arbitrary social convention. The savage, the hermit in the forest, would have been bound to invent language for himself even though he had never spoken it. His language was an agreement of the soul with itself, and it was an agreement as necessary as it was for human beings to be human from the start. To others it seems incomprehensible how a human soul could have invented language. To me it is incomprehensible how a human soul, given what it is, could exist without necessarily inventing language, even devoid of speech organs or society.

Nothing serves to elaborate this origin more than the objections of its opponents. By penetrating below the surface that others only skimmed, the most thorough, comprehensive defender of the divine origin of language[27] almost becomes a defender of its human origin. He left off exactly at the point his proof began, and his main objection, if merely explained more correctly, becomes an objection against himself and a demonstration of the opposite theory, that is, the possible human origin of language. He intended to prove "that the use of language was necessary for the use of reason!" Had he been able to do so, I do not know what else would have been proved thereby other than "since the use of reason is natural to human beings, the use of language must be so, too!" Unfortunately, he did not prove his proposition. He merely explained in a laborious way that intricate, complex actions, such as attention, reflection, abstraction, and so on, cannot be performed "very well" without signs on which the soul depends. However, the "not very well," "not easily," "not likely" does not demonstrate anything at all. If we assume that we are able, with limited powers of abstraction, to think even a bit abstractly without sentient signs, then we must conclude that other beings could be able to think more abstractly without signs. At any rate, we cannot conclude [from such an assumption] that absolutely no abstraction is possible without a sentient sign. It is not simply a matter of not being able to use reason "very well" without language; rather, I have demonstrated that not even the slightest use of reason, not even the most basic distinctions, not even the simplest judgment of human reflection is possible without language. For the difference between two things can only be recognized through a third. This third—this distinguishing sign—becomes an inner, distinguishing word. Language is, therefore, an entirely natural corollary of the first act of reason.

27. [Johann Peter] Süssmilch.

Süssmilch attempts to prove that the higher uses of reason are not possible without language. In order to support his point he quotes Wolff. But Wolff speaks here, too, only in terms of probabilities. The point is essentially irrelevant, for the higher uses of reason, as found in the speculative sciences, were not necessary for laying the initial foundation of language. Just the same, Mr. Süssmilch merely discusses and does not prove even this easily demonstrable point, while I believe to have proven that not even the first, most elementary use of reason could take place without language. He then goes on to argue that human beings could not have invented language themselves because the invention of language requires reason, and he concludes that language must have already existed before reason. At this point I need to stop this vicious circle and examine it closely. When I do, it pronounces an entirely different conclusion: *ratio et oratio!*[28] If human reason is impossible without language, then the invention of language is to human beings as natural, as ancient, as original, and as characteristic as the use of reason.

I have called Süssmilch's manner of arguing a "vicious circle" because I can turn his argument against him as easily as he can turn it against me, and we get nowhere. Without language human beings have no reason, and without reason no language; without language and reason they are not capable of receiving divine instruction; and without divine instruction they have neither reason nor language. Where could such an argument ever lead us? How can human beings learn language through divine instruction, as Süssmilch claims, if they lack reason? And if they do not have the slightest use of reason without language, then how can they possess language before they have it, or are capable of having it? How can they be rational without the slightest use of reason? In order to receive the first syllable of divine instruction, they had to be, as Süssmilch himself admits, human beings, that is, they had to be able to think clearly, and with the first distinct thought, language was already present in the soul. Language was, therefore, invented by human means and not through divine instruction. I know very well what people usually have in mind when they speak about this divine instruction: the way that parents teach their children language. But this is not at all the case. Parents never teach their children language without the children themselves inventing language along with them. The parents only draw the children's attention to differences between objects by means of certain words. Thus, they do not substitute but only facilitate and promote the use of reason through language. If for other reasons this kind of supernatural, facile argument is used, then it has no bearing on my purpose. God did not in any way invent any language for human beings. Rather, they have always invented language themselves by means of their own powers, albeit under a superior guidance. In order to be

28. [Latin for "reason and spoken language."]

able to grasp the first word, even from the mouth of God, as a word, that is, as a distinguishing sign of reason, reason was necessary. And human beings had to apply the same conscious reflection to *understand* this word as they did to *invent* it in the first place. Hence, all the arms of my opponent can be used against himself. Human beings had to possess the actual use of reason in order to learn divine language. All learning children also possess this unless they merely repeat words, like a parrot, without thinking. Could people learning in this way, however, be properly considered worthy pupils of God? If they had always learned in this way, how did our rational language ever arise? . . .

I do not want to pursue the hypothesis of the divine origin of language from a metaphysical standpoint any further, for its lack of foundation can be seen from a psychological standpoint by the fact that in order to understand the language of the Olympian gods, human beings already must have had reason and therefore language. Still less can I pursue in detail the discussion of animal languages, for they are all, as we have seen, totally and immeasurably different from human language. What I most regret not pursuing in this essay are the diverse views that lead from this genetic point of language in the human soul to the broad fields of logic, aesthetics, and psychology, especially by way of the question: How far can we think without language? What must we think *with* language? The subsequent applications of this question would extend to practically all disciplines. Let it suffice to recognize here that *language is the external distinguishing character of our species, just as reason is the internal one.*

In more than one language "word" and "reason," "concept" and "word," "language" and "cause" have *one* term, and this synonymy contains their full genetic origin. Among peoples of the Near East one of the most common idioms is to call the act of apperceiving a thing "giving it a name," for in the depths of the soul the two actions are one and the same. They call human beings "the speaking animals," and animals without reason "the mutes." These Near Eastern expressions elucidate the point in a tangible way. The Greek term *alogos*[29] captures both the ideas. Language, then, is a natural organ of understanding. It is a *sense of the human soul*, just as the power of sight, according to the sensitive soul of the ancients, built for itself the eye, and as the instinct of the bee built for itself its honeycomb. How excellent it is that this new, self-made sense of the human mind, even in its very origin, constitutes a means of relationship. I cannot think the first human thought, cannot order the first reflective argument, without forming a dialogue in my soul or without attempting to form a dialogue. The first human thought in its very essence prepares us to be able to be in dialogue with others. The first

29. [The Greek term *alogos* can mean both "without language" and "without reason."]

distinguishing mark that I conceive is a distinguishing word for me and a communicating word for others!

Sic verba, quibus voces sensusque notarent
Nominaque invenere. (Horace)[30] . . .

Part Two: The Way Human Beings Could and Must Have Most Easily Invented Language for Themselves

Nature bestows no powers in vain. Since she not only gave human beings the ability to invent language but also made this ability the distinguishing characteristic of human nature and the motivating power of its chief tendency, this power must have come *full of life* from the hand of nature. It could not, therefore, have been placed anywhere except in a sphere in which it could be effective. Let us look more closely at some of the circumstances and conditions that directly gave rise to language among human beings as soon as they entered the world with the ability to form language for themselves. Since these conditions are numerous, I will bring them under certain principal laws of human nature and of the human race.

1. Human beings are free-thinking and active beings whose powers operate in a continuous progression. This is why they are creatures of language. . . .

2. Human beings are by nature gregarious, social creatures. It is therefore natural, essential, and necessary for them that their language continuously develop. . . .

3. Just as it was impossible for the entire human race to remain as one homogeneous group, it was impossible for the race to retain one language. There followed, then, the formation of diverse national languages. . . .

4. In all probability the human race constitutes one progressive whole that stems from *one* source and forms *one vast household. The same can be said about all languages and about the entire chain of chain of human development* [Kette der Bildung]. . . .

---

30. ["They discovered words/ At last, verbs to express their feelings, nouns for ideas." Horace, *The Satires*, Book I, Satire 3, lines 103-4; translation by Smith P. Bovie (Chicago: University of Chicago Press, 1959).]

2

Myth and
Religion

CONCERNING THE VARIOUS RELIGIONS

. . . As disparate as heat is from cold, and as one pole from the other, so diverse are the various religions.[1] Their dissimilarity constantly provides us with a far more secure means of unlocking the spirit of a nation than the structure of the face provides in judging the temperament of an individual. Thinking about the religions in their diversity especially involves the examination of three observable distinctions: (1) the kind of ideas with which every religion fills the gaps in its understanding of the material world, (2) the types of rein and bit with which religions bridle sacrilege and spur virtue, (3) the diverse spirit of religious ceremonies. These are the signposts that historians of religion use as guides when they observe all religions primarily as natural phenomena, as phenomena in their relation to the physical world.

We do not show disrespect even to the best religion when we recognize its political purpose. The diverse means employed for carrying out this purpose make up the second level of inquiry that a "Xenophon of religions" must examine.[2] The diversity of these means can originate either in the thought of the political innovator who made them into divine laws, seeking through these laws to become a god in the eyes of the people; or it can originate in the thought of the people. The stability, renovation, or reformation of religious systems belongs here: before the judgment seat of politics. Religion has always

1. [SW 32:146-47. See also SW 32:148-52.]
2. [Xenophon (ca. 428-354 B.C.E.) was a Greek historian, essayist, and soldier. In this particular passage, Herder is apparently referring to Xenophon's well-known sense of the practical and his interest in political questions. Perhaps Herder also has in mind Xenophon's humanity and his ability to appreciate other cultures. See, for example, *Cyropaedia (The Education of Cyrus)*.]

been a cornerstone of governments, even according to the principles of atheists (with the exception of the unique LaMettrie).[3] Thus, we could use religion to explain diverse structures in forms of government and in domestic, matrimonial, and civil society. From this perspective we would find that many contracts, political ceremonies, and political institutions are based above all on ancestral religions. We would also discover that religion is the unnoticed mainspring of great changes in politics and of metamorphoses in the fine arts. We would find the intimate connections between nations and would lift their veils in order to see the maxims whereby they are secretly acting.

Are not these sufficient enticements for evoking in me the passionate desire to possess one day the "phlegm and fire"[4] to practice such a history of religions? Practicing this task requires the following: the political insight of a Montesquieu, Hume, and Beaumelle;[5] the knowledge of the human heart whose depths only a Rousseau can fathom; the cheerful phlegm of a Mosheim when dealing with his Cudworth;[6] and the knowledge of an all-knowing world historian. I say merely "practicing" because you obviously need to strain every nerve in your body just to be able to practice such a task tolerably well in the eyes of the public. By the way, the public even expects history from that most worthy among them all, from that poetic fencing champion of historiography, Voltaire.

You need an Argus[7] in order to observe calmly all of these religions with the same sharp and careful eye. It is, however, not possible to learn the same amount from all of them. Instead of making my own religion and the mythology of politically sophisticated nations the main object [in my history of religions], I am going to find increasing nourishment in the simple religions of primitive peoples who, close to the state of nature, provide less insight for poets but all the more for humanity in general. The simplest, most ancient religions expose the bosom of the human race. The middle religions expose the mind of the founder of a nation. The most recent religions are a curio-collection created by the poet. Fortunately, few peoples have risen to the fourth stage—that of the scientific systematist. It is evident that if I want to speak as a philosopher, then I must consider all religions to be equally natural and human.

3. [Julien Offray de LaMettrie, (1709-51). French physician, philosopher, and atheist.]

4. [An expression indicating an ideal mixture of humors. According to medieval physiology, humors are bodily fluids that determine by their proportion a person's health and temperament.]

5. [Montesqueieu, Baron de (1689-1755); philosopher and political theorist. David Hume, (1711-76); Scottish philosopher and historian. Laurent Angliviel de LaBeaumelle, (1726-73); French author.]

6. [Johann Lorenz von Mosheim, (1694-1755). German professor and Lutheran pastor. Translated Ralph Cudworth's *Intellectual System* into Latin.]

7. [In Greek mythology Argus is the hundred-eyed monster sent by Hera to guard the goddess Io after Io had been turned into a heifer by Zeus. Hermes then killed Argus, and Hera put his eyes into the tail of a peacock. Any guard who keeps conscientious or zealous watch is "Argus-eyed."]

I must do this, however, without placing either my nature over against the supernatural or my humanity over against divinity. . . .

FRAGMENT OF AN ESSAY
ON MYTHOLOGY

If we consider the mythologies of peoples to be merely teachings about false gods, lapses of human reason, or lamentable cases of blind superstition, then in my opinion our outlook is too narrow.[8] Although the mythologies of most peoples on earth from almost every walk of life have included or still include such characteristics and are consequently treated by scholars of religion from this perspective, there nevertheless remains another, more subtle view for the philosopher of humankind. Such a philosopher observes mythologies, even if they wander in false directions, as activities of human reason, as the first, elementary attempts to order human surroundings into ideas or images, to make present the spirit of existing things or of events, to express feelings about them, and through customs, songs, narratives, and tradition not only to establish this small treasure of human abstraction but also to commend it to later generations. The mythology of a people gives us, so to speak, the entire metaphysics of that people's earliest condition in all the shades of their way of thinking. Mythical expressions also provide us with a people's oldest symbolism and tactics of the heart and mind. Undeniably, mythology is an invaluable gold mine of human thoughts and institutions, not just for the historian in tracing the origins of peoples, but even more so for the philosopher in perceiving the strengths and weaknesses of human reason, its pet procedures and errors of abstraction and poetry, and its clever and lazy way of substituting images for those things it does not want to capture or to hold on to as ideas. Through mythologies, the philosopher also recognizes both the recurrent uniformity amidst diversity and the unmistakable limits within which the earliest poetry as well as the most astute abstraction operated. The examination of several mythologies becomes then not only a history but also an applied critique of human reasoning about God, the world, creation, the order of things, destiny, purpose, and the historical changes and origin of everything that our eyes apprehend and our imagination dreams. Yet this history of humankind also needs to be observed and treated with humanity. In other words, we must examine even erring nations without prejudice, anger, hatred, envy, or slander; we must view them as brothers or as children. For are they not all brothers of human reason and of every error of reason? Are they not all children of

8. ["Fragment einer Abhandlung über die Mythologie" was published for the first time from Herder's *Nachlass* by Ulrich Faust in *Mythologien und Religionen des Ostens bei Johann Gottfried Herder* (Münster: Aschendorff, 1977), 43-46, 154-55.]

one God and Father? God let the peoples of the earth go their own ways and revealed himself to them all.

In order to gain an overview of the entire subject, you must initially examine the common "rational charter" of individual peoples. It is obvious that among them the pure, ancient, civilized nations are the most remarkable, at least the most appropriate, for a more general study. In these nations you see not only uniqueness and originality that can also be noticed among barbarous peoples, but also the way that the operations of their human powers developed to a point beyond which they could no longer develop and, therefore, either came to a standstill or were thrown into confusion. The best field for such a study continues to be Greek mythology and poetry. The Egyptians and the mythologies of the Near East would rival this field, if we knew more about them from their earliest times. The tiny fragments of their tradition and period are, nevertheless, very remarkable. The peoples of the Far East give us, in contrast, an even greater harvest. India, Tibet, China, Japan, and their neighboring countries are magnificent temples of the gods in which reason and imagination have invented many strange forms and have exhibited and immortalized many fabulous images. The pictorial representations of such forms and images can seem repulsive and often revolting to our eyes. This should not, however, bewilder but rather please the observer. The observer can thereby more properly grasp these forms and images directly from the hands of invention: Pictorial art did not spoil them either by carving or reshaping them. This art did not make foreign children into slaves of its foreign realm. Rather, pictorial art itself has remained only a simple servant of the concepts that sects and nations conceived.

All nations of the earth have this in common: They initially conceived of God not outside the world but within it, assuming that they also placed God above them, that is, in heaven. The first thing human beings perceive outside themselves is the active powers of nature. Because human beings do not know the ground and the inner source of these powers, they are bound to perceive the instrument and vehicle through which this power reveals itself as the body and, consequently, as the symbol of this power. Human beings are bound to bring this instrument to mind and believe that it is inseparable from the power. This is the origin of fetishism, which predominated for a long time among all peoples of the earth in either "coarse" or "refined" forms, and it still predominates among most. Nevertheless, it predominates in very diverse forms, even within one and the same nation, according to the worshipers' diverse ways of thinking and powers of perception. Coarse human beings remain attached to the whole material form, believe that their god is locked up in it, and over time through sheer laziness make this form into God himself. Refined human beings see it only as the symbol and instrument of the penetrating power that reveals itself in and through this form. If idolatry is defined

as the act of considering something to be God that is not God, then this error
of human understanding obviously penetrates a long line of almost all religions
on earth, even the most refined. It is not the form of the object that matters.
What one thinks about the object and how one imagines that the deity is
present within this object is what counts. Whether one worships the sun, the
moon, the stars, or a cow's horn full of dung, whether a storm, a stone, a
picture, or a tiny piece of bread—it is not the object itself that distinguishes
idolatry from religion but rather the worshiper's way of thinking. This is what
either makes God into a stump and the stump into God and regards both as
a true unity; or considers the object to be a symbol and a symbolic reminder
of one certain power of God and no other, that is, as the symbol of an active
power of nature. We cannot compartmentalize peoples and their levels of
existence according to these objects anymore than we can according to historical periods, for both coarse and more refined thinking people can be found
everywhere. Even in the purest religion, idolatry is possible and bound to
arise as soon as this religion possesses symbols. The crudest slave of fetishism
often stands next to the purest worshiper of God. In order to avoid idolatry
you, like Moses, would have to prohibit absolutely all symbols of God.
Otherwise, as soon as symbols exist, try as you might to establish and transmit
proper ideas of their use, you cannot suppress the imagination of those reflective people who consistently think about God only according to their own
powers of perception, according to the level of their inner, pure understanding,
and even according to the circumstances of their life, and who consequently
think about God in one way during situations of fear, hope, or any other
strong emotion, and in another way during moments of pure contemplation.

Let us take the [East] Indians as an example. From many conversations
and responses of even common people reported by Danish missionaries, it is
obvious that the Indians possess many images of God that are not regarded
as idols or, at least, are not intended as such. The Indians say, "The images
express attributes, powers, and activities of the supreme God from which all
things flow and to which all things return. One rises, as if by stages, to God
through these images. God reveals himself as a spirit to those who want to
worship him as spirit; he makes himself visible in the object of the thoughts
of those who want to worship him in a visible way. If one directs one's faith
toward a certain object (whether it be the sun, ocean, or tree), believes that
God is within that object, and prays to God within it, then God will be in it
and will hear one's prayers. God is present in creatures in the same way that
many features constitute a face. God is not air, not earth, not the sound of
the law, not numbers, not letters, not a face, not the radiance of the sun, not
man, not woman; God is, rather, "inexpressible." The Indians say, "The letter
'a' has to die; the twenty-five powers of the body must die; anger must die;
all learning must die. The true theologian is the one, then, who disposes all

'black things' (sins), who is like refined gold, and who sees and hears nothing else; and who says nothing except at the place where no language exists. I do not worship an image but rather the God who fills all things; God is the supreme being who has no form. God is an ever-present light in the eight regions, in the eighteen corners of the earth, and in the fourteen worlds; those who do not understand God chain him to their sleeve, wrap him up, and carry him under their arm and not in their hearts. They are great sinners, for they call the day night. Nevertheless, God especially filled this place with his presence, which shines everywhere like the sun, and which only burns when focused through a burning glass, and so on." It is obvious that forms of representation of this kind can be raised to the purest idea or can be lowered to the most thoughtless idolatry by lazy, sensual souls. The lazy Indian bathes in the Ganges River as if he were washing in God himself; he places flowers before images of God as if he had brought them to the eternal throne itself, even though he knows that no material throne exists for God. The pure-thinking soul, in contrast, worships God in this form of representation only in spirit and truth; this is why in India so many sects of individual thinkers arose who reject all images and symbols of God and try to worship the supreme being with an intuition that rises above the senses and with a pure, meditative heart. In all this it is obvious that everything depends on the shallowness or the depth of the vessel that draws from this ocean of concepts. Among Christians, too, just as everywhere, there are perhaps more idols and even false gods than one thinks. The character of these Christians creates such idols, despite any mysterious religious formulas they might have learned, even if they prayed such formulas seven times a day. The purest concept of human understanding is the idea of God; whoever does not reach this concept, or whoever does not recognize this idea, possesses only symbols, for that person is concerned with symbols alone and thereby practices idolatry in the most naive way. How empty indeed, therefore, are all verbal squabbles about God! How awkward is every substitution of new symbols!

IDEAS TOWARD A PHILOSOPHY
OF HISTORY

Religion is the highest expression of our humanity.[9] No one should be too surprised that I refer to religion in this context. Understanding is the noblest gift of human beings; it is the business of understanding to trace the relation between cause and effect and to sense this relation where it is not apparent. Human understanding does this in all activities, from manual labor to the fine arts, for even where human understanding follows an established practice,

9. [SW 13:161-65, 387-95.]

some understanding of a previous time must have determined the relation between cause and effect, and thus introduced this skill. Now, strictly speaking, we cannot observe the innermost causes of natural phenomena. We do not know ourselves, and do not understand how things function inside us. Similarly, the way things function outside us is but a dream, a conjecture, a name. We consider this dream to be reality, however, as soon as we observe time and again that the same effects are linked to the same causes. This is the way that philosophy proceeds, and the first and last philosophy has always been religion. Even the most primitive peoples have practiced it, for no people on earth has been found entirely without religion, just as no people has been found without rational capacities and human bodies, without language and marriage, without some social morals and customs. Where these primitive peoples could see no visible author of events, they believed in an invisible one, and they continued to investigate the causes of things despite the darkness. They focused, of course, more on the events of nature than on its essence: They paid more attention to the terrifying and transitory aspects of nature than to its pleasant and permanent qualities. They also seldom advanced so far as to order all causes under one basic cause. Nevertheless, even these kind of early endeavors constituted religion. It is absurd to say that *fear* invented the gods of most peoples. Fear, as such, invents nothing; it merely rouses the understanding to speculate and to sense whether something is true or false. As soon as human beings, therefore, learned to use their understanding at the slightest stimulation, that is to say, as soon as they observed the world in a manner different from the animals, they were bound to assume that there were more powerful invisible beings that helped or harmed them. They tried to make friends or preserve friendship with these invisible beings. In this way, religion, true or false, right or wrong, was carried on. It instructed and comforted human beings in a life fraught with darkness and full of danger and confusion.

No! Eternal source of all life, all being, and all form, you have not left your creatures without evidence of yourself! The animal on all fours obscurely feels your power and goodness when it exercises its powers and tendencies according to its design: To the animal, human beings are the visible divinity of the earth. But you have exalted human beings so that they observe, even unconsciously and unintentionally, the causes of things, suspect their relation, and thus discover you, oh great coherence of all things, oh being of beings! They do not know your innermost nature, for they cannot see the essence of the power of any one thing. If they tried to give you a particular form, they would err and would have to err, for you are without form, even though you are the first and only cause of all forms. However, even every false glimmer of you is nevertheless light; every dubious altar erected to you by human beings is an indubitable monument not only to your existence but also to the human power to know and to worship you. Religion is, therefore, even when considered to be only an exercise of the understanding, the height of humanity, the human soul's most sublime blossom.

But religion is more than this; it is an exercise of the human heart and the purest direction of its abilities and powers. Human beings are created free and in this life have only those laws that they themselves impose; it follows that they would become the most savage of all creatures, if they did not quickly recognize God's law in nature and strive as children to imitate their Father's perfection. Animals are born as servants in the great family of this earthly household; servile fear of laws and punishments is the surest sign of brutish human beings. True human beings are free and obey out of goodness and love, for all the laws of nature, insofar as human beings can understand them, are good; and insofar as they do not understand these laws, they learn to follow them with childlike simplicity. The wise say that if you do not go willingly, then you will be forced to go; in other words, the law of nature does not change on your account. However, the more you discover its perfection, goodness, and beauty, the more this living form will shape you during your earthly life into *the image of God*. True religion is, therefore, the childlike worship of God, the imitation of what is highest and most beautiful in the human form. Consequently, religion is the most heartfelt contentment, the most powerful goodness and the love of others.

It is obvious now why in all religions of the world the notion of an analogy between God and human beings was more or less inevitable; either human beings were raised up to the form of the divine or the Father of the world was pulled down to the form of a human being. We know no form superior to our own, and those things that move us and make us human have to be thought and felt in human terms. Thus, nations that thought in more sensual terms exalted the human form to divine beauty; other nations that thought in more abstract terms represented the ideal attributes of what is invisible by means of visible symbols. Even the deity, because it wanted to reveal itself to us, spoke and acted among us in human terms and in a way that was appropriate to each particular period in time. Nothing has ennobled our form and nature as much as religion precisely because it has led them back to their purest destination.

The hope of and belief in immortality were connected to religion and established among human beings via religion. This is bound to be the case, for the notion of immortality is almost inseparable from the concept of God and humankind. How is this the case? We are children of the eternal one, whom we should learn by imitation to know and love; all things inspire our knowledge of God, and both our joys and sorrows compel us to imitate God. Yet we continue to know God so obscurely; we imitate God so feebly and childishly; we even understand the reasons we cannot know and imitate God in any other way in our present design. Is there no other design possible for us? Is there really no advancement for our genuinely best tendency? This does not seem to be the case, because our noblest powers are so little adapted to this world: They strive beyond this world, for everything here serves necessity. Yet we feel that the nobler part of ourselves continually struggles against necessity: The apparent goal of the human design finds its birthplace indeed upon the earth, but by no means its state of perfection. Did God, then, break the thread with creation and, despite all preparations for the human form, finally produce an immature creature, who was deceived about its whole purpose? Are all things on earth only fragments? Will they remain imperfect fragments forever? Similarly, will the human race remain a mere shadowy herd that hounds itself with illusions? In the face of such questions, religion knit all the imperfections and hopes of our species together into *faith* and created for humanity an *immortal* crown. . . .

Religion is the most ancient and most sacred tradition on earth.

Weary and tired of all the changes that we see in relation to various regions, times, and peoples, are we not able to find anything among them that might be the common property and excellence of the human race? Yes! Nothing but the predisposition toward *reason, humanity, and religion*—the three graces of human life. All political states arose late in history, and arts and sciences arose in them still later; but families are the eternal work of nature, a dynamic household in which nature plants the seed of humanity in the human race and fosters its growth. Languages vary with every people and in every climate; but in all languages we can recognize one and the same human reason, which seeks out distinguishing traits of surrounding objects. In the end, however different its garb may be, religion can be found even among the poorest and rudest peoples on the edge of the earth. The natives of Greenland and Kamchatka, of Tierra del Fuego and Papua New Guinea, have religious expressions, illustrated by their sagas and customs. Were there a single people who had no religion at all among the Ansicans[10] of West Africa or the forest people of the Indian Islands, who were driven from their region, this very lack of religion would testify to their utterly savage stage of existence.

Now what is the origin of the religion of these peoples? Did each unfortunate person invent their worship along the order of a natural theology? Certainly not! Those in hardship invent nothing; rather, in all things they follow the traditions of their ancestors. Besides, no external object of nature occasioned the invention of religion. They learned to make bows and arrows, fishing hooks and clothing, from animals or from nature. But from what beast or

10. [*Anziken. Ansiko* was an eighteenth century German term for a region in West Africa near the mouth of the Congo River. See the *Grosses Universal Lexicon* (Halle, Leipzig: Zedler, 1732); here *Ansiko* is "ein Königreich in Africa unter der Aequinotial-Linien zwischen Loango und dem Flusse Zaire."]

from what natural object could they learn religion? Or how to worship? *Tradition*, therefore, *is the propagating mother not only of their language and modicum of culture but also of their religion and sacred practices.*

Hence, it follows that *a religious tradition could use no other means than those that are used by reason and language, that is, symbols.* If thoughts must become words in order to be transmitted, and if every institution must have a visible sign in order to be handed down to later generations, then how can the invisible be rendered visible, and how can past history be preserved for future generations, except through words or signs? This is why even among the most uncultivated peoples the language of religion is always the most ancient and most obscure language. It is often unintelligible even to the initiated and certainly more so to outsiders. The most meaningful sacred symbols of every people, no matter how well-adapted to the climate and nation, frequently lose their meaning within a few generations. This should come as no surprise, for this is bound to happen to every language and to every institution that has arbitrary signs as soon as these signs are not frequently compared to their objects through active use and thus retain their significance in the memory of the people. In religion this kind of active comparison is difficult, if not impossible, for the sign refers either to an invisible idea or to past history.

Moreover, it was inevitable that *priests, the original philosophers of a nation, could not remain its philosophers forever.* As soon as they lost the meaning of the symbols, they had to become either the silent servants of idolatry or the loquacious liars of superstition. They did become this almost everywhere, not out of any particular propensity to deception, but out of the natural course of things. The same fate prevails in every language, in every science, in every art and institution: If the one who is supposed to speak or transmit an art is ignorant of its meaning, then that one must conceal, fabricate, and simulate. False appearance replaces the lost truth. This is the *history of all the mysteries* on earth. At first, these mysteries concealed much that was worth knowing, but in the end, especially when human wisdom separated itself from them, they degenerated into terrible trifles. The priests of such empty, sacred mysteries at length became wretched deceivers.

Sovereigns and philosophers are the ones who most often portrayed the priests in this way. The rulers who carried out their high, powerful rank with an almost unconstrained independence thought it was their professional duty to restrain even the invisible superior powers. Consequently, they believed it was their duty either to tolerate the symbols of these powers as a puppet show for the masses or to annihilate these symbols altogether. This explains the unhappy conflict that occurred between the throne and the altar in all half-civilized nations, until people at length attempted to unite them, bringing into the world the deformed structure of a throne on the altar or an altar on the throne. The degenerate priests necessarily had to lose in this unequal conflict, for invisible belief had to contend against visible power, and the shadow of an ancient tradition against the splendor of a golden scepter, which the priests themselves had formerly consecrated and placed in the hand of the monarch. Thus, with increasing culture, the days of priestly rule passed away: Despots who originally wore their crowns in the name of God now found it easier to wear them in their own names; and through the work of the sovereigns and the philosophers the people became accustomed to this other scepter.

First of all, there is no denying that *religion alone introduced the first elements of culture and science to all peoples; more precisely, culture and science were originally nothing more than a kind of religious tradition.* Even now, the less cultivated forms of culture and science that we find among all primitive peoples are connected with their religion. The language of their religion is a sublime ceremonial language, which not only accompanies their sacred practices with song and dance but also usually proceeds from the sagas of the primeval world. Consequently, this religious language is the only remnant these peoples have of ancient reports, of the memory of former ages, and of a glimmer of science. In all cases the numbering and observance of days, the foundation of all chronology, is, or was, a sacred act. Magi from all corners of the world acquired knowledge of the heavens and of nature, however humble this science was. Priests were in charge of medicine, prophecy, the occult sciences, the interpretation of dreams, the knowledge of writing, acts of atonement to the gods and of satisfaction to the dead, communication with the dead; in short, they were in charge of the whole obscure realm of questions and explanations about which human beings so readily seek to put their minds at ease. Thus, among many peoples the common worship and religious festivals were practically the only things that connected independent, extended families to the vague whole. The history of culture will show that this was the case with the most cultivated nations too. The science of the Egyptians and of all peoples from the Ancient Near East to the utmost end of Asia, as well as of all the cultivated nations of antiquity in Europe such as the Etruscans, Greeks, and Romans, began in the bosom and under the veil of religious traditions. This is the way poetry and art, music and writing, history and medicine, physics and metaphysics, astronomy and chronology, and even moral philosophy and political science were imparted to them. The most ancient philosophers did nothing but sort the seeds that were given to them from religious tradition and raise their own plants from them. These plants continued to be developed throughout the centuries. We northern Europeans have also received our sciences in no other way but in the garb of religion. Thus, we can boldly say with the history of all peoples, "the earth is indebted to oral or written religious traditions for the seeds of all more highly cultivated forms of culture."

Second, we cannot deny that the nature of the subject itself confirms the following historical assertion: If we were to ask, "What raised human beings above the animals and prevented them, even in their rudest state, from sinking to the level of animals?" then most people would reply, "Reason and language." Nevertheless, just as human beings cannot have reason without language, they cannot acquire either reason or language except by noticing unity in multiplicity, consequently by representing the invisible in the visible, and by connecting cause and effect. This means that a kind of religious feeling of invisible, active powers in the whole chaos of being that surrounds human beings must have preceded and formed the basis of every initial formation and connection of rational, abstract ideas. Primitive peoples possess this feeling of nature's powers even when they have no precise concept of God. It is a lively and active feeling, as even their forms of idolatry and their superstition indicate. In all their intellectual conceptions [*Verstandesbegriffen*] of merely visible things, human beings function much like animals. It is the representation of something invisible into the visible—of a power into its effect—that lifts human beings to the initial levels of higher reason. This representation is virtually all that uncultivated nations possess of transcendent reason, and other peoples have simply developed it more verbally. The same is true of the notion of the life of the soul after death. Regardless of the way human beings acquired this concept, it is the only universal concept on earth that distinguishes human beings from animals in death. No primitive nation can philosophically demonstrate the immortality of the human soul, just as perhaps no one philosopher can, for even the philosopher can only confirm through rational arguments the belief in immortality that is rooted in the human heart. Yet this belief is universal. The man of Kamchatka expresses it when he offers his dead to the animals; the man of Australia does when he sinks the corpse into the sea. No nation buries its dead as it would bury an animal. Every primitive person departs at death for the realm of the ancestors, for the land of souls. Thus, religious tradition about immortality and the ardent feeling of an existence that knows no end precede ever-evolving reason. Otherwise, reason would have scarcely thought of the concept of immortality, or would have presented it in a very abstract, impotent form. Consequently, the universal belief in the continuance of our existence is the pyramid erected by religion over the graves of all peoples.

Finally, could humanity's divine laws and rules, even if expressed only in fragments by the most primitive people, have been discovered by reason after the lapse of perhaps thousands of years? Could these laws and rules be based on this variable form of human abstraction? I cannot believe this, even on the ground of history. If human beings had been dispersed over the earth like animals in order to invent the central form of humanity for themselves, then we would still be able to find nations on earth without language, without reason, without religion, and without morals; for as human beings have been, so are they still today. However, no history and no experience tell us that human orangutans exist somewhere on earth. The tales that Diodorus and later Pliny narrate[11] about human beings without feelings and about other inhuman peoples either are self-evidently grounded in the fantastic or at least do not deserve to be believed on the basis of the testimony of these writers. The sagas about primeval peoples that poets recite, in order to exalt the merits of their Orpheus and Cadmus,[12] are also certainly exaggerated because the times in which these poets lived and the purpose of their account already exclude them from the rank of historical witnesses. No people of Europe, let alone of Greece, has ever been more savage than the people of New Zealand or of Tierra del Fuego. This can be expected if one takes the analogy of climate into consideration. These inhumane peoples nevertheless possess humanity, reason, and language. No cannibals devour their own children or brothers; their inhumane practice is in their eyes a ruthless custom of war that preserves their courage and terrifies their enemies. It is, therefore, nothing more or less than the work of a crude form of political reasoning, which repressed the humanity of these peoples in the face of these few sacrifices to their country. The same repression of our humanity takes place in Europe, even today, in the face of other situations. In front of strangers the cannibals are ashamed of this ruthless practice, while we Europeans do not blush at slaughtering other human beings. They even behave nobly and brotherly to every prisoner of war on whom the fatal lot does not fall. All these traits, even when the Hottentot buries his child alive and the Eskimo shortens the days of his aging father, are the result of lamentable necessity; they never completely suppress the original feeling of humanity. Misguided reason or unbridled luxury has produced many more strange atrocities and excesses among us, to which the polygamy of the African can hardly compare. No one among us will deny, therefore, that the form of humanity is buried in the heart of sodomites, oppressors, or assassins, although this form might almost be effaced by passions and licentious behavior. In the same vein, permit me, after all I have read and examined concerning the nations of the earth, to consider this innate tendency toward humanity to be as universal as human nature, or more precisely, to consider this to be human nature itself. It is older

11. [Diodorus Siculus was a Greek historian of the first century B.C.E. He wrote a world history *(Bibliothēkē)*, beginning from the mythical era down to 54 B.C.E. The work is undistinguished and at times confuses different traditions and chronologies. Pliny the Elder was a Roman official and author of the first century C.E. He wrote a natural history *(Naturalis Historia)*, which is considered to be a major work in classical Latin literature. Although the work is uniquely comprehensive and a valuable storehouse of facts, it contains much information that was obsolete or even absurd.]

12. [According to Greek mythology Orpheus was a poet and skilled musician, and Cadmus introduced the alphabet into Greece.]

than speculative reason, which first formed itself in human beings by means of observation and language; reason would have had no standard in practical cases, had it not borrowed one from that mysterious form within us. The rational syllogism claims: If all the duties of human beings were only conventions invented by us as means of happiness and established through experience, then they would instantly cease to be my duties the moment I renounced their end, that is, happiness. This rational syllogism is thereby brought to a close. However, how did these duties enter the hearts of those who never speculated on happiness and the means to attain it? How did the duties of marriage, or parental and filial love, of family and society enter the minds of human beings before they had gathered experiences of the good and evil related to each one of these duties? Did they initially in a thousand ways have to be something less than human before they became human beings? No! Oh, benevolent God, you did not leave your creature to such murderous chance. You gave instinct to the animals; you engraved your image, religion, and humanity on the human soul. The outline of the statue lies there hidden in dark, deep marble, but this outline cannot hew or fashion itself. Tradition and teaching, reason and experience must do this; and you have sufficiently supplied the means for attaining them. The rule of justice, the principles of social rights, even monogamy as the kind of marriage and love most natural to human beings, affection toward children, gratitude toward friends and benefactors, and even the feeling of the most mighty and benevolent of all beings are traces of this image, which are sometimes repressed and other times developed, but which always continue to reveal the original tendency of human beings. As soon as human beings perceive this tendency, they may not renounce it. The realm of these tendencies and their development form the actual city of God on earth, of which all human beings are citizens, but all in accordance with very different classes and levels. Happy is the one who can contribute to the expansion of this realm of the true, inherent creation of humanity! This person envies neither the inventor's knowledge nor the king's crown.

CONCERNING RELIGION, DOCTRINES, AND PRACTICES

Preface

A text that deals with religion should be written religiously, that is, conscientiously, and it seeks to be read in the same way.[13] Why not hope that it be read this way?

13. [SW 20:135-36, 140-42, 159-61, 240-42.]

Religion touches one's entire being;[14] it inspires calm conviction. In all ranks and classes of society human beings may only be human in the recognition and practice of religion. Religion touches all human tendencies *[Neigungen]* and desires *[Triebe]* in order to harmonize them all and guide them to the right path.

By distinguishing itself from all kinds of doctrines, religion allows each of them its own place. Religion does not, however, want to be doctrine. Doctrines separate and embitter. Religion unifies, for in all human hearts religion is but one.

If the following text speaks too sharply against some doctrines, then it does so only insofar as these doctrines attempted either to become religion themselves or to supersede it. This especially happens when young teachers of religion, who do not know left from right, equate religion with doctrines and believe they must force them on the people. As long as human beings possess freedom and conscience, the lines between opinion and religion may be plainly and freely drawn. Religion belongs to the people. Doctrines are to be debated in the universities.

No one should be surprised that my interpretation of the Bible takes an approach that requires an understanding of the original languages. Many false doctrines can result from one incorrect interpretation. Speculation never ceases once it is permitted to begin. If our ancestors had possessed, for example, a clear, complete idea of a symbolic act, then the Protestant churches would never have separated and no religious wars would have broken out over misunderstood words of the Bible.

In discussing religion, I speak against lifeless, verbal rules because I consider this to be a duty of humankind. Humankind is a living organism full of senses, powers, and desires. It wants to be stirred and directed, not merely commanded. Its nature is to create pleasure and joy. No arrogant set of rules *[Gesetzgebung]* can replace this. Nevertheless, religion has been defined in legal terms. Moreover, the Christian religion has been boldly alleged to be nothing other than a set of rules. It has been claimed that what Christ said weakly and in a popular tone, that is, very imperfectly, has now been expressed perfectly. For these reasons, I must point to the difference between religion and rules. They are as different as Christ and Moses.

It is remarkable that after Christianity, idolatry no longer holds water. Idolatry can be the worship of words and syllables as gods themselves. The

14. [*Gemüt*. Herder later defines *Gemüt* as the innermost connection of all human powers (SW 20:161). *Gemüt* had several meanings at the turn of the eighteenth century, and they indicate that *Gemüt* was an encompassing term for the entire inner world of human beings and for the place of ideas, having roots in the latin *animus* and the Greek *thumos*. It was only in the nineteenth century that *Gemüt* was taken to be an introspective term, and concepts that it once encompassed, such as thought, understanding, and reason, on the one hand, and soul, heart, and feeling, on the other, were often placed in opposition to one another. See HWP.]

frenzy lasts for a time and then subsides. All that remains is a sophistic
scaffolding. Religion, in contrast, is a living fountain. Even when it is dammed
and blocked, it breaks forth again from its depths, purifies itself, refreshes,
and gives life.

I invite both Christians and non-Christians to read my book. In all human
souls truth is the same.

Part One: On the Difference between Religion and Doctrines in General

1. Doctrines[15] (*dogmata*) are what the German word for doctrine *[Lehr-meinung]* implies: philosophical opinions about things that are not known but
are considered to be either probable or determined by means of debate.
Philosophers lectured about such opinions to their students. Students often
reformulated them and debated them with other philosophical schools, for
every school had its own dogmas. These dogmas did not require a commitment
of faith because they helped to frame knowledge but were not self-evident
truths, that is, axioms. The value of dogmas was that they corresponded to
one another, they provided the student with a certain way of thinking and a
certain language, and they led the student to a deeper investigation of the
truth.

2. The doctrines of all philosophical schools without exception have done
a great service to human reason and the power of investigation. They were
the means by which people lifted or tried to lift the golden vessel of philosophical truth, which was to be investigated, up out of the depths.[16]

3. What do doctrines, however, have to do with religion? Religion is, as
its name indicates, a matter of *our entire being,* of our innermost *conscious-ness.*[17] According to its etymology, the word designates the extremely careful
attempt "not to stumble, not to do anything against the rules." This meaning
was connected to the respect paid to the gods and to divine things, to the

15. *[Lehrmeinungen.* The literal translation of *Lehrmeinung* is "opinion that is taught."]
16. See the Greek terms *dogmata, zētēmata,* and *prostagmata* in the lexicon of Hesychius
of Alexandria. The Greek verb *dogmatizein* means "to set forth one's opinions (*doxa*)." The
Greek noun *dogmata* can have two meanings: (1) the thing about which you have an opinion
(*to doxazomenon*), (2) the opinion itself (*hē doxa*). Of these two things, the former is the *protasis*
["major premise of a syllogism"]; the latter is the *hypolēpsis* ["opinion"]. According to Suidas
[see *Suidae Historica* (Basileae: Eusebium Episcop, 1581)] there were *dogmata* that were moral
teachings, especially in the Stoic school. But we are not talking about them here. The first book
of Sextus Empericus's *hypotypōseis [Outlines of Pyrrhonism],* edited by J[o]. A[lbertus] Fabricius
[Lipsiae: J. F. Gleditschii et Filii, 1718], gives information about the modes of "thetic" debate,
that is, debate that proceeds through propositions. [Sextus Empiricus was a Greek skeptical
philosopher whose works are one of the best sources for the doctrine of the Sceptic school and
for Stoic logic.]
17. *[des innersten Bewusstseins.* Herder later equates *Bewusstsein* with the Latin word,
conscientia (SW 20:142), which can mean both consciousness and moral sense or conscience.]

vows taken in their name, to the precise observance of all legal and institutional duties owed to the native country, which was established and protected by these duties, and to *good faith*. The confession that "this duty, this activity, this love for you, and everything that this love requires shall be for me *religion*" indicates the innermost commitment *[Verbindlichkeit]* of the will to practice such duty, activity, and such love most faithfully. Religion can be defined, then, if I am allowed to use such expressions, as "the *backbone* of the sentiments[18] of a human being, a citizen, a friend," "the most careful conscientiousness *[Gewissenhaftigkeit]* of our inward consciousness," "the altar of our entire being."[19]

4. What does or can this conception of our being have to do with doctrines? Doctrines are propositions which we can argue for and against. In this sense, doctrines stand in opposition to religion. Religion does not require pro and con arguments. Rather, it requires the conscientious observance of an inviolable duty, of a truth that is recognized in our innermost being. Religion is not the investigation of something that is called into question. Rather, it is the acting out of something that is unquestionable. When investigation itself becomes a religion, then all doubting ceases, and investigation becomes *concern, duty, sentiment*. In the same way, as soon as arbitrary doctrines are able to make what is taken to be *religion* falter, then it ceases to be religion, and it becomes *a problem, a hypothesis,* and *a proposition* or *doctrine* established by a certain school of thought. We can all have different opinions. Where there is opinion alone, however, no one is thinking about religion. Arbitrary doctrines have meant the death of all religions and always will.

5. Religion presupposes the innermost *consciousness (conscientia), conviction*. It requires *faith*, builds upon *faith*, and creates *faith*. Without the conviction of our entire being, the word "religion" is just a name, a mockery of things that are made out to be religion without being religion for us inwardly; consequently, religion is a delusion, a masquerade. If religion, doctrine, dogma, hypothesis, and problem were one and the same, then why not call every thoughtless *cultus* that does not embrace our entire being religion? . . .

18. [*Gesinnungen*. In another text Herder equates the word with the power of both the mind and heart (SW 24:48). *Gesinnung* had a rich and varied meaning in the late eighteenth century. For example, Lessing used it as a translation of the French work, *sentiment*, which can mean sentiment, feeling, or consciousness. Fichte defined *pflichtmässige Gesinnung* as the foundation for the belief in God and immortality. See HWP.]

19. See "religio" [in *Novus linguae et eruditionis Romanae Thesaurus*, 4 vols. (Lipsiae: Breitkopf, 1749)], edited by J[ohann Matthias] Gesner [1691-1761] and [Gerhard Johannes] Voss [1577-1649]. The various assumed etymologies of the word do not change anything. In each section of the definition it preserves its strict meaning. [Johann Joachim] Spalding [1714-1804] has written a good book entitled *Religion, eine Angelegenheit des Menschen* (Berlin[: Voss,] 1798), [2d ed.]. [First edition was published in 1797.] He defines religion with an expression well suited to its name and concept as "my ultimate concern (*was mir innigste Angelegenheit ist*)."

Part Two: On the Difference between Religion
and Doctrine According to the
Symbols of Christianity

15. *Religion* is this conviction: the innermost consciousness of what we
are as parts of creation and of what we ought to be and do as human beings.
Religion neither derives its prestige and power from mathematical demonstration nor expects to do so. Does the animal know what it is to do and how
it should carry this out? Why should human beings not know what they are
to do in human community? Why should they not perceive either obscurely
or clearly the natural laws that not only are available to them but also are the
means by which they become themselves—the sole means by which they are
able to be what they ought to be? The most ancient law of wisdom was "follow
nature and live according to it." In order to be recognized and followed, this
law presupposed a specific order of nature, salutary laws, and binding duties.
The returning seasons, the stars in heaven, and the animals on earth taught
this order of nature. This order was to be followed constantly, for nature
rigorously avenges violations against itself. Nature itself, therefore, accustoms
human beings to *religion,* that is, to recognizing the rules of our existence in
our innermost consciousness, following these rules precisely, not wavering
from the law which the *Mother-of-all-things* prescribed for us, or (in other
words) obeying the great ruler-of-all-things (Pantocrator).[20]

16. Human beings possess reason in order to follow these rules joyfully,
willingly. Reason taught them to obey even when they did not want to obey.
They enjoy the pleasant illusion that they are able to make rules for themselves;
this illusion helps them carry out such rules more joyously and correctly. If
they stray from the right path and attempt to master or betray nature, then it
will rigorously seek revenge. Thus, the voice of God in all creation entered
the heart, like the *Holy of Holies.* It spoke through the very thoughts of each
person. Those who interpreted nature became the first mighty servants of
God's voice, the first religious priests. All sensible human beings have recognized this sacred element in the innermost consciousness of our being and
have praised its dictum as religion.

17. *Conscience [Gewissen]* is a word that has been misused and even
despised by many people. Nevertheless, it is the sole, true temple of a human
religion because nothing remains for those without a conscience except empty
devotion, opinions, and practices. The careless pay no attention to conscience.

20. Religion is the opposite of negligence, inattentiveness, and all inharmonious and dissolute
elements of thoughts and deeds. Thus, attentiveness, *fear of God*, was the first religion and
wisdom of human beings. Understanding meant to avoid evil and learn to protect oneself from
doing wrong. In Job and other books, this kind of religion is highly praised. All of nature appears
as the temple of God; all creatures proclaim the great order of nature and salvation. The word,
"religion," "human religion," is empty without this genuine, rigorous, and sacred naturalism.

The impudent mock it. Both are willing to learn that there is a conscience only under the scourge of the furies.[21] Conscience does exist! It is given to human beings in their sphere just as certainly and appropriately as trait, as instinct, is given to animals in their spheres. Conscience awakens reason; it spurs and warns. Joining itself to each desire, it guides every duty, calling "no further!" Those who quarrel or argue with it, bind or confuse it, have, in no time at all, childishly shredded and spoiled the standard measure of their most ultimate concern. It is only the faithful, free soul who enjoys conscience as a gentle but exact guide by becoming accustomed to its slightest warning. Only this kind of soul possesses religion because such a soul has faith in a divine order in nature—faith in a moral, paternal "nomocracy"[22] in the human race. . . .

Part Six: On the Difference between Religion and Science, and Mysteries and other Misused Words

Perhaps someone will say to me, "You have set the bounds of religion too narrowly, not just by relating religious truth to religious duty but by uniting them as one." I had to do this. Not only the concept of religion but also the Bible itself demand this. Further, this strict definition is necessary in an age in which the word "religion" has degenerated to such a point that we practically understand it to mean only what religion is not. It is precisely this weak homonym that has created so much contempt for this most venerable word that many righteous people are ashamed to possess that through which they become righteous.

1. No truth is religion unless it binds the innermost consciousness that contains both conviction and duty. This is why the Bible always stresses the *entire being, the mind of our being (phronēma, kardia, pneuma)*,[23] and *the open eyes of understanding and of inner knowledge.* Heart and mind are not separated in the Bible. They are one. This strict definition distinguishes religion

21. Unfortunately, this is the reason that the Latin word *conscientia* has also been used to mean more *flagrum post peccatum* ["penalty after the sin"] than *frenum ante peccatum* ["restraint before the sin"] or "the pure and certain guide of life." Alas, *perfecto demum scelere magnitudo eius intelligitur* ["after the crime is already committed, its magnitude is understood"]. Those passages from antiquity that stress the power and integrity of the conscience are stated with energy and religion, conviction and warmth. *Conscientiam a Diis immortalibus accepimus, quae divelli a nobis non potest,* and so on. ["We have received conscience from the immortal gods, and it cannot be taken away from us."]

22. [*Nomokratie.* Nomocracy, for Herder, is rule by law without coercion; laws are followed freely, and rulers are not necessary. For a discussion of his view of nomocracy, see F. M. Barnard, *Self-Direction and Political Legitimacy: Rousseau and Herder* (Oxford: Clarendon Press, 1988), 246, 262-68.)

23. [Greek for "mind, heart, spirit."]

from everything foreign, indifferent, and contrary to it. It becomes what it ought to be, thereby becoming more energetic, more powerful.

2. Religion distinguishes itself, then, not only from unnecessary doctrines (speculations) but even from the *sciences* and from *legal principles* insofar as these principles establish a science. Any confusion about science and legal principles is harmful to religion.

3. You will have noticed, for example, that in a certain respect the principles of the three articles of the Christian creed establish sciences. The First Article, for example, prompts natural science and so-called natural law. The Second Article prompts historical studies of the human race and so-called international law. Through the notion of the community of many in one Spirit, the Third Article prompts social sciences and civil law. All these sciences must obviously refer to religion, that is, to an innermost consciousness. The lines between them would be confused, however, if religion crowded its way into these sciences or disturbed either the process or the results of their research.

4. If religion forced its way into *natural science*, for example, in order to theologize about each wing of a gnat; into *historical studies* in order to moralize about each event; into *political science* in order to contrast it step by step with the supreme principle of religion; then religion would deny its own dignity and would debase itself unnecessarily. If it forced its way into the *law of nature, of peoples, and of society* and tried to complain about every abuse within them, then how burdensome and overloaded would be its zeal!

5. If each of these sciences is what it ought to be, then religion, that is, inner moral conviction, issues forth from all of them according to their own purest principles. The same principle of power, wisdom, and goodness can be seen, for example, in the wing of a gnat as well as in the movement of the universe—a principle that both the human mind and heart adopt as their most precious gift. The history of the human race clearly reveals the rule that the human race is *one species* and that every human being belongs to the whole. The history of social and civil society expresses the law that the union of the many into the one necessarily brings about the good; this is the purpose of our race. The following rule arises from natural, national, and domestic law: "Be a human being! Be a human being for others, be a human being together with all those with whom you can be." Consequently, from all of these laws emerge the principle of Christianity, that is, the pure religion of nature, peoples, and the human race. This principle speaks to us in these terms: "Your power shall be directed by wisdom and your wisdom by goodness. Be a human being with human beings and for the whole human race according to the ideal *[Urbild]* of the Father of this race and according to the ideal of the Father's image, who appeared in human form and who paid this sacrifice in fullest measure. If you become this image with innermost devotion and righteousness, then you will become what you ought to be." Every true

science comes back, without coercion, to genuine religion. Religion, however, should not attempt to replace the sciences; otherwise it will ruin them and lose itself.

6. The sciences, in turn, should not oppress or confuse religion. If, for example, the natural sciences investigated some phenomena that they could not immediately place under the supreme rule, then why should religion worry? At one time people did not yet know how to place night and day, light and darkness, under the one principle that both follow. As a result they invented a double principle of good and evil. How childish it would be for the natural sciences to use this double principle today! How tasteless it would be for philosophy to try to establish supposedly insoluble quarrels about nature (antinomies) on the basis of the same phenomena! The natural sciences are destined to follow their own method of observing laws and discovering higher ones; they have an infinite road ahead of them. For religion, in contrast, the center of its sphere, the principle that interweaves *power, wisdom, and goodness,* is already at hand in all things great and small. Religion can rejoice over every new scientific discovery without being disturbed by any new, seeming incongruities. The same applies to human history. If it portrays the most horrible abuses of human reason, human rights, and human nature not only between people and nations but also in every more intimate relationship, then religion does not worry about this. True to its inner consciousness it says, "You are not what you ought to be, but you can become so."

FIRST DIALOGUE CONCERNING
NATIONAL RELIGIONS

DIETRICH: You are reading so earnestly, Winnfried.[24]

WINNFRIED: I am reading a dialogue between the aged Ossian and St. Patrick, more precisely, between the oppressed Gaelic religion and monastic religion.[25] Read it with me.

OSSIAN: Relate the tale, O Patrick; I beseech you, by the books that you read, tell me truly is heaven in the possession of the noble Fians of Ireland?

24. [SW 24:38-49.]
25. [The dialogue, entitled "The Prayer of Ossian" or "The Conversation of Ossian and St. Patrick," was collected by Rev. Matthew Young and published in English and Gaelic in the *Transactions of the Royal Irish Academy* of 1787 (vol. 1, part 3, 96-104). Herder used Fr. L. W. Meyer's German translation of the dialogue but revised it at central points. Here, the English translation in the *Transactions* is used except that archaic spellings and forms of verbs and nouns have been modernized.]

PATRICK: I assure you, O Ossian of great deeds, that heaven is not in the possession of your father, nor of Oscar, nor of Gaul.

OSSIAN: This is a pitiful tale, O Patrick, that you tell me of my ancestors; why should I be religious if heaven be not in possession of the Fians of Ireland?

PATRICK: O Ossian! long sleep has taken hold of you, rise to hear the psalms. Your strength and your valour are gone, nor are you longer able to stand the fury of the day of battle.

OSSIAN: If I have lost my strength and my valour, and none of Fingal's heroes survive, I will pay little respect to your clerkship, nor care I to listen to your singing.

PATRICK: Such sweet songs as mine you never heard 'till this night since the beginning of the world; you aged and unwise old man, who often has arranged your valiant troops upon the mountain.

OSSIAN: Often have I arranged the valiant troops upon the mountain, O Patrick of evil designs; but it is wrong in you to dispraise my appearance, which once was not despised.
  Fin had twelve hounds; we let them loose in the valleys of Smail; and sweeter to my ears was the cry of the hounds, than the ringing of your bells, O clerk.

PATRICK: Since it was the height of your happiness to listen to the hounds, and to marshal your troops every day, and not to offer up your prayers to God, Fin and his heroes are for this bound in captivity.

OSSIAN: It is hard to believe your tale, O clerk of the white book, that Fin, or one so generous, should be in captivity with God or man.

PATRICK: He is now in captivity in hell, who used to distribute gold; since he did not give honor to God, he is in sorrow in the house of torture.

OSSIAN: If the clan of Boisgnè were alive, and the descendants of Mornè of valiant deeds, we would force Fin out of hell, or the house would be our own.

PATRICK: Although the five provinces of Ireland, which you so highly esteem, were to assist you, you would not force Fin out of hell, nor would the house ever be your own.

OSSIAN: What kind of a place is this hell, O Patrick of deep learning? Is it not as good as heaven; and shall we not there find deer and hounds?

PATRICK: Little as is the humming fly, or the mote in the sun, it cannot get under the cover of his shield without the knowledge of the king of glory.

OSSIAN: Then he is not like Fin-ma-Cual, our king of the Fians; every man upon the face of the earth might enter his court without seeking permission.

PATRICK: Compare not any man to God, O grey-haired old man, who knows not what he is. Long is it since his government began, and his right will live for ever.

OSSIAN: I would compare Fin-ma-Cual to God himself . . .

PATRICK: This it is that has occasioned your ruin; you not having believed in the God of the elements. For this not one of your race has survived except yourself, the noble Ossian.

OSSIAN: This was not the cause of our misfortunes, but the two voyages of Fin to Rome; we were obliged, by ourselves, to engage in the battle of Gabhra, and great was the slaughter of the Fians.
   One day, as we were on the mountain Fuad, Caolt of the steel sword was there, and Osgar, and the hospitable Fin. Loud was the cry of the hounds in the plain, and furious were they in the valleys.
   Fin-ma-Cual of great strength was king over us at the time; and, O clerk of the crooked staff, we would not suffer God to rule over us.

PATRICK: How wicked is that, O Ossian, you man of blasphemous words! God is forever greater than all the heroes of Ireland.

OSSIAN: I would prefer one great battle fought by Fin and his heroes to the Lord of your worship, and to yourself, O clerk.

PATRICK: Listen to the advice of the humble, and seek heaven for yourself tonight; you are now sinking under years, therefore at length lay aside your folly, O grey-haired old man.

OSSIAN: I ask the protection of the twelve apostles for myself tonight; and if I have committed any heavy sins, let them be thrown into my grave upon the hill.

DIETRICH: Does this dialogue make you sad?

WINNFRIED: I am not indifferent to anything that concerns humankind. This poetic dialogue expresses the feeling of all nations whose ancestral religion was torn from them. With the loss of their religion, they lost their spirit and character, indeed, their language, their heart, their land, their history. This is the reason for the silent and shrill laments of the Gaels and the Irish, the Kurds, Estonians, Latvians, Livonians, and so on. This is the reason for their indelible, irreconcilable hatred for the foreigners who, on the one hand, forced a foreign religion upon them and, on the other, took their land and their ancestors. More precisely, the foreigners did not simply take their ancestors; they shoved their beloved, venerated ancestors, whose memory meant victory and joy to them, down into the torments of hell. Is this not bound to distress these peoples? Remember how our tribal ancestors, the Teutons and the Goths, fought on the graves of their ancestors for their honor and religion. Remember with what faithfulness other nations have preserved for a thousand years the practices of their ancestors, which others called "superstitions," despite prohibition and punishment. Remember—

D: Let's sit beneath this linden tree, Winnfried. The sun is setting so beautifully—

W: —and it leaves all the plants in *their own* colors, and shares its mild radiance with *all things*.

D: This is precisely what delights me. Just before sunset we can speak peacefully and confidentially about the extinct national religions that you appear to hold in such high regard. Would you be annoyed with me, Winnfried, if I nevertheless hold Christianity to be the religion *of all religions,* of all peoples? "*One* shepherd and *one* flock" is Christianity's implicit motto. You are familiar with this image. It is a common Christian symbol that is found on the most ancient Christian monuments.

W: The miraculous draught of fish, too, no doubt. Tell me, Dietrich, what distinguishes and what separates nations? Is it something like streams and rivers?

D: You can cross these with a ship. You have to climb over mountains and walls. What genetically distinguishes peoples is this: *Bildung* and *language*. By *Bildung* I mean not simply "cultivation," but rather "the physiognomy of the soul and the body."

W: And what do you mean by "religion"?

D: I use the word in the Roman sense of "awe before the gods, sacred commitment."

W: All right, then: In which language will the heart commit itself to the gods most lovingly and most intimately? Does it not have to be in the language of the heart, that is, in our very own mother tongue? The language in which we *love, pray, and dream* is our very own religious language.

D: You have got something there. It is unusual for one language to be equally proper for every kind of conversation.

W: And for our conversation with the author of our being, the one who searches our hearts and knows our thoughts, would we want to speak with this author in any other way but from the depth of our hearts? Would we want to recite formulas to God in a secondary, foreign language of the ruling class?[26]

D: But what if this secondary language were more suitable or more powerful for expressing religious ideas?

W: If this language is not suitable for expressing *my* ideas, if it has not sprung from my very own needs and feelings, then no matter how powerful it is to others, it is not *my* religious language. Stop playing the hypocrite, Dietrich! Friendship and love, like the innermost recognition of truth, require one's very own language of the heart.

D: And *cultus*?

W: What do you mean by *cultus*? If it is the way that we act toward God and our protective spirit, toward all saints and souls, then it cannot be heartfelt and intimate enough. For this service, any secondary, foreign, and fashionable language of the ruling class is hypocrisy, deception, falsehood. It is precisely the worst kind of falsehood, for if one is not faithful to God in one's own words and with gestures that reflect one's own sentiment, then how can one prove to be faithful to oneself and to others? If we recite formulas in front of God that we do not understand, if we mimic practices that are borrowed from foreign peoples and times, that are foreign to our inner sense, then we damn ourselves to Hades as we live and breathe. We are doomed either to turn empty barrels, like the daughters of Danaus,[27] or to walk in leaden coats, like the hypocrites of Dante's *Inferno*. Our mind and our heart languish beneath them *without religion*, without inner conscientiousness and active truth.

D: It seems to me we are speaking about an *individual* religion. We wanted to speak, however, about *national religions*.

W: National religions develop from individual ones. A people springs from families; a national language springs from the language of related tribes. The same is true with national religions. Examine all the most ancient regions of the earth. Springing from the ground of tradition, national religions were and continue to be founded on the oral sagas of the tribe, on the needs and views of the family, on the most subtle physiognomy of the people, on the deepest

26. *[Hofsprache*. In eighteenth century Germany, the language of the courts was French, and the language of the Catholic liturgy was Latin.]

27. [According to Greek mythology, when the fifty daughters of Danaus were forced to marry the fifty sons of Aegyptus, all but one slew their husbands on their wedding night. They were condemned to fill and carry water in leaking jars eternally in the underworld.]

traits of a people's *national character*. Was not even the religion of the ancient Jews wholly a religion of Palestine?

D: Yes, according to the circumstances of the time and place in which it was established. But as the times changed, ancient Judaism itself was no longer suitable for Palestine. Christianity appeared, therefore, in order to—

W:—to destroy all dead or dying national religions.

D: Wait a minute, my friend! Why did the founder of Christianity send out his disciples to all peoples? In order to destroy or *to teach?*

W: By teaching they destroyed things such as idols, sacrificial vessels, practices, and temples.

D: It may be that they did destroy these things at appropriate and inappropriate moments. Nevertheless, they still *taught*. In which language? What was the symbol that signified the dawn after the passing of the night of ancient national religions? After the "inauguration" of Christianity? Was it not precisely the spirit of *national tongues and languages?* "Parthians and Medes and Elamites, etc., heard the mighty works of God in their own tongues."[28] This was the *initial appeal* of Christianity, and this was to become its main characteristic. For Christianity, *cultus* meant teaching (or, as we say, *cultivating*) the people in *their own* native languages, teaching them to observe what Christ commanded, the pure laws of humankind, and to address God in spirit and in truth, in the most genuine language of the mind and heart. Christianity was not supposed to *destroy* national religions, but rather to purify them, to improve them. Every nation loves God in its very own way and serves the neighbor in the way that most pleases God. "To the Jews I became a Jew, to the Greeks a Greek, to the weak I became weak that I might win the Jews, the Greeks, and the weak."[29] Do you know who said this, Winnfried?

W: The same man who knew how to relate his teaching in Athens even to the altar of the *unknown God*.[30]

D: He acted everywhere according to the above principle. Every one of his letters is written so *idiosyncratically,* as only he was able to do, for the city or for the small group of people to whom the letter is directed. What do you think about the fact that not one of the original documents of Christianity was written either in the so-called holy, ancient Hebrew language or in the language that the founder of Christianity himself spoke? Can there be any clearer proof that in Christianity there is no "holy" language that is foreign to the people? There can be no clearer proof that no language should be forced on the nations under the pretext of being the official language of God; that no language should fog their thinking or to imprison their understanding for thousands of years.

28. [Reference to Acts 2:5-13.]
29. [Reference to 1 Cor. 9:19-23.]
30. [Acts 17:22-23.]

W: Nevertheless, Latin, the language of the Romans, did this and continues to do so. It chains, as much as it can, the particular religion of the peoples. When a priest speaks strange formulas that the people cannot understand, he places himself between God and the people, separating instead of connecting the two. Did Jesus speak Latin?

D: Jesus scarcely understood the language of the Roman rulers.

W: And God is still supposed to be addressed among all peoples and for all peoples in this long dead *Vulgata* that is foreign to them all?

D: This language is used so that the holy does not become vulgar—

W:—and so that the pearls . . . I know the story. As soon as something holy, however, is locked up in a casket and treated like a mummy, then it is, indeed, a mummy—a dead, holy relic that can hardly guard against decay and that one always wants to bury. Who wants to be weighed down each and every day with the coffin, with the casket in which the mummy lies? How does the genuine, living culture of a people always begin, Dietrich?

D: With the revival and development of its own language.

W: And this depends on religion.

D: To be sure! Thus, you are getting yourself upset over nothing. Remember the admirable Ulphilas.[31] He cultivated the Goths through his translation of the Gospels, that is, through his cultivation of the Gothic language. How did the enlightenment of all of Europe begin in the dark Middle Ages? Through the translation of the Bible into the language of Limousin[32] and into other national languages. As soon as the language of the people was returned to them, their mind, heart, and soul were also returned to them. They felt that they were able to think, and they did think. This is what Christianity did, and this is what every intelligent missionary also does.

W: This is what those religious relics in the coffin do not do. The coffin preserves a foreign, dead language.

D: Let it be. All such attempts to preserve and limit a language are in vain. Truth can be hidden for a time but never buried. The human heart needs to feel religion for itself; human understanding needs to understand truth for itself. To be sure, you have often felt distressed when people speak the truth in a false way, speak what is most living in dead formulas. I feel the same. It is as if someone wrapped a budding young woman in burial clothing and covered her face with old masks.

W: Every conscience feels this way. This is why peoples rebel when someone takes the religion of their ancestors from them by taking away their language. This is why human feeling and a special joy reawaken after a long

31. [Ulphilias (ca. 311-383 c.e.) was an Arian bishop and missionary to the Goths who translated the Bible (except the two books of Kings) from Greek into the Gothic language.]
32. [Limousin is a province in France.]

sleep under the oppressive yoke of foreign words and practices. Dietrich, do you know the German who called back true religion, that is, conviction, faith, mind, and heart, to his people through their genuine language? It was Protestantism against everything improper, everything foreign.

D: You mean Luther. It is unfortunate that this great man did not achieve what would have been so desirable—a *national church, that is, a German church.*

W: *A German church,* Dietrich!? This would have been unworthy of the great man. Look what became of Henry VIII's Church of England, and look what became of every other exclusive church. They rot as they live. Luther wanted to give *religion* to his German people—the pure, free religion of the conscientiousness of mind and heart. And he gave this to them, insofar as his time allowed.

D: Unfortunately, however, he did not give it to all Germans. His language, too, has become archaic in some aspects.

W: We should rejuvenate it! But language rejuvenates itself automatically, continually, and irresistibly. Do you not agree that ever since Luther wrote, every German who wants to be read by the better part of the country must write, perhaps even unwillingly, in an *evangelical, Protestant, Lutheran* way. The masquerade, the time of aping foreign peoples and times, is over. Authors must write in a Protestant way against errors and superstitions—according to *their own* convictions. Otherwise, they will be mocked and will not be read.

D: What happens when none of our great thinkers reads German?

W: All the worse for them. Those who are ashamed of their nation and their language tear apart the *religion* of their people and hence the bond that ties them to the nation. I continue to believe that whoever lays pure sentiments, the power of the mind and heart, on the altar of the country continues the work of Luther and contributes to national religion in the strictest sense of the word, that is, *conscientiousness and conviction.*

D: This is a genuine Protestant, Lutheran belief. In this sense, Winnfried, would you like "national religions" of all peoples on earth?

W: Yes, in this sense. This would further peace on earth and the development of every people out of its own trunk into its diverse branches. In this way no foreign language or religion will tyrannize the language and character of another nation. No one will even think of a supreme shepherding nation of all the herds of humanity that does not understand their languages and does not know their innermost needs. Every nation blossoms like a tree from its own roots. Christianity, that is, *the true conviction about God and human beings,* is nothing but the pure dew of heaven for all nations that, moreover, does not change any tree's character or type of fruit and that does not strip any human beings of their own nature. In this way there will be peace on earth—

D:—and good will to all. (Look how beautifully the sun is setting.) And good will to all. Solyman the Magnificent[33] understood his kingdom to be a field full of *various* kinds of flowers, a garden full of *various* kinds of fruits. In the same way, the human race would become one family, which it truly is and must be, with the most diverse characters and national religions, and it would *strive toward one purpose*.

W: Every religion would strive, according to and within its own context, to be the better, no, the best of its kind without measuring and comparing itself to others. Do not peoples differ from one another in every respect—in poetry and pleasure, in physiognomy and taste, in customs, morals, and languages? Does not religion, which participates in this "everything," also have to be distinguished nationally?

D: Even individually, so that in the end all individuals would possess *their own* religions, just as they would possess *their own* hearts, *their own* convictions and languages.

W: And no one would be allowed to judge the innermost heart of another. If one is humble, then one will never ask about this mystery. I do not need to tell you that in this way the so-called propagation and expansion of Christianity would win a different character.

D: You also do not need to tell me that some useless trouble could have been spared in this way. The sun has set. It set just a few moments ago, as we thought that we still saw its image. Let us speak together again tomorrow, as the sun rises. Farewell, *alma mater!* And bring a joyous morning to other nations! Farewell, Winnfried!

---

33. [Soleiman the Magnificent (1494-1566); Ottoman Sultan.]

3

God and Nature

THE OLDEST DOCUMENT OF THE HUMAN RACE

[An interpretation of the first chapter of Genesis in relation to a description of the sky before the dawn.][1]

Come with me, young lad, into the open field, and take note! *The most ancient, most glorious revelation of God appears to you every morning as a fact, as the mighty work of God in nature.*

Heaven and earth! Look how they still lie mingled together around us! *Heaven set upon the earth! Earth lifted to heaven!*

The earth was without form and void,
And darkness covered the face of the deep.[2]

Can you think of a more graphic way, even in other passages of the Bible, to depict the vast *grave of night, the shudder of midnight*, than through this infinite, dark void? Now, feel the *spirit of the night* moving through all things! Feel the *shiver of the earliest hours* before the dawn! Feel how the Spirit moves through oceans, trees, and all things.

And the Spirit of God swept over the face of the deep![3]

Just before the first glimmer of daylight, when we are deeply stirred by it, who does not feel God breathing like a stirring, rousing power of nature? Behold! There is God! There is the first ray of light!

1. [SW 6:258-63.]
2. [Gen. 1:2. Some translations of Biblical passages in this section are revised from the NRSV to reflect Herder's own translation of the Hebrew text.]
3. [Gen. 1:2.]

—Light! And there is light![4]

Not even the briefest syllable of the Bible can capture it![5]

Behold! This *delight,* this *ineffable feeling at daybreak* seems to seize all creatures! To touch everything in nature! Everything lay in night and darkness, and then the moving Spirit came and prepared all that lay in expectation. The birds are still resting; their heads are tucked under their wings. The city lies buried, as if it had never seen the morning light. Even the morning lark does not yet rise. Nature is a dark temple of God, waiting in expectation. Living wind moves and—

—Light! There was light!

The temple is consecrated in a calm, quiet way! Perhaps the blossom of the tree, the flower, the bud feel this! *Oh, ray of light! You are the golden chord that resonates upon the great lute of nature!* The lark wakes and rises. Woe to those who have no feeling, who behold this scene and do not feel God! That ancient sage of nature paints the scene in this way: *the dawn raises its eyes and grasps the end of the earth, the great dark skirt of night*—

—at its hem
and shakes the wicked out of it![6]
—Light! And there was light!

Do you see that calm glory? Do you see how that soft flutter of the eye of dawn casts its shimmering light farther with every passing moment, how it changes the color of the clouds with every passing moment? What colors! What dancing brilliance! Who is the one who dipped the paintbrush here? And how tranquil! The eye lingers on this tender place—*the gentle face of God!* Revelation! Manifestation! Think what I have said about the light, and yet I still have not expressed it. Who cannot help but fall to the ground, worship, and silently sigh, "Oh, that my soul were eternal like *the light,* like this first manifestation of God!"

What dawns on us at such moments is always expressed in monosyllabic words. I wager that the same is true with every untainted, natural prayer. This is the sigh and praise of God at dawn!

No noise or sound surrounded him,
when he created the world from nothing.

4. [Gen. 1:3.]
5. Brief as the lightening in the collied night that, in a spleen, unfolds both heaven and earth and ere a man had power to say, behold!
From Shakespeare, Midsummer Night's Dream [I,i,145-47].
6. Job 38:[13.]

All peoples of nature whom we call "savages" have this reverent feeling before the first light of day. (Perhaps the animals do too. Who knows?) Later, this feeling is thought about more abstractly and expressed in words:

Behold, the light is good![7]

What dread, what darkness, is chased away! Look how the night gradually lifts in dark, vast waves! "God separated the light from the darkness!"[8] Look how the two masses stand next to one another in all their difference! (Certainly this relation between light and darkness is different than that of massive, fertile fields that stand next to one another.) The great difference is now visible! *Light! Darkness!*

The light is called day!
The darkness is called night![9]

Can there be a more striking moment in this scene of nature? Every morning both light and darkness are festively visible *next to one another.*

Behold! As the daylight now increases, nature weaves all things with an even hand, visibly spinning the *delicate gossamer of air and sky.* Everything was once *gray or black*—heaven was set upon the earth, the earth was lifted toward heaven. The color gray then *expands* on all sides! The heaven *lifts and rises!* The dark clouds *descend into fog!* It is as if light and water contend with one other.

Above, the color blue *emerges, vaulting and weaving* ever further. All those who depict the dawn see their best art in these phenomena: the gradual *lifting of the sky!* The *buoyant refining of the air* from the deepest grey to the most beautiful, most joyous and brilliant color of blue! The *fragrance of the morning* that drifts through all beings, especially in the far distance *where Aurora sleeps,* where we lose our sense of perspective and discover, so to speak, a new galaxy within a galaxy!

What are magic carpets of the most fortunate compared to this *all-encompassing painting of nature* itself? Behold! The *daily, active, obvious illustration of nature* gives us the simplest explanation of the most debated and confusing passage of the Bible:

"Let there be a dome in the midst of the waters,
and let it separate the waters from the waters."
So God made the dome
and separated the waters that were under the dome
from the waters that were above the dome!
And God called the dome sky.[10]

7. [Gen. 1:4a.]
8. [Gen. 1:4b.]
9. [Gen. 1:5.]
10. [Gen. 1:6-8.]

At the same time that the heaven refines and separates itself above, *the earth separates and refines itself below!* Behold! The two masses separate into *light* and *darkness*, like a great mountain that seems to rise as it is revealed! Now the earth *blossoms beneath the dew and morning light.* The rose gradually opens its bosom, and the violet finishes its fragrant cup! The early zephyr weaves blossoms and pollen around the young plant—brides that are reflected in the morning dew! The young tree weaves and shudders, feeling its branches in the first breath of waking creation! Here is the first *family* of creation! There is development in this picture of nature. The heavenly Father blesses the *plants, herbs, and trees* beneath the light of the dawn.

Behold! *The sun is rising!* The most glorious manifestation of nature! Flame! Face of splendor! King! The eye can endure only one glance! The sun surpasses and completes everything! Through it everything in creation becomes splendor, radiance, sound!

Who wonders now why the morning light was created so much earlier than the morning sun? Who can now hear yet another demonstration?

Now everything awakens! All things are—

By this lively fire
Disturbed! Disturbed from their sleep!

The stillness of the silver lake is *unraveled by living creatures:* The fish play in the rays of the sun! Air and the treetops are filled with morning song.

The lively choir of birds fills the air and forests.
With early song and early flight.

Everything is full of motion, *song, joy, and blessing!*

The earth brought forth living creatures of every kind,
Animals, reptiles, and wild beasts of every kind.[11]

And behold! The *human being! There you stand!* The *image of God!* The likeness of God! The *reigning thought of creation!* Call your scattered, stunned attention away from heaven and earth and back to yourself! Turn inward!

Oh human being, ruler of the earth, you dissolve
Into harmonies completely.
God favored you above everything else;
He gave you a spirit
That penetrates the structure of the universe.

Contemplate your *happiness!* Your *form!* Your *powers!* Your magnificent *character!* Listen to God's design! See what he has done!

11. [Gen. 1:24-25.]

People go out to their work
And to their labor until the evening.[12]

Human beings think, write poetry, govern, nourish themselves. The eye of God rests upon them.

God made everything!
Behold, it was very good![13]

Creation is completed! This painting of the morning is also completed! With what simplicity and natural order! Unity and diversity! Splendor! Sublimity! Started and completed!

Even the author who described this painting could say *epoiese!*[14] But he was not the author! All this appeared to him! It was revealed to him! It lives and moves each morning! *Oh, most glorious, most ancient, most simple revelation of God!*

LOVE AND SELFHOOD
(A POSTSCRIPT TO MR. HEMSTERHUIS'S LETTER ABOUT DESIRE)

A beautiful saga of ancient poetry claims that love drew the world out of chaos and linked all creatures reciprocally to one another with bonds of desire and longing, and that with these tender bonds love preserves the order of all things and directs them to the one who is the great source of all light and of all love.[15] Regardless of the various names and forms in which this poetic system was presented, this universal law is recognizable in them all: Love unites beings, strife divides them; every pleasure, divine and human, consists in love and the union of similar things; longing and desire are, however, like the bridesmaids of love, like the strong yet tender arms that prepare and attract all delight; indeed, they themselves provide the greatest pleasure through the presentiment of it.

Soon, however, the other side of the system also became visible: Love has *limits,* and a complete union of beings in our universe rarely or never takes place; the bonds of this union—desire and longing—necessarily subside precisely under the greatest strain, and unfortunately they often provide *ennui* and satiety instead of pleasure. It was soon noticed that this law also contained

12. [Ps. 104:23.]
13. [Gen. 1:31.]
14. [Greek for "I did it!"]
15. [*Liebe und Selbstheit (Ein Nachtrag zum Briefe des Hr. Hemsterhuis über das Verlangen),* SW 15:304-26.] See [Frans] Hemsterhuis [1721-90], *Vermischte Philosophische Schriften* (Leipzig: Weidmanns, 1782), 1:71.

wisdom because through it the Creator cared as much for the *definite existence of individual beings* as for the *union* and *gentle association* of several creatures through love and longing. It was seen that the two powers of love and strife, which are to the spiritual world what *attraction* and *repulsion* are to the physical world, belong to the maintenance and preservation of the universe. I believe it was *Empedocles* who already claimed that strife and love sketch the structure of all creatures. "Through strife," he said, "things are separated, and each *individual being* remains what it is; through love they are united and joined to one another"[16]—insofar as their nature allows them to be joined. For even love, the Greeks said, is ruled by *fate,* and *necessity,* the eldest of gods, is more powerful than love. According to the ideas of Plato, love was born of *poverty* and *resourcefulness* in the gardens of Jupiter.[17] Love has, therefore, the nature of both and is ever dependent on its parents.

I believe it will not be unpleasant to pursue both sides of this system, especially since Mr. *Hemsterhuis* has nicely guided us more on the one side. He saved the other side for another essay[18] that either he has not yet written or I have not yet seen.

Hemsterhuis demonstrated that love *unites* beings and that all *longing,* all *desire, strives* only for this *union,* as the only possible *pleasure of separated beings.* He has done this with such well-chosen examples that supplementing the discussion at length would only be superfluous. Every deep longing for sensual and spiritual pleasure, every desire for friendship and love thirsts for union with the object of desire because in this object desire has a presentiment of a new, sweet pleasure of its own reality. The deity has wisely and benevolently created us so that we are to feel our own existence not *within ourselves* but rather only through *reaction;* we are to feel it, so to speak, only in an object outside of us toward which we strive, for which we live, within which we are doubled and manifold. Nature places a *host* of attractive objects around us at so many different *distances* and gifted with such diverse *levels* and *kinds* of attractiveness that in this way a rich and tender lyre of feelings with diverse tones and modes became possible inside us. Our heart and life became, so to speak, a "harmonic instrument"[19] of desire, the artistic creation of an ever *purer, insatiable, eternal* longing.

Crude pleasure of the senses is transformed within itself and destroys the object of our desire. The pleasure of the senses is therefore *vivid,* for in this

16. [This is not a direct quote, but it summarizes a central point in the *Fragments* of Empedocles.]

17. [See Plato's *Symposium,* 203b. In the Greek, love is born of *penia* and *poros.*]

18. Hemsterhuis, *Philosophische Schriften,* 1:108. [The same passage can be found in the *Teuscher Merkur* November 1781:122.]

19. [*Harmonika.* Since the mouth harmonica was not developed until the nineteenth century, Herder is probably referring either to the glass harmonica (a musical instrument developed in the eighteenth century consisting of a chromatic set of glass bowls and played by rubbing the finger along the wet rims of the glass) or to the concertina.]

case complete union occurs. Yet such pleasure is also *crude* and *transitory*. There are people who speak about the pleasure of the tongue alone. (This is why in everyday life the German verb *geniessen*[20] is most often used in this sense.) In regard to eating and drinking, the pleasure is *union*, the dissolution of the finest humors. Yet with this union the pleasure also ends, for the object has been swallowed, destroyed. In a certain sense even here the finest pleasure is before the pleasure itself: The appetite for a lovely fruit is more pleasing than the fruit itself. The eye fills the tongue with desire in the most delightful way. As Lucretius says about another sense: *Voluptatem praesagit muta cupido.*[21] The same is true with the pleasure of smells and even of sounds. We draw them into ourselves, we drink the stream of sensual pleasure with long drafts. We only say that we "take pleasure in" music when it has melted our hearts, when it becomes one with the inner chords of our feelings. The stream of pleasing sound, however delicate, is nevertheless also *devoured*. It continues only in the harmonic effects, in the pleasant vibrations that it creates in us.

The more spiritual the pleasure, the more it *endures* and the more its object also endures *outside* of us. However, let us always also add that the more spiritual the pleasure, the *weaker* it is, for an object *exists* and *continues to exist* outside of us and can only really become *one* with us metaphorically, that is, hardly or not at all. The eye is never satiated with seeing, for how little does the heart receive in seeing! How little is the mere ray of light able to give us the innermost pleasure! . . .

Let us begin then by discussing the more genuine kinds of spiritual desire: *friendship* and *love*. I will mention only a few points given what Hemsterhuis has said about them.

The image of *friendship* in the ancient world was *two intertwined hands*. This image seems to be the most appropriate symbol of its union, its purpose, and its pleasure. It is a more meaningful image than that of *two lyres identically tuned*. This latter image expresses nothing but *affiliation*, which is far from being *friendship*. An affiliate is readily and harmoniously attuned to each member of the affiliation, and the members are in turn attuned to one another. They oppress no one with their existence, they constrict no one. Thus, everyone is at ease in their company. They are to a certain degree trusted because no one feels they are malicious. Characters of this kind are adequate for the dealings of everyday life. But *friendship!* What a different, holy bond it is! It links hearts and hands together into *one common purpose*. Where this

20. ["To take pleasure in" or to "enjoy." *Geniessen* can refer to pleasure in general, but often refers specifically to the pleasures of eating and drinking.]

21. [Latin for "desire, though wordless, tells of joys to be." The *Loeb* translation is "dumb desire presages delight." Lucretius, *De rerum Natura*, IV.1057 (Loeb edition; Cambridge: Harvard University Press, 1959). Here Lucretius is speaking about sexual desire.]

purpose is *evident*, where it is *ongoing and arduous* and even stands under or beyond dangers, there the bond of friendship is often so exact, solid, and heartfelt that nothing but death can divide it. . . .

Marriage should also be friendship, and woe to those for whom it is not, for whom it is only love and appetite! A noble woman finds it sweet to suffer for the sake of her husband, not to mention to rejoice with him, and for him to feel active, cheerful, honorable, treasured, and happy in her, and for her to feel this way in him. The common raising of children is the lovely guiding purpose of their friendship, a purpose that continues to reward them both in old age. They stand there as two intertwined trees and will continue to do so surrounded by a circle of young, budding trees and branches.

In general a life in common is the mark of true friendship: the *disclosing* and *sharing* of hearts, taking deep *joy* in one another, *grieving* together, offering one another *advice, consolation, care,* and *help*—these are the signs, the desserts, the inner rewards of friendship. There are such tender mysteries in it! Delicacies! It is as if one soul directly feels itself in the soul of another, and one soul has a presentiment of the thoughts of the other as clearly as if they were its own. Certainly, the soul has the power now and then to know another's thoughts in this way, to dwell directly and intimately in the heart of another. There are moments of sympathy even in our thoughts that occur without the slightest external stimulus. Psychology cannot explain them, but experience teaches and confirms them. There are memories, even distant memories of absent friends, that are often of the most marvelous, most powerful kind. If the soul ever did possess the mysterious power to act directly, without mediation, in another soul, then where would it be more natural than in friendship? This is purer and thus certainly also more powerful than love, for if love would elevate itself to the strength and duration of an eternity, then it must first become genuine and true friendship purified of crude sensuality. How seldom does love reach this point! Love destroys either itself or its object with penetrating, consuming flames, and both lover and beloved then lie there like a pile of ashes. But the fire of friendship is pure, refreshing, human warmth.The two flames on one altar play into one another, they jubilantly lift and carry one another, and often even in the hour of grievous separation they joyously soar upward in union into the land of purest union, of the most faithful, inseparable friendship.

Forgive me, my reader, for elaborating on this point. Yet I hold friendship to be the true, sole, and most beautiful union of souls and thus also the noblest and sweetest pleasure of which human beings are capable. Indeed, even love serves friendship. There are various levels of friendship from easy acquaintance to the most sublime, quiet, enduring self-sacrifice, which of course is bestowed upon only very select souls in very rare situations and relationships and yet is given to them as the most sublime privilege, as the genuine foretaste of a future, higher existence. In short, there is in friendship a union that is practically unmediated, pure, complete, active, and ever-growing. For all these reasons friendship appears to me to be the climax of every desire, and precisely under the greatest strain and pressure it becomes the purest happiness on earth. It is here where the true magnetism of human souls is at work, and we know that a magnet attracts most powerfully when it is used. Friendship that is not exercised is dead; without trust and well-tried loyalty no friendship, no exchange of hearts, is possible.

Nature saw, however, that these pure, heavenly flames would usually be too delicate for us on earth. Thus, it covered them with mortal, sensual attraction. At this point Venus Urania[22] appeared as Aphrodite. Love should invite us to friendship, love itself should become the most intimate friendship.

I do not seek the highest level of love's delight where, as Mr. Hemsterhuis says, nature deludes us with a moment of earthly union (a moment that loses itself everywhere in raw need). I seek love rather in the first happy find, in the sweet, indescribable moment, when both lovers are aware that they love one another and say it to one another so confidently, sweetly, harmoniously, however imperfectly or involuntarily. Why must I use the word "say"? This poor word! What can the dead tongue, the thirsting language, say in this moment when even the soul-filled, fiery glance lowers its wings and veils its radiance? If there is a moment of heavenly, sensual pleasure and of pure union of two bodily entities here on earth, then it is this one. This is a completely different kind of pleasure than what starving pleasure grants us. In the mythology of an Asian people, whose name I cannot recall, the periods of primeval times are divided in such a way that human beings (who at that time were still spirits in paradise) for thousands of years first loved one another through glances, later through a kiss, through a mere touch. It was only after many ages that they gradually sank to the lowest kind of pleasure. The moment of that spiritual recognition, of that disclosure of the soul through a single glance, takes us back, so to speak, to that primeval time and thereby to the joys of paradise. In it we take pleasure in what we sought for so long and what we did not dare express to ourselves *by feeling all that has gone before;* in it we take pleasure in all the joys of the future *by having a presentiment of what lies ahead.* We do not just anticipate these joys but rather possess them—no, if I may say so, we do more than possess them. The future can only unfold, and it rarely adds something independently; it often removes something— with every pleasure it decreases the illusion of pleasure. That moment is the one in which Psyche sees [Cupid] the god of love whom she had loved so

22. [Venus Urania is the representation of Venus (or Aphrodite, the goddess of love) as the goddess of heavenly or spiritual love.]

long beneath his veil. Oh why, unhappy one, did you let the spark fall and thereby end all your joy for so long a time?[23] . . .

Magnificent passages in the fourth book of Lucretius[24] describe this striving, this vain, insatiable striving for the union of beings with such strength, so philosophically and powerfully, that it seems as though either Lucretius wrote of the philosophical system of Hemsterhuis or that the latter used Lucretius's philosophical system of pleasure and love. Fortunately, nature couples this brief, deceptive illusion of intimate union with *friendship* on the part of the spirit, and favors it with the electric spark of nature's omniscience on the part of the body. Through this spark, which arises from the incomprehensible union of two beings, a third emerges who is, so to speak, a creature of love, a creature of desire and unfinished longing. The fiery chain thus expands further: A new link is attached to it between poverty and resourcefulness, and in this link the spark of longing is lit again. In general, I observe that the Creator allowed no level of the union of beings in nature without fruit. The lowest level of sensual pleasure, which an infant already sucks, gives us *life blood:* It prepares for us something *nobler* from a weaker material. The *more refined* the organ of pleasure becomes, the *more spiritual* are the offspring of its conception: *fragrances* strengthen and refresh the soul; *music* comforts and refreshes the heart with a heavenly drink; *images—simulacra, pabula amoris*[25]—guide more tender thoughts than their material counterparts to the mind; finally, *friendship,* the marriage of spirits, and *love,* the marriage of bodies, bring us a cup of pleasure crowned with the most lovely fruits. *Friendship* arouses noble feelings, yearnings, and deeds; *love,* like the divine springtime sun, animates the tender, maternal vine with foliage and fruits. The *creative power* of the first author lies within both of them.

It also seems that nature took care to replace and reward the brief, fleeting pleasure of love with a gift that nature took directly from pleasure's lap, a gift that honors even the slightest living creature with a divine spark. This gift is the *affection of parents—paternal and maternal* love. This love is *divine* because it is selfless and very often thankless. It is *heavenly* because it can divide itself into many parts and yet remain whole, undivided, and free from envy. Finally, it is also *eternal and endless* because it surpasses physical love and death. . . .

23. [Herder is referring to Apuleius's account of Cupid and Psyche in *The Golden Ass*, 5:22-5:24 (Loeb edition; New York: Putnam, 1935). Here Psyche loved Cupid, who came to her only at night so that she never saw him. He warned her that she must never try to see him. One night when Cupid had fallen asleep, Psyche, encouraged by her sisters, lifted a lamp and saw his glorious body. In her great joy, she let a drop of burning oil fall on Cupid's shoulder. He woke, perceived that she had not heeded his warning, and fled.]

24. [Lucretius, *De Rerum Natura,* Book IV.]

25. [Latin for "images, the food of love."]

To whom can I ascend from the tender, divine, eternal affection of parents except to you, great universal Mother, tender supreme Father! My language has no word to name the feeling by means of which you placed yourself in every creature, in every nerve and corner of each beating heart, and with which you gave each creature a pleasure that cannot be measured, explained, and perceived by others. Your whole creation is a woven fabric that *power* drew out of nothingness, that *wisdom* entwined, and in which *love* wove its meaningful and tender figures in a thousand different forms. Who ought not but love you, for every creature draws toward you, points to you? And yet who can love you as one should, since one drowns in the sea of your thoughts and your presentient feelings and sinks into the deepest depth only beyond oneself. You share the fate of all parents: They love more than they are loved. But you have an advantage over all others in that you have created the longing for you in me, and you can bring me ever closer to you by the bonds of knowledge and love. My whole heart says to me that you will and must do this, for the small spark of knowledge and love in me is nothing but a reflection of the eternal flame of your heart. You must recognize, name, seek, and love me a thousand times more deeply than I can name and seek you. This eternal pull of your heart to mine is for me an innate guarantee of my eternal affection for you and of the ever-growing pleasure in you.

But how do we take pleasure in the eternal one? Through intuition? Or through feeling? Hemsterhuis made a critical comment about the Enthusiasts[26] that, if well examined, unfortunately may be only too true. His comment refers to the common experience that women have been involved in all actions of Enthusiasts. Men were often only infected by women through whom they were, as the saying goes, "reborn." Women were, so to speak, "mediators of God" for the men. The way these women thought about and felt God, especially God in human form, can be found in many writings and letters. If the ecstasy felt by Teresa of Avila before the altar, when heavenly *amour* touched her heart, were observed at the very moment of ecstasy from a physical point of view alone, then it could hardly be distinguished from the kind of ecstasy found in love. In the bodily humors, love and love of the effects are the same no matter who might be the object of love. With all feelings of this kind, the greatest caution is necessary even for the most innocent heart. Even in the current of divine love, the heart remains a mere human heart. Every female mediator, even if she were the mother of God herself, is dangerous for the male heart; just as every earthly male mediator, even the heavenly mediator himself (if felt too sensually), can be dangerous for the female heart. God wants to be loved by our whole being, by all our powers, and not by nerves brewing in a sick, convulsive body.

26. Hemsterhuis, *Philosophische Schriften*, 1:88. [*Teuscher Merkur* (November 1781): 108.]

We automatically come to the limits placed on our love and longing in every pleasurable experience. These limits are not merely our bodily organs, as Mr. Hemsterhuis seems to believe, but rather, as he himself finally discovers, our *isolated, individual existence* [*Dasein*]. . . .

We are *individual beings,* and we must be so if we do not want to give up the *ground* of every pleasure—our own *consciousness* of pleasure—and if we do not want to lose *ourselves* in order to find ourselves again in another being that we never are and never can be. Even if I were to lose myself in God, as mysticism strives to do, and were to lose myself in God without any further feeling or consciousness of *myself,* then *I* would no longer be experiencing pleasure. The deity would have devoured me; and instead of me, the deity would have experienced the pleasure. How wise therefore is providence! It rouses the chords of our feelings only gradually in very different tones and ways. It calls upon our longing and then curtails it, exercises our desires here actively and there passively. And yet everywhere, even after the sweetest pleasure, it throws us back upon our poor *self,* saying "You are indeed a limited, individual creature! You thirst for perfection, but you never attain it! Do not pine away at the fountain of this one individual pleasure, rather pull yourself together and strive on!" Let us examine a few striking illustrations and examples of this.

All rapacious pleasure, which ravages its object, is given to us as a mere *need* from the hand of *necessity.* It wears itself out and dies away in itself. Human beings are tyrants of the universe; yet how quickly even these little tyrants, if they want to remain within the limits of nature, are satiated with pillaging! Every pleasure of the senses is actually only an *appeased need.* Where the destruction of the other ends there first begins a freer, more beautiful pleasure, a cheerful *coexistence* of many creatures who *mutually* seek and love one another. A tyrant who wants to be all things alone, who wants to devour everything, as Saturn devoured his children, is capable neither of friendship, nor love, nor even fatherly affection. He presses and oppresses. Nothing can grow next to him, let alone grow together with him into one common crown.

As soon as several creatures coexist peacefully and mutually seek to take pleasure in one another, it follows that none of them must seek either the *exclusive* or the *highest* pleasure. Otherwise, the creature destroys everything around it. It has to give and take, endure and act, draw inward toward itself and gently open itself to others. Of course, this means that all pleasure is incomplete. But this is the true measure and pulse of life: the *modulation* and *balance* of desire, of love, and of all the delights of longing. Here I must mention the beautiful wisdom of nature. It divides and, so to speak, gently rocks all things into this pulse of passive and active, giving and receiving creatures according to sex, particular moments in time, temporal circumstances, periods of life, situations, and so on. Just as God created two lights in heaven, God created two sexes on earth that counterbalance one another in the swing of feelings. The one compensates for the lack of tenderness or strength in the other, and in the realm of love, tenderness is more powerful than strength. God compensated for the fragility of woman and wrapped it in beauty. Where God had to depart from rules of beauty out of necessity, God wrapped the belt of love around this fragility, endowing it with the *desire* that, as that goddess [of love] said, overpowers all strength. In friendship, too, one partner is always more active and the other is more supportive and passive; the former is "masculine," the latter is "feminine." Often these roles are reversed between men and women. In this marriage of souls, unison is neither pleasant nor useful nor possible. *Consonant,* not *unisonant,* tones must be the ones that create the melody of life and pleasure. Otherwise friendship soon fades away into mere affiliation.

It is thus clear that the attractiveness of an *individual* human being neither can nor may expand into *infinity.* Nature has drawn narrow limits around every *individual.* It is the most dangerous dream to think oneself unlimited when one is limited—to believe oneself despot of the universe when one lives from nothing but individual alms. It sounds beautiful to embrace the whole creation with love, but love begins with the individual, with the neighbor. If one does not deeply, intimately, and totally love the neighbor, then how can one love what is distant, what casts down only weak rays from a foreign star, such that even this might earn the title of love? The most universal cosmopolitans are in most cases the poorest beggars: Those who embrace the whole universe with love usually love nothing but their own narrow selves. . . .

Nature always begins with the *individual.* Only when nature has ordered and satisfied the inclinations of the individual being in its small sphere does it relate several individual beings to one another and order their feelings toward communal happiness. The well-being of the state consists of happy families, otherwise its happiness is an illusion. Once an individual's physical and spiritual pleasures, friendship and love, paternal affection and individual virtue are well ordered and well combined, that individual possesses individual happiness and is happy for others. It is impossible for an individual to flow together with *everything* like mud. It is impossible to love, praise, and approve everything *to the same degree*—to try to change every particle of dust into a ray of sunlight so that the particle of dust can be loved as a ray of light. In this way an individual damages the good as much as the bad and in the end completely loses his or her own judgment and standpoint. Whoever cannot repel is also unable to attract. Both powers are only *one pulse* of the soul.

This is the way we are in *this* world, and it is hard to imagine that it will be different in our eternal journey. The existence of others rests only upon our *own individual existence* and *consciousness* insofar as others are linked together with *us* through love and longing. If we were to lose our own individual existence and consciousness, then we would also no longer have pleasure from love and longing. By giving and acting, rather than receiving and being passive, our existence necessarily will become ever freer and more effective from stage to stage, our pleasure will become less damaging and destructive, and we will learn to taste ever more joy. Nevertheless, the mutual relation that constitutes the sum of this entire happiness does not seem to be capable of ever completely coming to an end. In order to give there must always be objects that can receive; in order to act there must be others for whom we act. Friendship and love are not possible except between creatures who are mutually free and consonant, but not unisonant, let alone identical. Finally, when it comes to the pleasure of the supreme being, this always remains and must remain a *hyperbole with its asymptote,* as Hemsterhuis says.[27] The hyperbole approaches asymptote, but never reaches it. In the same way, in regard to *our* supreme happiness we can never *lose* the idea of our own existence and *arrive* at the *infinite* idea that we are *God.* We always remain creatures, even if we would become the creators of great worlds. We approach perfection, but we never become infinitely perfect. The supreme good that God could grant all creatures was and is individual existence. It is precisely in this that God is, and ever more will be, the all in all for all creatures.

LETTERS TO JACOBI

[These letters were written to Friedrich Heinrich Jacobi just before the "Pantheism Controversy" between Jacobi and Moses Mendelssohn was made public in 1785.][28]

Weimar, February 6, 1784

Hen kai pan.[29]
I need all the forgiveness you can offer, dear Jacobi, not only for replying so late to your letter, which I deeply enjoyed, but also for keeping the text on your and Lessing's views of God so long. I have been in such a state of "contraction" toward my philosophy of history that there was very little room left for other thoughts, and with the cold weather I simply forgot to write. Goethe reminded me to do so when he spoke about one of your letters to him

---

27. Hemsterhuis, *Philosophische Schriften,* 1: 108. [*Teuscher Merkur* (November 1781): 121-22.]
28. [Briefe 5:27-29,90-91.]
29. [Greek for "one and all."]

(I am very sorry to learn through the letter about your recurring illness), so now I am finally taking some time to write to you nothing but *hen kai pan*— a motto that I myself once read in Gleim's[30] garden house, where Lessing had written it. At that time, however, I did not know how to explain it. More precisely, I did not know how to explain it in relation to Lessing's soul. I could not imagine that you ever would have carried on metaphysics in such a dismal way with that old Anacreon [Gleim]. I suppose on account of a sort of prudishness and decency, his kind, spinster-like character did not alert me to any of these blasphemies. Otherwise, I would have written *hen kai pan* seven times beneath Lessing's words, after having so unexpectedly found him to be a fellow believer in my own philosophical credo.

Seriously, dearest Jacobi, ever since taking up philosophy, I have been again and again convinced of the truth of Lessing's statement that in fact the philosophy of Spinoza alone is *internally consistent in a complete sense*. This is not to say I agree with it completely, for even Spinoza's philosophy contains, it seems to me, undeveloped concepts too closely tied to the thought of Descartes, who deeply influenced him. Thus, I would never call my system Spinozism, for the seeds of this system lie in an almost purer form in the most ancient of all enlightened nations. Spinoza was, however, the first person who dared to combine this into a system with a method appropriate to our time. At the same time he had the misfortune of tracing precisely those delicate philosophical problems through which he discredited his system among Jews, Christians, and pagans. Mendelssohn, it seems to me, correctly claims that Bayle[31] misunderstood Spinoza's system. At least Bayle did much damage to it through the awkward comparisons he used in order to explain it. I am of the opinion, therefore, that no one has done justice to the system of *hen kai pan* since Spinoza's death (not even Mendelssohn in his *Conversation* about Spinoza). Oh why did not Lessing do it?! Fear certainly did not prevent him from going ahead with this task, because he never shrank from the consequences of expressing an opinion that he held to be true, and all kinds of indirect methods of expression were at his disposal. No, it was wicked death that overtook him!

For more than seven years I have intended to compare Spinoza, Shaftesbury, and Leibniz, but I could not find time. Last summer I started the project anew. I read the first two authors, but then the weather was so hot and my mind fell into such a state of "expansion" that I had to discontinue the project again. I would like to pick it up again soon.

30. [Johann Wilhelm Ludwig Gleim (1719-1803) was one of the main representatives of the *Anakreontiker,* a German group of eighteenth century poets who wrote about wine and love in the style of Anacreon, the last great lyric poet of ancient Greece.]
31. [The entry on Spinoza in Pierre Bayle's *Dictionnaire Historique et Critique* (1697) provided a stereotype that was held to be definitive until the controversy of the late eighteenth century. In this entry Bayle denounced Spinoza as an atheist.]

I ask you kindly, therefore, dear Jacobi:

1. Please have your conversation with Lessing copied. (I have not dared to do so without permission.) The conversation interests me a great deal. Write as much as you can to me about the foolish stuff that still comes to your mind. I ask you to do this because as a matter of fact, I do not yet understand Lessing's idea about the "contraction" of God into the individuality of an appearance, and I do not yet comprehend the law of this "expansion and contraction." You would delight my most secret, favorite ideas, for I cannot tell you how much I agree with Lessing about these central principles, even about what he says of Leibniz against Spinoza. I can write about this later, when my spirit wakes up, and Lessing's spirit will surely excite my own in the future.

2. May I request that, before Lessing's ideas are published by Mendelssohn in the form of a refutation, you publish the conversation outside this context in a more agreeable form? You can send your letter to Mendelssohn, but with the request that it not be published until you publish what you want from the conversation with Lessing. If he wants to take this conversation into consideration in his refutation, then he may publish it. You are responsible, however, for making the discourse public, for he will refute you as well as the discourse, and I do not know why you want to place both at his footstool.

3. In addition, my dear and good extramundane personalist,[32] I ask you most kindly and sincerely to think more about what Lessing said and to support your own system by giving several grounds for it. If there is no need to make a *salto mortale*,[33] then why make one? I am sure that we are not allowed to perform a *salto mortale* because we are on solid ground in creation. The *proton pseudos*,[34] dear Jacobi, in your and in every anti-Spinozist system is that by understanding God to be the great *ens entium*, the first cause of being, that is eternally active in all phenomena, you take God to be a nullity, an abstract concept that we formulate according to our mental capacities. According to Spinoza, however, God is not this. Instead, God is the most real, most active *one* that alone says: "I am what I am, and I will be what I will be" (in all changes of my appearance). (These changes refer to the phenomena among themselves, not to God.) The philosophy of true being does not begin with the rejection of the proposition, *ex nihilo nihil fit*.[35] Rather, it begins with the eternal proposition, *quidquid est, illud est*.[36] This was precisely the

32. [In his *God, Some Conversations* Herder criticizes Jacobi for viewing God too anthropocentrically as an extramundane personality.]

33. [Italian phrase which literally means "a mortal leap" and refers to a somersault that begins with a standing jump. Hence it is used to express a critical moment in life, or crucial undertaking and is often translated as "a leap of faith."]

34. [Greek for "first falsehood."]

35. [Latin for "nothing is made out of nothing."]

36. [Latin for "whatever exists, that thing exists."]

concept of being that Spinoza so fruitfully developed. Further, it seems to me that Spinoza correctly raised this concept not only above all ways of representing and thinking about individual phenomena, but also above all the limited kinds of existence in space. I do not understand what you dear people mean by "existing *outside* the world." If God does not exist *in* the world, and *everywhere* in the world, and precisely without measure, wholly and indivisibly (for the whole world is but an appearance of God's greatness in forms appearing to us), then God exists nowhere. "Outside the world" there is no space; space comes into being in that a world for us comes into being, only by means of abstraction from an appearance. The notion of limited personality is applied just as inappropriately to that infinite being, for in our world "person" is constituted only through limitation, as a kind of *modus,* or as an operative aggregate of being with the illusion of unity. In God this illusion falls away, for God is the highest, most living, most active *one*—not *in* all things, as if they were something outside God, but rather *through* all things, which appear only as a sensory display for creatures with senses. The image of God as the "soul of the world" is, like all analogies, imperfect because the world is not like a body for God, but rather like a whole soul. If the human soul had as clear an idea of itself and of its body as God has, then the soul would be so advanced that the body would no longer be a mere body for the soul but rather the soul itself, acting within specific powers and according to them and no other. But the soul would then be what it never could become no matter how it strived—God, that is, *hen kai pan.*

How I would love to keep talking about these things! But time and space prevent me. These are the two *modi* that limit all limited entities. Forgive me for going on and on, dear Jacobi. I would be very happy to receive a copy of your *Conversations* and your *Turgot.* As soon as my philosophy of history is finished, I will send a copy to you.

Again, I would very much wish that Lessing's thoughts be published initially as an open conversation, without any refutation, indeed without any suggestion that they are heretical. Berkeley has his idealistic system, Shaftesbury has his own *hen kai pan,* and you can offer your system and what Lessing said [in your conversation with him]. Let the reader decide who is correct and victorious over the others. For me, the most beautiful ending to every philosophical dialogue is ultimately the resulting divergence of opinions. This is exactly what you have done in your text. By the way, you present Lessing in such a way that I can see and hear him speaking. Adieu, dear friend. Stay well, and think of me with love. For love is the supreme being, and God is love. . . .

Weimar, December 20, 1784

. . . I am afraid, dear friend, that it is not I who am confused about Spinoza's intention, but you. While you were away I reread him, although sections of his writings and not his complete works; my first impression of him was reconfirmed. His notion of a single substance is that *ens realissimum*,[37] in which everything that constitutes truth, intimacy, and existence is united *intus* and *radicaliter*;[38] it is that substance alone through which all things can be conceived; and in all the appearances of individual things, as modifications of the supreme, eternal intimate existence, these attributes are only conceivable insofar as they are of its nature and insofar as that single, dynamic existence *continually* dwells in them. Do not make this being into an abstract concept! This being alone *exists;* I exist through it, only insofar as I blossom like a small branch on this eternal and unending root of the tree of life. God is, of course, outside you and yet acts for, in, and through all creatures. (I myself do not know the extramundane God.) What should God mean to you, however, if he is not in you, and if you do not feel and taste his existence in an infinitely intimate way, and if he does not also enjoy his own being in you as one part of his thousand million parts? You want God in human form, as a friend who thinks about you. Bear in mind that if God is understood in this way, then God would have to think about you in a human, that is, in a limited way. Further, if God favored you, God would have to be against others. Tell me, then, why do you need to view God in *one* human form? He speaks to you and affects you through all noble human forms who have been his agents, especially through the agent of agents, his only-begotten son, who is the heart of the spiritual creation. Yet God acted through his son only insofar as he was a mortal human being like you and me. In order to enjoy the divinity within him, you yourself must become a human being of God. In other words, there must be something in you that participates in God's nature. You can take pleasure in God only and always according to your innermost self. In this way God, as source and root of this spiritual, eternal existence, is unchangeably and ineradicably within you. This is the teaching of Christ, of Moses, and of all apostles, sages, and prophets. But they all expressed this according to the diverse times in which they lived and according to the measure of their depth of knowledge and capacity for pleasure. If this peace of God in the heart of an individual being to whom God has revealed himself is higher than all reason, then how infinitely higher must God be above all power of thought and the movements of all individual beings in him, who is the heart of all hearts, the supreme concept of all individual ways of thinking, and the most intimate pleasure of all kinds of pleasure which find their source, root, sum, purpose, and center in him. If you understand this innermost, supreme, all-embracing concept to be an empty name, then you are the atheist, not Spinoza. According to him, this concept is the essence of essences, Yahweh.

37. [Latin for "most real being."]
38. [Latin for "within itself" and "from its root."]

See, you are, after all, a heretic, and this is what I wanted. I am just about finished and say *Quod erat demonstrandum.*[39]

Rather, dear Jacobi, I want you to read Spinoza's *Ethics* again from this perspective. Do not stumble against its Cartesian form, which is always only the words. Rather, think about what he intends with this offensive way of speaking. Does he not express the most necessary, supreme truth when he says, for example: God is sublime above all individual ways of thinking, thoughts, inclinations, movements of the will, and so on, even though God possesses them all in individual creatures as His modifications? Otherwise God could not understand and love them so intimately and could not operate through them as he now does. Nevertheless, God enjoys the most blessed internal peace as the unity of all entities, powers, and spaces. I must confess to you that this philosophy makes me very happy. If only I could open my innermost sensibilities in order to enjoy it completely and unreservedly! I hope for you the same, for it is the only philosophy that unites all ways of thinking and systems. Since you left, Goethe has read Spinoza. I believe it is a significant sign that he understood Spinoza the way I do. You have to join our camp!

GOD, SOME CONVERSATIONS

Fifth Conversation

THEANO: . . . Yesterday, Philolaus, you wanted to know the laws of God's economy in the world, or, as you put it, symbols that express his reality, power, wisdom, and goodness.[40] How is it possible, however, that Theophron should draw so few drops out of the ocean which flows around us? Yesterday I heard almost with disgust how you expressed opinions as if the existence of God could not be proven, and I was astonished, Theophron, that you wanted to engage in these petty subtleties. The existence of an entity can be known, it seems to me, only through the existence and the intuition[41] of that entity; it cannot be known through arbitrary concepts and empty words any more than it can be eliminated by them. There is a saying that we become neither rich nor satisfied through dreams; the same can be said about words. We are human beings, and as such, it seems to me, we must learn to know God in the way that he actually *gave* and revealed himself to us. Through concepts we apprehend him only as a concept, through words only as a word. But through intuitions[42] of nature, through the use of our powers, through the

39. [Latin for "I have proved what I set out to prove." It is used at the end of logical proofs.]
40. [SW 16:532-72. See also Herder's *Versuch über das Sein,* 1764.]
41. [*Anschauung.* Anschauung can also mean "experience" or "observation." In the second edition, Herder uses the word *Erfahrung,* which means experience, instead of *Anschauung.*]
42. [*Anschauungen* (pl.). In the second edition, Herder uses *Anschauung* in the singular.]

pleasures of life, we take pleasure in God as actual existence full of power and life [*wirkliches Dasein voll Kraft und Leben*]. If you call this Enthusiasm, then I wish to be an Enthusiast, for I would rather see and enjoy the actual rose than drearily speculate about an imagined or a painted rose.

THEOPHRON: Well said, Theano! But you do, after all, see the rose that gives you pleasure, and you would not blindfold your eyes because of that pleasure. And what are you working on there? Oh, you are embroidering this flower yourself. You are then imitating the art of nature, which your attentive eye made visible to you, and which now your mind's eye, your lively memory, "traces" for the needle. Do not, therefore, exclude thought from any feeling or from any pleasure you take in creation. Thought is as necessary for our experience[43] of God, as the image of the sketch in your soul is necessary to your working needle. Whoever seeks only to taste and to feel the Creator, without seeing or knowing him, also misunderstands humankind.

THEANO: Do not reproach me, Theophron, for I am warning Philolaus precisely against a similar error of one-sidedness. I take great pleasure in philosophy when it confines itself to objects of nature and illuminates them. I was very happy when you drew your friend's attention to the beauty, goodness, and truth that is not arbitrarily tacked onto objects, but rather lies in every being as reality itself and constitutes that being. Since then I have tried to discover this point of pure necessity in everything around me, and I always perceive truth, goodness, and beauty in it. I wish that I could arrange my whole life, all my affairs, my slightest art, yes, even this insignificant embroidered flower, in such a way that Minerva herself at her loom would have to say, "It could not have been done in any other way." . . .

THEOPHRON: . . . Necessity is not compulsion, not internal or external pressure, although it seems to be to an inexperienced, lazy, and capricious person. Its yoke is gentle and its burden light once one becomes accustomed to it. Woe to those who become hardened in evil habits! But joy to all thinking, active beings for whom duty and the best way of practicing it become their nature, that is, their necessity. They possess within themselves the reward of the good angels of whom religion says that they are secure in goodness and can no longer either fall or want to fall because their duty is their nature, because their virtue is their heaven and their supreme happiness. Let us also strive, my friends, to take pleasure in the inner reward of these blessed beings. But why should we only take them as an example? All around us in nature we are guided by the model of our Father himself who acts in the smallest and largest affairs without any weak arbitrariness, but with the whole beauty and goodness of an independent reason, truth, and necessity.

43. [*Anschauen*. In the second edition, Herder uses *zum Innewerden Gottes*.]

I see, Philolaus, that you are getting your notebook ready. But first you and our friend, Theano, must help me discover the propositions that you want to write down.

PHILOLAUS: I will do this gladly, as soon as you show me the way.

THEOPHRON: All right, then, my friends! The deity itself will assist us because we are striving to unfold the nature of its being and of its works as the wisest, supreme necessity. In creating beings in a way that is incomprehensible to us, is there anything higher that the deity could give them than what is supreme in the deity itself: *existence* [*Dasein*]? In God, existence is the ground and essence of all pleasure, the root of all God's infinite powers; the same is true in every existing thing. Despite all our dependence, we are or think ourselves to be substances, and we feel our existence with such inner certainty, with such tender love and joy, that we not only do not like thinking about the destruction of our existence but also cannot, try as we might, conceive of it. It is the nature of the thinking mind that it has absolutely no conception of nothingness, and it requires a strange barrenness of mind even to imagine that nothingness is a conceivable idea. The mind can conceive a sign for nothingness, such as "0" or "the division of -1," and when it recognizes two things as contradictory, it can negate one through the other. That is to say, it can clearly understand that while it conceives one part of the contradiction, it cannot at the same time also conceive the other as the first. Yet the mind has no idea at all of absolute nothingness. Instead of the full space of the world, it can imagine, for example, a tremendous, black, empty space. But it thereby still does not imagine nothingness. In short, nothing is nothing; therefore, nothingness is completely unthinkable to every being that exists, let alone to the essence of all reality—God Himself. Do you see, Philolaus, what depends on this inner necessity of the concept of existence for every thinking being?

PHILOLAUS: The most beautiful truth depends on it, namely, that nothingness does not exist in nature, that there never was nor will be nothingness because nothingness is something inconceivable, it is nothing. . . .

THEANO: . . . There can be no higher, more blessed existence than what gives all things existence, what gives all things enjoyment and life. If the existence of everything rests on an inner necessity of God's supreme wisdom and goodness, then God cannot sustain anything laboriously. Everything sustains itself in the same way that a sphere rests on its center of gravity, for everything that exists is grounded in God's own eternal essence [*Wesen*],[44] in his power, goodness, and wisdom. You have, indeed, warned us against using images [of God], Theophron, but is it so intolerable to think of [the image of] the root that sustains the tree? The root would die, it would not be

44. [In the second edition, Herder uses *Dasein*.]

a root, if it did not have to sustain that beautiful creation of the trunk along with its branches, twigs, blossoms, and fruit. In the same way, God is the eternal root of the immeasurable tree of life that spreads throughout the universe. God is the infinite source of existence, the source of the greatest gift that only he could impart.

THEOPHRON: And what a pledge this gift offers us, my friends, for the continuance of our lives! Existence is an indivisible concept, an essence. Existence can no more be reduced to nothingness than there can be nothingness or than the deity could annihilate itself. I am not now speaking about appearances, about combinations of some sort of form in what we call space and time. Everything that appears must also disappear: Every temporal flower carries within itself the seed of decay, which provides that it does not last forever in its particular appearance. What is composed is decomposed, for precisely this composition and decomposition is the order of the world and the ever-active life of the world-spirit. I am also not yet speaking about the immortality of the human soul, and I am not at all willing to describe to you any phantoms of the imagination, such as how the soul will take on other organs and renew the exercise of its powers in space and time, that is, in the great order of the world. Our subject at hand is a simple concept—existence—in which the lowest as well as the highest being participate. Nothing can perish, nothing can be annihilated. Otherwise, God would have to annihilate himself. Yet everything composed is decomposed; everything that occupies space and time shifts. Hence, since everything that can and does exist is grounded in infinite existence, how infinite the world becomes, my friend—infinite in space and time and in itself infinitely enduring. God has imparted the ground of His own supreme happiness to entities, the smallest and the greatest, who take pleasure in existence, as God does. To use your simile, Theano, all beings, like branches, draw the eternal sap of life from his root. I think, Philolaus, that we have outlined the first natural law of sacred necessity.

PHILOLAUS: 1.*The supreme existence* [Dasein] *knew nothing greater to give His creatures than existence* [Dasein].

THEOPHRON: But, my friend, as simple as the concept is, one existence and another are very different in regard to their condition. Philolaus, what do you think designates their gradations and differences?

PHILOLAUS: Nothing but *forces* [*Kräfte*]. We found no higher conception in God himself; all his forces, however, were but *one* force. The supreme power [*höchste Macht*] could be nothing but the supreme wisdom and goodness that is ever-living, ever-active.

THEOPHRON: Now you yourself see, Philolaus, that the supreme one, or rather the all (for God is not the supreme being in a progressive scale of beings like himself), could reveal himself as active in nothing else but in the *universe*. Nothing could lie dormant in him, and what he expressed was himself—an indivisible wisdom, goodness, and omnipotence. The world of God is thus the best, not because he chose it among worse worlds, but rather because neither good nor bad existed without God and because, according to the inner necessity of his existence, he could effect nothing bad. Therefore, all powers exist that could exist; all of them are an expression of the all-wise, all-good, and all-beautiful. He is active in the smallest and in the largest, in every point of space and time, that is, in every lively force[45] of the universe. For space and time are but phantoms of our imagination; they are the measuring instruments of a limited understanding that must acquaint itself with things in succession and side by side. For God, neither time nor space exist, but rather everything exists in an eternal union. *He is before all things, and all things exist in him.* The whole world is an expression, an appearance, of his ever-living, ever-active forces.

THEANO: We can be so glad that, even though we are insignificant appearances, there dwells within us an expression of the three supreme forces of God and the world: *power, understanding, and goodness.* I can imagine no other, let alone higher, attributes than these. This is because what I see as divine in all the works of nature leads back to these three attributes. They explain one another, and their supreme essence and origin dwells in God. Thus, we also have the essential law of God in us: to order our limited power according to ideas of truth and goodness, as the almighty himself practices them in accordance with his most perfect nature. He thereby imparted something of his essence to us and made us into images of his perfection, for it is the nature of a divine force not to operate blindly, but to operate with supreme understanding and with a goodness that drives out all nothingness. Yet how far do we depart from this law with every arbitrary, irrational, and evil use of these powers!

THEOPHRON: Do not worry, Theano, for if it lies within the essence of every divine power to operate not blindly but rather according to wisdom and goodness, then this apparent shadow in creation will also clear itself up for us. It seems to me, Philolaus, that we can now write down the second great proposition of divine necessity.

2. *The deity, in whom there is but one essential force that we call power, wisdom, and goodness, could create nothing but a living copy of the same, which consequently is itself power, wisdom, and goodness, and these three powers inseparably form the essence of every existence appearing in the world.*

PHILOLAUS: I have written down the proposition and understand it on the basis of the nature of God. I wish, however, that you would illustrate it for Theano and me with specific examples. The levels of perfection in the world are so innumerably diverse that the lowest of them seem to us imperfections.

45. [*lebendige Kraft.* This expression is probably a translation of Leibniz's *vis viva*—the monads as living forces.]

THEOPHRON: Could it be otherwise, Philolaus? If everything possible exists and must exist, according to the principle of an infinite divine force, then the lowest as well as the highest perfection must exist in this universe. They are all united, however, by the wisest goodness, and even in the lowest of them there is no nothingness, that is, nothing that is essentially evil. . . . You know, Philolaus, what great things Leibniz claimed for his simple substances. "They are mirrors of the universe endowed with powers of perception to present and reflect the universe, each according to its point of view. The infinite sees the all in the smallest thing and the smallest thing in the all." Although this idea was sublime and is necessary, as soon as the world was viewed as a work of the supreme perfection, in which all parts are connected, many people understood the idea falsely. The infinitesimally simple mirrors of the universe were especially interpreted in an unworthy way. Let us, therefore, do away with this deceptive image because images do not belong in philosophy. Instead let us say, "Every substantial force according to its essence is an expression of the supreme power, wisdom, and goodness as it could exhibit and reveal itself in a particular place within the universe, that is, in relation to all other forces." In order to understand this, we need only to observe how each one of these substantial forces operates in the world. You agree with me, do you not, Philolaus, that it functions *organically* [*organisch*]?

PHILOLAUS: Indeed, for I am unaware of any force that demonstrates itself outside of bodies, without organs, but I am equally unaware of how these forces and these organs have come together.

THEOPHRON: Through their reciprocal nature, Philolaus. In the interconnected realm of the most perfect power and wisdom, they could not do otherwise, for what are we calling "body"? What are we calling "organs"? In the human body, for example, nothing is inanimate. From the tip of the hair to the end of the nail, everything is permeated with a sustaining, nourishing force; and as soon as this force leaves the smallest or greatest part of the body, that part separates itself from the body. With this separation, the part no longer exists in the field of the lively forces of our human race; but this part never falls out of the realm of the forces of nature. The faded hair, the discarded nail, now enters another region of the world's interconnectedness, in which it once again acts or is acted upon in no other way than according to its present nature. Look closely at the miracles that the physiology of the human body or of any animal body presents to us. You see nothing other than a *realm of living forces;* each in its own place is creating by virtue of its effects the interconnection, structure, and life of the whole and is ensuing from its own essential nature. Thus, the body forms and sustains itself, daily decomposes, and finally decomposes altogether. Everything that we call "matter" is, therefore, more or less self-animated; everything is a realm of active forces that *form a whole,* not only in appearance for our senses but also in accordance with their nature and their relation. One force dominates. Otherwise, there would be no unity, no whole. Various forces serve on the most diverse levels; but all parts of this diversity, each of which is perfectly determined, nevertheless possess something common, active, interactive. Otherwise, they would not form a unity, a whole. Because everything is most wisely interconnected in the realm of the most perfect power and wisdom; and because nothing in this realm can combine, sustain, or form itself except according to the inherent, necessary laws of the things themselves; we therefore see everywhere in nature *innumerable "organic wholes"* [*Organizationen*], and each in its own way is not simply wise, good, and beautiful but rather is something complete, that is, a copy of the wisdom, goodness, and beauty such as can be made visible in this interconnection. Thus, arbitrariness does not prevail anywhere in the world—not in a leaf of a tree, in a grain of sand, in a fibril of our body; everything is determined, placed, and ordered by forces that act in every point of creation according to the most perfect wisdom and goodness. Examine, my friends, the history of deformities, cases of corruption, and atrocities, when the laws of nature seem to have been thrown in disarray through foreign causes. The laws of nature were never thrown into disarray: Every force operates true to its nature, even when another force disrupts it, for even this disruption cannot bring about anything except that the disrupted force seeks to compensate for itself in another way. I have made special observations about these cases of compensation in a system of disrupted forces. We can discuss them at another time. But everywhere, even in the apparently greatest chaos, I have found *constant nature,* that is, unchangeable laws of supreme necessity, goodness, and wisdom that are active in every force.

PHILOLAUS: I am happy, Theophron, that you have clarified the obscure concept of matter for me. For although I gladly agreed with Leibniz's system that stated matter could be nothing but a phenomenon of our senses, an aggregate of substantial monads, the so-called "ideal connection between substances" in this system remained a mystery to me. . . . Now, matter remains for me not merely an appearance *in my idea* or something merely united through the ideas of perceiving creatures; matter is united through its nature and truth, through the intimate interconnection of active forces. Nothing in nature is isolated: Nothing is without cause, nothing without effect. And because everything exists in union and everything possible exists, it follows that there is also nothing in nature that is not part of an organic whole. Every force stands in union with other forces that either serve it or rule over it. Consequently, if my soul is a substantial force and its present realm of activity is destroyed, then it can never lack a new organ in a creation in which there is no gap, no leap, no island. New, serving forces will assist the soul and form a new sphere of activity for it in its new interconnection with a world in which everything is interconnected . . .

THEOPHRON: And what a necessary duty follows, dear Philolaus, to make sure that the soul proceeds in a well-ordered way from within itself, within the system of its forces, for the soul can act only as it is; its external form can also only appear according to the form of its inner forces. Our body is only an instrument, a mirror of the soul; every organic whole is an external copy of internal efforts that make its appearance endure.

PHILOLAUS: This reminds me of many beautiful remarks Spinoza made about the relation between body and soul. For although in accordance with the Cartesian system, he viewed the body and soul, like thought and extension, as totally independent of one another, an intelligent spirit like Spinoza could not fail to present his views on the harmony of the two. . . .

THEANO: I enjoy your conversation very much, my friends. You have appointed me to guide you back to the path, however, if you wander from it, so I would like you to end the discussion of this endless matter of phys- iognomy and return to the more general theme of your conversation. I am always satisfied with little, and it is enough for me to know that every organic whole is the appearance of a system of inner, living forces that, according to the laws of wisdom and goodness, form a kind of miniature world, a whole. I wish that I could charm the spirit of the rose, which is the object of my embroidering, so that it would tell me how it formed the rose's beautiful structure; or since the rose is only a daughter of the rosebush, I wish that its dryad could explain to me how it animates the little rosebush from the root to its smallest branch. As a child I often stood quietly before a tree or a flower and gazed in wonder at the amazing harmony that is found from top to bottom in every living creature. I compared many of them and idled away several hours examining the leaves, branches, blossoms, stems, and entire devel- opment of trees and plants. The longing to draw such original, beautiful forms in a vivid way sharpened my attention, and I often entered into such an intimate conversation with the flower, the tree, the plant, that I believed its captured essence would have to enter into my small creation. But this was all in vain. My creation remained a dead imitation, and that beautiful, transitory creature stood there in all the fullness of its calm self-sufficiency and the fullness of, so to speak, an *existence complete in and for itself*. Please discuss this matter more fully, and help my stammering language about nature.

THEOPHRON: Dear Theano, this language will probably always be stam- mering. We have no senses to see into the inner essence of things; we stand on the outside and have to observe. The clearer and calmer the eye with which we do this, the more the living harmony of nature reveals itself to us—a harmony in which everything is the most perfect unity, and yet everything is interwoven with every other thing in such multifarious and diverse ways. Art follows this observation of nature, and the recent, more attentive discipline of natural science is its sister. It observes in every thing what it is, how it is formed, and how it acts and is acted upon. It has collected treasures of experiences of plants, trees, minerals, animals, and so on, and of their origin, development, blossom and decay, about their diseases, death and life. These experiences show us with each individual object a world of self-subsisting harmony, goodness, and wisdom. But we are not going to speak about this subject now. It is better to look at all of this in the beautiful days of summer and spring than to hear about this now in a conversation in the evening. I do want to draw your attention to the simple laws, according to which all living forces of nature produce their thousandfold organic wholes, for everything that the supreme wisdom does must be supremely simple. The laws seem to me, then, to lie in three words that are fundamentally only one vital concept: (1) *persistence,* that is, the inherent continuance of every entity; (2) the *union* of likes and the separation of opposites; and (3) the *resemblance* of a being with itself, and the reproduction of its essence in another. If, Theano, to use your expression, you want to hear me also "stammer" about these, then my speech is at your service. At least you and I, Philolaus, will crown our conversation about Spinoza, for you know that he himself built his ethics on these concepts.

First, *every being is what it is* and has neither a conception of nor a longing for nothingness. The whole perfection of a thing is its *reality*; the feeling of this reality is the inherent reward of a thing's existence, its inner joy. In the so-called moral world, which is also the natural world, Spinoza sought to reduce all human passions and strivings to this inner love for existence and for persistence in this existence; in the physical world, various names, some of which were unworthy, were given to the appearances that follow from this natural law. Sometimes this is called the "force of inertia" because every thing continues to be what it is and does not change without cause. Other times, from another perspective, this is called the "force of gravity," according to which each thing has its center of gravity on which it rests. Inertia and gravity, like their opponent, motion, are mere appearances because space and bodies themselves are only appearances. What is true and essential in them is persistence—continuation of a thing's existence—through which it neither may nor can destroy itself. The structure itself of each thing shows that each thing strives toward a state of persistence, and you, dear Theano, as one artist of nature, will be able to explain much in the form of things, if you turn your attention to this. . . .

THEANO: . . . You spoke of a second law of nature: *All likes unite, and opposites separate.* Do you not want to give an example of this?

THEOPHRON: . . . You are certainly familiar, Theano, with the stone of hate and love in the natural world.

THEANO: You mean the magnet.

THEOPHRON: Exactly. Although theories about it are still very obscure, experiences of it are all the more clear. Do you know the two poles of the magnet and their friendly or inimical effect?

THEANO: Yes, and I also know that on its axis there is a point of greatest love and a point of complete indifference.

THEOPHRON: So you know everything necessary for understanding my example. Think of the magnet as a round drop in which the magnetic force is distributed so uniformly and evenly that its opposite ends form the north and south poles. You are aware that one cannot come into being without the other.

THEANO: Yes, and I also know that if you change one or the other, then you change both.

THEOPHRON: The magnet gives you the most beautiful image of the nature of hate and love in creation, and I am certain that the very same thing will be found in many, perhaps in all fluids.

PHILOLAUS: And what is this very same thing?

THEOPHRON: Whenever a system of similar forces acquires an axis, they settle around the axis and its center in such a way that according to geometric laws likes flow to one pole, and the powers arrange themselves from this pole through all grades of progression to a culmination, and then arrange themselves through the point of neutrality to the opposite pole. In this way, every sphere would be a union of two half-spheres with opposite poles, just as every ellipse has its two foci; and according to fixed rules, the laws of this construction would lie in the active forces of the system that is thereby formed. Just as in a sphere there can be no north pole without a south pole, in a system of forces that is formed according to laws there can be no structure in which the friendly and the inimical do not likewise separate. Consequently, it forms a whole precisely through the counterbalance that is accomplished by the two increasing and decreasing levels of the union. . . .

Because everything in the world exists that can exist, opposites must also exist, and a law of supreme wisdom must everywhere form a system from this opposition, from the north and south poles. In every sphere of nature there is the entire series of thirty-two winds; in every ray of sunshine there is the whole range of colors; and it is only a question of which wind blows at this moment or that one, which color appears here or there. As soon as a solid emerges from a fluid, everything is crystalized and formed according to the inherent laws that lie in this system of active forces. Everything attracts, repels, or remains indifferent in relation to other things, and the axis of these active forces goes through all levels of existence. The chemist brings about nothing but marriages and divorces; nature brings them about in a much richer, more intimate way. Everything seeks and finds what it loves, and physics itself had no choice but to adopt the expression "elective attraction" for the combination of bodies. Opposites repel and come together only through the point of indifference. The forces often alternate rapidly: Whole systems behave differently than the individual forces of a system in relation to one another. Hate can become love, love can become hate; all this is done for one and the same reason because every individual system *endeavors to persist in itself and orders its forces to this end.* You can see how careful one must be when making analogies between external appearances; one is not immediately justified in holding magnetism and, for example, electricity to be one thing just because one finds a few similar laws operating in both. The systems of forces can radically differ from one another and yet operate according to the same sort of laws, because in nature everything must finally be interconnected, and only one principal law can exist according to which even the most diverse powers are arranged.

THEANO: It seems to me that your law of persistence, of hate and love, comes very close to this principal law, because it appears everywhere in spite of all the innumerable differences and oppositions in nature. I would like to be a higher spirit for a few moments so that I could observe this great workshop from the inside.

THEOPHRON: Do not wish this, Theano. The external observer has a better, at least a more pleasant, situation than the internal observer who could never survey the whole. The spectator who stands before the stage is more comfortable than the one who listens from backstage. Searching for truth is more attractive; possessing the truth might make one satisfied and lazy. The very value of human life consists in this: investigating nature, surmising its great laws; then observing, demonstrating, and confirming them; next finding them verified in a thousand ways and applying them in new ways; and finally perceiving, appreciating, and appropriating the same supremely wise law, the same sacred necessity. After all, dear Theano, are we merely spectators? Are we not ourselves actors, nature's assistants and its imitators? Do not love and hate also reign in the realm of human beings? Are not both equally necessary for the formation of the whole? Whoever cannot hate, cannot love; one must learn, however, to love properly and to hate properly. There is also a point of indifference among human beings. But thank goodness that it is only one point in the whole magnetic axis.

PHILOLAUS: I must remind you, Theophron, that you still owe us your third part of the great law of nature, that is, *how entities resemble one another and in their reproduction form a continuous series.*

THEANO: I do not need to leave now, do I, Theophron?

THEOPHRON: Heavens, no, Theano! For we are speaking about the holiest and certainly a most divine law. All things that love one another, resemble one another. Just as two colors shine together so that a third, intermediate one comes into being, through sympathetic union human beings resemble one another in a wonderful way, even in bearing and facial expressions and in the most subtle tactics of thought and action. Mental illness, disease, enthusiasm, fear, and any emotional disturbance are infectious evils, not because of something evil or insignificant in them, but rather because of the strength of their active forces. How then should the effect of regular forces, that is, order, harmony, beauty not extend and impart itself to others with much more essential power? We saw that organic wholes come into being only when stronger forces draw the weaker ones into their realm and form them into a structure according to innate laws of a necessary goodness and truth. All goodness imparts itself: It has the nature of God, who cannot do other than impart himself. Goodness also has God's infallible efficacy. . . .

THEANO: . . . I like your way of thinking, Theophron, because it makes the all-active one present to me everywhere—the one who acts upon us with essential laws of harmony and beauty through the existence of his creatures themselves. I feel now that everything that lives in God's realm should become like God, indeed, if I may say so, must become like him. Even against our will, his essence, his thoughts and actions force themselves upon us as immutable laws in thousands upon thousands of demonstrations of his order, goodness, and beauty. Those who do follow willingly, must follow, for we are drawn by everything, and we cannot escape the all-powerful chain. Happy are those who follow willingly! They inwardly possess the sweet, illusive reward of forming themselves, even though God constantly forms them. By obeying with reason and serving with love, they are marked among all creatures and events with the character of the deity. They become rational, good, orderly, happy; they become like God.

But let us go back to the economy of nature. Is there not coercion in the fact that one force overcomes another, draws that force to itself, and unites with its nature? When I notice that the entire life of creatures rests on the destruction of other species, that human beings live on animals, and animals live on other animals or on plants and fruits, then I see organic wholes that are, of course, forming themselves but at the same time destroying others. In other words, I see murder and death in creation. Is not a blade of grass, a flower, a fruit from the tree, and finally an animal that becomes the food of another just as beautiful an organic whole as the one that destructively converts it into itself? Theophron, drive this dark cloud away! Like a veil, it is covering up my view of the sun that shines forth for me from every creature!

THEOPHRON: It will fly away, Theano, as soon as you realize that without this seeming death in creation, everything would be a genuine death, that is, an inactive rest, an empty realm of shadows in which all genuine, active existence would perish. A moment ago you were speaking like a disciple of Plato. Did you not discover through your teacher that in flux *everything* is change, that on the wings of time *everything* is process, haste, migration? If you stopped one wheel in creation, then all wheels would stand still; if you allowed one point of what we call matter to be inactive and dead, then death would be everywhere. Philolaus, you are not under the unphilosophical illusion, are you, that there is, for example, an absolutely solid body in nature?

PHILOLAUS: How could I be? If such a body existed, then all motion would be frustrated; and no matter how small the body were, it would stop the wheels of the whole creation.

THEOPHRON: Well, then, if there can be no absolute rest, no complete impenetrability, solidity, inactivity that would be an all-devitalizing nothingness and hence a contradiction, then, my friends, we have to venture to think in line with Plato that everything changeable is one wave, that everything temporal is one dream. Are you afraid, Theano? Do not be afraid! It is the wave of a river which is entirely *existence* itself; it is the dream of an independent, essential *truth*. The eternal one, who wanted to become visible in the appearances of time, the indivisible one, who wanted to become visible in the shapes of space, could not do otherwise than to give each form the shortest and, at the same time, the longest existence that its appearance required according to the image of space and time. Everything that appears must disappear; everything disappears as soon as it can, yet remains as long as it can. Here, as everywhere, the two extremes fall together and are actually one and the same. Every limited being, as an appearance, brings with itself the seed of destruction. With unremitting pace, it hastens toward the highest point so that it can hurry down and become, to our senses, the smallest thing. . . . Thus, there is no death in creation. Death is a *hastening away of what cannot remain, that is, it is the effect of an eternally young, restless, enduring force.* In accordance with its nature, this force cannot for one moment be idle, motionless, or inactive; it always operates in the richest, most beautiful way for its own existence and for the existence of as many others as it is able to produce and impart. In a world in which everything is transformed, each individual force operates eternally and hence its parts are in an eternal process of transformation, for this transformation itself is but the expression of an indestructible activity full of wisdom, goodness, and beauty. . . . Can you think of a more beautiful law of wisdom and goodness in what we call change, Theano, than the law that everything presses with utmost haste toward new life, toward new, youthful power and beauty, and thus changes every moment?

THEANO: I see a lovely glimmer, Theophron, but I do not yet see the dawn.

THEOPHRON: Now think about all of the forces of nature in this restless work, in this haste toward change on the wings of time. The minutest part of a leaf cannot be idle for a moment; otherwise, there would be death in creation. It attracts, it repels, it evaporates. That is why, Theano, the two sides of the leaf are formed so differently; the forces that dwell within it are formed so differently; the forces that dwell within it are changing their organic dress. Life is, therefore, motion, activity; *the activity of an inner force that is connected to the deepest pleasure of and the striving toward persistence.* Because nothing can remain unchanged in the realm of change, and yet everything wants to and must maintain its existence, everything is in this restless motion, in this eternal palingenesis, so that it will last forever and appear eternally young.

THEANO: Is this change also progress?

THEOPHRON: Let us suppose it is not. Change would still be the sole means of escaping death and an eternal death. In other words, change would maintain our living force in continual activity, in inward existence. If this were the case, change would still be as desirable a benefit as eternal life is in comparison to eternal death. But, Theano, can you easily think of a continual life, a continually active force, without a continuation of activity [*Fortwirkung*]? In other words, can you think of a progression without progress?

THEANO: It seems to be a contradiction.

THEOPHRON: It is one! Every force that takes on appearances in space and time must of course keep within the limits that are given to it precisely by space and time. But with every activity, its subsequent activity becomes easier; and because it cannot do this except according to innate, internal laws of harmony, wisdom, and goodness, which, as you yourself claimed, are lovingly forced and impressed upon every creature, and which assist every creature in every one of its activities, you see everywhere a *progress from chaos to order, an inner increase and enhancement* of forces in ever-expanding limits according to laws of harmony and order which are increasingly observed. Light imposes itself upon every blind force; reason and goodness impose themselves on every lawless force. None of its operations, no activity in nature was in vain. *Hence, there must be progress in the kingdom of God, for there can be no point of inactivity in it, and still less a retrogression.* By the way, our eyes should not be offended by forms of death, for if there is no death in creation, there is also no form of death. Whether we call this form decay, nourishment, or pulverization, it is the transition to a new, young, organic whole—the old, worn-out caterpillar spinning its cocoon so that it may appear as a new creation. Are you satisfied, Theano?

THEANO: I am, and I rely on the wisest, supreme goodness that brought me here, gave me so many powers that I did not merit but that were certainly not given in vain, and surrounded me with a thousand forces full of love and goodness to order my understanding, my heart, and my actions according to one eternal law of necessary, self-grounded wisdom and goodness.

Philolaus, you are not saying a word, and you let me, the one who should be and intended to be quiet, do all the talking. You even forgot about your notebook.

PHILOLAUS: I will catch up now and immediately add a list of conclusions that seem to me to follow undeniably from Theophron's system of an intrinsically necessary truth and goodness. I stopped at the second principle. To continue, then:

3. *All the forces of nature operate organically. Each organic whole is nothing but a system of living forces that serve a principal force in accordance with eternal laws of wisdom, goodness, and beauty.*

4. The laws according to which the latter principal force rules and the former forces serve are: *inherent continuance of each being, the union of likes and separation of opposites, and finally, resemblance of a thing with itself and the reproduction of its essence in another.* These are activities through which the deity has revealed itself; and no other, higher activities are conceivable.

5. *There is no death in creation; rather, there is transformation.* This transformation occurs in accordance with the wisest, best law of necessity. According to this law every force in the realm of change seeks to maintain itself in ever new and active ways, and thus each force continually changes its organic dress through attraction and repulsion, through friendship and enmity.

6. *There is no rest in creation,* for idle rest would be death. Every lively force acts and continues to act: With every continuation of activity, the force progresses and perfects itself according to inherent, eternal laws of wisdom and goodness which impose themselves upon this force and lie within it.

7. *The more a force perfects itself, the more it affects others,* expands its limits, and organizes and impresses upon them the image of goodness and beauty that lies within it. Thus, in the whole of nature, one necessary law prevails: *Order emerges from chaos, active forces emerge from dormant capacities.* The activity of this law cannot be stopped.

8. *Evil as a reality does not exist in the kingdom of God.* All that is evil is nothing. But we call evil that which is *limitation, opposition, or transition.* None of these three deserves this name.

Theophron, I would like to speak to you about this point. I am thinking about a theodicy of wise necessity.

9. Just as limits belong to the measure of every existence in space and time, and just as opposites must also exist in the kingdom of God in which everything exists, so it belongs to the supreme goodness of this kingdom that *opposites themselves help and advance one another,* for only through the union of both does a world come into existence in every substance, that is, an existing whole that is wholly good and beautiful.

10. *Even human errors are good in the eyes of the wise,* for these errors necessarily soon reveal themselves as errors to the wise and thus help them by way of contrast toward greater light, toward purer goodness and truth.

Are you satisfied with my conclusions, Theophron?

THEOPHRON: Absolutely! Your keen mind always hastens me forward, Philolaus, like a noble steed who needs only to be shown the racetrack and flies to the goal. I am grateful for the shade of Spinoza that provided me with such pleasant hours of conversation with you. I rarely have the opportunity to speak about matters of this kind, and yet they advance our thinking in such a unique way and educate it toward the clear, sharp, unique, necessary truth. These conversations with you have also provided me with a second pleasure in that they bring me back to the ideas of my youth with which I spent, and certainly did more than dream away, many sweet hours in the bosom of *Leibniz, Shaftesbury, and Plato.*

4

Literature and
the Bible

CONCLUSIONS DRAWN FROM THE COMPARISON
OF THE POETRY OF DIVERSE PEOPLES
OF ANCIENT AND MODERN TIMES

Poetry is a Proteus among peoples: It changes its form in accordance with a people's language, morals, habits, temperament, climate, and even with their accent.[1]

Nations migrate; languages mix with other languages and change; human beings come into contact with new things; their tendencies assume different directions, their strivings take on different purposes; new archetypes influence the structure of their images and ideas; even that tiny part of the body, the tongue, moves differently, and the ear becomes accustomed to new sounds. In the same way, poetry assumes different forms not only among diverse nations but also within one people. Greek poetry was something different at the time of Homer than it was at the time of Longinus.[2] The very concept of poetry differed in these two periods. Poetry meant something completely different to the Roman and to the monk; to the Arab and to the crusader; to the scholar who uncovers other ages and to the poet and the people in diverse periods of diverse nations. The word itself is such an abstract idea with so many meanings that if it is not clearly supported by concrete examples, then it vanishes in the clouds like a phantom. This is why the quarrel about the *superiority of either ancient or modern literature* was meaningless, for it was often carried on without reference to specific examples.

1. [SW 18:134-40.]
2. [Cassius Longinus (ca. 213-73). Greek rhetorician and philosopher who was more celebrated for his critical and rhetorical work than for his philosophical writings.]

This quarrel became even more meaningless as people adopted either a false standard of comparison or none at all. For on what grounds should the criteria in such a debate be determined? Should we judge the art of poetry on the basis of *the text themselves?* What a number of subtle specifications would be required to discover the perfect ideal of each literary form and genre in accordance with time and place, with means and ends, and to apply these specifications unbiasedly to every object of comparison! Or should we judge the art of the poet on the basis of *the poets themselves?* We would have to compare their possession of natural talents, who was granted more favorable circumstances, who more diligently made use of the tradition and resources at hand, who proclaimed a nobler goal, who demonstrated a wiser use of the powers to reach this goal. What another ocean of comparisons! The more one has tried to establish the standard for the poets of one or several peoples, the more one has worked in vain. People judge and rank poets according to their own favorite notions, according to the kind of poets they have known, according to the effect this or that poet has had on them. Educated people possess not only their own personal ideal of perfection but also their own standard of how to reach it, and they do not gladly trade this standard for somebody else's.

We cannot blame a nation for loving *its* poets above all others and not wanting to abandon them for foreign ones. The poets of a nation are, after all, *its* poets. They have thought in *its* language; they have used their imaginations within *its* context; they have felt the needs of the nation in which they were raised, and to those needs they have addressed themselves. Why should not a nation, therefore, empathize with *its own* poets, for a nation and its poets are tightly interconnected by a common bond of language, thoughts, needs, and feelings.

The Italians, the French, and the English biasedly esteem their own poets, often unfairly treating the poets of other peoples with contempt. Only the Germans have been tempted to overemphasize excessively the merits of foreign peoples, especially of the French and the English, thereby neglecting themselves. I am certainly in favor of the (albeit somewhat exaggerated) German adoration of Young when he was introduced through Ebert's translation (for we are not speaking here about Shakespeare, Milton, Thomson, Fielding, Goldsmith, and Sterne).[3] The translation not only has all the merits of a text

3. [Edward Young (1683-1765). English poet and literary critic. His poem, *Night Thoughts on Life, Death, and Immortality* (1742-45), was translated into German by J.A. Ebert in 1751, was extremely popular in Europe, and had a great impact on the *Sturm und Drang* and on German Romanticism. Shakespeare (1564-1616), John Milton (1608-74), James Thomson (1700-48), Henry Fielding (1707-54), Oliver Goldsmith (1730-74), and Laurence Sterne (1713-68) are all significant figures in English literature. Herder is saying in this passage that he is not concerned about the high estimation of the these authors, but about the Germans' exaggerated praise of less important English writers.]

in the original language but also cleans up and mitigates the exaggerations of the original English text by creating a harmonic prose and by adding the rich, moral commentaries from other nations. But the Germans should be reproached for the unwavering indifference with which they neglect and ignore the best poets of their own language in their schools and in the education of their young in general. No other neighboring nation does this. Through what means is our taste, our style of writing, supposed to develop? Through what means is our language supposed to take on structure and rules? How else except through the best writers of our nation? Through what means are we supposed to acquire patriotism and love of country except through our country's language, except through the most excellent thoughts and feelings that are expressed in this language and lie like a treasure within it? We would certainly not continue to be so unsure about matters of syntax after a thousand years of possessing a written language, if we had become acquainted with our best writers at childhood and chosen them as our guides.

Nevertheless, no love of country should prevent us from recognizing *everywhere* the good that could be increasingly produced only in the *great progression of times and peoples*. That sultan of old[4] rejoiced over the many religions in his kingdom, each glorifying God in its own way. For him, it was like a beautiful, colorful meadow in which all kinds of flowers blossomed. The same is true with the poetry of the peoples and periods on our earth. In every period and language, poetry embodied the imperfections and the perfections of a nation; poetry was a mirror of a nation's sentiments, the expression of its highest aspirations *(oratio sensitiva animi perfecta)*.[5] Juxtaposing these portraits (less and more perfect ideals, true and false ones) offers instructive delight. In poetry's gallery of diverse ways of thinking, diverse aspirations, and diverse desires, we come to know periods and nations far more intimately than we can through the misleading and pathetic method of studying their political and military history. From this latter kind of history, we rarely learn more about a people than how it was ruled and how it was wiped out. From its poetry, we learn about its way of thinking, its desires and wants, the ways it rejoiced, and the ways it was guided either by its principles or its inclinations. Granted, we still lack many resources for achieving this kind of general view into the souls of various peoples. Except for our view of Greek and Roman literature, dark clouds still hang over the Middle Ages, from which everything European emerged. Meinhard's weak *Essay on Italian Poets*[6] does not even get as far as Tasso,[7] to say nothing of similar weakness in essays about other

4. [Reference to Soleiman the Magnificent.]
5. [Latin for "speech that is sensitive to the perfections of the mind."]
6. [Johann Nicolaus Meinhard (1727-67). Herder is referring to Meinhard's book, *Versuche über den Charakter und die Werke der besten italienischen Dichter* (Braunschweig: Fürstliche Waysenhaus-Buchhandlung, 1763-64).]
7. [Torquato Tasso (1544-95). One of the great Italian poets.]

nations. The *Essay on Spanish Poets* died along with Dieze, the learned scholar of Spanish literature who edited Velazquez.[8]

There are three methods for achieving a general view of this field of human thought, which is filled with flowers and fruits, and each method has been used.

In accordance with his theory, Eschenburg[9] chose the method of *genres and literary forms* for his popular collection of literature. This is an instructive method for young students if they are guided by a bright teacher, for they can be completely misled by a term that is used to refer to extremely different things. The works of Homer, Virgil, Ariosto,[10] Milton, and Klopstock[11] are all called epics, and yet even according to the idea of art within these works, not to mention the spirit that inspires them, they are totally different works. Sophocles, Corneille,[12] and Shakespeare have in common only the title "writer of tragedy." The spirit behind their plays is totally different. The same is true with all genres of literature, right down to the epigram.

Others have classified poets according to *feelings,* especially since Schiller[13] has said many subtle and superb things about this. But look at the extent to which feelings flow into one another! What poet remains faithful to *one* kind of feeling to such an extent that it could designate his character, especially as it is expressed in different works? The poet often touches a string of many, even all, tones that soar precisely through dissonance. The world of feelings is a mysterious and often indivisible realm. Only the hand of the creator is able to classify the forms within it.

The third method is, if I may say so, the natural one: to leave each flower in its own context and from here to study it from its roots to its top just as it is, in reference to its own time and nature. The truly humble genius hates ranking and comparison. Genius prefers to be the first in the village rather than the second in rank behind Caesar. Lichen, moss, fern—each plant flourishes in its own context in the divine order.

Poetry has been classified "subjectively" and "objectively": according to the objects it depicts and according to the feelings that the author uses to present those objects. This is a genuine and useful approach that appears

8. [Luis Jose Velazquez de Velasco (1722-72) was a Spanish historian and poet. J. A. Dieze provided a copiously annotated German translation of his *Origenes de la poesia castellana* in 1769.]

9. [Johann Joachim Eschenburg (1743-1820). German literary historian.]

10. [Ludovico Ariosto (1474-1533). Italian poet and playwright. His most famous work is the epic poem, *Orlando furioso.*]

11. [Friedrich Gottlieb Klopstock (1724-1803). German poet who was well known for his epic poem, *Der Messias.*]

12. [Pierre Corneille (1606-84). French poet and dramatist who is considered to be the creator of French classical tragedy.]

13. See *Die Horen* (November/December 1795) and (January 1796). [This is a publication of Schiller's *Über naive und sentimentalische Dichtung.*]

suitable for characterizing individual poets such as Homer and Ossian, Thomson[14] and Kleist,[15] and so on. Homer narrates the stories of his prehistoric world without evidence of much involvement on his part; Ossian sings these stories from his wounded heart, from his bittersweet memories. Thomson depicts the seasons in a natural way; Kleist sings about his spring in a rhapsody of views inspired by feeling, often interrupting this rhapsody with thoughts about himself and his friends. However, even this kind of classification characterizes poets and periods of poetry very weakly. For even Homer is involved in the objects that he depicts but as a Greek, as a narrator, like the balladeers and fabulists of the Middle Ages, and like Ariosto, Spenser,[16] Cervantes,[17] and Wieland[18] in more recent times. For Homer to have done more would have been outside his calling and would have disturbed his narrative. Yet in the arrangement and depiction of characters Homer also sings most humanly. Where this does not seem to be the case, the difference can be found in the ways of thinking of particular periods and is easily explained. I am sure that I could track down every pure, human sentiment among the Greeks and perhaps find it expressed in the finest meter and the most beautiful way, but everything would have to be viewed in relation to time and place. Aristotle's *Poetics* unsurpassably categorizes plot, characters, passions, and sentiments.

Human nature has remained the same throughout history, but the way human beings express themselves always varies according to the context in which they live. Greek and Roman poetry is extremely diverse in its expressions of desires and complaints, in its descriptions of passion and joy! The same is true of the poetry of monks, Arabs, and modern writers. The great difference that emerged between the East and the West, between the Greeks and us Europeans, was not brought about by any category, but rather was caused by the mixing of peoples, religions, and languages and eventually by the historical progression of customs, feelings, knowledge, and experiences. It is difficult to express this difference in *one word*. If I were to use the expression "poet of reflection" to characterize some modern writers, then this expression would also be imperfect because a poet who writes out of *reflection alone* is actually no poet.

The ground and soil of poetry is *imagination* and one's *very being, the realm of the soul.* Through words and characters poetry rouses the ideal of

14. [James Thomson's masterpiece, *The Seasons,* was the first sustained nature poem in English. His verse foreshadowed several attitudes of the Romantic movement.]

15. [Ewald Christian von Kleist (1715-59). German lyric poet best known for his poem, *Der Frühling.* The poem presents realistic details of nature and expresses a passionate love for it.]

16. [Edmund Spenser (1552-99). English poet, author of *The Faerie Queene.]*

17. [Miguel de Cervantes Saavedra (1547-1616). Spanish author of novels, plays, and tales; author of *Don Quixote.]*

18. [Christoph Martin Wieland (1733-1813). German poet and author of the German novel, *Die Geschichte des Agathon,* which initiated the German tradition of *Bildungsroman.]*

happiness, of beauty and of integrity, that slumbers in the heart. Poetry is the most perfect expression of the language, the senses, and one's entire being. No poet can avoid the inherent law of poetry. This law shows poets what they do and do not possess.

One cannot separate *ear and eye* in poetry. Poetry is not mere painting or sculpture that can represent objects just as they are, without involving a special purpose. Poetry is *speech* and has *purpose*. Poetry affects the internal sense, not the artist's external eye. Among the educated and those being educated, this internal sense involves *one's very being, one's sense of morality*. Among poets, it involves a *reasonable* and *humanitarian* purpose. Speech possesses something eternal. It creates deep impressions, and poetry intensifies them through its harmonic art. A poet could never want to be merely a painter. Poets are artists because they are able to speak in a way that reaches one's innermost being. This speech paints the object that it depicts or represents on an *intellectual, ethical, and eternal background* right into *one's very being,* right into *one's soul.*

Is not progress *[Fortgang]* inevitable in this succession of poetry throughout history, just as it is in every succession of the continual workings of nature? I do not doubt it at all (if progress is understood properly). We will never become Greeks or Romans in our language and speech. We do not want to do so! But does not the spirit of poetry attempt, throughout all the oscillations and eccentricities in which it has until now striven, from nation to nation and from age to age, to cast off increasingly every rude feeling and every false embellishment and to seek the center of all human endeavors, that is, the *true, whole, moral nature of humanity, the philosophy of life?* Even in the times of the worst forms of bad taste we can say, in accordance with the great natural law: *Tendimus in Arcadiam, tendimus!*[19] Our way proceeds toward the realm of simplicity, truth, and morality.

SHAKESPEARE

"Sitting high upon a peak! At his feet the storm, thunder, and the roar of the sea; but his head in the rays of the sun!"[20] If there is any man who comes to mind with this marvelous image, then it is Shakespeare! But, of course, he comes to mind only with an additional image: At the very bottom of his rocky throne stands a murmuring crowd that explains, saves, condemns, excuses, idolizes, defames, translates, and slanders him! A crowd that he does not hear at all!

What a library has already been written about, for, and against him! And I have no desire to add to the collection. I would much rather wish that in

19. [Latin for "We press toward Arcadia!"—toward the pastoral life.]
20. [SW 5:208-31.]

the small circle in which Shakespeare is read it would no longer occur to anyone to write about, for, or against him; to excuse or to defame him; but rather to understand him, to feel the way he is, to use him, and—wherever possible!—to present him to us Germans. May this essay contribute something to this task!

The most audacious foes of Shakespeare have accused and mocked him in many different ways, saying that even if he were a great poet, he was certainly not a good playwright, and even if he were also a good playwright, he was truly not as classical a writer of tragedy as Sophocles, Euripides, Corneille, or Voltaire, who exhausted everything supreme and complete in this art form.

The most audacious friends of Shakespeare have usually merely been content to excuse and defend him by weighing and counter-balancing his beauties over against attacks against his use of the rules of aesthetics; they treat him as a defendant and try to absolve him from these rules; and then the more they idolize his greatness, the more they have to shrug their shoulders over his mistakes. This is the case even with the most recent editors and commentators of his work. I hope that my essay can change this perspective so that his image can be seen in a clearer light.

But is not this hope itself too audacious? Is it not too presumptuous considering the many great people who have already dealt with Shakespeare? I do not believe so. If I can show that both sides of the debate are built merely on a *prejudice,* on an empty illusion, if I can simply take one cloud away from the eyes or adjust the image more sharply without changing anything either in the eye or in the image, then we can perhaps blame either time or circumstance that I reach the place where I can take hold of the reader and say, "Stand here! Otherwise you will see nothing but a caricature!" If our task is to be nothing but continually winding and unwinding the great coiled ball of scholarship without ever getting anywhere with it, then what a sad fate awaits us because of this infernal kind of weaving.

We have inherited the words "drama, tragedy, and comedy" from Greece. The belles lettres of the human race made its way on a narrow strip of the earth only through *tradition,* and the same can be said about the dramatic arts. They had their beginnings in Greece and in the Greek language, and it was therefore natural to assume that Greek theatrical rules were inseparable from the dramatic arts. The education of a child cannot possibly take place through reason but through imitation, impressions, the divinity of examples and habits. In the same way, nations are children in everything that they learn. The seed would not grow without the husk, and nations would never receive the seed without the husk, even if they had no use at all for the husk. This is the case with the drama of Greece and of the North.

In Greece, drama developed in a way that it never could have developed in the North. In Greece, drama was something that it cannot be in the North. In the North, therefore, drama is not and may not be what it was in Greece. The drama of Sophocles and the drama of Shakespeare are, therefore, two things that from a certain perspective can hardly share the same name. By using Greece itself as my example, I believe that I can prove these propositions and thereby decipher the nature of Northern drama and of the greatest dramatist of the North, Shakespeare. By comparing the origin and development of one thing with another, you will see that it does not remain the same at all.

Greek tragedy came in, so to speak, from one dramatic entrance: from the improvisation of the dithyramb, of the mimetic dance, of the chorus.[21] This improvisation grew and took on new forms. Aeschylus brought two actors on the stage instead of one, invented the concept of a main character, and diminished the size of the chorus. Sophocles introduced the third actor and invented the stage. From such an origin, though much later on, Greek tragedy arose to its greatness and became a masterpiece of the human spirit, the height of literature. This is the tragedy that Aristotle praised so highly, and we cannot admire it deeply enough in Sophocles and Euripides.

At the same time, we see that from this origin certain things become understandable that are usually misunderstood terribly when they are gaped at in wonder as dead rules of aesthetics. That *simplicity of the Greek plot,* that *austerity of Greek customs,* that *enduring tragic style of diction, melody, spectacle, unity of time and place*—all these characteristics of Greek tragedy lay so naturally and essentially, without art and magic, in its origin that it could not have possibly existed had it not been grafted to them. All of these characteristics were the husk in which the fruit grew.

Go back to the childhood of that period: Simplicity of the plot lay so deeply in the *action of ancient times, of the republic, of the homeland, of the religion*— in what was called the heroic deeds—that the poet probably had more trouble discovering parts in this simple, vast material, that is, introducing a beginning, middle and end in a dramatic way, than either forcefully separating these parts, mangling them, or knitting a whole from many, separate events. Whoever has read Aeschylus or Sophocles would never question this. For what was tragedy other than an allegorical, mythological, semi-epic portrait almost devoid of successive entrances, of story line, of emotional continuity? It was, as the ancients said, almost chorus alone with a small amount of story interspersed in it. In this case could there be the least bit of effort and art involved in creating simplicity of the plot? And was this not so in the majority of Sophocles's works? His Philoctet, Ajax, exiled Oedipus, and so on, still always come so very close to their unique origin—the *dramatic scene amidst the chorus.* No doubt about it! This is the birth of the Greek stage.

21. [See Aristotle's *Poetics,* 4.1449a10 ff.]

Now let us see what follows from this simple observation. It is nothing less than the artistic character of the Greek rules of tragedy was not embedded in art, but in nature! *The unity of the plot* was the unity of the action that lay before them; according to their temporal, political, religious, and moral circumstances, this action could be nothing but such a unity. *The unity of place* was unity of their location; for the one, brief, festive action could only take place at one location in the temple or the palace—the action happened, so to speak, on one marketplace of the country. Thus, in the beginning, this unity was simply imitated mimetically and through narration and was interspersed throughout the play. Later, entrances and scenes were added, but everything still naturally remained one scene, with the chorus uniting everything, with the stage naturally never remaining empty, and so on. What child cannot see that the unity of place was a logical consequence of this and naturally accompanied it? All of these things were so embedded in nature that the poet with all his art could never have done anything without it.

It is also evident that the art of the Greek poets took a totally opposite road than the one attributed to them today. I believe that the Greeks did not *simplify* but rather *multiplied:* Aeschylus built on the chorus, Sophocles built on Aeschylus. If you simply compare the most artistic works of Sophocles and his great masterpiece, *Oedipus Rex,* with *Prometheus* or with reports of the ancient dithyramb, then you will see the amazing art that enabled him to write these works. But it was never the case that he had to create a whole from many parts; rather, many parts had to be created from a whole. He had to create a beautiful labyrinth of scenes, in which his greatest concern was to move his audience with the illusion of the previous unity at the most complex point in this labyrinth, to unwind the coiled ball of their feelings so gently and gradually that it seemed as though they still completely possessed the previous dithyrambic feeling. For this reason he introduced painted scenery for them, kept the choruses, made the choruses into places of rest of the action, held everyone in suspense, in the frenzy of the not yet and already, by writing each word with reference to the whole. (This is something that the learned Euripedes immediately, just after the stage had been invented, omitted again!) In short, Sophocles gave the action (something that has been terribly misinterpreted!) greatness.

It must be clear to everyone who has read Aristotle with a clear mind and from the standpoint of his time that he knew how to treasure the art of Sophocles's genius and that the whole situation was practically the opposite of what modern times try to make of it. Aristotle left Thespis and Aeschylus behind and concentrated exclusively on the diverse, poetic Sophocles. He began with the innovations of Sophocles and defined the essence of the new literary genre in relation to them. His favorite idea was to create a new Homer who would compare favorably to the old one. Aristotle did not overlook any minor detail that might support his conception of the main action in the performance. All of this indicates that the great Aristotle also philosophized in accordance with his time and that it is the fault of narrow, childish trifles that people have tried to make Aristotle into a paper framework for the stage.[22] According to his excellent chapter on the essence of the plot, he apparently neither knew nor recognized any rules other than regard for the audience, for the soul, and for illusion.[23] He says clearly that no other rules should determine the parameters of length, the temperament of the play's structure, or its time and space. Oh, if Aristotle were alive and could see the false, ridiculous use of his rules for drama! But let us stick to a quiet, calm examination of the subject.

Just as everything in the world changes, the temperament that created Greek drama also had to change. The worldview, the customs, the state of the republic, the tradition of the heroic era, faith, even music, diction, and the degree to which illusion was possible changed. Naturally the material for the plot, the opportunities for adapting it for the stage, and the reasons for attempting this also faded away. One could, of course, retrieve ancient material or even foreign material from other nations and clothe it in the prescribed way. But all this did not have the effect or consequently the spirit. It was no longer (Why should we play with words?) the thing that it had been. It was a puppet, a copy, an ape; it was like a statue animated by a demon that only the most rapt audience could conjure up. Let us turn directly to the modern Athenizers of Europe (for the Romans were either too stupid or too clever, either too wild or too extravagant, to establish a completely Greek form of theater), and I suspect that the matter will become clear.

Undoubtedly, no puppet of the Greek theater could have been more thoroughly conceived of and more perfectly executed than it was in France. I am not speaking merely about the so-called "rules of the theater" that have been ascribed to the good Aristotle—unity of time, place, action, relation between scenes, and probability of plot, and so on. Rather, I wish genuinely to ask if something could possibly exist that goes beyond the glittering, classical thing that has been given to us by Corneille, Racine, Voltaire, something that goes beyond the series of lovely entrances, dialogues, verse, and rhyme with their proportion, richness, clarity? I believe so, but all admirers of Voltaire and of the French and these noble Athenizers themselves are the first to deny it. They have already denied it repeatedly, continue to do so, and will do so in

22. [At the beginning of the sixteenth century there was an attempt to establish rules for the use of ancient genres based on Aristotle's *Poetics*. Subsequent theoreticians created a rigid framework of rules. The most well-known rules were the dramatic unities of time, place, and action. These rules won great support in France. See "Neo Classical Rules" in the *Oxford Companion to English Literature*.]

23. [For Aristotle's chapter on the plot, see his *Poetics* 7.1451a1-14.1454a15.]

the future: "Nothing can exceed this! This can never be surpassed!" And in the light of such unanimity that places the puppet on the stage, they are correct, and they are bound to prevail from day to day as more and more people throughout Europe go crazy over this glittering thing and ape it. . . .

Let us look at a people who, for whatever reasons, wished to invent its own drama instead of aping that of another people and running away with the walnut shell. It seems to me that the first questions are: When? Where? Under what circumstances? From what sources should a people do this? There is no need to prove that the invention of theater in this case can and will consist entirely of the answers to these questions. If a people does not create its drama from the chorus, from the dithyramb, then it cannot have elements of the chorus, of the dithyramb. If it was not exposed to such *simplicity of historical facts, tradition, domestic customs, and political and religious relations,* then naturally it cannot possess anything from all of these things. A people will wherever possible invent its drama according to its own history, spirit of the times, customs, opinions, language, national biases, traditions, and inclinations. It will even invent its drama out of farces and puppet plays (just as the noble Greeks invented it out of the chorus). And the invention becomes drama when it reaches a dramatic purpose among its people. You see that we have come *toto divisis ab orbe Britannis*[24] and their great Shakespeare.

No *pullulus Aristotelis*[25] will deny that Britain during Shakespeare's time and prior to it was not Greece. To demand that Greek drama would *naturally* arise in this setting (we are not speaking here about aping) is worse than expecting a sheep to give birth to a lion. The first and last question must be: What is the soil like? For what has the soil been prepared? What is planted in it? What should it be able to yield? Heavens! How far removed Britain is from Greece! History, tradition, customs, religion, spirit of the times, of the people, of the emotions, of the language—how far removed from Greece! Whether readers know little or much about either age, they will nevertheless not confuse for one moment two things that have no similarity. And if there were in this happy or unhappy different era a man, a genius, who developed a dramatic creation from his material in as natural, great, and original a way as the Greeks did from theirs; and if this creation reached the same goal but did it in the most different ways; and if it were at least in itself a complex unity or a unified complexity, that is, a perfect whole (in any metaphysical sense); then what fool would compare it and even go so far as to condemn it because this second form of drama was not the same as the first? Its entire essence, virtue, and perfection lies in the fact that it is not the first: A different plant grew out of the soil of the time.

24. [Latin for "to the British who were distinct from the whole world."]
25. [Latin for "sprout of Aristotle."]

Shakespeare was exposed to anything but the simplicity of national customs, deeds, inclinations, and historical traditions that had built Greek drama. Following the metaphysical proposition of wisdom "from nothing comes nothing," and if left up to the philosophers, this would mean that there would not and could not have been either Greek drama or, if we may speak of another nothing, any other drama in the world. Nevertheless, because genius is, as you know, greater than philosophy, and a creator is a different creature than a dissector, there was a mortal, gifted with divine power, who was able to create the same effects of fear and pity from totally different material and in the most different way. And he was able to evoke both effects to a degree that the first material and manner could hardly do! Oh, happy divine son over his undertaking! It is precisely the new, original, and totally different quality that shows the primordial power of your calling.

Shakespeare was not exposed to the chorus but to political farces and puppet plays. From these, from this meager lime, he created the glorious creation that stands and lives before us! He was not faced with a simple national character but rather with a diversity of social classes, life-styles, ways of thinking, peoples, and dialects. Grieving over the lack of a simple national character would have been in vain. He, therefore, poetically wove together classes and individuals, peoples and dialects, the king and the fools, fools and the king into a glorious whole. He was not exposed to such a simple story, plot, or sense of action. He took the story as he found it, and with creative genius he combined the most diverse elements into a miraculous whole—a whole that we might call, if not "action" in the Greek sense, then "activity" in the medieval sense, or "event," "great occurrence" in the modern sense. Oh, Aristotle, were you to appear, how you would Homericize about the new Sophocles! You would compose a unique theory about him that the people of his own native country—Home and Hurd, Pope and Johnson[26]— have not yet composed. You would rejoice to be able to draw lines in each work between action, character, thought, diction, spectacle—like drawing the lines between two points in a triangle. All lines meet above in one point of purpose, of perfection. You would say to Sophocles: Sketch the holy drawing of this altar! And to the northern bard, you would say: Paint all sides and walls of this temple in your immortal fresco!

Let me continue as interpreter and rhapsodist, for I am closer to Shakespeare than to Sophocles. For Sophocles, the unity of *action* dominates; Shakespeare tries to create the whole of an *event,* an *occurrence.* For Sophocles, *one tone* of the characters dominates; Shakespeare shapes the main tone of his concert from all the characters, social classes, and life-styles that he can and must.

---

26. [John Home (1722-1808), Scottish dramatist; Richard Hurd (1720-1808), English bishop and literary critic; Alexander Pope, (1688-1744), English poet; Samuel Johnson (1709-84), English literary figure.]

In the work of Sophocles, one melodious, delicate language resounds, as if in etherial heights; Shakespeare speaks the language of all ages, people, and kinds of people—he is the interpreter of nature in all its languages. Can both playwrights be intimate with the one God in such different ways? As Sophocles presents and teaches and moves and forms the Greeks, so Shakespeare moves and forms the people of the North! When I read Shakespeare, the theater, actors, and coulisse disappear! All kinds of individual pages blowing in the rage of time from the book of events, of providence, of the world—individual impressions of peoples, social classes, souls! All of the most diverse and distinct actors, all of the unknowing, blind instruments—what we are in the hand of the Creator of the world—used for the unity of a theatrical image, of a great event, which only the poet can survey. Who can imagine a greater poet for the people of the north and for this period in history? . . .

Examine, my reader, anything you like! Examine *King Lear* and the historical plays about the Richards, *Julius Caesar* and the historical plays about the Henrys, even the mystery plays and comedies; examine especially *Romeo and Juliet,* that sweet play about love, that story spanning all times; examine setting, dream, and poetry. Examine it all and try to eliminate or exchange any of it. See if you can simplify it for the French stage, transforming a living world with all its attestation of its truth into this structure. What a hapless exchange! What a ridiculous transformation! If you take away the soil, sap, and power from these plants and plant them in the air, if you take away the context, time, and individual existence of these human beings, then you have taken away their breath and soul, and they become a false creation.

Shakespeare is Sophocles's brother precisely where he appears to be very dissimilar to him, but is at heart exactly the same. All illusion is reached by way of the story's element of attestation, truth, creativity. Without them not only would nothing be accomplished but also no other element of Shakespeare's drama and dramatic spirit would exist. (Otherwise I would have written in vain.) It is apparent, therefore, that the whole world is the body for this great mind: All movements of nature are the limbs of this body, just as all characters and ways of thinking are the features of this mind. The whole thing might be called Spinoza's great God, Pan! Universe! Sophocles remained true to nature because he worked with unity of action of one time and one place. Shakespeare could only be true to nature by waltzing his event of worldwide significance and human fate through all times and places in which they occurred. God bless the amusing Frenchman who arrives at Shakespeare's play during the final act in order to gulp down the emotion in its quintessence. This might work at some French plays because everything is put into verse only for the theater and arranged into specific scenes. But at Shakespeare's play the Frenchman leaves empty-handed. The event of worldwide significance is already over. He sees only the last, most wretched consequences, sees

human beings fall like flies; he goes to the play and scoffs. For him, Shakespeare is a scandal and his drama is utter foolishness.

The whole tangled ball of questions about time and place would be unraveled
if a philosophical mind would have taken the trouble to ask the following
about drama: What is, then, place and time? Is it the stage itself and the space
of time of a *divertissement au théâtre?* If so, then no one in the world except
the French have unity of place, the proper proportions of time and of scenes.
The Greeks, with their grand kind of illusion of which we can hardly conceive,
thought of anything but this in their preparations for the public stage and in
their devotions at the temple previous to it. To what extent can illusion thrive
in those who look at their watches after each entrance on the stage in order
to see if such a thing could have happened in such an amount of time? Whose
greatest joy is to discover that the author did not deceive them for one second
but rather took exactly that much time on the stage as they would see in the
snail's pace of their own lives? What a strange creature who takes greatest
joy in this! And what a strange author who made this the main goal and who
boasted with the pack of rules, "Look how well I have squeezed and fit so
many beautiful plays onto the narrow slats of this stage called French theater
and into the given time span of the *visite!* Look how well I have crocheted
and darned the scenes! Everything is patched and fastened precisely!" What
a poor master of ceremonies! A Savoyard of the theater, not a creator! Oh,
poet! Dramatic god! No clock on the tower or the temple sets your pace!
Rather you are to create time and space! And if you are able to create a world
that does not exist in space and time, then your measure of time and space
lies within you. You must cast a spell over the whole audience with this
measure, you must press it on them all. Otherwise you are, as I have said,
anything but a dramatic poet.

Does anyone in the world need to prove that time and space are actually
nothing in themselves; that they are relative to existence, action, passion, the
train of thought, or the amount of attention inside or outside of the soul? Have
you, oh gentle timekeeper of the theater, never experienced times in your life
in which hours seemed like moments to you and days like hours, or in which
hours seemed like days and night watches became years? Have you never
experienced situations in your life in which your soul suddenly dwelled in a
place outside yourself such as in the romantic room of your beloved, or in a
rigid corpse, or in some oppressive, extreme, disgraceful need? Have you
never imagined that your soul flew beyond world and time, traversed spaces
and regions, forgot everything around it, and you were in the heaven, in the
soul, in the heart of the one whose existence you felt? And if this is possible
in your dull, sleepy life in which, as in the life of a tree, plenty of roots hold
you in the dead soil of your context and in which, as in the life of a worm,
you tread each sphere slowly enough for you to measure your worm's pace,

then can you imagine yourself for a moment in another world, in the world of a poet, even if only in a dream? Have you never felt how time and place seem to vanish as if in a dream? Have you felt what unessential things, what shadows, time and place are compared to *action* and *effect?* Have you never felt how it all depends on the soul to create space, world, and time in whatever way and wherever it wills? And if you had felt this just once in your life and were wakened after a quarter of an hour, and the dark remainder of your dream had made you swear that you had been sleeping, dreaming, and acting for nights, then how could Mohammad's dream, as a dream, seem for one moment to you as absurd? Is it not the first and only duty of every genius, every poet, and every dramatic poet to place you in such a dream? Now think about what worlds you confuse when you show your watch or your drawing room to the poet so that he can instruct you to dream according to them.

Time and space lie in the sequence of a poet's event, in *ordine successivorum* and *simultaneorum*[27] of the *poet's* world. How and in what direction does the poet pull you? At what moment does the poet pull you there? This is all up to the poet. The pace of the sequence of events is determined by the poet; the poet impresses this sequence of events on you. This is the poet's pace. And what a master Shakespeare is here! His chain of events begins slowly and ponderously in his nature as they do in nature, for he presents these events on a diminished scale. How laborious the play begins before the main threads are pulled together! But once they are, how quickly the scenes move! The speeches shorten and the souls, the passion, the action fly faster! And how powerful the succession of scenes becomes and the strewing of words as everyone's time runs out. Toward the end of the play, when Shakespeare sees that his readers are totally caught up in the play and are lost in the abyss of his world and passion, how bold he becomes, what sequence of events he allows! Lear dies after Cordelia, and Kent after Lear! This moment in the play is at the same time the end of the world that Shakespeare has created; it is the day of judgment, when everything collapses, and heaven is enveloped and the mountains tumble. The measure of time is over. Certainly, however, it is not over for the amusing, cheerful calculating Frenchman who arrived at the theater with flushed cheeks during the fifth act in order to measure with a stopwatch how many died there and how long it took. Oh, God, if this is supposed to be criticism, theater, and illusion, then where does this leave criticism? Illusion? Theater? What did all these empty words mean?

Now the heart of my study begins with the following questions: What kind of art and creativity did Shakespeare use to create such a lively whole from poor romances, novellas, and fables? What kind of laws from our *historical, philosophical, dramatic art* lie behind each of his steps and artistic footholds?

27. [Latin for "in the order of successive things—simultaneous things."]

What a study this would be! How much there is for our construction of history, philosophical anthropology, and drama! But I am not a member of all our academies of history, philosophy, and the fine arts in which one thinks of everything but such things. Even people from Shakespeare's native country do not think about them. His commentators have accused him of all kinds of historical mistakes! For example, look at what historical beauties the fat Warburton[28] blamed on Shakespeare! And did the most recent author of the *Study of Shakespeare* take up my question about how Shakespeare created drama out of romances and novellas? This question hardly occurred to him, just as it did not occur to Lord Home, the Aristotle of this British Sophocles.

Let us take just a peek at the classifications of his works. Recently, it occurred to an author,[29] who certainly knew his Shakespeare, to make Polonius—that honest fishmonger, that man of the court with grey beard and wrinkled face, sunken eyes and "plentiful lack of wit, together with weak hams," that "baby"[30]—into the Aristotle of poets and to suggest that the series of "-ls" and "-cals" which Polonius spouts off in his babble should be a serious classification of all works. I have my doubts. Shakespeare certainly preferred putting trickery, empty *locos communes,* morals and classifications, into the mouths of babes and fools. He used these classifications in a hundred situations, and they were appropriate to all and yet to none. The English already possess, in part, a new *stobaei* and *florilegii*—a *cornucopia* of Shakespeare's wisdom. Recently, we Germans supposedly have acquired it as well. A Polonius, Lancelot, Arlequin,[31] fool, foolish Richard, or arrogant knight would have the most to celebrate about such a development because every person with common sense does not say more about these characters than necessary. Yet I still have my doubts. In *Hamlet* Polonius is probably just the old child who takes the clouds for camels and camels for double basses,[32] who also played Julius Caesar once in his youth, was a good actor, and was

28. [William Warburton (1698-1779). Anglican bishop and literary critic. He brought out an edition of Shakespeare in 1747 that was criticized as unscholarly, and he is mentioned in the history of literary criticism as probably the worst of Shakespeare's many editors.]

29. [Heinrich Wilhelm von Gerstenberg], *Briefe über Merkwürdigkeiten der Litteratur*, Dritte Sammlung (Schleswig und Leipzig: Joachim Friedrich Hansen, 1767). Herder cites the third collection, but he is referring to the second, published in 1766, pp. 139-40. Here Gerstenberg claims that the following lines of Polonius can be used to classify the works of Shakespeare himself: "The best actors in the world, either for tragedy, comedy, history, pastoral, pastoral-comical [tragical-historical, tragical-comical, historical-pastoral] scene individable, or poem unlimited" (*Hamlet* II,ii,396-400). All references to Shakespeare's plays are from the RS.]

30. [In *Hamlet,* Hamlet describes Polonius (Lord Chamberlain) as a fishmonger (II, ii, 173-176), speaks to him of old men (II, ii, 199-200), and calls him a "great baby" (II, ii, 382).]

31. [*Lancelot* was a hero of Arthurian legend; *Arlequin* (Harlequin) was a stock character of the *commedia dell'arte.*]

32. [Hamlet: "Do you see yonder cloud that's almost in shape of a camel?" Polonius: "By the mass and 'tis, like a camel indeed." (*Hamlet* III, ii, 376-77).]

killed by Brutus,[33] and probably knows "Why day is day, night is night and time is time"[34] and thus *also* spins in this line a whirl of dramatic winds. But who wants to make more of all this? And what use are the divisions of "tragedy, comedy, history, pastoral, tragical-historical, historical-pastoral, and pastoral-comical, and comical-historical-pastoral?" And if we mix the "-cals" a hundred times, then what would we have in the end? No work would be Greek tragedy, comedy, pastoral, and no work should be. Every work is history in the broadest sense of the term, and each work is certainly more or less nuanced in tragedy, comedy, and so on. The colors float, however, into eternity; and in the end each work remains what it is and what it must remain: History [*Historie*]! The action of heros and of nations that create the illusion of the Middle Ages! In other words, with the exception of a few plays and divertissements, each work remains a sensational occurrence of an event of worldwide significance, a sensational occurrence of human fate.

It is sadder and more important to think that this great creator of history and the human spirit is becoming more and more antiquated! We are already so far removed from these great ruins of knighthood, because the words and customs and genres of the period wilt and decay like leaves in autumn. Even Garrik,[35] the one who has revived Shakespeare and protected his grave, has to change, edit, and garble so much. Because everything has become blurred and tends to change, perhaps soon it will even become impossible to present his plays on the stage. His drama will become the ruin of a colossus, of a pyramid, at which everyone gazes in wonder but which no one understands. It is fortunate that I live in a period of time in which I can understand Shakespeare. And you, the friend who recognizes and experiences yourself in this essay, and whom I have embraced more than once before his holy image, you live in a time in which you can still possess the sweet and worthy vision of presenting his monument from the times of knights into our language, into our country, which is so different from Shakespeare's own.[36] I envy your vision. Do not let your noble German work subside until the wreath has been hung. And if you should later see how the ground is shifting beneath your edifice, how the crowd is standing still and staring or sneering at the play, and how the enduring pyramid is not able to revive the ancient Egyptian spirit, then your work will remain, and a true successor will seek your grave and

33. [Polonius: "I did enact Julius Caesar. I was kill'd i' th' Capitol; Brutus kill'd me." (*Hamlet* III, ii, 103-4).]

34. [Line of Polonius (*Hamlet* II, ii, 88).]

35. [David Garrik (1717-79). English actor, dramatist, and adapter of plays by other dramatists. According to the *Cambridge Guide to Literature in English*, none of Garrik's adaptations from Shakespeare "say much for the 18th century's understanding of the original."]

36. [Herder is referring to Goethe, who was writing a play, *Götz von Berlichingen*, based on the sixteenth century knight. It was published in 1773.]

write to you in a devout hand what life has been for almost all worthy people in the world: *Voluit! quiescit!*[37]

<h1 style="text-align:center">THE SPIRIT OF HEBREW POETRY</h1>

Preface

The foundation of theology is the Bible, and the foundation of the New Testament is the Old.[38] It is impossible to understand the New Testament properly without understanding the Old, for Christianity arose out of Judaism, and the genius of the language is the same in both books. We cannot study the genius of a language better, that is, with more truth, depth, comprehensiveness, and pleasure than by studying its poetry, and especially its most ancient poetry. It is false and misleading to commend the New Testament to young theologians while excluding the Old. Without the Old, the New Testament can never be understood in an informed manner. Besides, in the Old Testament there is such a rich variety of stories, images, characters, and scenes! In it we see the multicolored dawn, the beautiful rising of the sun; in the New Testament the sun stands at its zenith. And everyone knows which time of day is the most refreshing and invigorating to the sentient eye. If one studies the Old Testament with passion and love, even if one regards it as simply a human book full of ancient poetry, then the New Testament will automatically arise in its purity, sublimity, and divine beauty. If one gathers the abundant riches of the Old Testament on its own terms, then one will not chatter about the New in a meaningless, tasteless, or even profane manner.

First Dialogue

ALCIPHRON: So, I find you still devoted to the study of this poor, barbaric language! This proves how much the impressions of our youth can affect us, and how absolutely necessary it is that from childhood on we be spared the stale rubbish of the times. Otherwise, you will not be able to free yourself from these impressions later in life.

EUTHYPHRON: You are speaking like one of the modern representatives of the Enlightenment who would free human beings not only from all prejudices of childhood, but if possible from childhood itself. Are you acquainted with this "poor, barbaric" language? And why do you have this opinion of it?

A: I am sad to say that I am acquainted with [Ancient Hebrew] all too well. I was tormented by it in my childhood, and I am still tormented every

37. [Latin for "He wanted it! He is at rest!".]
38. [SW 11:222-42.]

time that I hear the echo of its lofty nonsense in theology, philosophy, history, and what not. The rattling of ancient cymbals and kettledrums, in short, the whole janizary music of savage peoples, which people love to call "Ancient Near Eastern parallelism," is still ringing in my ears. I can still see David dancing before the ark of the covenant or the prophet summoning a musician to inspire him.

E: It seems, then, that you have acquainted yourself with the language, but not out of love for it.

A: That is not my fault! I studied it according to the standard method with all the rules of Danz.[39] I could even recite the rules by heart without knowing their meaning.

E: So much the worse! And now I understand why you have such an aversion to this language. But, my friend, do we necessarily have to hate a subject that we unfortunately first learned under a bad method? Do you judge a man by his clothes alone, especially when the clothes are not his own, but were forced upon him?

A: Of course not! And I am willing to abandon all prejudices, if you can prove that they are prejudices. I believe, however, that this will be difficult, for I have examined fairly well both the language and its content.

E: Let us try, and one of us will become the teacher of the other. It would be a sad situation for truth if human beings could not agree on it. And I would curse all the impressions of my youth, if they bound me in chains like a slave for a lifetime. You should know, however, that my present opinion of the poetic spirit of this language does not stem from the impressions of my youth. I learned the language in the same way that you did. It took a long time before I acquired a taste for its beauties and then gradually came to consider it, as I now do, to be a sacred language, the mother of our most precious knowledge and of that early *education* of the human race—an education that spread within but a small portion of the earth and came to us undeservedly.

A: That is almost deifying the language!

E: Not at all! We will consider this language to be human and study its content only in human terms. Better yet, in order to strengthen your assurance of my perfect fairness, we will speak of it only as an instrument of ancient poetry. Are you pleased with this subject? It is not at all risky.

A: Indeed, it is a subject that pleases me greatly. I like to discuss ancient languages if we speak about them strictly in human terms. These languages are the form in which human thoughts, whether good or bad, have been shaped. When languages are instructively compared, they can exhibit the most distinctive characteristics of particular peoples and their ways of looking at

39. [Johann Andreas Danz (1654-1727). German theologian and Hebraist whose text books on Hebrew grammar were standard works for nearly a century.]

the world. If you start to discuss even this dialect of these Hurons of the Ancient Near East, then its simplicity will at least enrich us and spark our own ideas.

E: What do you think is most essential to a poetic language, whether that of the Huron Indians or the Tahitians? Is it not action, presentation, passion, song, rhythm?

A: Yes, indeed!

E: The language that develops these qualities in a superior way is a superior poetic language. Now you know, my friend, that the languages of rather primitive peoples can be superior poetic languages to a great degree; in fact, these languages are actually superior to some of the too finely cultivated modern languages. I do not need to remind you among what people Ossian sang, or in what period even Homer of Greece sang.

A: It does not follow, however, that every barbaric nation has its Homer and Ossian.

E: Perhaps many have more than this—except, of course, that they had poets for their own language, not for other ones. In order to judge a nation, one must enter its time, its own country, the sphere of its way of thinking and feeling. One must see how its people lived, how they were educated, what sort of objects they saw, what sort of things they loved passionately, the nature of their climate, their skies, the structure of their voices, their dance, and their music. One must get to know all of this, not as strangers or enemies, but as their brothers and compatriots. One can then ask whether or not in their own way and for their own particular needs they had a Homer or an Ossian. You can see that we have examined very few peoples in this way. With some peoples we are just beginning to be able to do so. We can certainly examine the Hebrews in this way; their poetry is available to us.

A: But what poetry! And in what a language! How imperfect it is! How poor in proper names and exact relations between things! How unfixed and uncertain are the tenses of its verbs! One never knows whether the text refers to today or yesterday, a thousand years ago, or a thousand years to come! The language hardly has any adjectives, which are so necessary for descriptions; it has to manage by combining a few paltry phrases. How vague and farfetched is the meaning of their root words, and how forced the derivations from them! This is the reason for the frightful, strained catachreses, the farfetched images, the abominable combinations of the most distantly related ideas. The parallelism of the Hebrew language is monotonous; it is an everlasting tautology with no metrical arrangement of words and syllables that can please the ear even slightly. *Aures perpetuis tautologiis laedunt,* says one of the greatest Hebrew scholars, *Orienti jucundis, Europae invisis, prudentioribus stomachaturis, dormitaturis reliquis.*[40] And this is the truth! This is

40. Latin for "Ears are annoyed by everlasting tautologies." "They are pleasing to the peoples of the Near East but loathsome to the Europeans; they will nauseate smarter people and will make the rest fall asleep."]

obvious in all the songs and speeches that breathe the spirit of this language. Finally, the language had no vowels at all, for these are a more modern invention. It stands as a lifeless hieroglyph, very often even without any key to or certainty of its meaning, in any event without any certain pronunciation and knowledge of its ancient rhythm. What do you find here of Homer and Ossian? You might as well be looking for these authors in Mexico or in the writings on the obelisks of Arabia.

E: Thank you for the clear thread you are giving our conversation. You have provided such rich material for our conversation, and you have reflected on it and arranged it as carefully as one might expect from someone so skilled in several languages. Let us first of all discuss the structure of the language.

Did you not say that action and presentation were the essence of poetry? Now what part of speech paints action, or more precisely presents action itself—the noun or the verb?

A: The verb.

E: We can conclude, then, that the language that abounds in expressive, descriptive verbs is a poetic language: The more this language is able to make nouns into verbs, the more poetic it is. A noun always presents only the subject at hand in a lifeless way; the verb puts it in action. This arouses feeling, for the subject at hand is, so to speak, animated with spirit. Remember what Lessing has shown about Homer:[41] in Homer's work everything is process, motion, action, and this is what constitutes the life, the effect, the very essence of all poetry. Now in Hebrew the verb is almost everything; in other words, everything lives and acts. The nouns are derived from verbs and, in a certain sense, are still verbs: They are like living beings that are taken up and formed under the effect of their root source itself. Examine the effect produced in the poetry of modern language when verbs and nouns are still closely related, and verbs can become nouns. Think about English or German. The language of which we are speaking is almost an abyss of verbs, a ocean of waves, where action rushes upon action without end.

A: It seems to me, however, that this abundance of verbs must always maintain a certain relation to the other parts of speech, for if everything is action, then there is nothing that acts. There must be a subject, predicate, and copula; this is what logic dictates.

E: This order is fine for logic and necessary for its masterpiece, the syllogism. But poetry is quite another thing, and no one could read a poem written in syllogisms. In poetry, the copula is the main thing; the other parts of speech are merely necessities or useful additions. Even if I admitted that the Hebrew language may not be the best language for an abstract thinker, it is, in accordance with this active form, all the more appropriate for the poet.

41. See Lessing's *Laokoon* (Berlin, 1766).

Everything in the Hebrew language proclaims, "I live, and move, and act. I was created by the senses and the passions, not by abstract thinkers and philosophers. I am, therefore, meant for the poet; indeed, my whole being is poetry."

A: What do you do when you need nouns, not to mention adjectives?

E: If they are needed, then they are there, for every language has what it needs. We should not, however, judge every language according to our own needs. There are hundreds of things for which this language has no names because the Hebrew people neither possessed nor were acquainted with the things themselves. However, it has hundreds of other terms that our language does not have. It is poor in abstractions, but rich in the sensual presentations of things; it has numerous synonyms to denote one and the same object precisely because the object is always mentioned and, so to speak, "painted" in its multifarious relations with all the sensuous conditions that accompany it. The lion, the sword, the serpent, and the camel have so many names in Near Eastern languages, especially in Arabic, the most cultivated of them, because each person initially described the object from a particular perspective, and later these streams flowed together. In Hebrew, too, this superabundance of sensuous terms is very noticeable, even though so little literature of that language is available to us today. More than 250 botanical terms can be found in the small volume that contains the remnants of the Hebrew writings that we possess today! These are writings of a very uniform character and are mostly history or poetry from the temple. Think how rich the language would be if we had Hebrew poetry concerned with everyday life in all its diverse scenes, or if we just had the writings that are mentioned in the works handed down to us. The situation of the Hebrew writings was probably similar to that of almost all peoples of antiquity: The flood of ages has passed over them, and only a small remnant, such as Noah could preserve in the ark, could be saved.

A: In my opinion we have enough writings as it is, for even in the few books we do possess, the same things are repeated over and over. But we are wandering from the subject at hand. I am quite convinced that the language of which we are speaking could have been refined in the hands of other peoples. Look how richly Arabic was developed! The Phoenicians may have had plenty of expressions for trade and numbers. But these poor shepherds and paupers? In which direction could they develop language?

E: In the direction that the spirit and needs of the people required. It would be unfair to expect from them the Phoenician language of trade or the Arabian language of speculation, since they neither traded nor speculated. Nevertheless, all this wealth must have been part of the Hebrew language, for Phoenician, Arabic, Aramaic, and Hebrew are essentially only one language. Hebrew has many numerical terms that are difficult for us to state briefly. It also has many terms for the products of nature and even for different kinds of ornaments and luxury with which the Hebrews were well acquainted from an early period. The Hebrew language was spoken in the neighborhood of the Phoenicians, the Ishmaelites, the Egyptians, the Babylonians, and, in short, the most cultivated peoples of antiquity; it was spoken, so to speak, in the "center" of the culture of that time. It adopted, therefore, a sufficient amount from all that surrounded it. Had it continued as a living language, it might have appropriated all that now belongs to Arabic, which can justly boast of being one of the richest and most refined languages in the world.

A: The rabbis have in fact contributed to the Arabic.

E: Neither significantly, however, nor in accordance with the genius of its original structure. This unfortunate people was dispersed throughout the world. Most of them, therefore, shaped their expressions according to the genius of the languages that were spoken around them, producing a sorry mixture that we cannot consider now. Our discussion today focuses on the Hebrew language when it was the living language of Canaan and on the period of its greatest beauty and purity, before it was mixed with Aramaic, Greek, and other foreign languages. From this standpoint you should accept it as a poor yet beautiful, pure country maiden, as a rustic and pastoral language. I would gladly remove the finery that it borrowed from its neighbors.

A: All right, I will accept it in this way! As a child I felt with joy the special traits of its simplicity, especially in its depictions of nature. Still, my friend, it does not seem to me that this trait is sufficient to redeem the language. Everything is repeated so monotonously; nothing has an outline; their poets are forever sketching, but cannot paint in a subtle way at all.

E: It seems to me that they sketch as few of our poets do: not subtly and in an overly refined way, but vigorously, completely, and full of life. We have already spoken about their *verbs;* they are all action and motion; the roots of the verbs are image [*Bild*] and feeling [*Empfindung*]. The *nouns,* still half verbs, are often active agents, and they appear in one endless poetic personification. Their *pronouns* stand out prominently, as they do in every language of the passions. The lack of adjectives is made up by the combination of other words so that the quality of a subject becomes the subject itself, that is, a particular, active agent. In all these ways, the language seems to me to be more poetic than any other language on earth.

A: It will be most productive for us to continue the discussion with a few examples. Please begin with the roots, with the verbs.

E: The roots of the Hebrew verbs, I said, are image and feeling, and I know no language in which the simple and deft combination of the two is so sensual and so remarkable. It is not sensual and remarkable, I admit, to an ear accustomed only to the tones of Northern languages. But you, my friend, are acquainted with the principles of word formation in Greek, and thus it will hardly be difficult for you to go a few steps further and sympathize with the bolder, albeit not clumsier, method of forming words in the Ancient Near East. Let me repeat once again that in the most pregnant words of the language there is image and feeling. The language was formed and uttered with a full expiration of the lungs, with vigorous and strong voices, but at the same time under a clear and peaceful sky, with a keen eye that practically gripped the very objects themselves and almost never without some trace of passion.

A: Image and feeling? Tranquility and passion? Strong and yet light tones? These are rare combinations.

E: Let us look at them separately. All languages of Northern peoples imitate the sounds of nature; however, they do so only roughly, that is, only externally. Like the objects they imitate, they abound with creaking, rustling, hissing, and crashing sounds. Wise poets employ this feature sparingly and with effect; and bad ones use it to an extreme. The cause of this can obviously be found in the climate and in the voice in and by which the languages were originally formed. The farther south, the more refined the imitation of nature will be. Homer's most sonorous verses do not creak and hiss, they resound. The words have already passed through a more refined medium—feeling—and been formed, as it were, in the region of the heart. Thus, they do not offer crude images of mere noise, but images on which feeling has pressed its gentler seal, images that feeling modifies from within. The languages of the Near East are, I say, the best models for this union of feeling from within and image from without, a union that is found within the tone and the root of the verbs.

A: For heaven's sake! Are you speaking about those barbarous and crude guttural sounds? And do you venture to compare them with the silvery tones of the Greek?

E: I am not comparing them. Every language suffers by such comparison. Nothing is more national and more individual than the modes of pleasing the ear and the characteristic inflections of voice. We Northerners, for example, think it elegant to utter our words only in the front part of the mouth, between the tongue and the lips, and to open our mouths just a little, as if we were living in a cloud of smoke and fog. The climate, customs, and prevailing habits require it, and the language itself has been gradually shaped according to these factors. The Italians, and still more the Greeks, think otherwise. The Italian language abounds in round vowels, and the Greek in diphthongs. Both peoples speak *ore rotundo* and do not bite their lips together when speaking. The Hebrews form sounds from deeper in the chest, from the heart. Elihu describes this when he exclaims,

For I am full of words,
The spirit within me constrains me.

My heart is indeed like wine that has no vent;
Like new wine skins, it is ready to burst.
I must speak, so that I may find relief;
I must open my lips and answer.[42]

When these lips were opened, it was certainly a lively sound, it was the image
of the object in the breath of feeling. This is, it seems to me, the spirit of
the Hebrew language. It is full of the breath of the soul. It does not resound
like the Greek, but it breathes, it lives. This is the way the language appears
to us who are but partially acquainted with its pronunciation, and who cannot
utter its deepest gutturals. In those ancient, more primitive times, what fullness
of the soul, what breath of the living word, must have inspired it! It was, as
the Hebrews say,

The spirit of God who spoke in them,
The breath of the Almighty that gave them life.[43]

A: Once more you are on the verge of deifying the language. However,
maybe this was the case with the sound of feeling when the thing itself was
seen and felt. But what about the derivations from these root words? What
are they but an overgrown bush of thorns, as on an island where no human
being has set foot?

E: In bad dictionaries this is indeed the case, and some of the most learned
philologists of Holland, hacking away at the language, have made the path
much more difficult for us. But a time will come when this overgrown bush
will become a pleasant grove of palms.

A: Your metaphor is Near Eastern.

E: So is the subject at hand. The root of the primitive word will be placed
in the center, and its offspring will form a grove around it. Through taste,
diligence, common sense, and the comparison of diverse dialects, we will
eventually be able to use dictionaries to distinguish essential from accidental
meanings of a word, to trace subtle changes of meaning. By studying the
derivation of words and the use of metaphors, we will perceive the human
spirit's genuine art of invention, the logic of the figurative language of former
times. I look forward to this time and to the first dictionary that is able to do
this well. For now, I use the best dictionaries that we have from Castell,
Simon, Cocceius, their rich contributors, Schultens, Schröder, Storr, Scheid,
and any one else who has individually or collectively contributed to the same.

A: It will take a long time before we stroll in your palm grove of a dictionary
of Near Eastern languages. In the meantime, please give me an example of
derivation.

42. [Job 32:18-20.]
43. [Allusion to Job 33:4.]

E: You can find examples everywhere, even in the dictionaries we already have. Look up the first root word. Look how the root "he has passed away" subtly forms its derivatives. A series of expressions for loss, disappearance, death, vain advice, and fruitless toil and trouble are derived from it in subtle changes of meaning; and if you imagine yourself in nomadic times and in all the situations of a shepherd's life, then the most distant meaning of the word will still resonate with something of its original sound, with something of the image of the original feeling. This is what makes the language so sensuous and its poetic expression so present and moving! The language abounds in roots of this kind, and our commentators, who tend to proceed more callously than cautiously, have sufficiently shown this. They cannot help it; they have to lay bare all possible roots and fibers of every tree, even where one would wish to see only the flowers and fruits.

A: I suppose these are the slaves upon your plantation of palms.

E: Very necessary and useful people! We must treat them kindly, for even when they do too much, they do it with good intentions. Have you any further objections against the Hebrew verbs?

A: Quite a few. What kind of an action is it that makes no distinction between tenses? For the two tenses of Hebrew are, after all, essentially aorists, that is, undefined tenses that fluctuate between the past, the present, and the future. Thus, Hebrew has as good as only one tense.

E: Does poetry need more? In poetry everything is present tense; everything is the presentation of an action, whether it be past, future, or continuous action. For the writing of history, the defect that you observe can be quite substantial. In fact, the languages that love fine distinctions between tenses have developed them most of all in the style of writing history. Among the Hebrews, history itself is actually poetry, that is, the passing on of a narrative that is also depicted as taking place in the present: The indefiniteness or fluctuation of the tenses explicitly helps to give evidence, to give the clear, vivid presence of what is described, narrated, or proclaimed. Is this not poetic to a high degree? Have you never felt, my friend, how beautifully the tenses change in the style of the poets or the prophets? What one hemistich declares in the past tense, the next expresses in the future! It is as if the latter makes the subject continually and forever present, while the former gives the discourse a certainty of former times, as if everything had already been completed. The one tense extends the expression forward, the other backward, and thus the ear is provided with an agreeable variety and the tangible immediacy of the presentation. In addition, the Hebrews, like children, want to say everything at once and to express the person, number, tense, action, and more with a single sound. How much this contributes to the sudden presentation of an entire image! They express in a single word what we must often express in five or more. Our words hobble along with little, often unaccented syllables at the beginning or end of them. In Hebrew, everything is joined to the main idea as an echo or as a sonorous suffix. The main idea stands in the center like a king; his ministers and servant, who closely surround him, who are one with him, suddenly emerge in step with him as one small metrical foot. Do you think this is of no importance to a poetic language? Sonorous verbs, which convey so many ideas at once, are the greatest strength of rhythm and imagery. If I can, for example, utter the words "as he has given me" in a single, well-sounding word, then is this not more poetic and harmonious than if I express the thought with many individual words and in such a fragmented way?

A: I have sometimes considered this language to be a collection of alphabetical paintings for the eye, which have to be deciphered like Chinese writing. I have often complained that the children or youth who are to learn it do not become accustomed early on to this way of deciphering, of analyzing with the eye, which would aid them more than many dull and meaningless rules. I have read about cases in which young people, especially those whose intuitive senses are acute, have made great progress in this way in a short time. Neither of us enjoyed this advantage.

E: We will gradually acquire it, however, if both the eye and the ear become used to it. You will then notice the harmonious arrangement of vowels and consonants and the correspondence of many particles and dominant sounds to the things they signify. With these few, diverse words the metrical feet are placed in relation to one another: The two hemistiches have a kind of symmetry; word balances word, thought balances thought, in an alternation that is parallel and yet at the same time yields a free, but very simple and harmonious rhythm.

A: You are now talking about the celebrated parallelism. I will hardly agree with you about it. If people have something to say, they should either say it all at once or continually elaborate the image, but they should not keep repeating themselves. People who must say everything twice thereby only prove that they have said it partially or imperfectly the first time.

E: Have you never seen a dance? Have you never heard anything of the choral odes of the Greeks, the strophe and antistrophe? Suppose we compare the poetry of the Hebrews to the movements of a dance or to a shorter and simpler form of the choral ode?

A: Add the sistrum, the timpani, and cymbals, and your primitive dance will be complete.

E: So be it! A name should never frighten us, if the thing itself is good. Tell me, does not all rhythm, dance, and harmony, indeed, does not everything that delights the eye as well as the ear, depend on symmetry? More precisely, on a symmetry that is easily apprehended, on balanced simplicity?

A: I will not deny that.

E: And does not Hebrew parallelism represent the simplest balance between the parts of its poems, between its images and sounds? The syllables were not yet precisely scanned and measured, or even numbered at all, but the dullest ear can perceive their symmetry.

A: But must all this be at the expense of the understanding?

E: Let us dwell a little longer upon the pleasure of the ear. All poetic meters of the Greeks, which were constructed with more art and refinement than that of any other language, depend entirely on symmetry and harmony. The hexameter, in which the most ancient poems were sung, is in regard to its sounds a continuous, though ever changing parallelism. In order to give this parallelism greater precision the pentameter was adopted, especially in the elegy. The structure of its two hemistiches indicates that the pentameter is obviously a parallelism. The finest and most natural genres of the ode depend so much on parallelism that one can almost say, the more a light parallelism is heard together with a harmonious alternation of sound in a strophe, the more pleasing the strophe becomes. I need only to cite, for example, Sapphic and Alcaic verse forms or choriambic meter. All these forms of poetic meter are ingenious circlets, finely woven garlands of words and sounds. In the Ancient Near East the two strings of pearl are not twisted into a garland, but simply hang across from the other. We could not expect a chorus of shepherds to produce a dance as intricate as the labyrinth of Daedalus or of Theseus! They respond and rejoice in alternating voices, and they dance across from one another. Even this simplicity seems to me to have its beauty.

A: What beauty does it lend to the meaning of parallelism?

E: The two parts of the parallelism confirm, elevate, and strengthen each other as they instruct or delight. In songs of jubilation this is obvious, and in those of lamentation the nature of the sigh and lament is strengthened. Drawing the breath strengthens and comforts the soul; the other part of the chorus takes part in our sorrow and is the echo or, as the Hebrews would say, "the daughter of the voice" of our sorrow. In didactic odes one saying confirms the other, as if the father were instructing his son, and the mother repeated the teaching. In this way the discourse becomes all the more true, sincere, and familiar. In love songs with alternating voices, the subject itself determines the form: Love desires sweet conversation, the interchange of hearts and minds. In short, the connection between these two parts of feeling is so simple and sisterly that I want to apply the following gentle Hebrew ode to them:

How very good and pleasant it is
    when kindred live together in unity!
It is like the precious oil on the head,
    running down upon the beard,
On the beard of Aaron,
    running down over the collar of his robes.

It is like the dew of Hermon,
   which falls on the mountains of Zion.
For there the LORD ordained his blessing,
   life forevermore.[44]

A: You are a great defender of parallelism! But granting that the ear may become accustomed to it, what about the understanding? It is constantly held back and cannot advance.

E: Poetry is not addressing understanding alone but feeling first and foremost. And does feeling not love parallelism? As soon as the heart pours itself out and wave follows upon wave, this is parallelism. The heart is never exhausted, for it always finds something new to say. As soon as the first wave has softly passed away or has broken mightily upon the rocks, the second wave swells again. This pulse of nature, this rhythmic breathing of feeling, appears in all language of emotion. And you would not have this in poetry, which is actually the language of emotion?

A: But what if it aims to be and must be the language of understanding?

E: Then it turns the image and exhibits it from the opposite side. It varies the saying and explains it or impresses it upon the heart. Once again, we have parallelism. What kind of verse do you consider to be most suitable for didactic poetry in the German language?

A: Without question Alexandrine meter.

E: And that is completely parallelism. If you carefully examine why this meter is able to instruct so powerfully, then you will discover that this is precisely because of its parallelism. All simple songs and church hymns are full of parallelism; and rhyme, the great delight of northern ears, is an ongoing parallelism.

A: We are indebted to the Near East both for rhyme and for the uniform rhythm of church hymns. The Saracens introduced rhyme, and doxologies introduced rhythm. Otherwise, we might very well have been without either.

E: Do you think so? Rhyme existed in Europe long before the Saracens arrived. There were assonances either at the beginning or end of words, to which the ears of the people were accustomed and which their language could bear. Even the Greeks had hymns and choral songs as simple as our own church hymns can be. The Hebrew parallelism admittedly has, however, an advantage over our northern languages: With its small number of words it beautifully orders a metrical foot of words and lets it ring magnificently in the air. This is why it is almost impossible for us to translate it. We often need ten words to express three of the Hebrew; our little words drag along or become muddled, and the end of the poem is either lifeless or wearisome. Thus, we must not so much imitate parallelism as study it. In our languages

44. [Ps. 133.]

we must extend the images and round out their structure because we are accustomed to the meter of the Greeks and the Romans. But in translating Near Eastern languages, this must be laid aside. Otherwise, we lose a deal part of the original simplicity, dignity, and sublimity of the language. For here too:

> For he spoke, and it came to be;
>   he commanded, and it stood firm.[45]

A: And yet monosyllabic brevity also seems sublime to me.

E: A monosyllabic, laconic style is neither pleasant nor poetic. Even in the command of a monarch, we want to see the effect of the command, and so we find parallelism again, this time in the form of command and consequence. Finally, the concise structure of the Hebrew language almost always makes parallelism into a monarchic command. It knows nothing of the oratorical meter of a Greek or Latin sentence. The breath of its spirit called forth few words; these words were related to one another, and since the language possessed uniform inflections, the words became similar; and they became rhythmic through the sound of the words—each word through its position, and the whole through the predominant feeling. The two hemistiches correspond as word and deed, heart and hand, or, as the Hebrews say, entrance and exit. Thus, this simple structure of sound is complete. Do you have any other complaints against parallelism?

A: I even have something to add in its favor. In regard to understanding, I have often been thankful for the existence of parallelism. How could we explain so many obscure words and phrases, if parallelism did not serve as our guide? It is like the voice of a friend, calling out from a distance in the recesses of a wild forest, "Come here! Human beings live here!" But old ears are, of course, deaf to this friendly voice. They treat the echo as if it were the voice itself, and they always expect to find in the second part of the parallelism some new and miraculous meaning.

E: Ignore these people. Let us try to keep ourselves on the right path. I think you are exaggerating the part about the wild forest because at the beginning of our conversation, if you recall, you represented the Hebrew language as a lifeless hieroglyph without vowels and without any key to its meaning. Do you really believe that the people of the Ancient Near East wrote entirely without vowels?

A: Many people say so.

E: And by doing so, they say something contradictory. Who would write letters without the breath that brings them to life? For everything depends on that breath, and it is fundamentally easier to designate it in some general way

45. [Ps. 33:9.]

than the various consonants. As soon as the more difficult task was accomplished, the easier one was certainly not neglected, especially since the whole purpose of the work depended on it.

A: But then where are these vowels?

E: Read a book on the subject[46] that throws much light upon this and many other aspects of Hebrew antiquity. It is the first introduction to the language and writings of the Hebrews that equally combines good taste and scholarship. It is probable they had some, although few, vowels (for those we now have are a later device of the rabbis); the vowel markings appear to be a remnant of them. Grammatical precision, however, was not sought after in those ancient times, and the pronunciation was perhaps as irregular as Otfried[47] says it was in Old High German. Who has ever invented letters for every vowel of the dialect in which we speak? And who would use them if they were invented? The letters stand as general signs, and each person modifies the sound to suit his or her own voice. A series of refined grammatical rules on the change of vowels, the derivation of the conjugations, and so on, are, I fear, nothing but empty wind.

A: And yet the youth are tormented with these rules. I could imagine that a language as unrefined as the Hebrew could have as many regular and significantly different conjugations as young students are forced to find in every word. The multitude of irregularities and defective words show that I am right. The great number of such classifications have been derived from other Near Eastern languages according to which the rabbis liked to modify their own language. They took whatever they could into their little Hebrew tent.

E: Here again, we must not exaggerate. It is good and necessary for us to grasp the artificial grammatical structure of the language, even though it is highly unlikely that this is its earliest structure or that every Hebrew person thought about it in this way. How many authors even in our own language have the entire structure of their language down to its minutest inflection so fully in their heads that they never deviate from it? Further, look how much the structure of language varies with time! It is good that we finally have men who are thinking about the grammar of the Hebrew language.

A: It seems to me that we all have to create our own philosophical grammar. Once we omit the vowels and other marks now and then, the conjugations come closer together. We do not need to strangle a word seven times until it finally fits a structure.

E: Each person could become too, by this method, a second Masclef or Hutchinson.[48] The best course is to train the eye diligently with paradigms

46. [Johann Gottfried] Eichhorn's *Einleitung ins Alte Testament* (Leipzig: Weidmann, 1782) Part 1, 126. [The complete work is in 3 volumes, published 1780-83.]

47. [Otfried (or Otfrid), a monk and poet of the ninth century.]

48. [Francois Masclef (1662-1728), French Hebrew scholar; John Hutchinson (1674-1737), English theological writer who wrote on the Hebrew language.]

and the ear with the living sounds of the language and to bring both together. In this way one enters the genius of the language and shortens the path of rules. The language will then no longer be for us pedantic and rabbinical; rather, it will become the ancient Hebraic, that is, a poetic language. The child's attention must be roused by Hebrew poetry, and the youth rewarded by it. I am sure that not only young children but also adults would like the Bible as much as they like Homer or Ossian, if they knew what was in it.

A: Perhaps I would too, if you continued your conversation with me in the same way that you have started it.

E: Let's continue the discussion of the subject when we take our walks, preferably in the morning hours. The poetry of the Hebrews belongs under the open sky and, if possible, in the light of the early dawn.

A: Why does it belong there?

E: Because this poetry was itself the dawn of the enlightenment of the world, and it still is truly a poetry from the childhood of the human race. In this poetry we see the soul's earliest intuitions, its simplest ways of thinking, and the most basic elements that bound and guided it. Even if we believed nothing of its wondrous content, we would have to believe the language of nature in it, for we would feel it. We should appreciate the first human intuitions of things, for we can learn something from them. This poetry shows us the earliest logic of the senses, the most basic analysis of ideas, the primary principles of morals, in short, the most ancient history of the human mind and heart. Even if it were the poetry of cannibals, do you not think it would be worthy of our attention for this reason?

A: I will see you tomorrow.

The Psalms

No book of Scripture, except the Song of Solomon, has endured as many false interpretations and distortions of its original meaning as the book of Psalms.[49] In his own time, David made his feelings known and made his own style of singing the predominant style in the temple. It has been argued that this means the Psalms were intended to be a hymnbook for every time, for all peoples and all hearts, even for those who had no connection either with the spirit or the deeds of David. How could this happen? How else except by greatly stretching the meaning of the Psalms and by skewing their original themes and feelings? All commentators, all new versifiers, found in the Psalms their own time, their own needs, their own domestic and familial relations; and in this way they adapted the Psalms to the singing and reading of their own church. All the Psalms of David were sung as if every member of the

49. [SW 12:207-11.]

church had wandered upon the mountains of Judah and been persecuted by Saul. They sang against Doeg and Ahitophel, and they cursed the Edomites and the Moabites. When they could do no more, they put the curses in the mouth of the one who never returned rebuke for rebuke, nor threats for suffering. Read the devotional versifications of the most personal, the most characteristically beautiful songs of David, of Asaph, and of Korah, and then follow them back to their original context and source. Does one find even a trace of their original form remaining?

In order to attain your own view of the Psalms as lyric poetry of David's age, the following points are essential:

1. We should disregard all modern imitations and commentators, even if they were the most highly prized and the best for their time. They read the Psalms for their own time with their own purpose in mind; they applied the language, the consolation, and teaching of the Psalms to their own time. Our aim, however, is to view the Psalms in their original historical context and within that context to perceive the heart and mind of David and the poets associated with him.

2. In accordance with this aim we should seek first the subjects and situations to which these poems refer. These are cited in the superscription of many of the Psalms; in others they are determined by the contents; and in others they are not known. Here, however, the reader must guard against two things. First, do not insist upon finding a Psalm about every trivial event in the life of David. Second, do not make up a situation in his life for every minor trope in the Psalms. The former has been done to David, just as to every other lyric poet. People wanted to find a reference for everything; they wanted to have a memorial plaque *(miktam)*[50] for every minor circumstance. In pursuing the latter, that is, finding a situation to fit every word of a Psalm, people have imagined outrageous things (such as Psalms about smallpox and other things) about which the interpreter indeed might have known something, but of which the poet knew nothing at all.

3. We should study the peculiar langauge of David and his singers by comparing the different Psalms with each other and with the history of that period. It is obvious that the royal poet had his favorite expressions; they can all be explained in relation to his context. "The Lord is my shield," "he is on my right hand," "he sets me in a wide place," "he leads me to high places," and so on, are expressions of this kind. There are also a series of other expressions that have been common for centuries in the language of the church, but whose meaning have in part been badly distorted. A book about the poetical idioms in these songs would be useful, and indeed we are in need of a similar book for all the principal writers of the Old Testament.

50. [A Hebrew word that is found in the superscription of many Psalms and whose meaning is unknown; it is left untranslated in the NRSV.]

4. We should treat the feelings that are expressed so prevalently in the Psalms neither as an enemy nor as a blind defender of them. These feelings represent the character traits of individual human beings and should be explained as such without mistaking them for universal models of holy feelings. As a fugitive and a king, David had his own emotions and worries. We are neither of these. We should, therefore, neither curse enemies whom we do not have nor magnify ourselves as their conquerors. We must, however, learn to understand and appreciate these feelings. The Scripture itself gives us much information about them, since it does not conceal David's character, not even his failings. The man who sinned against Uriah and Bathsheba could also be hasty with his words. He was rash, persecuted, and a warrior. He often spoke not in his own name, but in the name of his people, as a father of his country. But in all circumstances he was a human being. His songs document his history, and history documents his songs. Anyone who tries to see everything in a supernatural glow will, in the end, see nothing at all.

5. When examining works of art, we should not use examples from other nations and languages as standards by which to judge them. The composition of a song must be judged with reference to the individual nature of the feelings, sentiments, and language out of which it grew. What does it mean when people call this or that Psalm "Pindaric"? Does it mean that it contains bold transitions, lofty maxims, and historical allusions? Must not the same necessarily be found in all songs of praise? In reference to his artistic composition, however, David has nothing more than this in common with Pindar. Pindar's lyrical language, his phrases and poetic meter, his use of material from mythology and ancient history, and the nature of his subject matter itself hardly allow for a comparison. We are sure to draw false conclusions if we let ourselves be blinded by the word "chorus." A Hebrew chorus is not at all the same thing as a Greek one.

6. Still less should we judge David according to our own structure of rules for lyric poetry. These rules are not even applicable to the odes of Horace, even though the rules were supposedly derived from them. Most often it was the literary critic's narrow perspective that was barely acquainted with the lyrical treasures of several languages, that confined its view to a few favorite works, and that framed this structure of rules according to them. How can they be applied, then, to an entirely different age? To a much simpler situation and language? Rules are appropriate when they flow from the nature of the feelings and the appropriation of the theme of which the poet sings; the character traits of the singer, the situation, and the language also play a role. Rules, therefore, should always be applied in a flexible and partial way. In short, if the rules are to be appropriate, then who would not prefer to feel and unfold them from the original song itself, instead of borrowing the rules from foreign models and poetics and thus violating the original simplicity of

ancient song through the artificial subtleties of modern lyrical invention? Whoever is not able to feel the beauty of lyrical poetry on its own terms will never learn to do so by force of artificial rules.

7. We should display Hebrew lyric poetry in its original nature and beauty. A teacher of the Psalms should point the student's attention to questions such as: What particular subject is addressed? What is the interest attached to it? In what manner is it sung? What feeling prevails in the song? What course does this feeling take? Into what sentiments does it unfold? How does it begin, proceed, and end? The more simply and impressively such questions are pointed out to the youthful reader without pedantry and without sentimentality, the more this poetry will find its way to the reader's heart. Vociferous praise of the poetry will not be necessary to help the readers love what is beautiful in it; the original strains of passion in the poetry will automatically make their impression upon them. If readers have a spark of lyrical sense in them, then Yahweh will inspire them. The simplicity of the development in Hebrew songs is an essential characteristic, for only very few of them were created as works of art. Instead, they sprang forth as genuine feelings from an impassioned heart. If only we had an edition of the Psalms in which David were treated like Horace! In which, without casuistry, the poet would be presented as a poet! The poet's beauty would not be shouted into our ears; but at the same time it would not be defaced by a patchwork of foreign languages and verse forms. In higher criticism of Hebrew poetry we are still in our infancy. We either strangle ourselves with variants of the original text or embellish the simplicity of the original with the modish attire of modern languages. . . .

ON THE GOSPELS

Preface (from *Concerning the Savior of the Human Race*)

This text, like the two previous texts in this series [*On the Gift of Tongues* and *On the Resurrection* (Riga: 1794)], was written several years ago.[51] The contents of the text itself may show why it has been published only now.

The purpose of this text is not to teach instructors, to inform the wise, to correct the masters, or to convince those who are demonstrating their own positions. At a certain age we like to stick to our own opinions, and it is foolish to try to force our own opinions on others. However, there are plenty of unbiased souls who do not yet have an opinion and perhaps do not even know left from right in these confusing times. It is my humble and, if I may

51. [SW 19:137-38,194-201,207-17. These selections on the Gospels are taken from two volumes of the *Christliche Schriften: Vom Erlöser der Menschen* (1797) and *Vom Gottes Sohn der Welt Heiland* (1797).]

say so, purely Christian intention to guide these people to the right path so
that they are able to say with certainty, "This is it, and this is not."

In order to achieve this aim I have avoided any dogmatism, mysticism,
unnecessary philological remarks, church history, and so on, and held fast to
the following questions: What are the Gospels? What is Christianity? What
was their nature and purpose in their genesis? What are they for us today?
The fourth Gospel, which was composed in such a unique way, will broaden
and complete this set of questions. We gladly give an account of those thoughts
belonging to our life's work. The contents of this text is part of my life's
work. I began this work early in my life, have gone back to it under the most
diverse circumstances, and have devoted very unbiased investigations to it.
I invite the unbiased reader to use these investigations with me. . . .

Part Four (from *Concerning the Savior* of the *Human Race*)

1. . . . How do the first three evangelists narrate all they have said about
Christ? Are their Gospels a *history* or a *biography* modeled after some Greek
or Roman ideal? No, and to expect this from them is completely inappropriate.
Historians belong to their particular nation, time, and language; and biog-
raphers belong precisely to that one whose life they depict.

2. The Greek style of writing history was initially modeled after their
manner of singing and the design of their rhapsodists and later after their
republican constitutions. In regard to the structure of his writing, Herodotus
was a Homer in prose. The *Attic historians* did not merely weave speeches
into their accounts of history, but rather modeled speeches about history after
the public addresses or special speeches that were influenced by the constitution
of their states, their stage of development, and ultimately by the spirit of the
people and the genius of their language. Rome modeled its history after the
Greek and after *its own* constitution. Again, historians of both nations are
individually characterized in terms of the time, circumstances, and period that
they describe.

3. The attempt to find *Attic* or *Roman* historians among the evangelists is
futile, not so much because of particular expressions but because of the whole
spirit of their way of thinking and writing. Scholars have devoted considerable
attention to locating in almost every classical Greek and Roman writer words
that are similar to those of the evangelists. But this research has not attained
its goal because *style,* in the profounder sense of the term, that is, *the spirit
of the way of thinking and writing,* is something altogether different than
individual words and formulae.[52] Justin called the gospels the "Memorabilia

52. The learned and intricate *observationes* of the New Testament by Raphel, Kypke, Elsner,

of the Apostles"; but it is a great mistake to expect from the Gospels "Socratic Memorabilia" after the model of Xenophon. The evangelists could no more write such memoirs than the early Christians could care to read them. Even among the sophisticated Arabs, the Greek style of history never took root, and what would a Persian or an Indian read in Tacitus?

4. The Hebrew style of writing history, like Hebrew poetry, belongs to the *childhood of the human race* and is an expression of it. Genealogies, ancestral sagas, prophets, and kings constitute its history; they are all expressed in the tone of the simplest narrative and include views of the world like those that are cherished in childhood, like those that were indispensable to the human race at that time; they include miraculous phenomena, poetic expressions, parabolic speeches, and the like. The very earliest history of the Greeks and Romans also possessed similar characteristics; but as the cultures of these people progressed, they mitigated and disguised the characteristics of this ancient way of thinking and seeing. Among the Hebrews, however, these characteristics remained as they had been. This is because the nation had not developed since Isaiah's time, and Isaiah lived in a very early era, during the time of the Greek rhapsodists, when they were barely acquainted with the Phoenician alphabet. Thus, after the probing of millennia, a more modern view of things and a closer acquaintance with the process of nature entered into the first rudiments of Greek culture, something that the Hebrews always lacked. Even in later times, and even when it was written in the Greek language, the history of the Hebrews still had the tone of the ancient prophetic sayings. This is evident in all of the apocryphal writings, which were written almost a thousand years after Moses, and even in the more sophisticated writers, the authors of the books of the Maccabees, Philo, and Josephus. In their view of things and even often in the structure of their speech, they seldom disguise their Hebrew authorship.

5. Putting aside everything that is foreign, then, we must place ourselves in the character of a nation *that was not acquainted with foreign literature and dwelt in the midst of its ancient holy books, which were* (in the original language or in translation) *"the sanctuary of all wisdom."* In these books every letter was divine, every parable a heavenly mystery; and whoever wrote something composed it in accordance with this way of thinking. The writings that especially had to be composed in this way were those that were to show the fulfillment of the spirit of *all* those ancient writings: the *Gospels*. The

---

and others are well known. They will always remain useful and were collected with very good intentions, although they have received exaggerated praise. For example, one philologist in 1732 wrote: "The Holy Spirit took great delight especially in the words and phrases of Polybius and deemed them worthy enough to imitate him." Similar eulogies are to be found in several places. What in recent times has been gathered from Philo, the Septuagint, and the apocryphal writings comes closer to the mark.

mere mention of their name informs us of their content, their structure, and
their style of writing.

6. The proclamation *(kērygma)* of John [the Baptist] was only the voice
of a herald, a servant preparing the way. As soon as a Messiah from heaven
was announced, the *gospel* began, the good news that "the long-awaited one
is here." Jesus came to Galilee with this good news (Mark 1:14, 15); and he
pointed to it in the Torah (Luke 4:17-19). His disciples proclaimed this gospel.
Christ explained the form, the duties, and hopes of his kingdom in parables
and teachings. He suffered and died for this gospel, and after his resurrection
he commissioned his disciples to spread it throughout the world. *Thus, before
a single one of our Gospels was written, the gospel was present* in the
proclamation of Christ and the apostles.

7. On the first Pentecost, Peter spoke of the man whom God had attested,
who was promised by the prophets and anointed with God's spirit, who had
brought the true kingdom of God to earth, who had shown himself alive after
his crucifixion, and who had gone to heaven in order to reveal himself and
his kingdom in his own time. These words of Peter constituted a *complete,
Christian gospel* (Acts 2:22-39). We find the very same content of this gospel
expressed in other words in all the speeches of Peter and the apostles (Acts
3:12-26; 4:10-12; 10:36-42; 13:26-41; 17:30-31). *He is the Christ, the son of
the living God; this was the rock on which the church was to be built* (Matt.
16:16-17). The apostles did not first of all need to come to an agreement over
this gospel and painstakingly achieve a unified understanding of it; they did
not first of all need to put it into writing and, according to the childish fable,
have each one of the twelve add a word to it. It was placed in their mouths
before and after the resurrection; it was the conception of the thing itself,
history.[53] Such a gospel, as testimony and message, lay at the basis of every
speech of the apostles.

8. Thus, it became a *symbol of the new church,* a symbol of the gathering
of all kinds of peoples. To be baptized in the name of Jesus meant to be
baptized on the basis of this confession; it meant to believe and accept the
gospel. Even the baptismal formula (Matt. 28:19) in its oldest form expressed
nothing but this. This was *canon,* the *ground* and the *rule* of Christianity
(norma fidei) that was even sung in hymns, such as in the one cited by Paul:

> I hope to come to you soon, but I am writing these instructions to you so that,
> if I am delayed, you may know how one ought to behave in the household of

53. If we insist on calling it an "agreement," then the rule of the agreement is clearly stated
in Acts 1:21-22: "So one of the men who have accompanied us during all the time that the Lord
Jesus went in and among us, beginning from the baptism of John until the day when he was
taken from us—one of these must become a witness with us to his resurrection."

God, which is the church of the living God, the pillar and bulwark of the truth.
Without any doubt, the mystery of our religion is great:

> He was revealed in flesh,
> vindicated in spirit,
> seen by angels,
> proclaimed among Gentiles,
> believed in throughout the
> world,
> taken up in glory. (1 Tim. 3:14-16)

Each symbol of the catechumens, like our second article, says the same thing,
but in simple terms.

9. If a *gospel* were therefore written in such a state of affairs, then it could
not be recorded other than *in this spirit*. Anecdotes from the private life of
Jesus were thereby neither aim nor intention, for the authors and people of
the Christian world for which they wrote did not constitute our modern public,
which is composed of avid writers and readers. No one from the Roman world
bothered about this prophet, and for the Jews he was an outrage. This is why
there is no reflection on Jesus in either Roman or Jewish history. Until his
thirtieth year he led a secluded life. Only his relatives could have known
anything about him from this time, but they recorded nothing of the sort (not
even his halfbrother, James). Since we know nothing about this period, and
since our Gospels are apparently written according to the basic features that
were sketched by the *oral gospel* that preceded them, who would want to fail
to recognize this *outline* in them and therefore misunderstand the *intention*
that was common to all of the disciples of Christ? *These Gospels were written
so that you might believe that Jesus is the Christ, the Son of God.* This was
the "rock," on which Christendom was to be built (Matt. 16:16-18), *the
"pillar" and the "bulwark of the truth"* (1 Tim. 3:15-18), on which it was
erected; this was *the great mystery that was to be confessed in every symbol*
and therefore the assigned form of teaching that, according to the nature of
the matter, was already called *"gospel."* Paul, who had also received this
gospel, was able to say: "If an angel from heaven preaches another to you,
may he be damned."

10. We can unbiasedly point to this "holy epic"[54] in our three Gospels as
they are. Since the return from Babylon, that is, for four centuries, people
had selected "signs of an awaited Messiah" from the Holy Scripture; at the
time of Christ, people wanted to know exactly whence he could and could

---

54. "Epic" does not mean "fiction" or "fable"; the latter terms fall under "myths." Peter
distinguished his gospel from cleverly derived myths *(sesophismenois mythois)*, calling the gospel
the testimony of an eyewitness (2 Pet. 1:16-18). "Epic" (speech) refers here to the speech of
the Gospels in terms of their *composition and intention;* they are neither mere biography nor
memoirs and anecdotes of a private individual, but rather Gospels of a Christ who was honored
as such in three parts of the world (Matt. 26:13).

not come. Thus, a certain formula, which had been handed down for a few thousand years (naturally with alterations) in the enslaved daughters of the tradition (the Jewish schools), was already established at the time of Christ (Matt. 2:4-6; John 7:41-43, 52), and perhaps even already at the time of the Maccabees, when on the iron tablet was written, "Until the great prophet comes." The Jewish interpreters of Scripture are full of these "signs of the Messiah," and they are still the same signs that we see clearly lying at the base of the evangelists. For example (according to Abarbanel, who lived in the fifteenth century and was certainly no friend of Christians), the Messiah had to be of the lineage of David, a wise prophet and discerner of the human heart, a friend of the people and its merciful servant, a peacemaker, a unifier of the scattered tribes, a king of all nations, a restorer of the ancient, golden time, one for whom songs of praise resound from all corners of the earth. It was natural that the evangelists did not simply take the same sort of ideas, as we say, "into consideration" when writing for their age and nation. Rather, these kinds of ideas were so fundamental to them that without this given "canon of the Messiah" no Gospel would have taken place. The apostles appeal everywhere to this "fixed prophetic word." Without it and without a canon that was derived from it and that served as the foundation of the Gospels, we cannot explain at all the structure of the Gospels at various points. With it, everything becomes clear.

11. For example, Matthew begins his gospel in this way: "An account of the genealogy of Jesus the Messiah, the *Son of David*." He counts the families (arranged numerically for memory's sake) up to Jesus, as does Luke in his own way. Both evangelists allege that Jesus, the son of a betrothed virgin, was born in "the city of David." Matthew adds that right after Jesus' birth, a delegation of wise men from the East recognized him, the future "king of the nations," as their own king. The brightness that hovered over him at his baptism is compared to a dove because the prophets said that "gentleness" was a trait of the Messiah and the dove was known as a symbol of gentleness. He appears everywhere as a "vanquisher of Satan," as a "destroyer of the kingdom of devils." All the evangelists noted that he was a "discerner of the human heart" and a warm "friend of the people"; the evangelists noted that as their "merciful helper" he marched into Jerusalem and performed not only more and greater miracles than Moses, Elijah, and Elisha, but also precisely the type of comforting, healing miracles that the coming Messiah was supposed to perform. "An Elijah went before him," as the prophecy would have it, but even the "Elijah in paradise" and Moses participated in his work. They visit him in his loneliness and see him, as they once did on Sinai and Horab, in the splendor of his apotheosis. The "sleeping saints" who, shaken by his death, rise from their graves and many of whom appear in the holy city, are noted by Matthew because they, too, as models of the final resurrection of

the dead, belong to the "signs of the Messiah."[55] The same is true in several other minor details, especially in quotations in the Gospels of individual passages from the Psalms and the prophets. It is not necessary to bicker with the evangelists about why they cite such passages in the places and in the senses that they do. These passages belonged to the canon of the signs of the Messiah, which had been accepted and passed on for two thousand years; this canon was the foundation of all the Gospels, *including the Gospel of John*. Allusions to this canon are even more frequent and subtle in the Gospel of John than in the other three Gospels.[56] . . .

13. One thing, to be sure, is indisputable: as soon as Christendom existed as *faith*, that is, as *oral gospel*, sooner or later, given the conditions of the time and the nature of the matter itself, *written gospels* could not fail to appear. The content of the oral gospel was prophetic-historical. Every speech about it, therefore, had to be interpretive-historical, that is, had to indicate the fulfillment of ancient prophecies in Jesus, which is to say that Jesus is the Christ. The historical part of this proof, the application of the prophecies, became therefore *gospel, a history of Christ*. Now who could have prevented all catechumens for the entire future from writing down for themselves this historical commentary of their faith that *Jesus is the Christ* or from troubling themselves any further with it? A gospel came into existence immediately. The introduction to the Gospel of Luke, Acts, and other traditions indicate that there were catechumens troubling themselves with it.

And had not apprentices applied themselves to it, *philosophers* were there who sought to attach this history to their theories or notions. As soon as they began distorting or undermining the confession of faith in which Christians believed, the true history had to be maintained in opposition to them, and thus a gospel had to be written. The first centuries show no lack of such distortions. Most of the apostolic epistles were also prompted by such errant teachers. Even if none of these errant teachers had existed, the rapid expansion of Christianity itself would have unavoidably produced *written gospels*. In Palestine and in Egypt, in both the Greek and the Latin tongues, people would have desired an *historical commentary on their confession of faith*. This is

55. See [Christian] Schöttgen [1687-1751], *Horae [Hebraicae et Talmdicae in universum Novum Testamentum* (Dresden: Apud C. Hekelii, 1733-42)] at Matt. 27:52] and *Jesus der wahre Messias* [Leipzig: Breitkopf, 1748], 803. In general these and other well-known collections become interesting even to those who do not want to convert Jews, inasmuch as one sees clearly in them the signs according to which the gospels were formulated and arranged.

56. This is so clear that if the evangelists themselves did not make it evident to us, the testimony of the entire early church would have made us believe it. "The gospel is *prescribed* in the prophets, and after them it is proclaimed by the apostles; the root is planted in the former, it sprouts forth in the latter." This is the way the teachers of the very early church speak of and refer to the prophets. The Gospel is for them the *fulfilled and condensed word (logos syntetmēnenos)*. They debate about the canon on the basis of the prophets, and clearly the apostles did the same (2 Pet. 1:19-21).

why Palestinian, Syrian, Egyptian, Greek, and Latin gospels came into existence. If they had not been composed by apostles or the assistants of the apostles, then they would have arisen on their own.

And since each province, each church, wished to be converted by an apostle or an assistant of an apostle, each naturally strove to have an *apostolic gospel*; that is, the instruction that they enjoyed concerning their confession of faith was to be given and confirmed by an apostle or his assistants. Therefore, there were *gospels of all the apostles who had planted churches, even if none of them had written one*. Their historical instruction in the faith that Jesus is the Christ was called their gospel. People raised an outcry over the plurality of the gospels and tried to discredit or disavow this plurality. This clearly indicates some ignorance about what "gospel" originally meant.[57] It was the nature of the case that many gospels came into being. Even if today we had ten such historical commentaries, instead of four, this greater number would be advantageous for the study of the history, but not damaging to Christianity. If they were built on the same foundation of faith, then their differences would be as harmless to Christianity as the variations among the gospels we do possess; if they deviated from this foundation, then they would not be Christian gospels. *The gospels have been written so that you might believe that Jesus is the Christ, the son of God. If any do not bring this doctrine, do not receive them as Christians* (John 20:31; 1 John 4:1-3; 2 John 9, 10). This is why the teachers of the church, who declared themselves so zealously opposed to every distortion of the symbol as an historical foundation of faith, not only allowed some diversity in the recounting of historical circumstances but even cite sayings of Christ from such provincial gospels. Why should they not have cited them since they were tradition, like the other gospels? No one could establish another foundation of faith beside the one that had been established, no matter how many gospels might have been written. Paul himself, in spite of all of his lofty revelations, had to travel to Jerusalem and come to an understanding with the witnesses of the history of Christ about the gospel that he preached. Otherwise, Paul would have "run far afield" and would not have been a Christian apostle (Gal. 2:1-3). He wanted to apply his doctrine as he was able and as he found appropriate. But the gospel itself as *historical*

---

57. I do not wish to mention the names of those who raised this outcry over the plurality of gospels any more than the names of the anguished defenders. [Isaac de] Beausobre [1659-1738] has written an essay about this subject that seems to me to be on the right track and scholarly, but it proceeds too fearfully and thus does not arrive at the natural reason for the plurality of these treatises. The beautiful essay is translated in J. A. Cramer's [1723-88] *Beiträge zur Beförderung theologischer [und andrer wichtigen] Käntnisse* [Kiel/Hamburg: Bohn, 1777-83], Part 2. In contrast, [Johann Salomo] Semler [1725-91], a highly esteemed name in the criticism of these writings and of early church history, which goes along with them, seems to me to be too liberal with the so-called evangelical treatises, for he works without authority, reference to the sources, and purpose. He seems neither to have thought entirely in the spirit of the first Christian century nor to have clearly organized his thoughts.

foundation was given to him, and even he held fast to this rule (Gal. 6:14, 16; 1 Cor. 3:10-15).

14. It was impossible therefore for Christendom, expanding at this time, in this region, and among these nations, to remain without written records, that is, without gospels; it is equally impossible to imagine for this age and situation an apostolic gospel-chancery in Jerusalem that sent treatises with each teacher for each congregation and certified him by means of written gospels. In Acts, which contains the most remarkable period of the first quarter of a century of Christendom, one finds not only no trace of such a chancery, but also an entirely different spirit in the cultivation of congregations. Apostles were sent *to teach,* not to pass around evangelical treatises. They expanded Christendom by means of *living speech;* they also installed teachers and dispatched assistants. Their sermon was a *sound, a voice,* a living epistle in the heart—not an edited letter (Rom. 10:8-18; 2 Cor. 3, 13). Such a letter would not have accomplished what they accomplished. The entire way of representing our evangelists as *scholarly writers (grammateis, scribae)* who collected, amplified, improved, collated, and compared treatises is utterly alien to the way they are represented in all ancient documents that speak of them, even more alien to the comparison of the evangelists themselves, and most alien to their vocation and the purpose of their gospels. Indeed, such a view of the evangelists is so strange that all justifications of it seem to me to be like the wind: No one knows either whence it came or wither it blows. Instead of wearily patching these things together, why did the evangelists not go and talk to eyewitnesses, who enjoyed respect in the church and were still alive? And what should we think of an *apostolic chancery* that produced such variations? What should we think of apostles who were so unsure of things that their closest daily friends and yearly companions had to patch together the entire historical foundation on which Christianity, the work of their entire lives, was based? People confuse themselves with hypotheses of this kind to such a degree that not only are all the evangelists' contradictions even more glaring, but in the end people do not even know which evangelist copied from, amplified, shortened, separated, improved, worsened, and stole from the other. Why indeed, that is, for what rational purpose, did they do all this so trivially, aimlessly, and miserably? It is certain that no evangelist was born in our century or wrote his Gospel in order to practice higher or lower criticism on his neighbor. No evangelist wanted to build over the others or to overpower them. On the contrary, each set down *his* narration for his own sake. Perhaps not one of the evangelists saw the gospel of another; if he did, then he did not use it as he wrote his own. We do not have 4 - 2 + ½ - ¾ + ⅐, but rather since the time of Irenaeus and Tertullian, the church has had *four* evangelists.

15. A complete view of them also indicates that they have not worked from one so-called *Urevangelium*. Neither apostolic nor church history is acquainted with this *Urevangelium*. No church father appeals to it as the original source of truth in the dispute over false gospels. Irenaeus, Tertullian, Origen are not acquainted with it, and the effort to derive our gospels from it or to reduce them to it ties not one knot but a hundred. . . .

16. "But what about the differences between the gospels?" They are so natural that if we just give up the strange notion that one evangelist wanted to amplify, shorten, improve the *others,* and if instead we view each evangelist on his own terms, and with each, as if he were the only one, try to put ourselves back in the era of early Christianity, then everything sorts itself out automatically. As *apostles and eyewitnesses,* Matthew and John stand on their own, while Mark and Luke are *evangelists.* With these words everything is explained.

17. A law is written; good news is *proclaimed.* This is what the *apostles and evangelists* preached. Evangelists were *assistants, representatives of the apostles.* They accompanied them on trips, carried on their instruction, interpreted them at those points where the apostles did not speak the language as fluently; and since the foundation of the apostolic teaching was history, the evangelists told this history. These are the reasons for their name: evangelists, co-workers, servants of the gospel, subordinates in service to the Word *(synergoi, diakonoi euaggeliou, hupēretai logou).* As such they traveled to the congregations *(periiontes ekērusson)* without having a specific place themselves, until they were established as permanent teachers of one or more congregations.[58] . . . Evangelists were, therefore, a *distinctive class of teachers* who stood behind the apostles and prophets, that is, the interpreters of the prophecies of the Old Testament. The central task of their office was to relate *the teaching and history of Jesus for the comprehension of everyone* (Eph. 4:11). From the mouth of the apostles, whom they thus also accompanied several years, the evangelists had received their gift; they communicated it to others as an *oral gospel.* In this age the act of entrusting *(paradosis)* was everything. Even Paul in his epistles, especially to Timothy and Titus, frequently referred to it (1 Tim. 1:2, 3-11, 18; 3:15, 16; 4:6, 14-16; 6:14,20,21; 2 Tim. 1:6, 12-14; 2:2-8; 3:10-14; 4:2-5). The oldest church fathers talk of nothing else from this age of oral tradition, and Papias explicitly cites what he received from this or that apostle or evangelist. With Luke it is no different. He appeals in the beginning of his gospel not to *writings* that he compiled, but to *news* which he received orally from eyewitnesses, the apostles, and servants of the word *(hypēretais logou),* evangelists (Luke 1:2).

58. [Johann Caspar] Suicerus, *Thesaurus [ecclesiasticus, e patribus graecis ordine alphabetico exhibens* (Amsterdam: Apud J. H. Wetstenium, 1682)], 1:1234; [Johann Friedrich] Schleusner, *Novum lexicon graeco-latinum in Novum Testamentum* [Leipzig: Weidmann, 1792], 1:834 et al.

18. Of course, the evangelists who transmitted the gospel orally had to receive during their instruction a circle (*cyclus*) which gave boundaries to their narrative, and this circle was the one that the apostles had from the beginning of their preaching. It is clearly cited in Acts (Acts 1:21–22; 2:23-36; 10:36-43). Since all the narratives came from a single source, from the apostles themselves, since everything at that time was intimately connected (Acts 2:34; 4:32), and since the instruction of the followers was the primary task of the apostles (Acts 6:3-7), the evangelists were educated in this way and by accompanying the apostles. In our three Gospels, for example, the *same* parables, miracles, stories, and speeches come up. From this one sees that the general tradition of these "evangelical rhapsodists" (if I may use this expression) closely follows what is narrated to them. Often, the material is narrated with the same words because this, too, is the very nature of an oral saying, especially an apostolic one, which was retold again and again, as we observe in Peter's sermons and in the letters of the apostles themselves. They were *established, sacred sayings*.

Yet this uniformity never went so far that each evangelist became a mouth-piece for the other, as our three Gospels testify once again. There is no parable, no miracle, almost no saying and no story that each evangelist does not say in his own way. There is a variety and freedom in their speech, which extend from the most irrelevant circumstance to the most important formulae, such as the Lord's Prayer, the words of institution, and all the speeches *[Reden]* of Christ. It is evident that *each of the narrators narrates freely*. Each evangelist, even the laconic Mark, relates circumstances, speeches, and miracles peculiar to his own Gospel. John relates ones unique to his Gospel. When Paul speaks about the resurrection, while preaching to the Corinthians, he refers to appearances of Jesus that none of our evangelists mention (1 Cor. 15:6, 7). Thus, none of the evangelists were collared like a slave by the yoke of words that are prescribed or learned by rote—a burden that is completely at odds with the word "gospel" and "evangelist." We know how freely evangelists and apostles cite passages of the prophets, even in written texts. We know how freely passages from them are cited by the church fathers, after this history was written down. Indeed, we know that one and the same writer can tell the same story in the same book with a different setting and under different circumstances. Luke's various accounts of the conversion of Paul are an example (Acts 9, 22, 26). All of this belongs to the *oral speech and instruction—to the catechetical teaching*—of those times. This free spirit of discourse breathes in every line of every evangelist; the *spirit* is not the *letter* (John 6:63; 2 Cor. 3:6). From this perspective, the differences between our Gospels are not only obviously necessary but also illuminate the genius of each individual Gospel to such a degree that it seems as if it were the only one.

19. *The Gospel of Mark.* Born in Jerusalem, Mark was an early adherent
to Christianity. The apostles were often at his house (Acts 12:12), and he had
adequate opportunity to learn precisely the history of Jesus. He became a
helper, evangelist, companion of the apostles on trips for several years, a
companion of Barnabas (he was the latter's [cousin, Col. 4:10]), of Paul (Acts
12:25; 15:37-40), and according to the undisputed legend of antiquity, even
of Peter, who named him his son (1 Pet. 5:15). Mark accompanied Peter
(according to the tradition of Irenaeus and Eusebius) as *student* and *interpreter
(hermēneutēs); in short, as evangelist. Why should he not write down, let be
written down, or dictate what he had often told as an evangelist? According
to the legend, the congregation asked him to do this. Peter praises their
eagerness and says neither yes nor no. The Gospel is written down, and Peter
corroborates it, in other words, he testifies that nothing in it is false. With
this saying[59] (without the well-intentioned addition that Peter may have dictated
the Gospel), we are led to the character of the writing itself.

a. No Gospel has so little the marks of a literary work and so much the
living sound of someone telling a story. This is the reason for the perpetual
"and" or "and then" or "and said to them" that begin all the sentences and
for the many Syrian expressions that are found in the Codex of Beza and the
old Latin translation. It is the highly popular tone of a *Palestinian storyteller.*
This is why here and there lists of miracles performed by Jesus and of the
illnesses cured by him are used as transitions and abridgements of the speech;
in turn, in the narrative of *particular* miracles, minor circumstances are drawn
out extensively, as is natural for a storyteller to do. Working with the same
stories, Matthew and Luke greatly condense these circumstances. This is
because they do not *speak,* they *write.* The slate pencil alters the tone of the
speech.

b. It follows from this living speech that Mark left out a series of moral
aphorisms, such as those that Christ spoke on the mount. They belonged in
a written text or sermon, but not in a narrative. This is also the reason that
Mark leaves out the interpretation of parables and abbreviates other parables
and speeches. Yet he stresses those that he does cite by ending them with a
powerful line, with some gentle sentiment, or even with repetition of the same
apothegms. For example: "Where its worm does not die and its fire is not
extinguished!"; "What I say, I say to everyone: Awake!"; "Carry salt with
you and have peace among one another"; "He has done everything well";
"Everyone who touched him was healed"; and "He began to cry." Mark is
particularly fond of such endings in his abbreviated stories. His Gospel is

59. These sagas are cited by Wetstein, Lardner, and in every introduction to the evangelists.
We see in Acts 14:12 from the story of Paul and Barnabas the nature of the interpreter *(hermēneutēs)*
who accompanied the apostle. The Lycaonians called Paul "Hermes" because, being the most
eloquent, he interpreted and amplified the brief address of Barnabas *(ho hēgoumenos tou logou).*

structured to be delivered aloud; he ends and abbreviates the speech for the heart and the ear.

c. It is even more clearly fitting for an evangelist, that is, for a vivacious rhapsodist of this story, to leave out what does not serve *the circle of those around him.* He leaves out, for example, the genealogy, the story of the temptation, which was certainly not fit for everyone, the parallels between John [the Baptist] and Christ, and so on. It was the evangelist's duty to narrate and recite *for his circle* (2 Tim. 4:3-5; 1 Cor. 9:22, 23).

d. It is quite proper for Mark and Peter that Mark included in the story neither Peter, who was present, nor the tribute that Peter paid to Mark. Even though our age may show little respect for such humility, it was actually part of *apostolic virtue,* as can be established by several witnesses. The apostles did not praise themselves and did not allow others to praise them to their face. In contrast, the story of Peter's denial is told in detail.

In short, the Gospel of Mark is an *ecclesiastical gospel* written on the basis of a living narrative for public delivery in the congregation.[60] In this respect it is narrated, abridged, organized. It is not known with what verse it originally ended. The present ending of the Gospel obviously indicates the transition to something following, to a kind of history of the apostles, which perhaps ended with a history of the miracles and martyrs of the church in which the Gospel had been preserved. Even the present ending indicates the Gospel's original distinctiveness as an *ecclesiastical gospel* and also indicates its character, in terms of which we can already explain almost everything about what is and what is not narrated in this Gospel. But why, in our distant times, in our estrangement from the situation of each individual congregation at that time, do we have to explain everything? . . .

On the Gospel Itself (from *Concerning the Savior of the Human Race*)

What we must read in the Gospels is the *gospel itself;*[61] this involves the *teaching,* the *character of Jesus,* and his *work,* that is, the provision that he intended to make for humanity's benefit. Since all three belong together, we will consider them in relation to one another.

1. The teaching of Jesus was simple and intelligible to all: *God is your Father; you are all brothers.*

2. "God is your father." Through this teaching Jesus excluded all servitude and slavish obedience, all empty ceremony, every national claim to a particular

---

60. (According to John the Presbyter or Papias in Eusebius) because Peter structured his teachings for his immediate needs, not intending to present the Lord's sayings in any particular order (*pros tas chreias epoieito tas didaschalias all' ouch' hosper syntaxin tōn kuriakōn poioumenos logōn*), Mark gave his gospel a historical framework.

61. [SW 19:239-50.]

god, and finally even the empty speculation that muses on the inner nature of God. A child does not speculate about the possible existence of its father, but assumes it as given in concrete acts of kindness, since the child regards its father as the author of its being, as its preserver, provider, and teacher. Likewise, the universal Father of all cannot be solved like a problem, demonstrated like a theory, or be worshiped with empty political ceremonies as an exclusive national deity. The God of Christ is "the only one who is *good*" (Matt. 19:17), the ideal of kindness and love; a Father who "sees in secret" and who rewards this hidden good (Matt. 6: 6, 18); a spirit who is worshiped only in spirit and in truth (John 4:24). Through Christianity the purest, most fruitful, and inwardmost conception of God thus became the most popular for all humanity. This concept of God is the foundation of the entire religion of Jesus.

3. For Jesus this concept of God involved not only a childlike respect for and love of God above all things, and an immeasurable trust in this fatherly being, but also the imitation of God as the original image of righteousness and justice, of universal goodness and generosity (Matt. 5:44-48). Jesus awakened the divine in human beings as children of God; he awakened an affinity with their universally active Father and made this feeling their principle: "We are of a divine nature, we are of God's race." We are not only to carry on a work of God here below (to do his will); rather, it is through human beings that providence carries on its noblest work. They are God's moral instrument of righteousness, goodness, and love. Christ portrayed this moral world of God and humanity as so interconnected that God can act toward us in no other way than we act toward one another. Thus, the law of requital, as any law of movement in nature, does not merely apply here and there, but rather *universally*—not arbitrarily or accidentally, but *essentially*. And for this reason, this law cannot be changed in this world or the next except through itself.

4. The same concept, God is the Father of all, links the human race as brothers—brothers of a noble stock of divine nature and quality. The more of this quality and character of the divine that human beings possess, and the more universal reason and a general idea of what is best, the more a universal charity in what is most necessarily the best takes shape in them; the more they feel like brothers according to this conception of the matter. Without knowing one another, they work toward the same plan, according to the same principles. They proceed toward what is most necessary first of all, to the root of things, and in the quietest manner. For this reason Christ speaks out so strongly against the Pharisees, the hypocrites, the superficial flatterers, the arrogant, and brings low the easy, superficial good that one performs in hope of reward or fame, out of habit, or to escape from boredom. We are to take care of those people whom no one else assists—to help the neglected, seek out the lost, heal the sick, fill the gaps and holes in the plan of providence,

and in this way become the most noble instrument of providence, its eye, ear, mind, heart, and helping hand. Such works are accomplished with God, and the more secretly and unassumingly they are performed, the more they are done for pure humanity, for the son of man (Matt. 25:40).

5. Since this good cannot occur without the resistance of evil, there is only one means against it: to endure and to overcome evil with good. The good by its nature is stronger and is the affair of God himself; thus, in the end the goal will be achieved. The strongest opposition is forbearance, patience, forgiveness, redoubled kindness and generosity. The sentiment of charity toward enemies that Christ enjoined is anything but dull indifference or intellectual laxity; rather, it is the most silent and strongest energy of a higher order. It is contrary to the original concept of Christianity to think that it manifests itself in a tepid indifference toward good and evil or in a dying lack of will power, since it was its author who made the most powerful will of a wise and gracious omnipotence not only his model but also the mainspring of his entire institution. Wherever a universal, eternal work of God is to be carried out in his stead, as an eye, a hand, or an instrument of providence regarding all of suffering humanity, then slumber is out of the question. There is work to be done until the task is completed; and as long as one evil exists, it is to be overcome with good. Whoever puts a hand to the plow and hesitates is not fit for this work. All good on earth must be done by godly folk; they are the active goodness and omnipotence.

6. What makes the teaching of Christ a predominant sentiment and an endless striving was perfectly and simply expressed by the *character of Jesus,* even down to his two names. He was called "son of God" and "son of man." For the beloved of God, the will of his Father was the most important rule, the driving force behind all his actions, even the most difficult, including the sacrifice of his life. He was indifferent to esteem, honor, riches, undeserved insult, and contempt. A work was to be carried out for which he bore the call: the work of God, the true and eternal business of providence to save our race and bless it. He carried out this work as son of man, that is, out of pure duty and for the highest interest of humanity. It had to be done from within, not from without, for the human race is responsible for its own misfortune. It is redeemed only when it is rescued from superstition, foolishness, vices, personal and national prejudices, bad tradition, corrupting habits (in whatever glistening forms they may appear), ill will, and indolence. It is not rescued by external force but through inner conviction, through higher activity, and by making an ever-effective impulse into habit. Beginning from within, humanity is made a holy, charitable, happy people, a family of children and brothers. Christ sacrificed himself for this plan with a zeal, a confidence in the good, with a kindness, patience, and gentleness whose equal in history

is unknown to me (however simply everything is presented here). Up to his last breath he was the son of God and son of man, lamb and lion.

7. *This character was unmistakably demonstrated in his fulfillment of his work,* for it was a work, not simply a teaching. His calling, his intention, was to bring among peoples a kingdom of God, that is, a true order and disposition worthy of God and humanity. This is why he immediately chose helpers who were not to be rabbinic students of a school of scriptural interpretation or new tradition, but rather the "light of the world", the "salt of the earth." He endeavored not merely to teach them, but to form their character. His association with them and even his instruction of them, built on those simple principles, was utterly practical. Consequently, he strove to remove their prejudices, to impart his sentiments about God and human beings, and to give them practice, heart, and courage for their appointed work. He said that everything, including their replies before tribunals, would turn out all right as long as his spirit was in them, as long as they acted with his sentiment. How could it be otherwise? If they entered his plan and participated actively in this work with conviction, then an ever-living kernel was planted for each one of their actions. The rest required time, effort, and experience. Thus, Jesus' association with his friends was an education that should be their model for the future education of human beings. Do not merely teach the people, said the risen one, but rather, "teach them to observe what I have commanded you; I will also be with you amidst this work." Christendom did not reach people's ears as preaching alone, but as a living, effective institution; not as a school, but as an active community.

8. Whether, as the history of the church has richly shown, it directly follows from this that all the faults and abuses of such an institution necessarily adhered to this human community, which was to be planted among all the nations, these abuses still cannot be blamed on the work itself or on the intention of its founder. The work had to be started; it is pure and necessary. One day humanity will recognize and honor the image of God within itself. One day everyone will learn to see that the human race is unhappy only through its own fault—through ignorance, prejudices, obstinacy, indolence, and vice, especially the vices that oppose universal righteousness and equity, love and active generosity. Among these vices are, for example, self-interest, violent lust for power, brutal pride, personal ambition, jealousy, slander, vengeance, fraud, oppression of others, and that disgraceful indolence that desires to maintain the status quo and to do nothing for the betterment of the whole. Someday the peoples will recognize that they are human beings and not robbers or wild animals who force themselves to devour and be devoured by one another. One day infidelity, oppression, luxury, vice, and indolence will appear equally shameful to all classes of human beings. For this reason this religion exists, and it will bring this about. Despite all the corruption that covered it,

this religion has undeniably helped to elevate consideration and respect for universal human feeling. The conclusions of the wise of all nations have embraced this religion. In conformity with its own principles, it has patiently taken these conclusions under its wing and made them the language of common sense, which now not even the most wicked person can oppose without being accused of nonsense or madness. Even the stagnant pond is covered with flowers, so that it does not appear in its real shape to the light of the sun.

9. And this work of God must continue throughout all times and nations. We can be certain of this because providence has either this work or none at all. And do we not see that everything contributes toward it? Sooner or later every wound must open; one day the mask will be torn from the face of every bit of nonsense and foolishness so that they are shown in their grotesque form. "Whatever is hidden," Christ says, "will be revealed. What I whisper in your ear now will someday be preached from the rooftops." This word of Christ has already been fulfilled in an extraordinary way. In the same way each of his words will be fulfilled. His religion is a "yeast" among the peoples (Matt. 13:33); with or without his name the whole loaf must be leavened by these principles. For they are the purest principles of reason and moral feeling, which the worst misery will finally bring to our attention if we continue to oppose the pure gospel of humanity. This gospel continues to speak and work in a thousand forms for humanity. The prince of the world need not first be judged; he has long since been judged in the gospel, and only gradually is his sentence being carried out. The kingdom does not come through outward preparations, but through inner conviction, strength, and truth.

10. *The abiding value of our Gospels will lie, then, in every word and feature of Christ.* The Gospels are valuable not only as the oldest documents of Christendom but also as sources for us without which we would not know the Savior's actual way of thinking, his intention, and the true quality of his work in *his* sense. Without the Gospels we would hear how Paul, Peter, and John regarded and understood the matter, but not what Christ initially and simply thought of it. The more occasional and the more Hebraic his words are, the more agreeable they are to us, for no reasonable person would have Christ be an Attic sage.

11. *Accordingly, the quarrel over the differences between the Gospels could be settled quite easily,* if those quarreling were concerned about a settlement.

One part of the Gospels, which deals with Jewish and Roman history, is merely *historical.* And just as the texts themselves (that is, their composition, style, materials, age, their transmission to us) must be tested simply according to historical-critical rules, so this part of the Gospels is at the disposal of every judge of Judaeo-Roman history. No such judge has denied this part of the Gospels; no one has been able to bring any fixed doubts against it as long as it is not mingled with one's religious system.

A second part of the Gospels is of concern to the *church;* it deals with what is *miraculous in history.* And as a Protestant, I do not hesitate to say with St. Augustine, the father of our Protestantism, "I would not believe it if the church had not handed it down to me."[62] Here, I use the word "church" in a very pure sense. Christ himself gathered together, formed, and educated the church in its beginnings *(ekklesian kyriakev)* in the small society of his friends. They were the only witnesses to what the evangelists narrated. What they did not witness (for example, the history of Jesus' childhood) was first collected by a learned man, who himself remarks (Acts 1:22) that in fact the report of the apostles begins only with the teaching of Jesus, but that he has carefully made inquiries into what had taken place before, that is, into the history from its beginning (Acts 1:2, 3). We accept his two writings as well as the other Gospels and epistles on the word of the church. On who else's witness should we accept them? Do we ask the Chinese and Tibetans in order to establish some fact about the Greeks and Romans? Yet the Greeks and Romans were as removed and alien to the core of this history as Tibetans and Chinese could be; and we have no writings at all from Jews of this time. According to the book of Acts, they behaved as they had to behave. They denied nothing, and they investigated nothing, because a national history to which their witnesses freely and openly appealed was neither to be denied nor deleted through investigation. They overlooked, and they suppressed. In the meantime, the witnesses expanded the history further; it became a confession of faith, orally transmitted and strictly observed; finally it passed over into written treatises—our Gospels. The audience that alone had interest in them—the church—collected them, sorted them, examined them, and, finally, catalogued them. Thus, we receive them from the hands of the church and upon its belief. *We* cannot question witnesses; *we* cannot retrieve any lost writings from the ashes or erase the decay of time. Apart from these writings, the entire first century is lost to us. Nevertheless, everything to which Roman authors testify concerning Christendom supports these writings, that is, supports the faith of Christianity in the history and teaching expounded here. This is a faith of the *church,* spread by tradition, confessions of faith, and gospels, received by word and witness of the apostles and handed down to us. We can go no further than this, and no reasonable person will demand anything more.

The situation is completely different in regard to *the part of the Gospels that is the gospel.* It stands as a work of providence that has been realized

62. *Evangelio non crederem, nisi auctoritas Ecclesiae me commoveret.* [Latin for "I would not believe the Gospel unless the authority of the church influenced me."] This ecclesiastical authority and motive power can only refer to one part of our Gospels.

and continues to be realized. It speaks to every heart and says: "This is the
need of our race, its situation, and the only way in which it can be helped;
this is the certain, well-founded, noblest way for all times and nations. This
is its dignity, its destiny, its eternal path. Right and left, power and cunning
are wayward paths. The narrow gate is pure truth, love that ceaselessly and
quietly operates even in suffering, and a more intense kind of energy." The
pearl has been found. No one can lay another foundation than the one laid
by Christ; all who are wise and good, whether or not they know Christ, build
on this foundation, each in his or her own way—gold, silver, straw, and
stubble. The more purely one ponders the need of humanity and labors for
it, reflects upon it, and writes about it, the nearer one comes to this point—
to the mind and the work of Christ. It does not deceive our race with a false
beauty; it shows to our race its true form and restores to it its dignity through
itself, through a mind awakened in him and a universal activity, one for the
other; it also restores to the human race the happiness for which it was destined.
As little as this gospel requires outward proof, since it is itself its most rigorous
proof, so little can it be discarded through a churchly or other type of suspicion.
Let history happen as it may; the plan of God for the human race moves
inexorably onward, and the call to it has been ineradicably written in every
heart. The mustard seed has been planted, and it has the power to become a
tree for all nations. Every kind of storm, good or evil, must advance its
growth.

12. *It is also the case that pure ecclesiastical faith increasingly loses itself
in the deed itself—in the pure, genuine gospel.* For hundreds and even
thousands of years this kind of faith was essential as confession, as conserving
tradition, as the documentation of history, and, finally, as symbol of the
acceptance of the community, the seal of the separation of the true from the
false. We thank the church fathers for all the rigor with which they held fast
to this faith. Nevertheless, this faith was and remains *symbol* or *sign;* it was
never *the thing itself*. A Christian was never obligated to it. This symbol was
added as a sign of entrance into the active community. The symbol called for
and consecrated active cooperation in this community, the mind of the spirit
of Christ to save oneself and others, in short, spirit and power. In the course
of the centuries the symbol has had to give way imperceptibly to the thing
itself; the sign has had to yield to the signified and will continue to do so.
At this time our confession can verify nothing more; our faith can confirm
or justify nothing that happened two thousand years ago. Christ's descent into
hell stays the same, whatever one believes about it. The history of Christ
stands in the Gospels; our oral tradition may not develop it further. Thus, for
us, every word of our confession of faith has no other point of reference than
the work of Christ itself, insofar as it belongs to us. Luther also expressed
this very well in his explanation of the Second Article [of the creed] when

he did not account for every historical fact but for the work of salvation, specifically the extent to which we are to have a share in it. For me, the salvation of Christ is that I live holy and upright voluntarily, as one set free in the kingdom of Christ, and it is the same for everyone. Through this or that formula, the ecclesiastical faith was the hull in which the fruit—the gospel itself—grew; it was the shell that held the seed. Certainly we will not throw the hull and shell away. We enjoy the fruit and the seed from them. But we still say that they are not the seed and fruit themselves. The ecclesiastical faith, even robed in the finest dogma, is merely *historical faith*. No one ever became righteous and holy either through this faith, according to its content, or for its own sake, because it is believed, that is, confessed. Christ dismisses those who merely cry "Lord, Lord," however they may say it; he knows only those who do the will of his father in heaven. With the passing of time the so-called *Religion about Jesus* must thus be changed to a *Religion of Jesus,* and do so, of course, imperceptibly and irresistibly. May his God be our God, his father our father! This is apparent in all of the speeches of Christ, for he always sets his followers in his own place—in trust in God, in action, love, and hope. They were his friends, not servants. They were the branches, he the vine; they were his representatives and brothers inspired by his spirit (John 14-17; 20:17, 21-23).

Whoever helps to lead the religion of Jesus back from meritorious servitude and painfully pious calling on the Lord to that genuine gospel of a friendly and brotherly sentiment, to a convinced, spontaneous, free, genial participation in the work and purpose of Jesus according to the clear sense of the Gospels, that person has had a share in the work of Christ and has promoted it. All dead words are lifeless. Let the dead bury their dead. Share in the living purpose and striving of Christ and follow him! There must come a time when salt learns to restore its taste, otherwise its fate is sealed (Matt. 5:13).

Principles for Comparing the Evangelists:
Principles that can be
Derived from the Evangelists
Themselves and from the History of the Time
(from *Concerning God's Son, the Redeemer of the World*)

1. *The comparison of the Gospels does not begin with words or phrases but with the events of that time and with the subject matter.*[63] All gospels began with oral proclamation and oral narrative; this passed through the lips of several people and was often repeated in various contexts to diverse audiences. People were satisfied with this form of transmission for a long time.

---

63. [SW 19:416-24.]

It was, therefore, impossible to avoid a diversity of words and of phrases, yes even discrepancies, within the narrative itself. This is self-evident.

2. *Consequently, the attempt to trace our synoptic Gospels to one nonexistent* Urtext *is a presumptuous race without a goal.* Such an unwritten *Urtext (graphē agraphos)* can never be traced with certainty from the words and phrases of a free narrative. Rather, the presumptuous attempt to do so destroys the natural view of our Gospels by heaping difficulty upon difficulty.

3. *Not everything is equally free in an unrestricted oral narrative.* Aphorisms, extended sayings, and parables are more likely to be retained in the same expression than minor details of the story; the narrator himself chooses the transitions and conjunctions. These differences are obvious in our Gospels. Certain expressions—especially strong, obscure, and parabolic expressions—are the same in all the Gospels, even when they are interpreted differently. The narratives differ most freely in their details, their transitions, and the arrangement of events. Painstaking attention applied equally to every part of the speech often determines the perspective of the whole.

4. *Our three Gospels are based on a common gospel* (evangelium commune)*; this is obvious in any genuine synopsis.*[64] This gospel, which was common to all three Gospels, is coherent; it presents a natural unfolding of the events, contains what is essential, and rarely varies in the main point. The most frequent and radical differences between the three Gospels are found in what is unique to each evangelist outside this common gospel. Separating out this additional unique material makes it much easier to achieve an unbiased view of the common material.[65]

5. *The common gospel consisted of specific units, narratives, parables, sayings, and pericopes.* A view of the Gospels themselves reveals this common material and the diverse order in which this or that parable or speech is placed. Even the earliest writers do not cite them differently. We read: "the Lord speaks" or "the parable says."[66] The fact that the Gospel consists of such parts speaks for its truth. For people such as the apostles could more easily remember a saying, parable, or apothegm that struck them than well-structured speeches through which John later portrayed his friend [Jesus]. Separating out these individual speeches (*rēmatōn, logōn*; Matt. 28:15; John 21:23) simplifies the view of the whole. Mark often includes only the title of the

---

64. See [Johann Jakob] Griesbach's exact and intelligible comparison of the Gospels in his *Libri historici Novi Testamenti Graece* (Halle, 1774-75).

65. In Eusebius's "Canon of the Harmony of the Gospels" there are ten classes of affinity between the Gospels. Many such diversions are unnecessary in light of a text that places the synoptics next to one another. Besides the editions of Eusebius, see that of Mills. [See Eusebius, *Canones decem harmoniae evangeliorum praemissa ad Corpianum epistola.*]

66. There are older comparisons of these *kephalaia* of the evangelists. These are called *peri tōn magōn, peri tōn anairethentōn paidiōn, peri tou leprou.* They were sometimes shorter, sometimes longer. In Matthew there are, for example, 64-94 of them and 107 in Luke.

speech *(logos, kephalaios)* that another evangelist narrates, for Mark's Gospel was originally only a sketch for oral delivery. Yet he still refers to it. To present the simplest view of the whole, the evangelists can only construct their Gospels from such specific speeches *(logois, kephalaiois)*, parables, miracles, narratives. Each evangelist arranged this material according to his own purpose and context.

6. *The common gospel obviously assumes a pattern of these sayings (diē-gēsin, hupotupōsin logōn, tupon paradoseōs)* that must have been composed early because all gospels contain it. Luke already fixes its limits (Act 1:1-3, 21, 22) by the very use of the term (Luke 1:1 = *diēgēsin*). We see this pattern observed in the earliest speeches of the apostles (Acts 2:22; 10:36-42; 13:23-38). Even in their letters, they often mention a specific, fixed act of being entrusted with the fundamental teaching of the faith (1 Cor. 11:23, 15:1-11; 1 Tim. 3:16; 2 Tim. 1:13, and so on). If evangelists who were not eyewitnesses were to go out and to tell the story, then the fundamental teachings had to be fixed. And they went out right away (Acts 8:5, 6:35).

7. Since the names of Peter, James, and John are often mentioned in this common gospel as guarantors of the most important events, to what period can this pattern belong if not to the time *when they were leaders of the church in Jerusalem and when Peter in particular was leader of and spokesman for the community* (Acts 1-12)? In this respect, the gospel's repeated guarantee on behalf of the three main apostles—that they were eyewitnesses—has a purpose and does honor to their character. Thus also in his epistle Peter vouches for himself (2 Pet. 1:16-18).

8. Since Mark, Peter's pupil (1 Pet. 5:13), was one of the *earliest* evangelists, to whose names may we attach this earliest pattern of the gospel sayings than to those of Mark and Peter? This is in fact the case. The Gospel of Mark evidently contains the briefest, simplest, and uncomplicated outline of the things to be narrated in the gospel. Further, in expression and in its transitions Mark's outline is the simplest and most primitive. It is, as it were, the original structure *(prōtoplasma)* of the oral Gospel, its vital Palestinian archaism. It breathes the spirit of those hopes with which Peter and the apostles first spoke to the Jewish nation, and it does not contain the harsh expressions against this nation found in the other Gospels. Mark is the unadorned central pillar of the other Gospels, their simple cornerstone, a witness to what first came into the world *(protaktikon prosōpon Euaggeliou)* as historical gospel.

9. *Mark is thus a separate Gospel.* It is neither an extract from Matthew nor a compilation from Matthew and Luke. Indeed the hypothesis of compilation comes as a surprise considering all we know about Mark (Acts 12:12, 25; 15:39; and 1 Pet. 5:13) and about the variegated, widespread oral tradition of church history concerning the origin of this Gospel and Mark's relation to

Peter in general. The ancient church knows nothing of this compilation hypothesis, and a perusal of the Gospels themselves contradicts it. No matter how many different ways this hypothesis is reformulated by the cleverest men, it remains unsatisfactory, for it only heaps response upon response.[67] The Gospel of Mark itself vouches for its originality; the first chapters of Acts are its vivid commentary. Further, at every step it can be explained why within the confines of their perspectives the other evangelists diverged here and there from the *protologen*. In contrast, we find no reason Mark should have abridged or stolen material from the later Gospels. From the very start of his office, the student and companion of Peter had to know of a gospel that Peter narrated. Did Mark need to compile it from others and from his younger co-worker, Luke, in such an aimless, poor, and measly way? Was Mark so stupid that he did not recognize what was superior in Luke?

10. Mark is thus not only a separate evangelist but also *our sole standard for measuring what was added in the other Gospels for their own purposes.* Without a common, standard measure how is a comparison possible? If this is surrendered, then what would be left for making comparisons except fancy or an ever-changing *Lesbia regula?*[68] As long as one imagines all the Gospels were written in one place, in one year, and in one language, one can do nothing but daydream in the cave of Epimenides[69] and forget the world, since it is known that Christianity quickly spread into three parts of the world, suffered persecution, and split into groups early in its history. Being the oldest version of the Gospel in its Palestinian outline does not make Mark the oldest version known in Greek. Mark, the Hebrew, learned it from Hebrews in his mother tongue. Our Greek text contains obvious traces of this. But although we know only the Greek version, which Mark wrote later, it still remains what it was—the oldest *diēgēsis peplērōmenōn* (Luke 1:1).[70] Thus, as an examination of the texts themselves shows, it remains the standard for separating what was added in the other Gospels. Explanatory passages added to the Greek for non-Jewish readers are obvious in the text itself.

11. *The gospel of the Nazarenes retains, then, its full integrity. It was the first composition to be circulated in written form, published prior to Mark.* It was a text written entirely from a Jewish perspective in order to prove that

---

67. See [Heinrich Wilhelm] Halfeld, *Commentatio de origine IV Evangeliorum* (Göttingen, diss., 1794). The situation is examined with critical precision in Eichhorn's *allgem. Bibliothek.*

68. *Lesbia regula dicitur quoties praepostere non ad rationem factum sed ratio ad factum accomodatur.* [Latin for "The Lesbian rule is said to establish how often the rationale is made to suit the deed and not the deed to suit the rationale."] Erasmus.

69. [Epimenides was a religious teacher of Crete (see Plato's *Laws*). Along with variations about the date of his life go legends of his great age and his miraculous sleep of fifty-seven years.]

70. [Greek for "narrative of the things that have been accomplished."]

Jesus is the Christ and to strengthen the Christians against the raging persecution by the Jews. As such it is self-explanatory from beginning to end, even
in our present Gospel of Matthew.

12. The basis for this gospel appears to be the *older Syro-Aramaic version
of Peter,* which this commentary freely used and applied for its own purpose.
This is why the two texts agree. Every addition and abridgement in Matthew
can be explained from this standpoint.

13. The Greek translation of Matthew was written after the Greek versions
of Mark and Luke. The Greek translator omitted from the original what was
not applicable to Christians of the Panhellenic world. We do not know if he
added material, because we do not have the gospel of the Hebrews.

14. *Luke wrote the first Christian history.* His Gospel is not, like Mark,
a collection of sayings of the oral gospel; and it is not, like Matthew, the
product of a Jewish context. Luke wrote his history in a purely *Hellenistic*
way.

15. Whether Luke was inspired by the gospel of Mark or did not see it at
all, he knew of its contents from Palestine through *autopten* and *hupereten*[71]
(Luke 1:1-3), for he was an evangelist for some twenty years. Most likely
he knew of it; he actually adopted some of his friend's archaic expressions.

16. Luke probably knew the gospel of the Hebrews as well. If he did not,
then he was at least acquainted with specific speeches and sayings that that
gospel combined in its own way. Luke combined them in accordance with
his own end. Luke did not know our *Greek* version of Matthew, for it had
not yet been written.

17. In general, our three Gospels quickly followed one another, and ecclesiastical tradition yields information about them that is worth noting. It is
said that the gospel of the Hebrews was written in Palestine when Christianity
in the Ancient Near East was being harshly oppressed, and when Paul and
Peter were in Rome starting a church.[72] At this time, it is said, the congregation
in Rome wanted the gospel from Mark and Peter, and the protoapostle agreed
to write it. At this point, it is said, Paul encouraged Luke to write his Gospel.
A gospel, which no one had thought of writing down for thirty years, which
had been transmitted orally or handed on as a sacred legacy, was suddenly
presented to the world in three different texts? The horizon of Christianity
had expanded; gospels written down in Greek were indispensable and continued to be so. Perhaps *all three gospels* appeared between 61 and 64 C.E.
(They shared one common oral gospel that had been proclaimed for about
thirty years without being written down.) The Greek translation of Matthew
could not be long in coming. This was a bright period in the life of Peter and

71. [Greek for "eyewitnesses" and "ministers of the word."]
72. Irenaeus, [Adversus Haereses], 3, 1, 1.

Paul, which in 66 or 67 C.E. would soon come to an end. Afterward, for thirty or forty years, a great period of silence took place until the end of the first century, when John gave voice to the higher Gospel, which we discussed above.

18. According to these principles for comparing the Gospels, I hold that a "harmony of the Gospels" (as the Greek church called it), which many people till now have doubted, is not only possible, but is genetic down to the most minor differences in details. It is a harmony in which each voice retains its own sound, its own character, in which nothing needs to be silenced or suppressed—a harmony in which everything is instructively explained in relation to its context. *Its sole canon is the emergence of the Gospels themselves according to time and place.*

19. The canon of the harmony of the Gospels.

a. *The common Gospel delivered orally from the school of the apostles (euaggelion koinin, didaskalia apostolon, diegesis ton peplērōmenōn).* This gospel was naturally conceived of and composed in Syro-Aramaic and was delivered in this form until Christianity spread among the Greeks. It is the basis of all our Gospels, to which they generally adhere even in their expression. It is clearly recognizable in all the Gospels. Our Gospel of Mark provides us with the clearest idea of it.

b. *The Gospel of the Hebrews.* This gospel was composed in Palestine more than twenty years later, in times of persecution and the utter decline of the Jewish nation. Written to prove messiahship, it was perhaps the first gospel to be circulated in written form. We are familiar with it through quotations and fragments, but more so through our Matthew, though with significant changes. The Gospel of Matthew is a liberal translation of this gospel; Luke used it even more freely.

c. *The Gospel of Mark.* This was most likely the first Greek gospel. It was faithful to the original outline, with a few explanations added for foreign readers.

d. *The Gospel of Luke was the first history of Christ.* It was a gospel written for Hellenists by a companion of Paul, who not only knew Mark, Peter's companion, but was also perhaps himself inspired by Mark's Gospel to write his own. He made use of both Mark and the gospel according to the Hebrews in a very liberal way.

e. *The Gospel of Matthew, the Greek version.* This was a liberal translation of the gospel of the Hebrews with omissions and no doubt also with additions. It was the latest of our first three Gospels, written after the destruction of Judaea.

f. *The Gospel of John.* This Gospel was composed at the end of the first century after a long period of silence. It echoes the earlier Gospels in a higher key.

20. This canon would present a harmony of the Gospels in which every dissonance would be self-explanatory. It would eliminate their being thrown together into one so-called "gospel story." Precise distinctions would be made between authors, languages, purposes, and times. Criticism of the text and of its content could prove to be the same for these historical writings as for any other: impartial and with room for distinctions and differences.

21. This approach yields insights at every turn. Guidance and instruction arise precisely from the obscurity of contradiction.

22. Such an approach brings to light the entire form of the Gospels. The very contradictions verify what underlies their content.

23. And criticism would be satisfied to such a degree that I would dare to look Casaubon, Bentley, and Lessing in the eye with this disharmonious harmony. Why can I not write this kind of criticism immediately?

5

Christianity and Theology

CONCERNING THE DIVINITY AND
USE OF THE BIBLE
(ROMANS 15:4-13)

If there is a fundamental truth of Christian doctrine against which people are wont to entertain deep, silent *doubts,* and which they usually apply to their *actions* in a very negative way, then it is the *doctrine of the Holy Scripture.*[1]

We all go by the name of all Christians. By this we confess: We accept a *revelation of God* through Jesus; we cannot understand anything very deeply with the *mere light of nature;* we regard the Bible as a *fulfillment,* a supplement, of this light; we consider what the Bible says to be altogether *divine* and thus believe it and bear witness to it; and through the promises this divine book shares about this life and a future one, we expect to be certainly and truly *happy.* All of these things are included in the name "Christian," for Christ based his revelation on the Old Testament and established the New Testament through his disciples. We would be *unchristian,* we would be *pagans,* if we did not accept this divine revelation. We would be *Jews,* if we accepted the Old Testament alone. We would be *naturalists* and *freethinkers,* if we believed to know all necessary truths from the light of reason alone. We only become Christians when we take the Bible to be the *language of God* to human beings, the *ground of knowledge* about our religious truths, religious duties, and religious hopes, according to which we believe, live, and await the future.

Nevertheless, there are many people hidden under the cloak of the name "Christian" who are *not at all Christians* in regard to this fundamental doctrine

1. [SW 31:96-121.]

201

of our religion. So many *secret doubts* against the truth of the Bible are germinating in some of these people, and so many *heretical practices* concerning the use of the Bible prevail in others that it would be a rare sight indeed to see each one's actual opinion on this point exposed. . . .

Our text for today is full of material that serves our aim, in the first sermon of the church year that I hold for this congregation, of discussing the primary truth of Christianity, that is, biblical revelation. The text confirms for us the truth of the Old Testament (Rom. 15:8). It explains for us the form in which the Christian religion appeared in the world. This form was beautifully built upon the Jewish religion, but in such a way that the Christian religion was to be a religion for the world and for all peoples (Rom. 15:9-12); that the first duty of Christianity was therefore to be like-minded, not to quarrel over opinions, and not to be full of hate in life (Rom. 15:5-7); and that the purpose of the Bible was not to feed disputing parties but to teach and to comfort (Rom. 15:4). In the final verse the text seals everything with a hope that should also sustain our sermon today (Rom. 15:13).

Part One

Let us rescue the *Christian faith in a divine revelation,* on the one hand, from several doubts of the human heart and, on the other hand, from many cases of abuse. Let us be persuaded and edified.

People have asked: How can this book be a Word of God, a divine series of thoughts for human beings, where I perceive so much that is human? Where there is so much worthless and insignificant material that I can hardly imagine to be worthy of the supreme deity? Where there is so much that pertains to the trivial matters of a miserable people with its kings and tribes and ceremonies, even though it is supposed to be a revelation for the entire world? Where so many things that I would gladly like to know are missing from the most important pages, and passages are instead filled with useless material? Where there is such a predominant tone of strange and often undignified images here, of confused regulations there, of such unsupported promises here, of such unimportant narratives there, that one does not know where to begin or end in order to hear the voice of God? Where the character of that particular period in which the book was written, and of that particular author who wrote it—down to his temperament, failures, and ignorance—are so conspicuous that I seem to hear the voice of ignorant Jews everywhere but that of an omniscient God nowhere? Where so much material is hidden in such riddles that since then and throughout all the centuries of Christianity new disputes have arisen about how this or that word should be understood, this or that verse interpreted, this or that truth presented? Among these hundreds of disputing parties, individuals were almost ready to be made martyrs over their own hypotheses, and yet they all referred to the Bible, to such an obscure and ambiguous book, as if they were referring to the voice of God that rang in their ears alone. It is asked, How can something be a divine book for the human race that carries so many signs of its low, pitiful origin?

I have, dear listeners, spoken very harshly against the Bible, but not nearly as harshly as some foolish and presumptuous people. Nevertheless, all these arguments do not express anything that holds a place in the eyes of an unbiased, rigorous lover of truth. It would be best for us to consider individually each of these harsh charges, which we have heaped together like great stones, and to examine whether or not they can be verified. However, because this is too much material to address in the few minutes I am to speak, I will limit myself to general remarks in order to stop the source from which these particular doubts are flowing. I will give, so to speak, a history of the biblical books according to the standards of our apostles. In this way, all the particular issues will certainly find the right solution automatically, as long as we are attentive, sincere, and true to our God.

1. What does it mean to say that the Bible is the Word of God? Does it mean that these are the precise thoughts of God when God is thinking about this or that subject? This is the way God speaks to Himself? This is the way God thinks? Does it mean that when you, a human being, look in the Bible, you know the nature of God's soul, the way God imagines everything, the way God speaks to himself and to others? Does it mean this? By no means! For God, the omniscient and perfect one, everything is one thought. God thinks without words, without a series of ideas. God thinks about all things from their essence and not merely, as we do, on the basis of their external qualities. We learn everything through the senses, and thus we understand things only from their external qualities, from the outer surface, from one perspective. We learn to think only by speaking, and from childhood on we learn to reflect only by imitating the words of others. We cannot think any universal truths, any abstract ideas, any rational thoughts without words: We speak to ourselves when we think, and we reason with ourselves when we speak. But none of this applies to God, who has nothing to do with the stupid opinion that God needs words in order to think. God thinks without veils, without meager, confusing signs, without series of representations, without classes of ideas. For God, everything is one, single, perfect thought.

Those who understand me see that the Bible is not called the *Word of God* in this sense, as if this Word were a series of thoughts expressing the way God speaks to himself, for God does not speak; as if this Word were, so to speak, the "language of the gods and the heavens," as the pagans called their poetry and revelations, for God in fact possesses for himself no words with which he must calculate, as if counting pennies, and teach himself, as if using ciphers. Seen from this perspective, the criticism of the Bible based on the meanness of the words in which God supposedly revealed himself becomes utterly ridiculous. Fools! If we are talking about God in himself, then even the most sublime, most splendid, most articulate, and most meaningful words are imperfect for him. They are the crutches with which we limited human beings are able to hobble along. God, however, who is all thought, does not need to limp along with words. They are signs of our imperfection. Do you think you can apply them to God, who is perfect? Do you think you can overhear God's thoughts and teach God which words would probably be worthy of him? Fools! Before God, no word, no language, is worthy.

2. Let us assume, however, that God wanted to reveal himself to human beings and that God wanted to do this in a different way than in his nature. How else would he do it but in a human language? This is not his language! These are not his words that drop from heaven! No! These are human words, this is a human language, and God nevertheless revealed himself in them. How can God speak to human beings other than in a human language—to imperfect human beings other than in an imperfect, faulty language, in which they can understand him and to which they are accustomed? I use far too weak a comparison when I say a father also speaks to his child in a childlike way, for between these two beings there still exists a rapport; father and child are both human beings, who can think only through words and have the language of reason in common. Between God and human beings, however, there is no rapport at all; they have, as it were, nothing at all in common for understanding one another. Thus, God has to explain himself to human beings completely in human terms, completely according to their nature and language, completely according to their weaknesses and within the limitations of their ideas: God cannot speak in a divine way but must speak in a completely human way.

If this had been kept in mind, then we could have avoided a lot of useless speculating about mysteries that human beings absolutely cannot understand. Take, for example, the story of creation. The wisest, most educated, most experienced natural scientists, if they have been honest, have readily and openly confessed that they have not even advanced so far as to be able to understand how it is possible that a body "continues to exist," let alone to understand how it comes into existence. It is, therefore, out of the question for them to be able to understand how one spirit continues to exist according to its inner essence, to understand what it is, how it comes into existence. If this is already completely incomprehensible to human beings, then how should they be able to understand that a world comes into existence that once was not, that a world of living spirits comes into existence and continues to exist, that every part in itself enjoys the whole world, and that every part is a world in itself? What human understanding could grasp this when even our own feelings are still obscure to us? What human language could express it?

Therefore, how must God have been bound to speak down to us much further in his revelation of creation than we have to speak down to children! What unwise children we are when we insist on speculating about something that is simply not for us and that God simply could not reveal to us, unless of course, in that moment we altogether stopped being human beings with senses and started to become gods. How miserable our subtle speculations and doubts become when we insist on speculating about the world's origin out of nothing into something, about time and eternity and their distinction from and relation to one another, about the decline and end of the world, about the nature of the Trinity in God and God's activity outside himself, and about the essence of human souls and all spirits. We quarrel with one another about these things and call one another heretics and thereby oppose and murder the Bible. In all these things we stand, as it were, on top of the world and say, "This is vanity. I cannot simply understand this, and God could not reveal it to me more clearly; it is very important to confess that I know nothing, that I remain a human being, and that I do not want to be God."

We would save ourselves a lot of trouble if we regarded the most important truths of the Christian religion accordingly to the above standard. If so, how many of our subtle speculations would be suddenly cut off, and how many unnecessary doubts and misgivings would fall away! Should it hinder me from being a Christian, for example, that I am not able to understand the Trinity rationally? I cannot even understand my human powers, how they act and exist together. How, then, does it profit my life or promote my welfare to pursue an investigation into matters that in no way pertain to human beings? Why should I be worried, for example, about the way the service of Christ is viewed by God, whether as a ransom and satisfaction for taking away the sins of the world or merely as the means for improving a sinful world so that it can be reconciled to God precisely through its improvement? In either interpretation Christ's service is a sacrifice; in either interpretation there is something whose deeper investigation is none of my business. It is a relation between God and Christ and between Christ and God. How can I know how they relate to one another when I only know that I am not at all released and spared from a virtue for Christ's sake. Rather, if I am pious and sincere, then it is a comfort to me as a religious person to think that one such sacrifice was sent once for the whole world of which I am a citizen. By the way, the attempt to determine the nature of redemption is not at all human and thus no object of human investigation. Why should I wrack my brains over the way that the Spirit works in my soul? It is enough to know that the Spirit acts only through my thoughts, and that the Spirit can act in me only through moral conviction and motivation. I feel this; thus, I will try to improve my thoughts and actions; this is enough for me. I cannot see more deeply into the essence of my soul, and I do not see how a human language could penetrate a place that the inner feeling of human beings does not penetrate.

The main perspective in the discussion of religious truths should always be this: In what sense is knowledge of these truths human? Am I able to understand them, given my nature? If I cannot, then how can I speculate about the way that God deemed it good to reveal himself to me? Here, too, dear listeners, the formation of the soul is the best way to find yourself in the ways of God, and here again the beginning of wisdom is the fear of God and reverence for God's revelation.

3. When God reveals himself to human beings, how else can he do it except in the language and way of thinking belonging to that people, that place, that century, and that period to which he spoke? Now everyone agrees that the way a people thinks and expresses itself is not the same among all peoples of the earth; still less does this remain the same over time. The people of the Near East express themselves differently than the people who dwell in cold regions of the earth; the peoples of the Near East have an entirely different environment, collect a treasure of entirely different ideas in their souls, and through the education of their region of the earth receive an entirely different direction, twist, tone, and structure of spirit than that of Western and Northern peoples. The most radical difference in the world extends from their facial features and clothes to the most subtle manners and deepest recesses of their spirit. The difference is too well known and too true for me to linger on it.

Since this religion was revealed to an Ancient Near Eastern country, how could it be revealed except in a way that would be intelligible to these people of the Ancient Near East and, thus, in the way of thinking that was prevalent among them? Otherwise, God would have completely missed his aim. Our Bible, therefore, carries the traces of this Ancient Near Eastern way of thinking on every page. Their style of writing is full of lofty, bold, and passionate images, especially in Job, the Psalms, and the Prophets. Even the story of creation is narrated in such a sublime tone and with such wording; the description of the travels of the Jews through Arabia also has traces of this figurative, metaphorical language; their history and the history of the kings in Canaan, the writings of Solomon—everything carries with it this character of Ancient Near Eastern, figurative, and metaphorical language.

It is not good, dear listeners, to attempt to prove the divinity of our books on the basis of such qualities, for the Turks talk in the same way about their Koran, which is written so poetically. But it is even worse to take such qualities as an opportunity to criticize and to mock the divinity of our books. A bit of reflection should bring home to us that all those who want to be understood must speak in accordance with their audience's way of thinking, their country, and their century. Otherwise, they will be unintelligible. Because the religion was given in the Ancient Near East and only came to us Northern Europeans after a long migration, because our way of thinking and our period differs greatly from theirs, and because a people's way of thinking and expressing itself changes almost every quarter of a century, it is natural that many images and ways of thinking, which were familiar in their own time and place, are bound to be foreign to us now.

Every one of my reflective listeners will agree that it is good and necessary to explain and elucidate even the Bible in relation to its historical context. There is no reason to criticize the Bible because it can and must be elucidated. Every book from a past time or from a foreign nation must, precisely because it is a book, be explained in relation to its context. It is absurd to require a text to be completely and equally intelligible to all human beings, peoples, and centuries. This is the case with all texts in the world. Even the clearest writings of our time will be in many respects just as strange to our descendants after two hundred years as the texts written two hundred years ago are for us. What is this compared to a time span of three thousand years, and compared to such a great distance between peoples and ways of thinking! Nothing in the world is, therefore, more petty and foolish than to take an obscure expression from the Bible or from a translation of the Bible, which is already over two hundred years old, and to make fun of it. Such ridicule, which is at times really over nothing at all, must appear to anyone who has reflected on the matter as the coldest and most foolish thing in the world. If we blame the Bible for not being "artistic, witty, polite, or learned" enough, then let us remember that it was not composed in our "artistic, witty, polite, learned, political" time. Rather, the authors of the Bible had to conform to the customs and way of thinking of those times in order to be understood. It is utterly absurd to require the Song of Solomon to be an anacreontic poem written according to modern tastes; or to require the sermon of Jesus to be a dogmatics written according to the standards of our century.

One can conclude that it is a good and praiseworthy thing to explain the Bible, to elucidate it, and to make it intelligible. If the ministry existed only for this purpose, then it would still be a far more necessary office than many imagine. What sort of barbarianism would most likely invade other parts of our intellectual education, too, if public discourses to the people disappeared in a few years? Who would still understand the Bible or even wish to read it then? Who would show the slightest taste for what transcends the senses? Who, for whom sermons and devotional books mean everything, would still profit from the way of thinking that is connected to a language other than one's everyday language? Who would then cultivate those aspects of their minds which have always been cultivated by the pastor so that the basis of the soul remains tender, the conscience is addressed in its own language, and human understanding gets used to thinking about worthy matters in a nobler, refined language.

I will go over the other consequences of my proposition. If the Bible is a divine book, then one should, my dear listeners, finally abandon the prejudice that nothing more is required from a pastor or an interpreter of the Bible than to write a tiresome sermon. If the Bible is a divine book, then in every Christian house there should be at least one book, in which the main and most instructive parts of the Bible are explained in a clear and simple way in the spirit of our own time. Thank God that a few of these kinds of explanatory texts are already available to us today. If the Bible is a divine book, then one should not miss the public speeches, in which the truths of religion are delivered in such a way that we can most easily understand them in our time. Indeed, if the Bible is divine, then it is appropriate for me to take the trouble in every sermon to refrain from using any expressions that we learned by heart in our catechism or that we know from the prayer book; to take the trouble every time I preach to translate the language of the Bible into the common language of our time and life,and precisely in this way to elucidate it; and to take the trouble to try to help every one of my listeners to think for themselves and to think along with me by using words that I "steal" from their tongues. I do this so that my listeners can finally learn to think about religious matters with the same free and uncoerced language that they use when they explain everything in the world to themselves, without using words that they have learned by heart and do not understand.

How much, oh how much would religion have gained if we had reflected as reasonably on it as we are able to reflect on the business matters that fill our lives! Believe me, my dear listeners, it is no victory for religion to renounce thinking. Rather, this marks the decline, the true decline, of humankind. Even the apostles, who were called by Jesus to be teachers, praised their listeners when they investigated the truth of the apostles' sayings. It would, therefore, also be the greatest satisfaction for me in my office to have awakened reflection upon and attention to religion and to have helped individuals to wake their own conscience, to develop feelings in themselves that were previously hidden, to train reason, and in short, to become wiser, more familiar with themselves, nobler, and better than they were before through my explanation of religion.In this way religion also promotes the education *[Bildung]* of our time. Religion has already heightened human understanding, and will continue to heighten it along with our virtue, humanity, and happiness. Oh, fortunate times, fortunate world!

4. God revealed himself in the soul of each person who became his writer. How did this happen? Did the writer stop thinking at that moment, and did God do all the thinking? Impossible! Thinking is the essence of the human soul; a soul that no longer thinks for itself has lost its reason, its free will, its essence. It is no longer a human soul; rather, it is an absurdity. Thus, the moment any being outside of me violently interrupts my train of thought and

directly shoves thoughts into me that are not my own, about which I know nothing, for which I can take no responsibility—at that moment I cease to be a human being. I may become a god, a devil, or an absurdity, but I am no longer a human being. I have lost my power to think and my freedom of choice; the train of my independent thoughts is torn asunder, and the essence of my soul has been annihilated. Even if God himself did this for only a brief moment through one thought, it would be as if God had miraculously destroyed an entire human soul. And if God allowed me to think for myself again after that brief moment, it would be as if God had created an entirely new human soul. What a contradiction!

No! It is clear to me, indeed to anyone who looks at the Bible, that all of its writers thought in a way that they could think and wanted to think in accordance with their own intellectual capacities, the tendency and measure of their human powers, the makeup of their temperaments, and even their acquired knowledge and their ability to write. Saint *John* writes like Saint John—tenderly, with sensitivity and feeling, according to a train of thoughts that are his own favorite thoughts, and according to a series of expressions that are his own favorite expressions. Saint *Paul* writes like Saint Paul—with fire, in haste, with one thought tumbling over the next; he is a lover of allegories and, in short, a converted Pharisee. *Isaiah* writes like Isaiah—sublimely, powerfully, like a eagle soaring toward the sun. *David* writes like David—as a lover of country living and of sweet, refreshing, joyful images. *Solomon* writes in his youth, in mid-life, and even in old age in a style that the particular character of his thinking dictates each time. Even *Jesus Christ* is, as Paul expresses it, a "servant of the law"; he was raised among Jews, was shaped by a Jewish way of thinking, lived and preached in the midst of Jews; he built his own better religion, so noble, so simple, so moral. His apostles expanded and developed this religion after him. Thus, all sacred authors consecrated their human powers on the altar of God; grace itself consecrated and sanctified their temperaments as instruments of God.

You see, therefore, that God is the author of the Bible in respect to its thoughts and words in a more worthy way that is also more suited to his nature. His omniscience had, if I may say so, a "closer eye" to the souls of his sacred writers; his grace, which abounds in the entire creation and sustains every being at every moment with a power as if it had been newly created in that moment, supported the depths of the writers' souls at that time in a wonderful and divine way. The soul brought images before the eye of its imagination, either in a dream or in an increased heightening of the senses, and directed its attention to the same. This is the way thoughts arose in their souls, and with these thoughts words, for these words flowed into their pens and became a book for posterity and a guide for the church. They thought under the most careful supervision of God and under the guidance of his grace. Nevertheless, as they wrote, they held onto their souls, their ways of thinking, their ways of speaking. God did not speak instead of them; rather, God spoke through them. They became teachers of the church. What is offensive or unworthy about this interpretation of the divinity of our Scriptures?

Just as all sacred authors used their particular gifts, we must do so to an even greater degree if we want to read and use the Scriptures. It would be ridiculous to expect that when we interpret the Bible the Spirit of God acts in us without any action on our part. It would be ridiculous to expect that we could let good thoughts affect us without ourselves thinking. Expecting this kind of divine help when using the word of God is totally irrational, absurd, and contrary to common sense. Nothing can function in a rational soul except on the grounds of reason and by means of motivations. I would have to be able to destroy the essence of my soul the moment I presumed that God was interrupting my own train of thought by inserting God's own thoughts and was changing me into something better than I am while I was inactive. This is an absurd and inhuman idea. Let us think more carefully when it comes to the best book in the world; let us summon our reason, our integrity, and thirst for knowledge each time we read or hear the Word of God. Let us not expect that it will affect us through some magical power without any thinking on our part; rather, let us summon our thoughts and talents in order to receive every ray of light that penetrates us and appropriate every conviction. In this way, we will also discover in the Word of God, my dear listeners, each according to our own way of thinking and our own way of reading, the seeds for edifying and improving our souls, and so be assured that this is the Word of God.

Part Two

1. It may be that the Bible contains many mistakes concerning geology, history, and astronomy (although it has been shown that these are not mistakes). Let us assume for the moment that this is the case. The Bible has certainly not been given to me in order that I might learn all these things from it but rather that I might learn about religion and virtue. Perhaps Joshua did indeed believe that the sun stood still or sat in the sky. Why should this bother me? He was able to believe this in accordance with his own historical context; and God found it beneath his dignity, as I showed in the first part of the sermon, to prove himself to be a professor of astrology and to explain to Joshua whether the sun or the earth moved. For God's purpose this would have had as little effect as it does in everyday life to say that the sun "rises" or "sets." It is extremely ridiculous to read and to judge the Bible from such perspectives. It is even more ridiculous, however, to make the Bible into a

cheap novel, into a wheel of fortune, or into a hocus-pocus of sudden inspirations about what I should or should not do this moment.

The Bible is truly not given to us for such nonsense; rather, it is given to us for the edification and improvement of our souls. When you approach the Holy Scriptures, enter as if you were entering a holy place of God in which you are to be given another mind. Do not feed your inquisitiveness, pride, or skepticism with questions or comments prompted by idle curiosity; rather, turn directly to that material that concerns you and can help you improve. Read "into your own soul," and summon all your powers in order to feel this Word of God. Let every great example that is introduced to you, every impressive and sublime truth that God holds before you, let all this come alive and work within you! Allow your soul to remain open to every good and excellent impression—See! This is the way to read the Word of God!

2. If we do this, then how quickly the popular way of reading the Bible by chapters will be abandoned. When we take this approach we cut up and mangle a biblical book in the stupidest way in the world in order to lay a chapter before God each day as if laying a sacrifice on his altar. . . . Instead of this, my dear sincere Christians, read an entire book of the Bible in one sitting, for no biblical book is very long; in this way, you will enter into the thread and tone of the writers and into their "train of thought." You will be animated by their spirit, and you will read as they wrote. Where can I recommend to do this more with the letters of the apostles and the speeches of Jesus? The letters of the apostles, like all letters, refer to certain spiritual events of their congregations; thus, they can be read only as a whole. Those who divide them, who read them chapter by chapter, who sever their meaning, are acting as if they had written down a coherent text on tiny pieces of paper and then made it a daily habit to read one piece of paper a day without any relation to the whole text and without purpose, choice, and order. How we mutilate the Bible in this way! . . .

What secular author would not be abused to an extreme if we were to read individual passages out of context, making out of them whatever we pleased, misconstruing them, ridiculing them, and misinterpreting them in any way we desire? Is it not odd that we do such things to the greatest book in the world—things that we would not approve doing with any other book in the world?

If one cannot understand everything, even in its context, then it is best for all sincere, Christian readers to rely primarily on those passages that they do understand and that they find useful. If you find a saying, my Christians, that in a special and impressive way shows you the rule and providence of your God, a saying that deciphers your own heart for you, or a saying that tells you your responsibilities in a more concise, more exact, and clearer way than you could have told yourself, then impress this saying on your soul as the voice of God. Let this saying be your guide in life and death.

3. Above all let us bring sincerity and a good heart when we read the divine Word. This is more necessary for reading it than unusual intelligence or a burning imagination. The purpose of reading the Bible or listening to a sermon is not to make critical remarks; it is not to start a discussion about whether or not the material was presented well. We should proceed, instead, by discussing the extent to which the material concerns, enlightens, and improves us. No one should bring to the Bible a heart that is loaded with prejudices, whether against the Bible or for this or that ecclesiastical doctrine. Armed with such prejudices, readers will, of course, see what they want to see; they will remain wrapped up in their cherished ideas or favorite inclinations and become worse than they were before. What a miserable situation! Let us pray instead:"Dear Lord, look at me as I approach your Word; look at my inner, sincere soul! I come knowing nothing and wanting to know nothing; I come preferring nothing and wanting to prefer nothing. I bring neither a preconceived idea nor, what is worse, a prejudice of the heart against this book that blinds my seeing eyes and hardens my feeling heart. Look, oh Lord, at the delicate, quiet ground of my soul. Oh Lord, persuade me, enlighten me, and improve me, for you teach human beings what they should know." . . .

I have already warned you that no duty in the service of God requires us to sink into a lazy stupor so that we do not think on our own but rather expect the voice of the Holy Spirit. I need to warn you again. Unfortunately, people have become accustomed to confusing devotion with indolence, piety with lazy thinking. This is one reason among others that we gain so little when we hear sermons or read the Bible. This is one reason that no one wants to think along with a preacher or biblical author. Rather, we all want the Holy Spirit to prepare our thoughts, and then none of us thinks at all. The Holy Spirit and God's grace function in human beings only humanly, in rational beings only rationally, in moral beings only morally. Thus, you must think thoughts, you must rouse the feelings of your heart, you must let your conscience speak, you must read the Bible as actively and as thoughtfully as any other instructive, moving, and edifying book. Approach the Bible with this prejudice: Behold! It is the most instructive, the most edifying book! With this approach, if you are righteous, your soul will open itself up, the feelings of your heart will speak, and your conscience will be roused. Then, and only then, will the Holy Spirit speak to you. Do not be an automaton-like Christian; do not bind yourself to a few moving words that, because they touched you in your youth, supposedly continue, although in some very mechanical or magical way, to bring tears to your eyes. Do not play with individual biblical words, such as "lamb," "blood," "sacrifice," "wounds," "child of God," and "bride of Christ," as if the sound of these words supposedly have some divine and heartrending effect on you. Perhaps these words can do this; perhaps they can wring a tear from your eye, or excite some kind of emotion. Certainly they can do this. If the emotion, however, is thought to be more than simply a preparation, then it is nothing. Tears dry up: The emotion is not transformed into good decisions and actions. Anything that does not go beyond this, that does not improve or ennoble me, is not from God, no matter how divine it seems. This is enthusiasm and the mechanical spasms of the fibers of our feeling. This is not a genuine emotion.

"No! Oh God, your book should serve to teach me, and to judge, to improve, and to lead me to blessedness and nothing more." . . . "My reading of the Bible should be a quiet, continual conversation with you. It should be an act of remembering you, a sincere, quiet prayer that lifts and edifies me." Again, if I am depressed, if there are hours when I lose my taste for all worldly things, if I am perplexed or afraid, then I go to my God, then the Word that has comforted so many, that has already healed the wounds of so many suffering people and comforted them in hours of trial, then the Word will comfort me; it will also cheer me, teach me to love others, bind me more closely to my God, satisfy me, and lift my spirits. May the Word be a light on my path! "And in the evening of my life, when my spirits grow weary in the final hours, and when they flare up a last time, only to be quenched again, like a lamp that is about to die out, let the passages of your Word, oh my God, that were passages for my heart, also lift my mind for the last time so that I can enter my future existence with peaceful, heavenly thoughts, with comforting hopes and expectations."

May the God of hope [bless and keep you. Amen.]

TO PREACHERS:
FIFTEEN PROVINCIAL LETTERS

For as the heavens are higher than the earth, so are God's thoughts higher than the thoughts of human beings (ref. Isaiah 55:9).

God is revealed to the human race at many times and in various ways.[2] As far as I can tell, however, God's revelations were not always, even rarely, *moral discourses, lectures, or sermons* that dealt directly with duty or with pointed arguments. They were *seeds,* concealed and sown in various ways, which contained much that was to develop only with the passing of time and with the extensive passing of time. The Bible consists of the *unfolding of developing times.*

2. [SW 7:242-47, 249-50,261-62,265.]

Moralists and Acroamatics[3] always complain that God is revealed in this way and not in *dogmatic sentences* or in Catonian distichs. The pastor, that is, the *teacher of the divine Word,* leaves the Word as it is, rejoices in it, and uses it in *the most comprehensive way* that he possibly can for the purpose it was given! Only in this way does he become a preacher of *the Word of God, of divine revelation.*

Children learn only from *experience and history.* The former opens the eye and the senses; the latter the ear and the mind. Religious instruction should, therefore, do both. Children can only grasp *what is tangible [Tatsache].* If during their life they therefore learn to sense and taste the good Lord *in nature* and in every *sphere of life* that opens itself to them at their tender age, then *the fear of God* will become their Eden from childhood on, just as *virtue* will become the framework for their health and joy. The voice of the parents, held in almost divine esteem, can only add *history.* God has developed the human race as a whole truly in the same way that the powers of an individual child develop. *Faith* and *obedience, love and hope* (although not in our philosophical education) are the first *virtues* that must be awakened in children and that guide and carry everything else for the rest of their lives. The *miraculous* and *ceremonial aspects* of the *narrative* give the picture all the light, bright color, and heroic enormity that it needs to have in order to wake the eye of the child. In short, as indemonstrable, coarse, and simple as it may seem, and despite all of the philosophical problems about catechism that it creates for the young, *the history of religion [Geschichte der Religion]* remains the primary, favorite, and only *educational tool [Bildungsbuch]* from which so much develops later in life! A childhood that is simpler, wholistic, and more full of life scorns torn out bouquets of words, wreaths of morality, and bundles of truths!

Just as in the sciences *natural history* is the "first Bible" of a child, the *history of religion* is the child's "first Bible" here. It is dogmatics, casuistry, theological ethics, everything! Try to teach children "just for the present," that is, as our teachers say, "by stooping down to their level"; try to "take them up to your level," that is, try to teach an entire religion in a philosophical way. Go ahead! But I will not go along with you. This is the way to nourish the soul of a child *in the deepest* and *most lasting way:* only *gradually,* yet by developing it *with all its powers.* Imagination begins to grow more perceptive; judgment, yet a closed, fragrant bud, begins to open; tendencies gradually sprout, like shoots from the seed of a tender plant; the little human beings develop their powers, just as they develop the use of their limbs.

3. [In ancient Greek philosophy, the *acroamata* were the oral teachings heard only by the initiated; the adjective "acroamatic" therefore means "orally communicated to chosen disciples only" or "secret." Herder makes the adjective into a noun to refer to those who prefer secret teachings or material calculated only for those adept or proficient in the subject.]

Behold! The same is true with *the great vehicle of education [Bildung]: the history of religion.* Currents and groups begin to single themselves out within this history; speeches, concepts, univeral truths automatically arise. Since it was not a matter of a mere book of examples of sweet ideals of virtue but rather the whole *development of human powers through the revelation of God,* how easily and powerfully the beautiful body grows over the years! *Simple dogmatics, morals,* and so on, gradually develop, but never dogmatics hung on moral propositions like some tail, or moral propositions merely extorted from the whole of history. The great plant of God grows from a dynamic seed of *fact,* of *history! Its* soil is *revelation! Its* inner sap and power is *faith!*

It is within this development that a preacher goes forth with his congregation. Every duty and teaching still grows out of this holy soil! It grows in relation to the great revelation that is greater than all human reason, or greater than the itemized list of current moral considerations and duties. The preacher strengthens the whole person: not only the sensual powers, based on faith alone, powers that rest on authority, powers obscure and yet so full of life and effective that everything in life depends on them, but also the limited, concrete power of comprehension that, of course, can only be effective in very peaceful, reflective situations. The Word of God nourishes and develops, sustains and strengthens, the whole soul. *Faith, hope, and love* are as much powers—and noble, effective powers—as that artificial construction "clear reason." *Not to see,* and yet to be compelled to believe, to act, is as much a part of human fate in this life—and is, indeed, the more difficult part—as it is to want to act wherever and to the extent one is able to see, only to *moralize* with God, with oneself, and with all that crawls on earth. Human beings grow from their childhood experiences, from which they take the seeds of *all of their powers.* Their education has a *similar* development. Yet they remain *children of a higher power* their whole lives. What they recognize within themselves and around them is *infinitely less* than what they see *through a glass darkly* before and after them. It is illusion or shortsightedness not to recognize this *expanse,* not to want to sense it, and only adhering to *the illuminated point* of the pin-head on which they stand and praising it *as the whole of our system of knowledge and practice.* I am only where I am now: on *one* enclosed, damned point that has become visible to me and is dimming. Before and after me is a *great chain* in which all my powers strive. I would be extremely handicapped if I did not look *on both sides of me* and develop myself in a way in which God grants me an outlook. *Religion* in the most genuine sense is the *only treasure for all human powers! In every respect, in their entire development, and for their entire existence!*

It seems to me that those who try to define and make the soul into *one power* do not understand it correctly. How little in life is done out of *clearly recognized, known* motivations, is done in the name of "philosophical duty!"

Even if an action is recognized as such, which happens one out of a hundred times, how often does it still have a *lively effect?* Does the soul even know its own body? Does it have the least bit of knowledge about its motivations in regard to tendencies or drives that become action? Does it have any understanding about this in the moment that it acts? According to philosophical ethics should not a soul act rather than wait until the time that it has knowledge of its action? Does human life not build on experience and go back to experience? Does it not build a thousand times more on *faith* than on *enlightened sentiments, motivations,* as that triumphal rubbish states? I know of nothing that would affect humankind, that is, the great, strong, active part of it (not the group suffering in philosophy and the theology), than *religion in the fullest sense of the word.* What pastor has not found that with a certain group of people he achieves as little with mere morality using praiseworthy, clear, known motivations than he does with another group merely using *stern, oppressive* authority! Forever philosophizing about *kalon k' agathon*[4] of morality is like a fragile cobweb: delicate and beautiful but not useful; it does not move the powers of the soul—those powers one finds among the great, noble *masses!* These powers must be awakened if they are to be effective. The masses, which are not yet developed toward reasoning, believe and act. If you take away their belief, then your eternal reasoning cannot *replace* anything and reason has *withered* and *died.* But give children and adults a word of God that is strongly believed and recognized, that goes directly to the heart, striving for action, *then something happens!* The miserable scene of human beings speculating about their duty becomes the scene of new *existence, activity, religion of God!*

But who will attempt to measure the whole broad circumference, the depths and heights of the souls of all human beings? Their direction and purpose? How they can and should be used in the most powerful and enduring way? Who other than one who has experienced the most extraordinary occurrences, on which often the repose and the duty of this and of almost every other noble and tender heart depend, if only they were challenged so profoundly! Call it superstition! Create for yourselves philosophical, utopian gods who dwell in the holy eather of ineffective speculation and yet act. I do not find them in the Word of God, and I have not yet found them in one single human soul. To my great comfort, I know that as a pastor I have no other news than faithfully to proclaim the Word of God in its entire range of strength and fullness as it is, *in the great course of revelation!* I see *all powers* striving from and toward it. *The kingdom of God is a seed of mustard,* a *pearl,* a *net.* What can the net not capture! The pearl not buy! The seed not produce! I dare to determine everything a priori with my morals as little as I dare to

4. [Greek for "the good and the beautiful."]

grow grass or to hear yeast rise. As when *one casts seed on the land, sleeps, wakes, and departs: The seed grows in a way one does not understand.* God lets his seed produce even though those who analyze or disturb it do not understand it in the least. *The Word of God* and the *power of God* through which it is activated: *the sower* sows the seed. . . .

First, is it not the purpose of the pastor, to *teach morality*, in the best sense of the word, without *necessarily needing doctrine?* No! *Christian* morality is impossible without *doctrine,* and the pastor is a Christian. The pastor is not a teacher of morality, but rather a *servant of religion, one who proclaims the Word of God.*This is clear, and one can say this confidently. Seneca and Epictetus were great, valuable people, but they were not *Christian pastors.*

Second, but should not the pastor weigh down the sermon so heavily with dogma that, like a clock, its hand points to duty? No! A sermon that is a time-piece of duty is *good;* its weights should and might as well have bearing on duty. But this kind of sermon is not the *one and only!* It is not *the stamp on everything!* It does not constitute *the essence of the pastor's office! This is the pure sum of the Bible:* speeches in which *doctrine* and the *history* of revelation are *central,* and *doctrine* in the most noble sense of the term: In my opinion this is the *foundation* from which the Christian pastor draws every moral duty. The pastor is no prime mover of moral duty and civil virtue but rather *the preacher of the Word of God, the preserver of faith, of revelation,* and of all that rests on it. The consequences of the difference between the two are immediately apparent to anyone.

Third, is then not teaching doctrine the primary task of the pastor and morality only a secondary matter? This is really strange! What can we call *primary* and *secondary* parts of a living body, when one part cannot exist without the other? Yet no part of Christian morality should take on such significance that *doctrine* (in the pure sense of revelation) becomes an *accidental addition*; no part of Christian morality should take on such significance that *the teaching of the Bible, the explanation of the Bible, revelation,* are called something like useful "private lessons of the pastor" instead of religion and nothing but religion! . . .

If morality is the main concern of the pastor and the Bible and the speeches of Jesus merely serve as citations—something that comes from God, as all truth comes from God—then farewell *Christianity, religion, revelation!* These words will be used for the sake of polite, outward appreanance but that is all. . . .

If God acts not "instead of a human soul" but rather *on, in, and through* it, then on which powers of the soul does God act?

The Bible says that God acts *on all powers.* . . .

Our souls have two powers or classes of powers that the philosopher calls "higher" and "lower" powers, but only the *philosopher* calls them this and does so as a *philosopher.* Yet it is clear that these classes are not divided rooms but rather abstractions; they are different names for *one* unified power whose effects, like the colors of a ray of light, appear to our eyes in diverse forms. We also divide the soul into "understanding" and "will." But tell me what act of the will can be done without understanding? What act of understanding can be done without the will's inclination toward action? Abstractions, limitations, and divisions of this kind, *when put into practice,* can hardly produce glowing and appropriate results. . . .

The foundation and essence of religion as a whole is *fact! History! [Tatsache! Geschichte!]* The *senses* and not only the "higher powers" attest to this. For the individual believer, religion is built on *faith, which arrests all powers.* Its purpose and content are directed to the people, the most noble and *more sentient part* of humanity, and not to the brooders. Its *nature* and *language recreate* and *direct* all powers along with *all desires.* This is the way that the apostles preached Jesus; they did not philosophize. The prophets spoke as the *voice of God!* Faith resulted from a sermon that spoke to the heart and to the senses and to the entire person. God speaks to and treats human beings like *children,* and *children* are sentient beings!

LETTERS CONCERNING THE STUDY
OF THEOLOGY

First Letter

It is still true, my dear friend, that the best way to study theology is to study the Bible,[5] and the best way to read this divine book is *in a human way [menschlich].* I use "human" in the broadest and most significant sense of the word.

The Bible must be read in a human way, for it is a book written by human beings for human beings; its language is human; it has been written and preserved by human means; finally, the mind whereby the Bible can be understood, every interpretative tool which elucidates it, and all the ends and uses to which it is to be applied are human. You can safely assume that the more you read the Word of God in a human way (in the best sense of the word), the nearer you will approach the purpose of its author who created human beings in his own image, and who acts for us in human terms in all the works and benefits whereby he reveals himself as God.

Do not think that I am trying to hand you an empty platitude. The consequences of this fundamental principle, if rightly understood and taken into full consideration, are important.

5. [SW 10:7-11]

First, reading the Bible in a human way dispels many superstitions, such as the view that the Bible is superhuman and supernatural in every way, right down the material used to write it, whether parchment or paper, stylus or quill; down to the writers who used one or the other; even down to every scratch or squiggle of the text and the language itself. Such a view also treats the Bible as something that has been extraordinarily and uniquely subject to neither fraud nor errors, something to be idolized instead of examined, studied, or tested. This is, indeed, a terrible principle that makes those who accept it on account of its supposed divinity all too human, that is, idle and stupid. Such a principle blindfolds them and then asks whether they can see the light. Does a person who transcribes the Bible suddenly become an infallible god? You can test this for yourself, if you like, by watching your own transcriber copy texts today. He will write today as transcribers have always written—according to his possession of accuracy, diligence, knowledge of the language and facts, time, patience, and legible handwriting. God will not miraculously alter any of these factors for him because he is presently copying the Bible. This has always been the case, not just since the invention of printing but to an even greater degree prior to it. No parchment takes on a firmer texture because the Bible is written on it. No ink becomes indelible on that account. Hebrew diacritical marks and letters do not shed their characteristics because they are part of the book of books. All the influences and changes that time exerts upon language do not come to a halt. These are not hypotheses but facts. My conclusions are also dependent on such facts. Banish everything that smacks of the opinion that this book in form and content is comparable to no other book. Abandon the opinion, for example, that no variant readings can exist in the Bible because it is a divine book. Variant readings actually do exist in it (even though only one variant can be the proper one). This is a fact, not an opinion. Consequently, we must work closely with these variant readings and distinguish and choose between them. This is why there is an academic discipline that examines such distinctions and choices, just as there is for every other human book. In this respect the Bible is to a certain extent the most human of all books because it is for the most part one of the oldest. It has been transmitted through so many hands, peoples, and ages! Although providence, as we shall soon see, has uniquely preserved it through natural means, and although we can be certain of the authenticity of its whole purpose and contents in so far as they are useful to us, we should never infer these things a priori, as if the Bible were written in heaven and not on earth, by angels and not by human beings. With such presuppositions we do not honor the Bible, but rather disgrace and injure it. Many of the most impudent objections against it have been taken from this arsenal built in the sky. Many opponents are still fighting on this kind of ground, as if they were fighting for Mohammad's Koran and for some Gabriel who brought it from heaven.

I do not want to be of this party, not because the enemy is formidable, but because the whole battleground is a fairyland. Such an unfounded hypothesis, which is to some extent obviously false and fictitious, is definitely harmful to young students of theology. It obstructs their vision and clogs their minds. It suppresses their desire to examine, collect, analyze, and explain soundly. It also paralyzes their natural intelligence and acumen if they possess any, both of which are great gifts of God. Many people have said outright, "I do not like to read a book that is not supposed to be like other books." Other people have eventually given up reading it after great labor and pain. Luther was a bright, first-rate thinker, and he did not concern himself at all with such leaden stupidities. I am certain that no intelligent person could or would be concerned with them. By the same token, I have witnessed in more than one case how difficult it is to bring people to a correct understanding and view of the use of the Bible, once they are stuck in such a putrid quagmire of nonsense. When they pick up the Bible they do not believe they are holding a book and therefore do not let themselves see what they see or hear what they hear. Their minds are clouded with heavenly shadows, with forms from the realm of Peris and Neris,[6] which can cloud their sense of truth, application, and proportion. Worst of all, through this darkness they learn in their youth to despise or neglect the tools for interpreting texts. The lack of these tools then plagues these people for life because it is practically impossible to learn to use them later. And because we do not willingly expose our weak spots, this deficiency may even impede them from seeing the brighter light of the proper use of such tools. They may not know their reasons for doing so. This worsens the situation, for they think they are fighting for God and the Bible, but in fact they are fighting for their own lack of true insight and tools of interpretation. In other words, they are fighting to protect their own blindness.

Therefore, my dear friend, do not scorn knowledge about the use of the Bible that is offered to you. It remains to be seen exactly *how* you will use this knowledge in your mature years. Do not let the misuse, the frequently downright impious application, of so-called *biblical criticism* frighten you. Instead, learn the biblical languages and their related languages. Get to know the principles of this fine, scholarly, and philosophical discipline. Gather everything that you can, even if it only remotely serves your purpose. As soon as possible buy an interleaved copy of the Bible in its original languages, in which you can note variant texts, insertions, tentative conclusions, comments, and rules for your future use and judgment. Save your judgments for now, however. You are still too young. Perhaps the whole discipline of biblical studies itself, especially the study of the Old Testament, is too young to make

6. [In Persian mythology Peris are evil female creatures who were attractive in appearance but demons in action.]

any mature, final judgments. In ten or twenty years, we will all be at a different level than we are today. We will have thrown away some of the scaffolding of biblical criticism because the wall of the building itself will be completed. We will accept other things as certain that seem precarious to us now, and we will not be any worse off for the changes. Until that time, be like the bees who gather their honey from all kinds of flowers. Just make sure you are gathering honey instead of poison or rubbish. Always preserve your childlike simplicity and respect for the Bible, even when you see that it has been profaned in the hands of its critics. Criticism itself is guilty of this act purely by accident. An expert in languages and an interpreter of texts are two very different creatures, as we see among so many contemporary experts in modern languages. The experts understand the languages, but they do not understand the author at all. A veil hangs between them and the simplest level of meaning, not to mention the subtlest. This can and will probably be the case for experts in the biblical languages precisely because the Bible is the most ancient, most unpretentious, and most comprehensive of all books. Nevertheless, experts in languages (apart from their rigidity) are good, useful, and indispensable people. Even their rigidity serves a purpose when applied to grammar and to the detailed aspects of criticism. In short, my friend, pay attention to all the tools and scaffolding of theology. Do not forget, however, that the tools are not the thing itself, and the scaffolding is not the building. This will protect you not only from critical pride—the genuinely nasty side of sound understanding—but also from uncritical laxity and excess enthusiasm.

Twenty-fifth Letter

. . . I do not know why one studying theology could not have as open a mind and as cheerful an attitude as one would have studying one of the other disciplines.[7] Theology is, in a sense, the most liberal of all disciplines. It is a free gift of God to the human race that it has contributed to the storehouse of human reason, to noble virtue and enlightenment. Theologians were the fathers of human reason, of the human mind and heart. The first wise men, the first lawgivers and poets proceeded from this sacred grove; and often only much later did various disciplines develop from the ancient theology into independent disciplines, just as the fruit grows from the blossom. Why should we not celebrate this origin and—with all the fire and all the love with which the poets, prophets, and the wisemen of old made known to the world, often imperfectly enough, their great truths—learn and teach theology today in a purer light, with a nobler kind of enthusiasm? If Orpheus and Homer, Pythagoras and Plato, Hesiod and Pindar can so energetically and ecstatically

7. [SW 10:276-81]

praise the birth and splendor, the rule and miracles of their gods, who were the initial buds of human doctrine and virtue, then why do we meekly lower our eyes when we speak about the true, eternal God and his miracles, about the care he has taken to direct the human race toward this same, eternal dignity? Do we believe that in the midst of light we see best with our eyes closed, with a blindfold over our minds and souls? Do we believe that we can feel the influence of the supreme, noble spirit only when our own spirits are most closed and least noble? Wake up, my dear young man, from this base illusion that breeds in such an unhealthy, oppressive valley of fog. The revelation of God is the rosy dawn, the rising of the sun in springtime for the human race with the dawn's whole light, with all its warmth and abundance of life. What is the revelation of God to make of this oppressed, morose attitude, as if this attitude goes along with the Bible and theology as a beggar's hat goes along with begging? . . .

Is it not strange, for example, what kind of stupid prejudices people have against *dogmatics, homiletics, polemics,* yes, and even against the *Bible* and *theology* in general? They seem to believe that all common sense in learning and teaching stops here and that only the meanest, most slavish spirit can find its place in them. What is *dogmatics,* correctly taught and correctly understood, but a system *of the noblest truths for the human race concerning the happiness of the human spirit and its eternal salvation?* What is *dogmatics* but a *scientia rerum divinarum et humanarum*[8] and, at the same time, the most beautiful, most important, truest philosophy—a *philosophia sacra,* as the church fathers called it? Dogmatics discusses everything that philosophy does; it uses what philosophy knows and possesses of the truth, for reason is a noble gift of God to it. Dogmatics upholds this truth, however, with more grounds; it pulls this truth out of a higher source and augments this truth with endless, new, beautiful perspectives. Should this make dogmatics into closed, oppressive, slavish doctrine? Is not truth everywhere, even in its application and amidst debate, *the same* truth? Is there not harmony in a set of doctrines that are presented in their proper relation and with reference to their grounds and purposes? Is this not even a harmony for the most noble human sense: understanding? Is there a wise man of old who could have given us the kind of structure, the kind of perspective on truths, doctrines, duties, and hopes that our Christian dogmatics truly ought to provide, which has been despised by Christians and non-Christians alike?

Polemics (a word that has shaken the fragile nervous system of our century, a word that has been despised, and not always unjustly so, and is awkward)— polemics in the proper sense of the word is nothing but a *philosophical history of dogmatics.* Is it not thereby the most interesting *history of a great sphere*

8. [Latin for "science of human and divine things."]

of influence on the human spirit? What thing has created more revolutions in the world than *religion*—revolution and religion in both the best and worst sense of the words? You know that fine image of religion from [Friedrich Gottlieb] Klopstock;[9] and *history* is the great commentary on this image. People have argued, persecuted, hated, and murdered with religion and over it; and yet they have also examined and taught religion and been refreshed and comforted by it. The human spirit has shaped itself to its true nature through the proper use of religion; and yet through its misuse, the human spirit has, of course, hindered and destroyed itself in the most brutal ways. Now imagine a history that examines all of this, that shows step by step how each Christian doctrine gradually developed, how each grew amidst dispute and became powerful amidst foes and opponents; which methods were employed in each case to show hostility toward or to defend the doctrine; which positive and negative terms were coined for it; how each word was used in different contexts; what kind of good and bad passions were mixed together, and continue to be so, in this alternating war of truth and falsehood, of light and darkness; what kind of ground, what kind of golden background and stone foundation, lies behind and under this sea of tides and opinions. From all this data, and from anything else that reveals the thing itself, present a *philosophical history* that is what it was meant to be and that follows its object in all its bends, corners, deviations, and creases. Can there be a more pleasant, more varied, more educational study than this? If the *study of the oral expression and elocution* of theological truths has something of those truths themselves, then those truths are what they are: the most important, most diverse, and yet most simple truths for humanity. If this is the case, then it seems to me that the study of their elocution, their oral expression, and their eloquent expression has all the attraction that true, useful *eloquence* can have. Truth and virtue are the most noble treasures of humankind. And the science that teaches and uses them is, it seems to me, the most noble science of all; and this science is *theology, the doctrine of God and of humanity.* . . .

Twenty-sixth Letter

So, you too are caught in the unfortunate quarrel between *nature and Scripture, nature and grace, reason and revelation!*[10] You are so deeply caught in it that you think there is no way out, and you believe you must give up one of them in order to keep the other. Please open your eyes, my friend! There is no quarrel between them! They are but different tracks on the same course that lead more or less to the same end. Listen!

9. "Religion of God, you holy friend of the human race/ But a sword in the hand of the mad."
10. [SW 10:284-91.]

It is not good to create oppositions where none exist. It is even worse to sow seeds of destruction between peaceful parties and to praise one party at the expense of the other simply because they are not the same. It seems to me that the least that can come of it is retaliation. Maybe this was the situation between *theologians* and the so-called *naturalists*. What did the theologians not demonstrate! What did they find that should not be demonstrated! They demonstrated the blindness of *reason,* and then they immediately tried to use this "blind reason" alone to demonstrate precisely the necessity, reality, structure and usefulness of *revelation*. Theologians proved that nature is *mute everywhere,* and yet along with all their condemnations, they praised the enlightened, *eloquent* pagans who *heard* only this "mute nature." And when the theme of nature and grace finally was discussed, heavens!, what extraordinary bickering arose between these two matrons—nature and grace! The one would under no circumstances accept what the other had prepared for her, even if it had been ambrosia and nectar. Before it could be accepted, it had to be cooked and distilled some other way. Neither nature nor grace could stand being together in the same place. They quarreled until the stronger one took the upper hand, tied up her enemy so that she could not move, and then rejoiced as the victor. What a fine way to think about the *one* noble work of God, about humankind and its formation! We divide it into pieces and undermine ourselves. What a peculiar kind of grace that tears apart and destroys nature, as Saturn did his children.

What a sad misunderstanding of the finest biblical words! It is very unfortunate when one language is translated into another in such a way that no trace remains of the source and of the original idea! Are not reason and Scripture, nature and grace, nature and revelation, all gifts of *one God?* And can this one giver be in conflict with himself over his finest gifts? And are two gifts *in opposition* to one another just because they are more than one? It seems to me that the greatest peace occurs and the intention of the Creator is carried out when *both* gifts are *used well*.

Let us consider, first of all, the theme of *reason and Scripture*. What does reason mean? What does Scripture mean? Scripture did not come into being at the same time as revelation. God looked after the human race from the beginning of its formation. Reading and writing were not the first things, however, that God could teach human beings, as if God had dictated to them. They had to do many things before they could read and write. They had to understand many things before they could understand and use the Scripture. This is my opinion, although I assume it to be self-evident that Scripture was used very early.[11] It goes beyond a rabbinistic way of thinking to say that

11. See Part One [of *The Letters Concerning the Study of Theology*], the end of the "Twelfth Letter" [SW 10:152].

God's teachings come to human beings only by way of pen and paper! Such a statement is inept and absurd! How young are the oldest books of the Bible in comparison to the beginning of the human race! During the whole time of both the Old and the New Testaments, how much more was said than written, how much more was heard than read! Writing is only a copy of speech: The best education and instruction in everyday life takes place in many more ways than merely in lessons of *reading and writing*. Whoever binds and chains the Spirit of God from the beginning of the world and throughout the history of all nations in this way truly possesses but a greatly limited, impoverished, and dead Spirit of God.

Thus, in order to understand the relation between *reason and Scripture,* we must first turn to the theme of *reason and revelation.* Yet here, too, I see no quarrel between them. If *revelation* is the *education of the human race,* as it indeed was and had to be, then it shaped and taught *reason:* The mother cannot oppose the daughter, and the daughter, if she is as she ought to be, should not want to oppose the mother. Reason (even when unclearly defined and used ambiguously) is the natural, active use of our human powers. Who else could have taught us to use these powers but the Creator who *educated* us? From the first moment of our existence God watched over his favorite creation—human beings. God gave them occasions to develop the powers of their minds and to practice, examine, order, and limit the inclinations of their hearts. God himself associated with them and constantly accompanied them as they took their first steps in the course of life, such as in the development of doctrines, laws, sanctions, inventions, worship, institutions, and so on. These traces of our God who walks with us like a father have spread throughout all nations. These traces are still visible everywhere, even after thousands of years. The most ancient traditions of all peoples, their simplest customs and institutions on which an entire culture depends (whether they have little or much of it), are so similar, so closely related, and share such simple lines of development that, regardless of what crooked paths or inscrutable byways these traditions may have taken, it is difficult to overlook or to deny the very beginnings of God's formation of the human race. It is not so necessary for us to understand the means of God's communication. The Bible itself tells us little about this. In the Bible the story of the first manifestation of God to the human race is told more in a few verses than in chapters and books. And the Bible allows us to deduce the cause from the effect. Wherever I see the effect, I am sure to deduce the cause. Some cases of *concordia rationis et fidei* and *osculum ethnicae et Christianae religionis*[12] may be exaggerated, particularly when people try to universalize subsequent phenomena which are merely

12. [Latin for "the harmony of reason and faith" and "the kiss of the pagan and Christian religion."]

historical. Nevertheless, it seems to me that the *first analogy,* the foundation of everything, is undeniable. Thus, do not be afraid of these sacred groves of ancient tradition and religious practices in which human reason was initially educated and shaped. We who now have more light can enjoy reason's dawn. It is very pleasing and edifying to perceive everywhere the traces of the Father walking with his children and to rejoice in the way God also revealed himself to those standing in the dawn and let himself be sought by them so that they might "grope for him and find him."[13] This is why I prefer these particular, dark traces of sacred practices, allegories, and traditions over much of the recent, malicious kind of aimless talk that is so full of retractions and rationalizations. These ancient peoples possessed and knew many things! Yet we think they did not possess and know these things because they did not express them *the way we do.* And where did they get these things except from the same source as we do—from the tradition of an original revelation that has been guiding the human race since its infancy. Some people constantly replace this dynamic, living culture with the word "reason." They speak about reason as if it were an automaton that is self-made and self-operating. It seems to me that these people speak in radical opposition to the common view of human education. Reason has to be formed; it does not fall from heaven. This is evident in many nations or individuals who lack education but are not stupid, and it is evident and in the education of every child. All things such as *law, teaching, truth, and practice* must first be concrete before they become abstract. This is the way children and all the rest of us are educated. There is no other course possible for the development of our human powers. Human beings would still be crawling on all fours, as that anatomist wanted to prove, if fatherly education had not raised them up and continued to develop positive doctrine and religion. If you break this chain, if you lift human beings out of the world of language, teaching, customs, instruction, and practice that surrounds them, then they are no longer human beings. Their reason cannot develop. They are citizens of the animal world in which they are placed. Intelligent, rational nations will remain within a narrow sphere of culture for hundreds and thousands of years if they are not constantly shaped and educated by external, "driving" forces. In short, the relation between reason and this most ancient revelation that always accompanies our race is like the relation between child and mother. If a child opposes its mother to her face, claiming that she never taught it how to walk because it now walks by itself, then the child behaves in neither a rational nor a childlike manner.

Perhaps you will say, "It may be that the daughter learned how to walk from her mother at one time. Now, however, she can walk by herself. She is no longer tied to her mother's apron strings. She does not want her mother

13. [Acts 17:27.]

always running after her." The mother can only reply, "Walk by yourself! I do not want to hinder you. I do not force myself on anyone. I hardly let you notice that I taught you how to walk!" But, my friend, all such analogies about reason and revelation are imperfect. Thus, let us not take this analogy to an extreme. As everyone knows, divine revelation wove itself into the history of a particular people, and it spread to many other peoples through this one. This revelation in and through history apparently possesses a larger range of hopes and teachings than the most sophisticated reason of the Greeks and Romans ventured to indicate. Nevertheless, this revelation appears in the most comprehensible form for human beings. It makes the infinite finite, for the Creator himself became incarnate and instructs, saves, and directs the human race toward eternity. The greatest truths and hopes in which the human soul finds pleasure and through which Christianity was expanded are connected to him, to the events and deeds of his life. At this point reason and revelation do indeed part company, not as enemies, but rather in the way that *abstraction* and *history* part company. If abstraction has reasons not to recognize history as authentic, then it should give these reasons and should also allow these grounds to be examined. It should also permit others, however, to recognize history as authentic, for abstraction has no laws over history. No history in the world stands a priori upon the foundations of abstraction. Let us suppose that abstraction says to history, "I part company with you because I do not want to place my teachings, my hopes, and my duties on such a dilapidated structure as history; I do not even want to make them dependent on history. In short, I do not want you as a neighbor." History might reply, "Go ahead! I cannot demonstrate historical facts with your methods. If you do not want to recognize facts the way I do, the way they must be recognized, then I do not envy the philosophical web that you claim to have spun by yourself, even though you are indebted to me for much of it. Go ahead and make it dependent on you, or create it so that it exists independently, but at least allow me to build my structure in another way, upon another foundation. I believe not only that everywhere reason and history are *connected,* but also that reason emerged out of history within particular circumstances and, so to speak, awakenings. You abstract from these circumstances and classify truths gathered from them in order to feel their beauty and harmony. I grant you your feeling and share it with you. I do not, however, deny my humanity and the particular sources from which these great truths have flowed, and I believe I posses more of these truths than you do by abstracting from them. Allow me this human weakness, for we both share powers of abstraction. Why do you insist on being intolerant when I am tolerant? Why should I become a mind of pure reason when I can only be human? Both in my being and in my knowing and believing I move like a wave on the sea of *history.* You admit that the scope of eternal truths is always *infinite.* You also admit that you, as finite reason,

cannot fully comprehend these truths and that you must and will learn them
in eternity. Allow me to believe that I have an image of what I cannot yet
fully comprehend in itself; allow me to have as *history* what will be my history
in eternity or what will determine it. My eternal Father gave me this childlike
disclosure,that is, this instruction *di esoptrou en ainigmati.*[14] I hold onto it
with faith, love, and hope; and I thankfully feel and enjoy your harmony of
eternal truths even in this higher light, where they are strengthened with divine
authority in conformity to my comprehension and made visible within the
horizon of human beings. Depart! At the proper time when your structure,
which perhaps depends on a single straw, one day totters, you will indeed
return." Farewell!

Twenty-seventh Letter

Now let us reflect on the second theme: *nature and Scripture.*[15] From what
has already been stated, it seems to me that the quarrel between nature and
Scripture is settled. For what is nature? What is Scripture? Is not nature also
a scripture, a very readable, noble book of God for human beings? The
exquisite Psalm 19 recognizes nature as such. How many psalms and chapters
of the Bible are nothing but *pages* of this book—*sounds* of this divine *language
of nature* made audible! This language is evident in the first chapter of the
Bible and in many descriptions of nature, some of which come from the voice
of God himself, in Job, the Prophets, and so on. Paul expresses it best when
he calls this language of the speaking creation a veritable *revelation* of God
that will release no pagans from their responsibility.[16] Thus Christ loves the
God and Father *of the whole world, of all nations and peoples,* and Paul
preaches him to the pagans. There are such candid passages in several of
Paul's speeches and letters that I am amazed how it could have occurred to
even one barbarian to destroy the language of nature, the book of God for
heaven and earth. People have done this because, foolishly enough, they
believe that the book of nature can be replaced by Scripture. Yet Scripture
speaks about the book of nature on every page.

Where there is *truth,* there is also *virtue that is in agreement with this
truth.* If pagans have law, as Paul and common sense explicitly say, and if
they have *responsibility* for the law and a *conscience,* whether it be one that
tortures or one that calms, as Paul explicitly says, then pagans also have
virtue! It is this virtue that Christ so often praises in pagans and Samaritans.
It also follows that pagans will have a judge who judges them and determines

14. [Greek for "through a glass darkly." Reference to 1 Corinthians 13:12.]
15. [SW 10:292-99.]
16. [Reference to Romans 1:18-23. For the idea of the creation that speaks see, for example,
Psalm 19.]

their fate according to this code of law that Paul clearly names. This is all so evident, and maintaining the opposite opinion is so inhumane and contrary to reason and Scripture, that I am once more amazed how such quarrels and walls between parties could have possibly been introduced by Pharisaic hands which held the keys to the kingdom of heaven. Even the Jews, whom one Roman called *odii humani generis convictos*,[17] did not quarrel and judge in this way. Since we possess no judgment seat for damning the pagans, my friend, who would have granted us a seat for canonizing them? Let the Father of nature rule and judge as he desires, not as we think it ought to be done. He can overlook times of ignorance and will punish times of crasser ignorance. This is not our concern. Chorazin and Bethsaida are not the judges of Tyre and Sidon; rather, they are the more strongly accused codefendants.[18]

In this sense there is no quarrel between nature and Scripture, between code of law and conscience. There is, however, a big *difference* between them that should not be overlooked. *Nature* is the work of God, but how much is necessary to *understand* this work? To *detect* its Creator within it? To discover exactly from it everything that is intended for us? How little the artist has in common with the work of art! And how little God, the infinite artist, has in common with his work which we can only survey from a *finite* perspective! God is the most perfect being, yet everything around us seems imperfect and defective. God is the one God, the sovereign, the most blessed one, the highest good, yet here on earth there seems to be misfortune, death, misery, the triviality of external forms. God is the eternal harmony of harmonies, yet here and there on earth there is strange confusion, chaos. We dwell in such a small corner of creation! And how little we see in this small corner! How briefly we see it! Through what cloudy lenses and dull senses! We arrive not knowing what we were and depart not knowing what we will become. Oh, you inhabitants of other worlds, other stars and planets, do you know more? Do you see around you a greater harmony and order among yourselves and between you and the nature of God? Or do you also see only *one* link ahead and one behind in the chain in which you are poised? Nature, speak to us! Nature, you are silent! I search everywhere in creation and do not find the image of God. How should I be able to find it? God has no image. Yet I long for this image, as if God had a form like my own. I long for God as I long for a dear friend who is hidden, close to me, and whose nearness I sense. Oh, how I wish one sound of God's voice would speak to me! And behold! God does speak to me! I cannot see God's form, but I can *hear* his fatherly *Word*. God opens, as in childhood, my eye and my soul through the ear. God speaks to me like a father about what I ought to see in creation and about the role I

17. [Latin for "those who are guilty of hating the human race."]
18. [See Matthew 11:21-24. Jesus says judgment day will be more bearable for the cities of Sidon and Tyre than for Chorazin and Bethsaida.]

do, should, and will take in it. At this point the holy, mute temple of nature comes alive for me. Beautiful chaos becomes harmony and order in the making. At least I receive a clue for fighting my way through the immense confusion of these incomprehensible scenes and for discovering my own part in it. Moreover, I could never have discovered this instructive voice of God's disclosure, this intermediate conception [not final revelation] of the *interpretation and relation of all things to me and my whole existence,* and now I will never lose it. It becomes a gentle, fatherly word for my *heart* that no image, no direct view, could ever be. The *voice* wakens me, as Isaiah says, "morning by morning" and inspires my harp and my soul: It "wakens my ear to listen as those who are taught . . . and I was not rebellious, I did not turn backward."[19] In this way God's voice lifted Adam from the earth, opened his eyes and ears, instructed and punished him, and never abandoned his fallen, sunken race. Precisely in times of most miserable confusion this voice returned and created wise people of God—holy, pure, dear souls who welcomed the voice, understood it, and were ready to express it to others and even to bear witness to it with their lives. The book of holy nature and of conscience was gradually *opened, interpreted, and explained* through the commentary of tradition. Over time certain sciences separated themselves from the great tangle of commentaries, and human reason spun its more delicate web. In this way this voice took up its dwelling over many centuries among all peoples of the earth and among one chosen people. Not only was the chain linking God and humankind noticed in the public institutions of worship and of politics, but it was now and then also newly realigned through chosen "instruments." This chain also extends in the history of this people from the first member of the human race, through the new Adam, and to the end of the human race. This second Adam, this eternally begotten son and teacher, brought to earth the voice of God that speaks most clearly and *most intimately to the human heart.* He was a teacher as no prophet of his nation had been. He proclaimed the true religion of humanity, made peace between heaven and earth, taught about and pointed to the *one God of both nature and the Scripture,* the one God of both Jews and Gentiles; the one God who is a Father to all people, a helper to all sinners. This is the way this second Adam taught and acted. His teaching spread to many lands and destroyed idols and vain systems. It assisted human reason and tried to purify and edify the human heart. This teaching has been so corrupted and misused for hundreds of years, and in part still is today, that it has been covered with atrocities and sophistry and has flooded almost all parts of the world with blood and wickedness! Nevertheless, it could not have become all this had it not been essentially good. Only a rare, powerful drink could become such a strong poison. Only a sharp

19. [Is. 50:4-5.]

tool could hone human reason and imagination to such a degree of misuse. In regard to its good, great, and wise teachings and instruction, this teaching is the simplest and most profound *interpretation of nature.* In regard to its history, it is the most encompassing plan for all *humanity* and certainly *that which develops our whole, earthly labyrinth* (for history can only be developed through history).

You see, my friend, how quickly the quarrel between nature and revelation disappears from this point of view! The one becomes the peaceful *interpreter* of the other: nature of Scripture, and Scripture of the revelation of nature. Nature is a book that is perhaps not directly intelligible to human beings; Scripture is the marginal commentary, no, rather the abstract of that very book. Nature is an open letter of God to all peoples; Scripture is a fatherly explanation, a secret interpretation and teaching for God's children and those who dwell in his creation. Nature is God's revelation for the eye, a revelation that is endless, clear, diverse, and enduring; Scripture is God's trusted *voice* for our ear, a voice that is intelligible, gentle, loving, and speaks to the heart. The blind deny nature; the deaf deny Scripture. Yet nature and Scripture, *like eye and ear,* like *present and future,* are in harmony. I am not willing to create a friendship between reason and revelation that Scripture itself does not make. I am even less willing to create one between corrupted nature and revelation. In this case it is more appropriate to speak in terms of the relation between illness and a doctor, between the poverty of our knowledge and the benevolent charity of a higher state of understanding. The two are so well matched that, even according to Sirach and the wise Solomon, they had to exist together for "the Lord arranged it this way." What diverse and contrary elements constitute *one* world in God's nature! Fire and water, earth and air! Can it be otherwise with the human spirit in the higher nature of God's economy? May it be otherwise? The cross of Christ and the ignorance of the wise are as well suited as the nothingness and the something from which a world came into existence.

May I add, dear lad, that I commend you for so warmly taking up Greek and Roman writers. Who would speak coldly about Xenophon and Plato, Homer and Pindar, Plutarch and Cicero, Seneca and Marcus Aurelius, if they were perceived as natural theologians? What they say well, no one can say better. And even if they do not say everything, or do not say everything correctly, is it their fault? Are we not able to find these things expressed in a purer form somewhere else? Well, then! Let us make worthy use of what is godly in them. And let us not violate the holy temple of the invisible one whom they worshiped in nature by slandering the servants in the outer court of the temple. In some Greek hymns, in some poetic delights of Plato's Socrates, and in other beautiful passages of Plutarch, Maximus of Tyre, Cicero, and others, are voices that are bound to bring people to their senses if they have any feeling for God at all. Similarly, a few modern writers and even very notorious naturalists and deists also express feelings for the deity and the developing of eternal truth, harmony, and virtue that one cannot find in many so-called pious books. I believe I have already mentioned to you Shaftesbury's *Moralists*,[20] for example, and especially his hymn of praise to God. There are similar, wonderful passages of philosophy and natural theology in Rousseau's *Confessions* and in other writings, some of which are said to be harmful. Continue to be as fond of your pagans as you have been, and learn what you can from them. Scripture, grace, and revelation do not forbid you this. No saint will appear to you in your sleep, as to Jerome, and lash you for reading Cicero. If so, it would not be a genuine saint. The church fathers borrowed much from the pagans. Some people wish they had borrowed even more so that they could have preserved a few more texts that are now lost to us. Let us, therefore, make up for this loss by using those texts that have been preserved.

Twenty-ninth Letter

Dogmatics is admittedly a philosophy and must be studied as such.[21] It is, however, a philosophy created *from the Bible*, and this must always remain its *source*. No matter what one says to the contrary, dogmatics took on a false method when Wolfian philosophy dominated it, established definitions in each doctrine, deduced from them whatever it pleased, and then for show ended with a few biblical passages that said virtually the same. This approach was essentially no better than the Aristotelian-scholastic approach of the Middle Ages, for it is irrelevant whether one appeals to Aristotle or Wolf.

Indisputably the better method is the *philological*, which begins with properly selected and sufficiently understood *scriptural texts* and then, using common sense, infers and gathers *doctrines* from them. We are indebted to those who preserved and confirmed this approach and to all those who continue to use it and who try with ever greater precision to select scriptural texts and to simplify, explain, and establish doctrines. In our church Melanchthon, who was as great a philosopher as a philologist, paved the way and had a number of students. When his approach was drowned out by a renewal of scholasticism, Calixtus[22] and his assistants came through again with an even better approach. Free-thinking arose; philosophy placed itself in opposition to it. Pietism reacted

20. [Anthony Ashley Cooper, third earl of Shaftesbury (1671-1713). *The Moralists* (London: John Wyat, 1709).]

21. [SW 10:314-23.]

22. [Georg Calixtus (1586-1656). Protestant theologian who had a high regard for Melanchthon. The sources for his theology were the Bible, the Apostles' Creed, and the faith of the first five centuries of Christianity.]

against philosophy, and everything seethed together until, with the help of
common sense and the study of languages, the *philological* method soared
and corrected many errors of its forebearers. Much useless terminology has
now been abandoned; much pious drivel has been cleared up and replaced by
more authentic concepts of the Bible, other doctrines have been arranged
more clearly, and in general the student is more carefully guided into a *literary
understanding* of the Bible that undoubtedly is a good approach in its own
way. But does one not omit something else with this approach? Are not (without
wanting to preach about it) some doctrines presented so dryly that often when
using this necessary kind of literary criticism the subject matter itself—its
nature, importance, integrity, benefit, use, application, in short, the *reality
to which dogmatics refers*—is somewhat neglected? This is what one suspects
if one speaks to some of the young men who come from the university. You,
my friend, are certainly not neglecting content for the sake of literary analysis.
Do not use words, as if they refer to nothing in reality. Do not handle the
Bible as if it only *becomes* a Bible through your critical analysis. This kind
of critical impertinence harms the wisdom, truth, and usefulness of your entire
study of dogmatics and the Bible more than you think. It would be terrible
if the Bible or dogmatics *came into existence* only through your efforts! And
it is also not necessarily advantageous if you have in your confessional writings
nothing but a factory of the same kind of *curae academicae*.[23] Later on, when
you enter the ministry, you will see how unprofitable such capriciousness is
for you. If you direct your own reading and study to an examination of
antiquity, then you will discover that much of what your teachers claim was
discovered yesterday had already been stated long ago. Melanchthon, Chemnitz, Hyperius, Strigelius, Chytraeus, Calixtus, and others were no fools when
it came to the proper method of dogmatics! Along with them you can also
use Calvin's *Institutes* and Gerhard's *Loci*,[24] especially the editions of Cotta,
which are a sea of scholarly learning and knowledge. In recent times, through
the work of a few learned exegetes such as Michaelis, Zachariä, Tellers, and
Döderlein, the study of the Bible has made strides in the proofing of texts.
You can take advantage of these gains quietly and modestly without either
losing the subject matter itself in a sea of critical fog or finding that you no
longer have a dogmatics because of using nothing but exegesis. Hold to a
clear-thinking, learned philologist who has a grasp of both the subject matter
and the text. Basilius said, *Theologein dei, ou technologein*.[25] Perhaps in our
time we should add: *Ou philologein monon*.[26] I wish you would read in [Johann

23. [Latin for "academic concerns."]
24. [Johann Gerhard (1582-1637). German Lutheran theologian. His *Loci theologici* (1610-
22) is the most significant dogmatic work of Lutheran orthodoxy.]
25. [Greek for "to theologize about God cannot be equated with speaking of technical things."]
26. [Greek for "not only to philologize."]

August] Ernesti's *Theologische Bibliothek* the reviews of the new dogmatic texts by Baumgarten, Clemm, Stackhouse, Heilmann, Barth, Teller, Michaelis, Gerhard, Zachariä, and others. Ernesti's judgments also about the presentation of specific doctrines are very precise and valuable. It would be even better if this meritorious old man would grace us with his own textbook.[27]

Up to this point I have praised biblical theology as the sole, true kind of theology. However, you recognize yourself, my friend, that I do not thereby exclude *acroamatic precision*[28] and in fact find it highly desireable. Any idiot can spew forth passages of the Bible, and all enthusiasts and lunatics have known how to couch their own crazy ideas in words from the Bible. I have intentionally called dogmatics a *philosophy*. A long time ago I sent a letter to my wife about *the history of dogmatics and its elocution* through all major themes and centuries. It is incredible to see how each doctrine becomes *genetically* bright and clear through this history, how even the driest terminology is brought to life. You see throughout this history how each new *terminus,* each classification and antithesis arose; which side was right and possessed the truth; whether we should still use the expression or the classification today or exchange them with something more appropriate to the present situation. This latter task is especially useful for catechesis and preaching. Why should children and those listening to a sermon be tormented with words whose original meaning was lost long ago? Why should they be tormented with words that (because of the nature of language and the way the common meaning of words can change) we tend to interpret with a different meaning than the original one? *Verba valent, sicut nummi.*[29] Just as philosophy and indeed every art and language change their lineaments, why should not *scholastic dogmatics* also change, in so far as it is mere *philosophy, art, language?*

I do not think that this perspective has been carefully observed in the dispute over whether or not scholarly terminology should be banished from theology. In my opinion this perspective is the sole, genuine perspective. But the question arises: From which theology should these words be banished? Not from acroamatic dogmatics. It would have to invent a new terminology in order to be an exact science. Far less from the history of dogmatics. For here the words are *res facti* that we might forget, not know, or (certainly) never have learned, but they remain what they are and will remain so throughout time. Indeed, the origin and structure of contemporary theology often clings to these words, as the many examples of Ernesti and others have shown, but who can doubt that the entangled, lifeless, extinct verbal rubbish can,

27. Since this has not happened, perhaps the same kind of book would be even more desirable from his predecessor, Morus.

28. [Precision available only to those proficient in the subject.]

29. [Latin for "Words, like money, have power."]

indeed must, be left out of the pulpit and catechesis? Does one go to battle with a rusty sword that neither strikes nor cuts? Does one go to bed with a helmet and a suit of armor? Does one cut grain with an ancient lance? It is no less ridiculous to go to the altar and the pulpit with the dead language of heresies and theological debates. Speak here as *your* time speaks; explain in a way that your listeners will understand and in a way that they would explain the *locum* to you if they were in your place. Leave the old armor in the armory of dogmatics at councils and synods. But you need to *know* where this armor is, where it belongs, the original grounds for its use, whether something should continue to be used or, thank God, no longer used at all.

I greatly treasure, my friend, a speech, whether it be a sermon or catechetical instruction, in which this measure of *dogmatic precision* is also correctly applied to the terminology without neglecting either the current understanding of the words or the concept of the doctrine. This is not as easy to do as one thinks. For example, I believe it is a mark of Socratic theology and wisdom to be able to explain the Second or Third Article of the Creed or the doctrine of the sacraments to children without repeating the useless, pedantic rubbish of earlier centuries, yet doing this in a way that enables the children to arm themselves against future errors that they might face, that is, doing this in a way that an evangelist or an apostle would do if he were alive today. Nothing comes of superficially philosophizing about these doctrines; it is even less effective simply to leave out what does not please us, what we cannot confess wholeheartedly. It is necessary to possess knowledge of the Bible, dogmatics and the history of dogmatics, knowledge of the historical context and the content of dogmatics. If only we had a *history of dogmatics* that included at the conclusion of each doctrine a practical judgment about how, on the basis of its own premises, this doctrine could best be presented *to our time*. Semler's writings have generously paved the way for us in reference to particular articles of faith. But the specific kind of work that I desire (which would be unbiased, complete, philosophical, and humane) has, as far as I know, not yet been written.[30]

A *history of dogmatic preaching* is also desireable because an amazing perspective can be gained by following the nature of preaching throughout the periods of church history and seeing the shade that it assumed in each period and in relation to the thinking that was in vogue at that time. . . .

Intentions and what determines them, drives and perfections, essence and possibility, perspectives, contexts, situations, characters, ideals, and the like are still found in the pulpit. Often they are needlessly misunderstood by the preachers themselves or used in the most improper way. In the earlier disputes

30. Those who have read Spittler's book on church history will not hesitate long in recognizing whom they would prefer to undertake such a project.

about the philosophical way to preach, other theological ideas arose in which a philosophical sermon was translated into good, intelligible German. How often do we have the opportunity to hear such translations today? And how often does the crowd regret that it cannot understand such a translation! Of course, our most recent book language that has forced its way into the pulpit has not been taken from Wolf's writings, which are no longer read. Rather, this language comes from France, England, Italy, and who knows elsewhere. The overabundance of translations (most of them by manual laborers who do not know the genius of our language) can ruin a sermon. But a sermon is spoiled even more by the immature, hasty, aimless reading of such translations. Given our human nature, which inherits what has come before us, and given our mania for imitation, we are always borrowing and begging in such a way that when we cannot easily grasp the subject matter at hand; we pick up only the *language,* that is, the empty, wooden vessels, and childishly present them for show. I knew a man from whose speech you could always tell what he had just read. I knew another man who was fascinated by Crebillon and who actually preached in a Crebillon style.[31] You can imagine what this sounded like! When Klopstock became popular, all the young people seeking to be sublime preached in a clumsy hexameter. If the craze over bards had lasted only a little while longer, then people would have preached in a bardic style. A few years ago when everyone wanted to be acquainted with *art,* art also appeared in the pulpit. Now that young men use biblical expressions in their romances and romantic poetry, it would be unthinkable for the pulpit not to follow them after a while and to borrow from this romantic tone. Oh Luther, when one thinks back on you and your pure, solid, completely intelligible language!

Thirtieth Letter

The central doctrine of all religions and the source of all knowledge, salvation, and virtue is the doctrine of God.[32]

1. The first warning I offer is this: *Do not profane God when you ought to be revering God as holy. Do not use God's name in vain* in the pulpit or at the altar. How often is God's name used in vain there! The word runs down the [preacher's] lips without thought, without feeling and emotion like an

---

31. [Claude-Prosper Jolyot de Crebillon *fils* (1707-77). A French author who wrote dialogues reflecting social problems. According to Clifton Cherpack, "On both sides of the Atlantic, Crebillon *fils* is either known as an eighteenth-century purveyor of frothy salaciousness, or is not known at all." One aspect of his style, "like some children's party balloons, often develops unexpected kinks and protuberances until it reaches grotesque proportions at its maximum point of inflation." See *An Essay on Crebillon fils* (Durham, N.C.: Duke University Press, 1962), vii, 171.]

32. [SW 10:323-29.]

empty symbol, an empty syllable. It makes a person shudder to hear this and
to think back on the devotion and respect with which virtuous pagans named
the eternal, supreme being. "The name of God is blasphemed among the
Gentiles because of you,"[33] said Paul about the Jews, and what better example
could there be?

Make sure, therefore, that you never speak about God or pray to God
without a feeling of reverence and honor. Christ says that God seeks to be
worshiped "in spirit and truth"[34] so that knowledge of God becomes "eternal—
life within us." How can this happen with thoughtless carelessness? When
Socrates, who was only investigating a philosophical truth, prayed to his
supreme god, how simple and sublime was his prayer! The Pythagoreans
preferred to honor God through silence, through quiet seeking and imitation,
instead of with empty twaddle. Many peoples believed it was best to worship
the "great unnameable one" with a quiet tremor of childlike love. The son
of God made God known to us Christians as the Father, as the active over-
flowing source of all life, of all happiness. Yet if you keep these examples
of non-Christians in mind, then you can see how far behind them we stand
in a good many books, sermons, deeds, and practices! This is not to say that
I would encourage either that dubious fountain of emotion—mysticism—or,
as a substitute for emotion, cold and arrogant lofty constructions of the imagination, flowery odes that go nowhere, and so on. God is dishonored not only
in these ways but also through every empty show of hypocrisy and idolatry.
A congregation is often tempted and vexed by this. Speak about God and to
God with simplicity of heart, the way you like, the way you know and feel
God. Learn to know God well, to sense him with confidence, not only through
words but through thoughts, through practice and experience. This is the
meditatio, oratio, and *tentatio* that Luther prescribes for the study of theology,[35]
for we cannot teach others what we ourselves do not know, and we cannot
give to others what we ourselves do not possess.

2. Do not, therefore, engage in *subtle inquiries about God's essence and
attributes* in front of a group of people who want to learn about salvation. It
is good, even necessary, to know these disputes and to what extent the human
capacity for disputation is developed through them. Get acquainted with this
aspect of the human spirit in all the changes and hidden corners [of history]
and with the ways it has for centuries raised the same questions and problems
albeit in different words. Do not, however, bother the congregation with it.

33. [Romans 2:24.]

34. [John 4:23-24.]

35. [Martin Luther, *Dr. Martin Luthers Werke: Kritische Gesamtausgabe* (Weimar: Böhlaus,
1883-) 50:657-61. In his 1539 preface to the first volume of the Wittenberg edition of his German
writings, Luther gives three guidelines for studying theology: meditation, prayer, and trial. He
says that one must constantly pray and meditateon the Scriptures. The devil will test anyone
studying the Word of God, and these temptations will help the student love God's Word.]

People have always struggled with questions such as, What is God? How can God be three in one, one in three? How did God become so? What has God been doing since eternity? How did he "step out" of himself (a monstrous expression!) and bring finite things into being? How does the "infinite one" relate to finite things now? How does God see and recognize them? Are they within God or outside of God? Is God in them, or are they in God? Is it possible that changes of finite things do not generate changes in God, even though God *acts* within time and became a human being? How is this possible? These and a hundred other questions will always remain stumbling blocks that baffle the most intelligent people. It is the work of fools rather than of human beings *to calculate* the infinite with the finite, *to measure* "inside" or "outside" God extensively or intensively, and so on. Whoever earns the crown of heresy with such questions carries it neither profitably nor honorably. We poor creatures! We do not even know what we ourselves are, and yet we want to know the being of beings as it knows itself! We are finite creatures enclosed within time and space, and yet we want to enter that which is immeasurable, where no time and space exist, and to substantiate God's omniscience, omnipresence, predestination, and justification! We do not know how we move our hands or how the mind affects the movements of the body, and yet we want to demonstrate how God affects the world, other minds, elements, and bodies! *Insania insaniarum!* In your own reflection on these matters, try to use the simplest, most natural expressions; do not discuss them, however, in front of the congregation.

When you speak to the congregation, use and explain the language of the Bible. This language speaks *humanly* to human beings. I do not know if divine eternity, immutability, omnipresence, omniscience and holiness, that is, the incomparability of God, can be expressed more sublimely, comprehensibly, and meaningfully than in Psalms 90, 102, and 139; in beautiful passages of the book of Job; in Isaiah; and in those passages of the Pentateuch and the Prophets that explain the name and nature of Yahweh. In the Gospel of John where Christ speaks so often about God, his Father, he always does so in the simplest, most intimate way. Christianty's finest teaching about God, which comes directly from God and God's Son, involves impressing these passages with their noble concepts on young people; instilling in them the view that everywhere in nature and in the Bible God is incomparable, great, and worthy of love; and always speaking about God with clarity, compassion, and awe. Christ often captures in one loving word and with a childlike simplicity what philosophers have only half proven with obscurity and with great effort, even though many of those philosophers have based their proofs on the words of Christ.

3. I do not appreciate *lofty doxologies about God or boring discourses about each and every one of God's attributes* either in sermons or in hymns

and prayers. The people of the Near East like them, but they express them
with more warmth than we do. The spirit and language of the Near East
became accustomed to them at some point in history. In our part of the world,
however, they usually develop into verbal ice floes, into cold abstractions
that take aim at God from all sides, or into monkish litanies. Christ forbids
all such absurd talk, viewing it as the babble of heathens. This is why he
taught his brief prayer, "Our Father, who art in heaven!" Are we Christians
supposed to forget this teaching and blather on by the hour in hymns with
boring melodies and in sermons that are even more boring? The less truth
people possess, the more they try to assist themselves with such babble. For
what would the people who understand practically nothing about articles of
religion sing or say hour after hour, if they were not able to squeeze yet
another grand, empty notion about God into prose or poetry? One should send
these people to the Persian Mobeds so that they can pray and rhyme their
Yashts.[36]

The Bible always speaks about God as a *present, living, active being* who
is living in all works of his creation and active in every single work, even in
the minutest affairs of our life. Understood in this way, the concept of God
takes on an urgency, and the doctrine of God becomes stimulating and delightful. This is indeed the only way we can "feel sure" about God, perceive
him, and draw the attention of others to him. In short, this view of God is
the basis of all religion on earth. I can neither comprehend nor be moved by
an infinite being who dwells outside the world, for such a being is distant
from me. But the God who surrounds me, who sees through me, who created
me, who created all things, who preserves and guides me—this is my God
and Father! Where there is power in nature, there is God; where there is spirit
in nature, there is the breath and power of God's Spirit. "God is in all things,
and all things exist in him." Where could I seek you, oh God, where you
would not be? Where could I go where you would not guide me? The pattern
of my thoughts is an embroidery stitched by your hand. The paths of my life
are a labyrinth arranged by your goodness. All of nature is your work, your
dwelling, your temple.[37] . . .

4. This final thought leads me to something I have often noticed, especially
among children. The sublime, vast, *astronomical proofs of the splendor of
God discovered in the endless galaxies of space* are too remote for children.
These proofs, even when presented clearly and persuasively, excite them much
less than, if I may say so, the "earthly proofs," which are human and visible
to us at once. I did not expect this. I have noticed the same thing among
ordinary adults. Presented with either accepted or almost-verified scientific

36. [Yashts are hymns of praise found in the *Avesta*.]
37. [Cf. Psalm 139.]

discoveries, they shake their heads and think at most *quae supra nos*.[38] Thus, for their sake too, I consider the speech of the Bible to be the *most human and best* speech. It speaks about heaven entirely within our earthly realm and speaks about everything on earth completely *kat' anthropon*.[39] Try to taste for yourself all the sublime delights that lie in the discoveries of Copernicus, Kepler, Galileo, Newton, Bradley, Herschel, and others, which Huygens, Kant, Lambert, Schmid, and others[40] have presented in part with exquisite warmth. Spare the pulpit, however, from sermons full of astronomical proofs. Instead, use as a model Psalms 8, 19, and 104, and the words of God in Job. In these texts there is sublimity enough for everyone's emotions; in these texts the "One who embraces all things" appears within the poor, limited horizon of our earth.

Even if you have appropriated everything that Ray,[41] Nieuwentyt, Derham and others in the area of natural theology have written, use it sparingly in the pulpit. Not all proofs of these theologies are equally good, for in all these facts lies really only one proof. The books multiplied, and this great theme became in the end just an ordinary title for yet more books! I do not need to introduce you to Bonnet's *Contemplation of Nature* and Plüche's *Nature Displayed*[42] (two works with the same subject but executed very differently). Reimarus wrote *Abhandlungen von der natürlichen Religion* [Essays on natural religion] and *Betrachtungen über die Triebe der Tiere* [Contemplations on the instincts of animals].[43]

How I wish that I could mention everything in this immense field! If someday you get a house in the country and the good Lord grants you the spare time, health, and the means, this study of *God and nature* would be

38. [From the Latin proverb *quae supra nos nihil ad nos*, which means "what is above us is nothing to us." The saying is ascribed to Socrates by various church fathers, and it sits well with Xenophon's portrait in which Socrates depreciates the study of geometry and higher mathematics on the grounds that they might not be useful. Cf. *Memorabilia* I,1,11-15; IV,7,3-18.]

39. [Greek for "in human terms."]

40. See, for example, [Christiaan] Huygens's *Kosmostheōros* [Hagae-Comitum: Apud A. Moetjens, 1698], Kant's *Allgemeine Naturgeschichte und Theorie des Himmels* (Königsberg:Peterson, 1755), [Johann] Lambert's *Kosmologische Briefe [über die Einrichtung des Weltbaues* (Augsburg:Kletts, 1761)], Schmid on *Weltkörpern*, and so on.[Nicolaus Copernicus (1473-1543), Johannes Kepler (1571-1630), Galileo (1564-1642), Sir Isaac Newton (1642-1727), James Bradley (1693-1762), Friedrich W. Herschel (1738-1822), Christiaan Huygens (1629-95), Johann H. Lambert (1728-77) all made contributions to the area of astronomy.]

41. [John Ray (1627-1705). English naturalist; often called the "father of English natural history."]

42. [Charles Bonnet (1720-93), *Contemplation de la nature* (Amsterdam: chez Marc-Michel Rey, 1764). The earliest German translation is entitled *Betrachtung über die Natur* (Liepzig: Junius, 1766). Noël Antoine Plüche (1688-1761), *Le spectacle de la nature* (Paris:Veuve Estienne, 1732). The earliest German translation is *Schauplatz der Natur* (Vienna, 1746-53).]

43. [Samuel Hermann Reimarus, *Abhandlungen von den vornehmsten Wahrheiten der natürlichen Religion* (Hamburg: J. C. Bohn, 1754) and *Allgemeine Betrachtungen über die Triebe der Tiere* (Hamburg: J. C. Bohn, 1760).]

your daily joy. The closer these studies adhere to the everyday blessings of God in the First Article [of the Creed], the better! Luther draws our attention especially to the *eye* and *ear* (as the finest, most noble senses—two unfathomable wonders), to *reason,* and to a number of fine, inscrutable *human powers,* as well as to the noble *structure* of the human body. Galen has already written an excellent book about the latter; and Haller's physiology, especially the part about the heart, the senses, and the human soul, together with what he has inserted about the whole economy of life, are an ocean of science and knowledge. Süssmilch's *Divine Order*[44] offers you a new area that is very relevant to the office of the ministry. If a general physical geography of the human race on earth were added to it, this would be a beautiful commentary on the words of the apostle in Acts 17:26, 27.

I would not finish if I tried to offer a thorough introduction to all the excellent works that have been and certainly will be done toward understanding God in nature. Do not, however, load yourself down with work in this enticing field. Too much reading can make you blind; and more than one scientist has been called a freethinker. They carried themselves too far with hypotheses and, in the end, placed a thing that they called "nature," "necessity," and "eternal order" on the throne of God. This "nature atheism," which can often be coupled with great superstition and with an extremely intolerant enthusiasm, is now a contagious disease, especially in France.

I have strayed so far from my dogmatic-homiletic Article that it is difficult to come back to it. So that is all for now!

Thirty-seventh Letter

From what I have said previously, my friend, you can see that you cannot stick closely and simply enough to the *history of Jesus.*[45] It is written for the simpleminded and for children. So become a child among children! Bring them closer to Jesus through Jesus himself, through his genuine *divine wisdom,* through his *calm, suffering human form* and eternal *loving kindness.* All of his deeds, speeches, parables, and his final fate were written in this way, and in no other, for this reason: He was to be more than a Socrates to us; he was to be not only the model but also the perfector of our faith and of the most enduring moral strength.

Even the Second Article of your Apostles' Creed points to this *historical* method of interpreting the Scripture. For what other reason are the stages of degradation and exaltation told in this article? It is because the earliest centuries

44. [Johann Peter Süssmilch, *Die göttliche Ordnung in den Veränderungen des menschlichen Geschlechts, aus der Geburt, dem Tode und der Fortpflanzung desselben erwiesen* (Berlin: J. C. Spener, 1741).]
45. [SW 10:392-95.]

of the church held them and the *history of Christ* to be the genuine foundation
of faith. Use the historical method with this article as well as the third. Even
though the parts of the creed stand separately, they have a beautiful unity.
This can been seen especially when you yourself examine the causes in the
history of the first centuries of the church. You must become familiar with
the following: King's *History of the Apostles' Creed*;[46] what Amyraut (Amyr-
aldus) Parker and others have written about it; and other works that examine
the faith of the first centuries from an historical and dogmatic perspective.
Several authors have excerpted passages from the church fathers for various
purposes. More about that later.

Ernesti maintains not without justification that the so-called "three offices
of Christ" are not the best teaching tool for dogmatic theology, in part because
they are metaphors, and in part because of their relation to one another and
to the work of Christ. Ernesti also demonstrates that our earliest theologians
did not use them. One can immediately avoid this shortcoming of using them
by pointing out the *names* and *images* that were used to portray the *person*
and *work* of Christ in the Old and the New Testaments. Then one can point
out why there are so many of them: Not one of them says *everything* that
should be said. Therefore one should *place them next to one another,* analyze
the figurative expressions, such as"lamb," "sacrifice," "guarantor," "high
priest," and so on, and create out of them *one* complete concept. Let individual
instructors do this in the way that they desire. As for myself, when speaking
before a popular audience I prefer to keep using Luther's concept [of Christ]
as expressed in his interpretation of the Second Article [of the Creed]. In my
opinion it is the easiest concept to understand, for both young and old, and
at the same time, it is a pregnant, fruitful concept, as all the words of Luther's
interpretation are. Here you have the best opportunity to avoid or to improve
crude and even false ideas about the power of the devil, from whom Christ
supposedly bought us, about the magical power of his blood, and many other
unworthy notions. The satisfaction and sacrifice of Jesus are presented in
Luther's interpretation from the purest perspective of a friend who has saved
me, who risked his blood, his whole being, his life and death, for me, and
who is now my Lord because of his justice and love. Even the *nature of his
service, the purpose of his sacrifice,* is decribed in such a worthy way here
that it is very difficult to misinterpret the doctrine of Jesus' reconciliation if
one follows the simplicity of this article of the Creed. Every time I read
Luther's Small Catechism, I am struck again and again by its pointed *com-
prehensibility* and *power.* Even the interpretation of the Third Article, which
is connected to the second in a very helpful way, is full of this powerful

46. [Lord Peter] King [1669-1734], *History of the Apostles' Creed* [London: W. B. Robinson,
1702].

intelligibility and truth. It deals not with enthusiasts' ravings about the effects of grace but rather with the many *gifts of the spirit*. They must, first of all, be understood *historically* in relation to the origin and foundation of the church and then related *to us*. The explanation is arranged in such a lovely way that it follows the Article itself word for word, step for step. It is a great joy to hear someone instruct catechumens with this natural simplicity and fullness of truth, just as the confession of faith would have been explained to those to be baptized in the early church. But we do not always appreciate this joy. Over the course of time so much chaff has been thrown over the two Articles that if the instructor wants to use all of it, oftentimes the most beautiful seedling, yielding a host of living fruits, becomes idle and dies. . . .

Thirty-eighth Letter

. . . Because no one learns disciplines merely for the sake of learning them, let us speak about the *use, benefit, and application* for which you learn and pursue theology.[47] For the goal determines the path leading to it.

The goal of theology, apart from the formation of your own *character,* is the *formation* and improvement of others through *elocution* [*Vortrag*]. I use the term "elocution" instead of "preaching" because this innocent word, "preaching," has a bad reputation and because the expression that I am using means something more to me than what is commonly called preaching. Our thoughts are determined and arranged by language; we learn something for ourselves best by teaching others; in general what one calls the *formation of the soul* cannot merely be measured by one's *thoughts* or by the *content* of what one knows but rather is also primarily measured by the *method* through which we know these things and express ourselves to others; in short, one's *way of thinking and way of living* also belong to our evaluation of one's *formation.* In all these illustrations and in regard to elocution, the first and last word is *action,* but in a much broader sense of the word than used by Demosthenes.[48] What good would it do to study the Bible, dogmatics, polemics, ethics, or any of the human sciences if they were to lie dormant like a dead seed inside of you and were not made useful through either language or experience? Unfortunately, in our overabundance of knowledge and learning today, we often lose the purpose for which we are learning. And we do not know if anything we are studying is *applicable* to our lives.

The Bible, the book of God that was written during so many periods and ages of the human race, is distinctive in that its elocution changes in very diverse ways in conformity to various times and people. Does a *type of*

47. [SW 11:5-10.]
48. [Demosthenes (384-322 B.C.). Greek orator whose speech was regarded as the mode of impassioned reason.]

elocution exist that cannot be found somewhere in the Bible? Amidst its unity and diversity we find all kinds of poetry and prose, the most diverse speeches of very diverse books and periods: a garden full of flowers and fruits where every bee can suck, every worm and human being can find nourishment. What does the Creator want to say to us with this rich perspective? What else but that God treasures *each gift* of nature, each innocent *tendency* of the human soul in its own way? God even accommodates himself with his heavenly power and truth to each person; God acts in each individual as that individual's needs require, giving each of us the spiritual nourishment that our individual souls, tastes, and senses can and may enjoy. The sun is effective through its rays, the dew and the rain through their fertile refreshment of the nature of each plant; in the same way God acts in nature and sought to act in Scripture. Nothing is more foreign to the Word of God than a restrictive formula of words—a uniform, wooden speech intended for every soul and thereby meaning nothing to anyone, for we are not formed in a uniform way by our God and Creator. Therefore the noble, magnanimous way for us to deal with the Bible is to be true to ourselves when learning truth, but to become all things to all people when proclaiming the truth. Otherwise, we do no good to anyone. As little as God lost of truth, clarity, and unity in his revelation by accommodating himself to each age, each writer, and each kind of person, so little must we believe that the Scripture, which is so full of variety, will lose something through our varied approaches to it. The firmer our character is, the more we are able to accommodate ourselves to others; the richer and stronger our character, the more flexibly and powerfully we can serve others.

Let us therefore do away with the restrictive method that presents syllables instead of the content itself to which the syllables only *refer!* Let us do away with a uniform kind of elocution that is born of our weakness and ignorance, or of our obstinacy and rigid habit, but not born of truth and divine understanding! The Bible does not, like some kind of instruction manual, provide us with a *pattern* for what we call preaching, let alone a uniform, unchanging pattern. Preaching, like every other form of elocution, originates within a certain time and according to the needs of the time: Preaching changes in relation to such things, and it must be measured, shaped, and judged according to them. Moses and the prophets, the prophets and the apostles, the apostles and Christ all spoke God's truth with divine power, but each of them spoke this truth in his own way, and no two prophets, no two apostles, are completely alike in this respect. Each speaks true to his impression of truth in accordance with what the Spirit gave him to speak. The seed for the entire living plant, the determination of its form and the whole appearance, lay in this impression of the truth, in this *material,* just as the spirit shapes the body, just as in every form of writing the meaning shapes the presentation of it.

Someday, when you are exhausted by certain aspects of your profession, you will experience how refreshing and cheering this rich diversity of the elocution in the Bible is. Who would want to or would be able to drone on year after year for one's whole life in the same way about a wooden metaphysics that had been given the same authority as the Bible and had thrust its scholasticism into an eternal whirlwind of words? How could the human spirit thrive when it had to chew for hundreds of years on an ill-conceived, Aristotelian metaphysics? And how does it fare today with those who voluntarily forge similar chains for themselves? It is fortunate that the Bible did not intend for us to forge such chains. The Bible is a garden, not a prison; it is a world full of diversity and fecundity of thought, not a workhouse in which one always eternally rasps away in the same way. Refresh yourself with this or that author, with his sayings, with his style of writing. The ancient truth will thereby become new to you and to your listeners; the new situation of the author, the new application of his teaching will renew your heart and soul. In this way the fresh air will cheer us and the dead air will be revived through new plants and herbs. There is no doubt that you will feel more comfortable with, more intimate with, and more affectionate toward one author or another. You always find a new friend in the ancient Word of God to help you carry the burden of your profession and your life, and you will praise God for the diverse powers, gifts, languages, and offices that Paul so highly extols as proof and signs of the Spirit.

Do not ever let one form of the Bible's elocution distance you, however, from the one truth that enlivens all of its forms. For if ignoring this diversity is slavery, then ignoring the truth is childish. In all cases the form is only the means of teaching; the truth itself is the end; and only the weak disregard the latter in favor of the former. It seems to me that this warning is particularly necessary in our time because people concentrate so heavily on individual parts of the Bible and spend so much time on minor details of the text that many people never learn to see the forest for the trees. You will recognize many examples of this and will perhaps learn to understand this even more later in life. It is not that I despise attention to detail; every whole is only composed of parts, and up to now my letters have encouraged paying the most careful attention to the parts. It is just that one must not miss the greatest aspect of all—the *content* of the whole Bible—by paying attention to its small and most minute aspects. It is only with a perspective for the whole that one becomes a hero in war, a success in business, an artist in the arts, a person of wisdom in the sciences, a theologian in the study of theology. Without this perspective, one is only a soldier in the first case, a day laborer in the second, an artisan in the third, a scholar, God willing, in the fourth, and a keeper of syllables in the last.

Fortieth Letter

I have intentionally noted, my friend, that the external form of our sermons has no model in the Bible.[49] What would this model of a sermon be? The patriarchs blessed their sons; they recommended the way of the Lord to them. Yet they did not preach in the same way that we do. Deuteronomy is a speech of Moses to the people, spoken from and about his whole life. It is the warmest, most powerful, most urgent speech, which closes with shouts of curse and blessing, followed by his eternal song and his humble prayer of blessing. This is not, however, the model for our common sermon. The same is true with the speeches of the prophets. They stand there like God's mountains. Who dares to say, "You mountains, come to me?" We have Christ's sayings and parables, including some with their interpretation. We also have a few heartfelt speeches to his disciples and to the people. They lack, however, the *form* of our sermons. The *letters* of the apostles are just that—letters; sometimes they include theoretical and practical parts. They have become *texts* for sermons, and we preach about them. But what a difference there is between a letter and a sermon! We are left with nothing but Luke's *account* of the sermons of the apostles. But this is only an account, only *historical summary,* not the form of a sermon that has been copied. In my opinion all of these speeches are different from one another, and which one among them would genuinely be *our* sermon?

You see then, my friend, that nothing depends on the *form;* the form is determined by the content, even though form is shaped by the historical context. The most essential element that all speeches of the Bible have in common and that our sermons should also have in common with them is that they *proclaim the will of God,* that they present *the word and counsel of God concerning our happiness* to the human heart and conscience. This is what they all did—patriarchs and prophets, Christ and the apostles—each in his own way. This is what we are to do in our own way, drawing *from the Bible and in accordance with it.* This is preaching.

The more we draw *from* the Bible, the more we speak in accordance with it and *with ourselves and those around us,* then the better we preach.

It seems to me that the first rule of a good sermon should be that it does not become *speech or idle chatter spoken in our own name.* We are preaching about the will of God, not our own; we are presenting *God's* theme, not our own. As soon as preaching stopped being what it was in the mouth of the apostles—*good news*—it became *an explanation of the Word of God, of its writings, and of its teaching* and *the application* of that which was *delivered* in a quiet, Christian group. This was called "homily" and was not truly oration or speech. The latter arose only later along with the pulpit and lectern,

49. [SW 11:16-23.]

and the most eloquent speakers among the church fathers, including Chrysostom himself, still distinguish between "homily" and "speech." It seems to me that the nature and purpose of the two are distinct and that the homily was the mother of the speech.

I consider the *interpretation of the Bible* to be the most refined, best kind of sermon. The words *post illa* should remind several inspired speakers how foreign the peacock feathers of their eloquence is to this time and this place. Their style goes along *post illa verba Christi et apostolorum* [after those words of Christ and the apostles], as the peacock follows the dove, as a local peddler hounds a shy man. Whoever simply takes the legal speeches of Demosthenes and Cicero as models for our sermons has no concept of either preaching or legal speeches and has not understood their purpose.

When the Word of God and good taste reemerged with the Reformation, the reformers immediately followed in the footsteps of the ancient church. They delivered homilies, they explained the Word of God and applied it. This was the character of the sermons of Luther, Chemnitz, Bullinger,[50] and others until this healthy, ancient, and popular kind of preaching was suppressed by a dogmatic-polemical spirit and eventually by philosophy and rhetoric, and people preferred preaching about themselves over preaching Christ and the Word of God.

Allow me, my friend, to further develop my thoughts about this most simple and most ancient method of preaching, which you may call the *analytical* or the *biblical method of preaching*. I consider this method of preaching to be the best in its place and especially in our time. It is the surest way to a rich and proper practice of preaching, especially for young people.

We have a Word of God that we are to read, understand, apply, and explain to others; preachers are truly *called* and taught to explain, teach, and apply this Word of God; and biblical texts are to be the basis for our sermons. All this leads us to *homily, to a method of preaching that explains and applies the texts*. We should certainly not choose a little word in the text, such as "and," spin a scholastic or rhetorical theme out of it, reel this off, and ignore the rest of the text and God's Word. To do this you do not need a Bible. In such sermons the Bible is not preached; the whole, lively view of the text is not used. In a pinch one could just as well preach about a philosophical compendium or, as Kaiserberg did, preach about Brant's *Ship of Fools*,[51] and at least the sermons would be more consistent. Now, as soon as this kind of speaker announces his bittersweet theme, does it not seem as though he spread over the assembly the seeds of the poppyhead that make you fall asleep? One part of the assembly thinks: What does this have to do with me? Can this

---

50. [Martin Chemnitz (1522-86). Lutheran theologian who helped to consolidate Lutheran doctrine and practice after Luther's death. Johann H. Bullinger (1504-75); Swiss reformer.]

51. [Sebastian Brant (1458-1521), *Das Narrenschiff* (Basel: J. Bergmann, 1494).]

sentence, which is so general and suspended in midair, which is wrapped in preaching-prattle, say anything to me about duty or virtue that I did not already know more clearly long ago from more solid sources and with the help of more distinct concepts and experiences? If one is preaching, then preach! The great, eternal theme of this kind of preacher is: If it does not help, then it does not harm; if it does not harm, then it does not help. He strictly carries out this theme in parts and sections, next to the *introitus* and the *exordium*, adding six kinds of *usus* and an illustration for every point. He proves his point for today and next week and for the next century. If he goes on living, he will continue proving his point.

In contrast to this approach, take hold of the Word of God or your text as it presents itself. Most of it is *story, parable,* interwoven with every kind of teaching. What would be more natural than for you to present the text as it is, to put life into the text or its context, and to apply them to each small part of the whole and of its development? You should introduce the content of your text humbly and attempt in a few words to make the situation in which the text was written interesting or to apply the teaching of the text to a particular situation. Then go through all parts of the story, teaching, or parable at hand in an animated and concise way. Universalize the particular, and particularize the universal. Make your text into a *universal* text, your story and parable into a story and parable about the human heart, the situation to which you refer in all its meanderings into a situation *of our own life.* In this way, no one will escape you, even if they try; no one will be waiting for an application of the text, because the whole sermon will be application; no one will fall asleep in disdain at the pronouncement of the theme, because it will not be a dry proposition, a *universum in nuce,* but rather the whole will be a theme of the *human life and spirit.* The constant theme would be *de te narratur fabula,*[52] even if it were not expressed in words. The *content* speaks, *the situation* touches us, embraces us, and does not relent until the sermon is over, until each person feels that it is over and wishes it were longer. You would not lead the listeners on a beaten, worn path, on which it is as little a joy to lead others as it is to go along yourself, especially since, as the saying goes, we can only go where our heart leads. If you lead your listeners through natural, uncharted, constantly varied, and yet coherent labyrinths to the goal of your pilgrimage, and you always keep the guiding thread in your own hand, then the listeners are bound to follow you. Moreover, your sermon should grow in *interest* and *passion* from beginning to end. The sermon should basically be a *story,* a *vivid situation,* a *drama of the human heart* (I know that this word is not an obstacle for you) with a center and with development; in short, it should a *unified whole.* With this method of preaching listeners

52. [Latin for "the story is told about you."]

have the advantage of always hearing *the Bible alone—the Bible, which has been enlivened for them*, which in a certain sense stands before them and encompasses them. They have the advantage of being able to remember part for part, word for word what was said in the sermon afterward, especially what was said for them. They only need *to pick up the text* and stroll alongside it like a rolling stream or down it like a promenade lined with statues that prompt the memory. In this way they enjoy the Bible more because they have learned to understand it, and they read on its every page *the story of their own hearts.* Through other methods they learned about everything except the Bible, which was presented to them only in strained passages that were torn from their context or in endless, hollow tones that ring in their ears, which were taken for the tones of the Bible but are not. You yourself will enjoy the Bible more, which presents to you in this way a *richness and variety;* the Bible never leaves you impoverished. Using the monastic method of preaching leaves you as poor as a church mouse in no time at all because with that method you have to live on generalizations alone and consume such generalizations all too soon. With the biblical method of preaching, you will always remain *fresh, like your text, like your story.* This story can be viewed from a variety of perspectives in different years, and it contains a thousand viewpoints, while cold, scholastic abstraction contains only one or none at all. The sun rises each morning with new grace, and each evening the sun sets with new beauty; every spring, each returning season, has its new, inexhaustible charm. The same is true with all living objects of nature and with all situations in the Bible. They rejuvenate themselves for our sake, and we are rejuvenated through them. It seems to me that we should not, could not, preach two sermons on the same text in different years that should or could be completely the same. For we are indeed always swimming further in the stream of time; our viewpoint and matters of the heart are therefore constantly changing. If you do fear monotony in preaching, then there are a multitude of *stories, parables, sayings, and situations* that lie beyond or often next to the text at hand; you may place these in relation to the text, connect them to one another, and thereby renew and enliven yourself and your sermon. Who, except a Tantalus,[53] could be thirsty in this stream? There are so many and various ways of thinking about *people, books, and periods* in the Bible, and people have freed this whole garden full of flowers and fruits for their use, have even obliged themselves to using the *whole* garden. Since this is the case, can those on heaven and earth forgive us for, instead of treating the Bible in this way, separating spider webs, preaching foreign, false rhetoric or narrow scholasticism, and thereby putting the world to sleep? Where is

53. [In Greek mythology Tantalus was a god who was punished in Hades by an eternally insatiable thirst and hunger.]

the Word of God, which we are to bring home to people *in all its parts?* Where is our conscience and our duty?

From the very start, my friend, practice this *analytical method of learning,* which points your attention to the *individual* and the *universal,* to the *old* and the *new,* and which opens you up to all the treasures of the Bible and of the human heart. The most appropriate symbol for the use of empty generalization would be the words of David, understood in a negative sense: "[God] will not cause to prosper all my help and my desire."[54] The most appropriate symbol for the analytical method is *fertility, application, lively presence in each moment.* At the beginning this method of instruction will be difficult, for it demands ever new and fresh materials and constant presence of mind and heart. It requires a cheerful spirit, which is constantly able to view the particular from the universal and to discover the most interesting universal within the particular. This method cannot be learned through rules, but can be learned through *examples,* through practical experience; above all, it re- quires a free, willing spirit that desires to serve God with one's whole heart and soul. It rejects the clank of empty words and sentences that are imitated or learned by rote. In short, it rejects the slavish, *thrashing method,* whereby one is always clubbing empty straw. The analytical method is worthwhile precisely because of its import and difficulty. It requires one to attend to the content; to get acquainted with the Bible, world history, the history of the kingdom of God; to read good examples, especially from the ancient world, of loving the *particular, the singular,* facts, particular situations, vivid and descriptive perspectives; to nourish oneself with their spirit; and to learn about the noblest purpose through their influence; not to want to be useless, big talkers on earth. Protect yourself early on, my friend, from such a hopeless abyss.

Fiftieth Letter

The undeniable merit of our theology rests no doubt in the *diligent pro- motion of the languages and the literary text.*[55] This is what makes us true Lutherans, for even Luther made this his starting point in his refutation of opponents and his creation of a purer doctrine.... All of his essays prove how much [Luther] held onto the pure, unshakeable sense of the word. My first concern [in these letters] was to direct you to this and to the *natural form* of the Scriptures, for a true, genuine theology cannot exist without a grasp of the languages and the Bible. It would be senseless not to use the many resources and efforts that have been generated in our time to aid us in this task.

54. 2 Sam. 23:5.
55. [SW 11:119-23.]

However, my friend, do not begin too quickly to translate or even criticize and mutilate the text. We still need a whole series of resources before we are prepared to present a detailed critique of the text; and it seems to me that our contemporary age is not the best suited for translating. We mutilate the language and either write without power or in an affected manner. In short, the pure, genuine German in which our ancestors wrote, before so many foreign languages were known in Germany, has nearly been lost in the last few years. It will reappear and perhaps a richer, more beautiful language will emerge out of our depravity. Therefore, wait and practice translating privately. In the meantime, use Luther's translation and write any corrections in your own copy of the Bible. Or if you want to practice, especially with the poetic books of the Old Testament, then translate them on your own. . . .

In dogmatics use the diligence of our age to verify the illustrative quotes, to place their correct meaning in context, and to make the concepts themselves intelligible. Except for certain abuses and exaggerations, this was the true method of Luther and the reformers, who are especially suited to the apprentice in theology. Protect yourself, however, against the unfounded mania for innovations, against prejudice, and against an aversion to certain doctrines that are apparently contained in the Scriptures. Some preferred to ridicule and ignore these doctrines rather than be uncertain about them. In such matters take a simple view and, as soon as theological disbutes emerge, avoid taking either side. Remain calm and use anything correct or more intelligible from either party. As that farmer amidst the debate said, the most hotheaded party is probably wrong.

It is an evil thing that parties exist in religion. But if you try to unify them too quickly or surreptitiously, then you have certainly done more harm than good. You forge new chains, which may be more refined, but yet, precisely because of their refined nature, are more difficult to remove than the old, rattling chains. A half-known truth, which is made into law, is often more oppressive than a stupid, crude lie. And as soon as political leaders meddle in religious matters, it is the end of unity and free inquiry. Only the *truth* can unite us; only an even, unconstrained, clear, and correct *interpretation of the Word of God* can remove the scales from the eyes of each party. Therefore, let us work toward this goal and continually strive toward it. Leave the rest up to God and time. What we have owed ourselves so long is tolerance and mutual freedom: *amici usque ad aram*.[56] It seems to me that the present age is not as advanced in these matters as it alleges to be and that those who speak the most about tolerance often practice it the least.

The *outward circumstances* of some churches and religions is such that the hope for improvement or the fear of total decline seem almost inevitable.

---

56. [Latin for "friends all the way to the altar."]

The so-called "guardians" and caretakers of the church have deep contempt for their younger generation. The situation of pastors has fallen in some places to the level of poverty and slavery and from time to time gets worse. This is occurring in conjunction with the prevailing economic spirit that affects all classes. Anything religious is treated with cold indifference, and this indifference has spread even among the masses. Such circumstances and others are bound to effect a necessary change over the course of time. Will it be for the better or the worse? Who knows? It is enough to know, my friend, that good must eventually come out of the bad. The dregs of the murky drink eventually sink: The drink becomes clear. The course of providence continues.

Deal with these matters in no other way than by acquiring the skills that in this regard even the present situation demands. The church of God swims on the ocean of this world, and therefore one must be familiar with its shallows, reefs, and waves. Study, therefore, canon law and secular, political history, insofar as it concerns your position, and wherever you can, seek to procure the practical wisdom that looks good even on a theologian.Often one man has created good for an entire country; often one man has done irreparable damage to the entire church polity of the same country. It is not good when a pastor deals with secular business that is foreign to him. But it is equally bad when he is carried along like a fifth wheel in matters in which he should participate.

In this regard, too, keep in mind the examples of our ancient theologians and reformers. All of them worked more or less happily or unhappily according to their powers, according to their gifts and insights, and according to the situation of their countries. Yet how diligent, courageous, and determined they were! We are all so idle compared to Luther, Melanchthon, Zwingli, and others. They acted, they organized more than they wrote; they wrote more than we are able to read. They spoke passionately, from the heart, about issues and not about words; even when they spoke about words, they spoke as if they were talking about issues. Our voices are weary and meek: Our greatest gift is caution, and our writings are so often an idle art. What a pile of rags has been written by the clergy, particularly in Germany! And who writes more wastepaper than the clergy? Try not, my friend, to let your writing ever become full-time work, a bread-and-butter job. It is one of the most disreputable professions of our time; with it you ruin more than paper. It would be better if you did some work with your hands that kept your head and heart healthy. It is difficult to express how miserable human beings become when truth, knowledge, and the cultivation of the human character become a matter of their daily wages.

Finally, my friend, theology is not the study of words, syllables, and books but rather knowledge of the truth that leads to godliness. In other words it is a matter of genuine concerns, activity, practice. For this task you should daily

acquaint yourself with piety and worldly wisdom. In this regard, I also recommend that you read the older writings of active theologians. Look at their
lack of selfishness, their zeal, the pure way in which they adhere to that which
they hold to be true and right. The life of these theologians was short, just
like ours. They lengthened their lives, however, through their efforts and
deeds, just as we shorten our own lives through useless erudition, timidity,
and cowardice. Those theologians live among us, as if they had just died.
We who are still living are often already dead. Who will remember us? What
public or Christian institution, what achieved good, what eternal, lovely seed
will celebrate our name and our life when we, like a dream, are gone?

Farewell! Because we will perhaps part for a long time, I enclose two
additional texts that can supplement my letters well.

[The letters close with selections from Franciscus Hemsterhuis's "Lettre
sur l'homme et sur ses rapports" and with reference to the Earl of Shaftesbury's
Several Letters Written by a Noble Lord to a Young Man at the University
(London: Roberts, 1716). Herder praises Shaftesbury for his view or theology,
his tolerance, and his Christian simplicity. Herder also claims that he referred
to the ten letters by Shaftesbury while writing his own letters (SW 11:124).]

LETTERS TO THEOPHRON

Second Letter

I suspected that your initial doubts would strike the chord that you had already
struck at times during your studies at the university: Your reading of the Bible
is very disturbed and profaned.[57] You cannot free yourself from the critical
view to which your eyes have become accustomed, that is, that the books of
the Old Testament impress you as ancient, as perhaps incomplete, as uncrit-
ically arranged or even mutilated remnants of the Near East, written for the
most part in poetic form, and which we would either have to keep repairing
and improving or would be at a loss to present in a sufficiently literary or
poetic way. The situation is almost worse for you with the New Testament.
The critical view of these books all but reduces them to bare stubble and
refuse reaped from false gospels and writings of idiots who obfuscated the
primitive church. You are not able to express how much this view confuses
your mind and tears your heart apart. You want to abandon much of the
critical erudition of your text books, desiring a return to the naivete, purity,
and simplicity with which in your childhood you read Moses and Job, the
Psalms and the Prophets, John and Christ.

Experience completely, my friend, the lack in your soul, and do not take
it lightly. But also trust your ability to overcome all distortions, to smooth

57. [SW 11:165-70.]

hill and dale, and to regain the simple meaning that once made you happy in your youth and without which we can never be happy. No book in the world can be read properly without inner pleasure and joy. Anyone who reads Homer in a merely critical way, as a pedant or schoolmaster, certainly reads him inappropriately and will not sense his depth—to say nothing of anyone who reads an Ancient Near Eastern book not written for the sake of criticism, of anyone who reads the *Word of God* in such a way. Listen for God's voice in the Bible like a child listens for the voice of its father, like a lover for the voice of his bride. Hear the sound of eternity ringing in it. I offer you a few tips that I found to be true when I suffered from this disease and, as you express it so forcefully and accurately, when the Word of God seemed like a squeezed lemon in the hands of criticism. Thank God it is once again a fruit for me that blossoms on its tree of life.

1. Do not read the Bible at random, but rather in individual books, living in them to the full for a time, during the best hours of the day. For this task choose the most cheerful hours of the day, such as the morning hours, and drink deeply the spirit of the authors. Do this at first with as little critique as possible. Avoid as much as possible the fashionable, new, clumsy translations of the Bible that are written in iambic meter or in even more artificial meters that usually eliminate completely the meaning and spirit of the original text. In the poetic books of the Bible, listen to the simple, repetitive choral hymn. In the historical texts, go back in the same way to the childhood of the world, to the poverty and need of their authors. God lives in this lowly dwelling; the Father speaks to this childhood.

2. Do not look for artifice, embellishment, or contrived beauty in these books, but for truth, feeling, simplicity. In this regard recall many of my past letters to you. Just as you sometimes could not understand me and contradicted me then, you will now praise God for this truth and simplicity. The supreme form of nature is always poetry: The deepest feelings always express themselves sublimely. All primitive peoples understand themselves through their powerful, sweeping images; and passion needs no philosophical poetics in order to present and portray itself as it is. As often as images of this kind seem foreign and farfetched to you, remember that you are reading an Ancient Near Eastern book. These people had a different horizon, a different language than we. What seems remote to us could have been closest to their hearts and their imagination. People who suffer today still speak and sigh as Job sighs, even if not in the same series of images or in the same sublime language. Perhaps it is the impressions of my childhood or a fancy of habit that the most striking passages in the Bible seem to me to possess such a sublime and, at the same time, simple nature that I would not want to replace them with anything in the world. When I hear it said in learned commentaries, paraphrases, or even in the pulpit that much of this metaphorical language

must be translated into good, "purely intelligible," that is, metaphysical, abstract, and intelligible German, I do not know where to turn. Everyone can understand the metaphorical language of the Bible because it is the *language of the human heart;* no one understands that metaphysical jargon.

3. In order to be lifted up into the simplicity, power, and inherent worth of the Scripture, pick up now and then one of the older commentaries, especially from the time of the Reformation. Do not do this in order to discover everything that each religious party of that time located in every passage, for in the heat of the quarrel of that time, every party came across its own system wherever it chose. Rather, look at these commentaries because people at that time still sought content in the Word of God, not merely syllables and literary form as seen from the pettiest perspective. Freely disregard the material that you find foreign or irrelevant. But appropriate these commentators' hearty way of proclaiming the truth. Further, in these commentaries the words of the biblical text are generally printed in large letters beneath the small letters of the commentary, like palaces beneath huts, like giants beneath dwarfs. This juxtaposition of the texts aids your eye and your very being, and ideas develop that are far afield of the merely one-sided, time-conditioned, and personal commentary. Break away completely, however, from any paraphrases of the Bible.

4. Do not let the glitter that people are currently tacking onto biblical poetry rob you of a sense for historical process, historical truth, or even divine revelation. Otherwise, you have won nothing and lost everything. The young poetic asses who can offer a Christian congregation nothing but a cornucopia of poetic blossoms instead of the Word of God are poor wretches indeed. If you lose your inner conviction that divine actions offer a refuge for the salvation of the world and the ennobling of humanity, then what good does the most colorful Persian carpet do you? If the whole language of God, if all the phenomena and miracles of the Bible, its most sublime characters of the human race, the Bible's richest prophecies and most beautiful points of view are dissolved into poetic foam and capricious or dead poetry, then please read the Greeks and Romans instead. Their poetry is obviously more rounded, and their poetic style clearer. Daedalus's[58] holy pillars of the Ancient Near East are, by comparison, crude works if one desires to seek nothing but human work in them.

I need to explain this last point more clearly, for it has serious implications. The oldest parts of the Bible are clearly written in the original language of humanity, that is, in images, in the language of passion and intuition. It would not be appropriate, it would be neither as moving nor as true to the documents, to describe them otherwise. Thus, we must also read and feel them in this

58. [Daedalus is a skilled artisan and architect in Greek myths.]

language. Indeed, as I have often pointed out to you before, we must use everything that helps draw us into its particular tone. But now, one hypothesis claims that it is mere "poetry" that God created the world, that he created human beings in paradise, that they left it through the first, childlike act of disobedience, that God appeared to human beings either directly or through angels, and that from the beginning God guided their education and culture. This hypothesis also claims that it is mere "poetic device" that God appeared to Abraham, that Sodom and Gomorrah fell, that God raised up Moses and led the Israelites through the sea, and that God gave his law on Sinai and spoke through the prophets. If this hypothesis were true, my friend, then I would curse all this poetry and wish to replace it with the barest, driest history. At least then I would know what happened and how it happened. If this hypothesis were correct, then I would know nothing at all. Read sometime the hundreds of hypotheses that people attach to the story of the fall, the flood, and Balaam. Read sometime the newest revelations. For example, the whale that swallowed Jonah was supposedly a ship called the "Whale," sent by God just as the king of England sends the "Swallow" or the "Pelican." Elijah was supposedly struck by nothing but lightning.[59] Elisha made the axhead float supposedly by lifting it from the bottom with a wooden stick;[60] he was apparently able to make the colocynth edible by mixing it with flour, because flour is supposed to make colocynths very edible.[61] Balaam himself was supposedly the donkey with whom he held the dialogue, "How is it that my old donkey suddenly becomes so shy? Could it be imagining that it sees an angel of God?"[62] Such hypotheses are inadequate, childish blather. In face of them, one would gladly go back to Hardt's hypothesis[63] that claimed Jonah slept at the hotel called "The Whale." Read the things that are exhibited from book fair to book fair! You will gladly return to the simplicity with which you read these stories in your childhood and did not think about poetry. Read most of the new, pretentious translations of the Old and New Testaments, which are stilted and clumsy. You will gladly return to the old, simple translation of Luther. This is, alas, the human lot: We exaggerate everything, even the best things and hypotheses, and precisely by exaggerating and by going to both extremes, we finally find the happy medium of truth.

It is, indeed, a delicate thread that runs through the Old and New Testaments, especially in those passages in which image and deed, history and

59. [2 Kings 2:11. Here a chariot of fire appears to Elijah, and he is taken up into heaven.]
60. [2 Kings 6:1-7. In this passage Elisha threw a stick in the water at the point where an axhead had fallen, and the axhead came to the surface of the water.]
61. [2 Kings 4:38-41.]
62. [Num. 22:1-40.]
63. [Hermann von der Hardt (1660-1746). Pietist who later became a rationalist theologian; professor of Ancient Near Eastern languages in Helmstedt until his rationalist criticism of the Bible lost him his chair.]

poetry are mixed. Clumsy hands can rarely follow this thread, let alone unravel it, without tearing it apart or tangling it up, without harming either the poetry or the history that is spun into a whole within this thread. The history of interpreters, especially of the Old Testament, proves this sufficiently, as Jerome and Erasmus already recognized. This history tells us directly that interpretation belongs to God or to the man upon whom rests the spirit of the gods, the genius of ancient times, and the spirit of the childhood of the human race. When people arrive on the scene who know nothing of this thread, for whom nothing is more foreign than poetic feeling, especially of the Ancient Near East, then, even if they were the world's greatest systematic theologians and critics, the plant loses its color from their breath, it wilts in their hands.

You see for yourself, my friend, that I cannot instruct you in the short space of this letter about how to follow this thread of biblical poetry and interpretation. Everything depends on local circumstances, on the author's time, place, context, intention, and genius, and above all on the reader's inherent good sense. Reading Near Eastern poetry, travel journals, and other poets in general arouses this sense, if it exists. If it does not, then it cannot be aroused. In this case, it would be better had some people read neither poetry nor travel journals. . . .

Third Letter

In order not to torture you with my great plan [for a book on Hebrew poetry] which I might never finish, I want to draw a few conclusions from it that pertain to questions you have raised about the *immoral and savage quality of some Hebrew poems*.[64] I hope my remarks can lay these questions to rest.

1. *Poetic expression is suited to a nation's times, morals, and way of thinking*. Description must correspond to the deed itself: Outer expression is always directed toward inner feeling. Since the morals of all nations and even the morals of one nation at different points in history vary, it would be inappropriate to demand bloody war songs from timid shepherds or courtly songs from a wild, nomadic people. Times of war produce different songs than times of peace; and the song of the heroine, Deborah, cannot sound like the Twenty-third Psalm or like the Song of Solomon.

2. We must be even more careful not to judge the *customary way of life or the common morality* of ancient nations according to our own time, for these nations did not live in our time, and both life-style and morality are the finest blossoms and fruits of the relations of temporal circumstances. Greeks and Romans have more offensive qualities than the Hebrews; yet we rectify

64. [SW 11:176-78, 181.]

and conceal these qualities among the Greeks and Romans while exposing and ridiculing them among the Hebrews. You err if you demand Western morals from a people of the Ancient Near East or expect Amos the herdsman or Ezekiel in captivity to provide the subtlety of expression found in the story of creation or in the writings of Solomon, especially in the Song of Solomon. The writings would not stem from a particular time, people, or author if they all looked either the same or like the books at our yearly book fairs.

3. We must therefore pay attention to the *individual and temporal circumstances* under which something occurred and not mix and throw everything together. Abraham's timidity in Egypt is as appropriate in its time and place as Samson's boldness. Moses' giving of the law was as relatively and comparatively good as every good legislation must be and cannot be otherwise. It is not suitable for just any situation. Christ himself says, "Moses gave you such laws because of the hardness of your heart"; if you had been more sensible, more tender, and more willing, then you would have received other laws, for "you did not even keep the ones you had." This is what Christ said. And what would he say if he visited us and saw us hanging onto these laws and still singing David's imprecatory Psalms in his Christian congregations? He would probably say, "Where are your Jebusites, Philistines, and enemies of the king whom you are cursing? How do you dare put such words into my mouth, for I myself never returned insult for insult and never cursed, even when I was rebuked? Let [David], an afflicted, passionate king whose rule and life turned sour, get everything off his chest, and in his circle, in the throes of this distress let him curse, pray, hope, and desire in the way he finds most appropriate. But who are you to parrot his words completely outside his context, outside his emotional world, and in this way not only disturb the sanctity of your meditation but also blaspheme my person? You should learn from all times and morals. This is why they are mapped out for you so faithfully. But do you learn anything from them when you just repeat them mechanically?"

4. The greatest abuse of all is to ascribe to God everything that is said and done in the Bible, even if Satan is the one who is speaking or acting in it. "It says so in the Bible," people argue. This abuse really becomes absurd, and yet people commit it more often than we think. It is assumed, for example, that because David is called a "man after God's heart," that is, an honest and praise-worthy ruler in most of his deeds and intentions, then he must have done everything in God's name. This would mean then that God must have also committed the sin against Uriah and Bathsheba through David, for which the guilty one had to pay dearly! Such distortions would be blasphemy if they were not obviously so absurd. Everything is written in the Book of God, the Bible, just as everything between heaven and earth, both good and bad, is

contained in God's book of nature. Annals must be written accurately, and these are the annals of humankind.

My dear friend, if you read through the Bible with a humane eye and heart, if you also follow the thread of God's development *[den Faden der Entwicklung Gottes]* according to times, life-styles, people, and morals, then what truth you will find, and with all that is miraculous in many a story, what powerful truth! Here there is no miraculous mixture of fables and poetry as in other ancient sagas, especially those of the Ancient Near East. How simple is the narrative from the earliest times of the world to the patriarchs, where the style of other nations would require the boldest lies and miraculous stories. Here there is nothing of that. Indeed here we find modest and natural enlightenment on some of those fantastic traditions, such as of giants, heavenly storms, and so on. The way that God deals with human beings in this period of time cannot be more naturally conceived. All pageantry and artifice is so far removed from the narrative that the text does not even state how God appeared or in what form God spoke to human beings. The same is true of the simple, pastoral narrative of the patriarchs. Nothing is dolled up, nothing exaggerated. Even what is miraculous is so natural that we ourselves would like to sit in their tents, among their huts and herds, and wait for the angels. . . .

Everything is narrated here in relation to the nation; every event is painted in the color that people saw in it; fortune and misfortune, vices and punishment, praise and blame, everything, yes everything, is connected to the name of Yahweh. Yahweh hardens the heart of Pharaoh and rouses Samson. He allows David to take a census of the people and punishes him for it. He commands Shimei to curse[65] and rewards his malice. Who does not see that all of this makes up the prophetic-theocratic style, the national tone, in short, the particular color of the events that also belongs to their accurate presentation? I am going on and on, and yet I could have said much more about the poetic history of this people, about what is miraculous and natural in it, and about the manifest purpose of God for and through this people. Another time. Take care, and study history with children so that you will discover its beautiful enlightenment everywhere.

Fifth Letter

Much more ground work needs to be done, my friend, before we achieve an entire *pragmatic survey of the history of Christianity.*[66] We must philosophically investigate the history of *sciences,* that is, *particular* sciences, such

65. [2 Sam. 16:5-14 and 19:16-23. Here Shimei curses David and throws stones at him. One man says his head should be cut off for cursing the king. David says, "Let him curse. If Yahweh has said to him, 'Curse David,' what right has anyone to say, 'Why have you done this'?" Later Shimei repents, and David spares his life.]
66. [SW 11:198-201.]

as dogmatics, Christian ethics, the interpretation of Scripture, mystics, and aesthetics. (We should not simply investigate the teachings; rather, we must understand how these sciences reigned and were effective within their historical contexts.) In other words, the influence of *external* circumstances, of ritual, of secular and ecclesiastical leadership must be observed philosophically and historically. Yet we cannot stop here. The history of *particular opinions, sects, and heresies*—how they changed and what they changed in the world—and the historical study of the religion of particular *countries and human beings* must lead to a general overview, and the history of the *customs of peoples* must be investigated much more thoroughly than it probably has been up to this time. The case is the same in church history as it is in intellectual and political history: We take the *head* to be the body, the *thoughts of particular human beings* to be the prevailing state of affairs.

Remember, my friend, what I have already told you: Once you have achieved a general view of the history of the Christian church through the author about whom you have heard or with whom you are familiar, then tackle the historical perspective of particular parties, churches, sects, countries, or even disciplines and forms of teaching. You gain the most by turning to the *particular*. For example, how illuminating, edifying, and pleasant is a history of dogmatics that is written historically and philosophically! It shows the way that the doctrine changed over the course and development of time; it shows the waxing and waning of the light and of the truth. Such a history gives us criteria for both light and truth. It shows the many opinions about the forms of *one* doctrine; it makes us unbiased, cool-headed, and tolerant; and it teaches us to thank God actively and from our hearts for the increase of the true light, of true simplicity and intellectual freedom. If only we possessed such a history of dogmatics! Several people wish that Semler would publish his scattered writings, part prefaces and part commentaries, on the history of dogmatics in one volume but arrange them in a clearer, more definitive form.

Poiret and Arnold have written a history of mystical theology; yet both of them were themselves mystics and did not therefore retain an open mind and perspective.[67]

As far as I know, no one has even thought of writing a *genuine history of ethics*. This would be very difficult to write if one aims, as one should, to include everything: rules, customs, natural law, civil law, and international law.

Even the *history of the interpretation of Scripture,* which would be the shortest work of them all, has hardly been gathered together and completed.

---

67. [See the works of Pierre Poiret (1646-1719) and Gottfried Arnold (1666-1714). Arnold's *Historia et descriptio theologicae mysticae* (Frankfurt: Apud Fritsch, 1702) contains a lengthy defense of mysticism by Poiret. Arnold's *Unpartheyischen Kirchen-und Ketzer-Historie* (Frankfurt: Fritsch, 1699-70) claims that mystics are the true Christians.]

Christianity and Theology

261

What Richard Simon accomplished in this field was carried on only here and
there in scattered works of Wetstein, Ernesti, and Michaelis.[68] Hetzel's history
of cricitism is incomplete, although it is useful as an index of more recent
works.

The history of *individual parties* has, in part, been treated with great
diligence. But most of the time it is written either by the party itself or by
its enemies. We need an open perspective somewhere between the two. . . .

We do not possess a *history of Protestantism* where Böhm and [Christian
August] Salig left off. . . .

I have said more than enough. You see, my friend, how far we still are
from possessing a true, complete, pragmatic *history of Christianity* that includes the influence that it did or did not have. If we did have such a history,
then we surely could have addressed the doubts raised in your question: How
can such different opinions and interpretations of the Bible exist within the
purpose of Christian revelation? You would see either that these differences
of erudite opinions had much less influence in the *framework of humanity*
than one thought and that the course of Christianity kept *progressing* because
it was based on something more essential; or that given the nature of the
situation, this is what had to happen and that every twilight, every eclipse,
achieves its *positive purpose*.

Sixth Letter

Do not be afraid, my friend, of our current revolutions and ferments in
Christianity, especially in the areas of dogmatics and biblical interpretation.[69]
According to all earlier examples in history, according to all analogies in the
household of God on earth, you have *nothing* to fear.

If Christianity and scholarship, if scholasticism and Christianity, are not
one and the same, as I believe that I have shown you very clearly, and as the
New Testament itself demonstrates as clear as day, then such changes can
neither subvert or destroy Christianity. In its own time it returns in a more
fitting and lovely form. And those efforts of the human spirit, whether they
are called large- or small-scale conflicts, have helped Christianity, as it later
becomes apparent, to achieve this more fitting, lovely form, even at their own
cost.

Nothing is more dreadful in regard to human understanding than for it to
be *standing still*. Indeed, such a complete static state is practically impossible
without the extreme pressure of barbarism and brutality. The pressure of
coercion does not stop the human spirit. Rather, such pressure encourages

68. [See the works of Richard Simon (1638-1712), a French biblical critic.]
69. [SW 11:201-9.]

the human spirit to bolt and cross over fields and gardens. As long as Europe was truly barbaric, nobler notions were not accepted. People brutalized such concepts in their own ways. But now that something was set in motion after hundreds and thousands of nudges, no one can stop this motion—neither excommunication nor inquisition, neither sword nor the burning of heretics. On the contrary, such foolish methods of coercion drive people from one extreme to the other: from ignorant barbarism to ignorant sophistry; from crude superstition to atheism, which reigned, as everyone knows, during the dark centuries of coercion by the church and during those years perhaps reigned exclusively.

The human spirit must have freedom, even if it sometimes misuses freedom. Human beings must be able to understand and interpret the Word of God in the way that they find correct and true, even if they sometimes interpret it falsely. God expected that Adam would fall, and yet God created him *free.* And God had to create him free if he was to be *God's* image, if he was to be a human being.

Freedom is the foundation of all Protestant churches, as their name suggests. Freedom is the foundation of common sense, of all freely expressed virtues of the human heart, of the entire welfare of the human ability *to strive forward.* One might ask, "Must it not be a kind of freedom, however, that is coupled with laws?" Indeed, with laws! But only those that common sense recognizes as such, those that freedom itself *chooses.* Freedom rests on them, that is, on choice and on a discipline for happiness. Laws are the essence of freedom and must continue to be. Otherwise, freedom is an empty word.

When Germany broke the chains of papalism, what right did it have to do so? *The human right of freedom.* Luther did not reform because the prince wanted this. Otherwise he would have been a bad reformer of religious matters who slavishly invalidated old truths and interpretations that the prince could not control. Luther reformed because his *conscience and conviction* drove him to do so. The princes allowed reform in part because of their own convictions and in part because, from the perspective of the necessities of their office, they found it to be *politically valuable.* Anyone who tries *to eliminate* conscience and clear conviction in the Lutheran church or in a Protestant church is the most wicked anti-Lutheran. That person eliminates the principle of the Reformation, indeed of all healthy religion, happiness and truth: *freedom of conscience.* Anyone who attempts this condemns Luther, all of his assistants, and all men of the past who have stood up for freedom and truth.

Do not allow any external guidelines determine that "freedom should be allowed to go this far and no further." True freedom must have its own *internal* limits. Indeed, freedom limits itself more strictly than any guidelines because it acts only out of *innermost* conviction, choosing and scrutinizing what is best. We are not speaking here about external connections, duties, and obligations but rather about the inner nature of truth. . . .

It is undeniably good that a fair, unbiased form of tolerance is growing even in some provinces of Germany. It is time that it did. How wonderful it would be if the Catholic provinces of Germany moved closer to the Protestant and all Germans recognized one another as *brothers,* as *parts of one nation and language,* and worked together toward *a common good*! I say "together" and not "identically" because this is impossible. I know no greater intolerance than its most recent form, which lables everything as "non-belief" and forcefully seeks to discard it. Let all people believe *according to their own, individual convictions.* If you want to change them, then do not demand, rebuke, and criticize, but rather *pursuade* them.

In addition, I do not see the dangerous consequences of recent *investigations* into religion that you, my friend,suspect. If they come up with nothing, then they go under automatically: They are like chaff that the wind scatters. If they do produce something, then they are useful to religion. They illuminate it, strengthen its foundation, examine it, and purify it. The ship on the sea needs wind: Human understanding needs continual, even controversial, investigation and examination. . . .

I offer you, my friend, a few observations that I have found to be true in the whole history of Christianity. Use them to encourage you and to give you hope and comfort in our time.

First, whenever there is ferment, whenever a scientific or religious revolution takes place, nothing is more difficult than *keeping oneself within limits.* One easily moved from one extreme to the other. You know that when the Reformation came into being, Socinianism and Enthusiasm were introduced along with it. These were two evils for which the noble reformers were only accidently responsible. . . .

Second, a party is most effective *in its first state of zeal.* A new future is more provocative. Whoever fears protest must either prepare for opposition or prevent it. Those who oppose are usually more daring than those who merely defend. . . .

Third, in every period of endeavor and advance there are always *opposing parties* that seem to be born for and against one another and that often exist in very close proximity. God has placed them in *one* period of time: Their powers check one another in such a way that from their combined efforts a third, intermediate good emerges. . . . I do not want to mention any specific parties in our time. Yet it seems to me that the modest, clever man and youth stays in the *middle* and learns what he can from *both sides.* The more he does this in an unbiased and peaceable manner, the more he secures his own peace of mind, what is *best* for him, and the *praise* of later generations.

Finally, let us least of all impose ourselves on others or suppress and persecute them. Is not Holland now ashamed that it expelled its Grotius?[70] Are not Saxons ashamed that they made Melanchthon so miserable? Now we see every unworthy vehicle of persecution in its own light and call it by name. Thus, as soon as the matter becomes knotty, one should say *non liquet*[71] and leave it up to the king *who created light and darkness and changes the hour and the day. He gives wisdom to the wise and understanding to the judicious. He hunts down the sophistry of the wise and dashes foolish council. He knows what lies in darkness, for he is pure light!*

---

70. [Hugo Grotius (1583-1645) was a Dutch lawyer and statesman who supported international law and humanist ideals. He was sentenced to life imprisonment after a theological dispute in which he criticized orthodox Calvinism. During his imprisonment, from which he later escaped, he wrote *De Veritate Religionis Christianae* (Leiden, 1627).]

71. [Latin for "it is not pleasing."]